ARCHEOLOGICAL EXPEDITION TO ARIZONA IN 1895

LECTOR HOUSE PUBLIC DOMAIN WORKS

ARCHEOLOGICAL EXPEDITION TO ARIZONA IN 1895

JESSE WALTER FEWKES

ISBN: 978-93-90015-59-7

Published: -

LECTOR HOUSE LLP
E-MAIL: lectorpublishing@gmail.com

ARCHEOLOGICAL EXPEDITION TO ARIZONA IN 1895

BY

JESSE WALTER FEWKES

CONTENTS

LIST OF PLATES

ARCHEOLOGICAL EXPEDITION
TO ARIZONA IN 1895

BY JESSE WALTER FEWKES
INTRODUCTORY NOTE

About the close of May, 1895, I was invited to make a collection of objects for the National Museum, illustrating the archeology of the Southwest, especially that phase of pueblo life pertaining to the so-called cliff houses. I was specially urged to make as large a collection as possible, and the choice of locality was generously left to my discretion.

Leaving Washington on the 25th of May, I obtained a collection and returned with it to that city on the 15th of September, having spent three months in the field. The material brought back by the expedition was catalogued under 966 entries, numbering somewhat over a thousand specimens. The majority of these objects are fine examples of mortuary pottery of excellent character, fully 500 of which are decorated.

I was particularly fortunate in my scientific collaborators. Mr F. W. Hodge, of the Bureau of American Ethnology, joined me at Sikyatki, and remained with the expedition until it disbanded, at the close of August. Much of my success in the work at that ruin was due to his advice and aid. He was constantly at the excavations, and the majority of the beautiful specimens were taken out of the graves by him. It is with the greatest pleasure that I am permitted to express my appreciation of his assistance in my archeological investigations at Sikyatki. Mr G. P. Winship, now librarian of the John Carter Brown Library at Providence, visited our camp at the ruin mentioned, and remained with us a few weeks, rendering important aid and adding an enthusiastic student to our number. Mr James S. Judd was a volunteer assistant while we were at Sikyatki, aiding me in many ways, especially in the management of our camp. I need only to refer to the beautiful drawings which accompany this memoir to show how much I am indebted to Mrs Hodge for faithful colored figures of the remarkable pottery uncovered from the Tusayan sands. My party included Mr S. Goddard, of Prescott, Arizona, who served as cook and driver, and Mr Erwin Baer, of the same city, as photographer. The manual work at the ruins was done by a number of young Indians from the East Mesa, who very properly were employed on the Moki reservation. An all too prevalent and often unjust criticism that Indians will not work if paid for their labor, was not voiced by any of our party. They gave many a weary hour's labor in the hot sun, in their enthusiasm to make the collection as large as possible.

On my return to Washington I was invited to prepare a preliminary account of my work in the field, which the Secretary of the Smithsonian Institution did me the honor to publish in his report for 1895. This report was of a very general character, and from necessity limited in pages; consequently it presented only the more salient features of my explorations.

The following account was prepared as a more exhaustive discussion of the results of my summer's work. The memoir is much more extended than I had expected to make it when I accepted the invitation to collect archeological objects for the Museum, and betrays, I fear, imperfections due to the limited time spent in the field. The main object of the expedition was a collection of specimens, the majority of which, now on exhibition in the National Museum, tell their own story regarding its success.

I am under deep obligations to the officers of the Smithsonian Institution, the National Museum, and the Bureau of American Ethnology for many kindnesses, and wish especially to express my thanks to Mr S. P. Langley, Secretary of the Smithsonian Institution, for the opportunity to study the ancient ruins of Tusayan. Nothing had a greater influence on my final decision to abandon other congenial work and undertake this, than my profound respect for the late Dr G. Brown Goode, who suggested the expedition to me and urged me to plan and undertake it.

JESSE WALTER FEWKES.

Washington, May, 1897.

PLAN OF THE EXPEDITION

It seemed to me in making a plan for archeological field work in 1895, that the prehistoric cliff houses, cave dwellings, and ruined pueblos of Arizona afforded valuable opportunities for research, and past experience induced me to turn my steps more especially to the northern and northeastern parts of the territory.[1] The ruins of ancient habitations in these regions had been partially, and, I believe, unsatisfactorily explored, especially those in a limited area called Tusayan, now inhabited by the Moki or Hopi Indians. These agricultural people claim to be descendants of those who once lived in the now deserted villages of that province.

I had some knowledge of the ethnology of the Hopi, derived from several summers' field work among them, and I believed this information could be successfully utilized in an attempt to solve certain archeological questions which presented themselves.[2] I desired, among other things, to obtain new information on the former extension, in one direction, of the ancestral abodes of certain clans of the sedentary people of Tusayan which are now limited to six pueblos in the northeastern part of the territory. In carrying out this general plan I made an examination of cliff dwellings and other ruins in Verde valley, and undertook an exploration of two old pueblos near the Hopi villages. The reason which determined my choice of the former as a field for investigation was a wish to obtain archeological data bearing on certain Tusayan traditions. It is claimed by the traditionists of Walpi, especially those of the Patki[3] or Water-house phratry, that their ancestors came from a land far to the south of Tusayan, to which they give the name Palatkwabi. The situation

---

[1] See "The Prehistoric Culture of Tusayan," *American Anthropologist*, May, 1896. "Two Ruins Recently Discovered in the Red Rock Country, Arizona," ibid., August, 1896. "The Cliff Villages of the Red Rock Country, and the Tusayan Ruins, Sikyatki and Awatobi, Arizona," Smithsonian Report for 1895.

[2] The reader's attention is called to the fact that this report is not intended to cover all the ruins in the section of Arizona through which the expedition passed; it is simply a description of those which were examined, with a brief mention of such others as would aid in a general comprehension of the subject. The ruins on the Little Colorado, near Winslow, Arizona, will be considered in a monograph to follow the present, which will be a report on the field work in 1896. If a series of monographs somewhat of this nature, but more comprehensive, recording explorations during many years in several different sections, were available, we would have sufficient material for a comprehensive treatment of southwestern archeology.

[3] It may be borne in mind that several other clans besides the Patki claim to have lived long ago in the region southward from modern Tusayan. Among these may be mentioned the Patuñ (Squash) and the Tawa (Sun) people who played an important part in the early colonization of Middle Mesa.

of this mythic place is a matter of considerable conjecture, but it was thought that an archeological examination of the country at or near the headwaters of the Rio Verde and its tributaries might shed light on this tradition.

It is not claimed, however, that all the ancestors of the Tusayan people migrated from the south, nor do I believe that those who came from that direction necessarily passed through Verde valley. Some, no doubt, came from Tonto Basin, but I believe it can be shown that a continuous line of ruins, similar in details of architecture, extend along this river from its junction with Salt river to well-established prehistoric dwelling places of the Hopi people. Similar lines may likewise be traced along other northern tributaries of the Salt or the Gila, which may be found to indicate early migration stages.

The ruins of Verde valley were discovered in 1854 by Antoine Leroux, a celebrated guide and trapper of his time, and were thus described by Whipple, Ewbank, and Turner in the following year:

> The river banks were covered with ruins of stone houses and regular fortifications; which, he [Leroux] says, appeared to have been the work of civilized men, but had not been occupied for centuries. They were built upon the most fertile tracts of the valley, where were signs of acequias and of cultivation. The walls were of solid masonry, of rectangular form, some twenty or thirty paces in length, and yet remaining ten or fifteen feet in height. The buildings were of two stories, with small apertures or loopholes for defence when besieged.... In other respects, however, Leroux says that they reminded him of the great pueblos of the Moquinos.[4]

A fragment of folklore, which is widely distributed among both the aboriginal peoples of Gila valley and the modern Tusayan Indians, recounts how the latter were at one time in communication with the people of the south, and traditions of both distinctly connect the sedentary people of Tusayan with those who formerly inhabited the great pueblos, now in ruins, dotting the plain in the delta between Gila and Salt rivers. That archeology might give valuable information on this question had long been my conviction, and was the main influence which led me to the studies recorded in the following pages.

An examination of a map of Arizona will show that one of the pathways or feasible routes of travel possible to have been used in any connection between the pueblos of the Gila and those of northern Arizona would naturally be along Rio Verde valley. Its tributaries rise at the foot of San Francisco mountains, and the main river empties into the Salt, traversing from north to south a comparatively fertile valley, in the main advantageous for the subsistence of semisedentary bands in their migrations. Here was a natural highway leading from the Gila

[4] Report upon the Indian Tribes, Pacific Railroad Survey, vol. iii, pt. iii, p. 14, Washington, 1856. The cavate dwellings of the Rio Verde were first described by Dr E. A. Mearns. Although it has sometimes been supposed that Coronado followed the trail along Verde valley, and then over the Mogollones to Rio Colorado Chiquito, Bandelier has conclusively shown a more easterly route.

pueblos, now in ruins, to the former villages in the north.

The study of the archeology of Verde valley had gone far enough to show that the banks of the river were formerly the sites of many and populous pueblos, while the neighboring mesas from one end to another are riddled with cavate dwellings or crowned with stone buildings. Northward from that famous crater-like depression in the Verde region, the so-called Montezuma Well on Beaver creek, one of the affluents of the Rio Verde, little archeological exploration had been attempted. There was, in other words, a break in the almost continuous series of ruins from Tusayan as far south as the Gila. Ruined towns had been reported as existing not far southward from San Francisco mountains,[5] and from there by easy stages the abodes of a former race had been detected at intervals all the way to the Tusayan pueblos. At either end the chain of ruins between the Tusayan towns and the Gila ruins was unbroken, but middle links were wanting. All conditions imply former habitations in this untrodden hiatus, the region between the Verde and the Tusayan series, ending near the present town of Flagstaff, Arizona; but southward from that town the country was broken and impassable, a land where the foot of the archeologist had not trodden. Remains of human habitations had, however, been reported by ranchmen, but these reports were vague and unsatisfactory. So far as they went they confirmed my suspicions, and there were other significant facts looking the same way. The color of the red cliffs fulfilled the Tusayan tradition of Palatkwabi, or their former home in the far south. Led by all these considerations, before I took to the field I had long been convinced that this must have been one of the homes of certain Hopi clans, and when the occasion presented itself I determined to follow the northward extension of the ancient people of the Verde into these rugged rocks. By my discoveries in this region of ruins indicative of dwellings of great size in ancient times I have supplied the missing links in the chain of ancient dwellings extending from the great towns of the Gila to the ruins west of the modern Tusayan towns. If this line of ruins, continuous from Gila valley to Tusayan and beyond, be taken in connection with legends ascribing Casa Grande to the Hopi and those of certain Tusayan clans which tell of the homes of their ancestors in the south, a plausible explanation is offered for the many similarities between two apparently widely different peoples, and the theory of a kinship between southern and northern sedentary tribes of Arizona does not seem as unlikely as it might otherwise appear.

The reader will notice that I accept without question the belief that the so-called cliff dwellers were not a distinct people, but a specially adaptive condition of life of a race whose place of habitation was determined by its environment. We are considering a people who sometimes built dwellings in caverns and sometimes in the plains, but often in both places at the same epoch. Moreover, as long ago pointed out by other students, the existing Pueblo Indians are descendants of a people who at times lived in cliffs, and some of the Tusayan clans have inhabited true cliff houses in the historic period. By intermarriage with nomadic races and from other causes the character of Pueblo consanguinity is no doubt somewhat

---

[5] See mention of cliff houses in Walnut canyon in the Fifth Annual Report of the Bureau of Ethnology.

different from that of their ancient kin, but the character of the culture, as shown by a comparison of cliff-house and modern objects, has not greatly changed.

While recognizing the kinship of the Pueblos and the Cliff villagers, this resemblance is not restricted to any one pueblo or group of modern pueblos to the exclusion of others. Of all modern differentiations of this ancient substratum of culture of which cliff villages are one adaptive expression, the Tusayan Indians are the nearest of all existing people of the Southwest[6] to the ancient people of Arizona.

The more southerly ruins of Tusayan, which I have been able satisfactorily to identify and to designate by a Hopi name, are those called Homolobi, situated not far from Winslow, Arizona, near where the railroad crosses the Little Colorado. These ruins are claimed by the Hopi as the former residences of their ancestors, and were halting places in the migration of certain clans from the south. They were examined by Mr Cosmos Mindeleff, of the Bureau of American Ethnology, in 1893,[7] but no report on them has yet been published.

While, however, the Homolobi group of ruins is the most southerly to which I have been able to affix a Hopi name, others still more to the southward are claimed by certain of their traditions.[8] The Hopi likewise regard as homes of their ancestors certain habitations, now in ruins, near San Francisco mountains. In a report on his exploration of Zuñi and Little Colorado rivers in 1852, Captain L. Sitgreaves called attention to several interesting ruins, one of which was not far from the "cascades" of the latter river. After ascending the plateau, which he found covered with volcanic detritus, he discovered that "all the prominent points" were "occupied by the ruins of stone houses, which were in some instances three stories in height. They are evidently," he says, "the remains of a large town, as they occurred at intervals for an extent of eight or nine miles, and the ground was thickly strewn with fragments of pottery in all directions."

In 1884 a portion of Colonel James Stevenson's expedition, under F. D. Bick-

[6] The kinship of Cliff dwellers and Pueblos was long ago recognized by ethnologists, both from resemblances of skulls, the character of architecture, and archeological objects found in each class of dwellings. It is only in later years, however, that the argument from similar ceremonial paraphernalia has been adduced, owing to an increase of our knowledge of this side of Pueblo life. See Bessels, Bull. U. S. Geological and Geographical Survey of the Territories, vol. II, 1876; Hoffman, Report on Chaco Cranium, ibid., 1877, p. 457. Holmes, in 1878, says: "The ancient peoples of the San Juan country were doubtless the ancestors of the present Pueblo tribes of New Mexico and Arizona." See, likewise, Cushing, Nordenskiöld, and later writers regarding the kinship of Cliff villagers and Pueblos.

[7] Report of the Director of the Bureau of American Ethnology for the year ending June 30, 1894; Smithsonian Report, 1894.

[8] The ruins in Chaves Pass, 110 miles south of Oraibi, will be considered in the report of the expedition of 1896, when extensive excavations were made at this point. About midway between the Chaves Pass ruins and those of Beaver creek, in Verde valley, there are other ruins, as at Rattlesnake Tanks, and as a well-marked trail passes by these former habitations and connects the Verde series with those of Chaves Pass, it is possible that early migrations may have followed this course. There is also a trail from Homolobi and the Colorado Chiquito ruins through Chaves Pass into Tonto Basin.

ford, examined the cliff houses in Walnut canyon, and in 1886 Major J. W. Powell and Colonel Stevenson found scattered ruins north of San Francisco mountains having one, two, or three rooms, each "built of basaltic cinders and blocks of lava." These explorers likewise reported ruins of extensive dwellings in the same region made of sandstone and limestone. At about 25 miles north of the mountains mentioned they discovered a small volcanic cone of cinders and basalt, which was formerly the site of a village or pueblo built around a crater, and estimated that this little pueblo contained 60 or 70 rooms, with a plaza occupying one-third of an acre of surface.[9]

Twelve miles eastward from San Francisco mountains they found another cinder cone resembling a dome, and on its southern slope, in a coherent cinder mass, were many chambers, of which one hundred and fifty are said to have been excavated. They mention the existence on the summit of this cone of a plaza inclosed by a rude wall of volcanic cinders, with a carefully leveled floor. The former inhabitants of these rooms apparently lived in underground chambers hewn from the volcanic formation. Eighteen miles farther eastward was another ruined village built about the crater of a volcanic cone. Several villages were discovered in this locality and many natural caves which had been utilized as dwellings by inclosing them in front with walls of volcanic rocks and cinders. These cavate rooms were arranged tier above tier in a very irregular way.

At this place three distinct kinds of ruins were found—cliff villages, cave dwellings, and pueblos. Eight miles southeastward from Flagstaff, in Oak creek canyon, a cliff house of several hundred rooms was discovered. It was concluded that all these ruins were abandoned at a comparatively recent date, or not more than three or four centuries ago, and the Havasupai Indians of Cataract canyon were regarded as descendants of the former inhabitants of these villages. The situation of some of these ruins and the published descriptions would indicate that some of them were similar to those described and figured by Sitgreaves,[10] to which reference has already been made.

In 1896 two amateur explorers, George Campbell and Everett Howell, of Flagstaff, reported that they had found, about eighteen miles from that place, several well-preserved cliff towns and a remarkable tunnel excavation. The whole region in the immediate neighborhood of San Francisco mountains appears, therefore, to have been populated in ancient times by an agricultural people, and legends ascribe some of these ruins to ancestors of the Hopi Indians.

There are several ruins due south of Tusayan which have not been investigated, but which would furnish important contributions to a study of Hopi migrations. Near Saint Johns, Arizona, likewise, there are ruins of considerable size, possibly referable to the Cibolan series; and south of Holbrook, which lies about due south of Walpi, there are ruins, the pottery from which I have examined and found to be of the black-and-white ware typical of the Cliff people. Perhaps, however, no ruined pueblo presents more interesting problems than the magnificent

[9] Smithsonian Report, 1883; Report of Major Powell, Director of the Bureau of Ethnology, p. 57 et seq. Explorations in the Southwest, ibid., 1886, p. 52 et seq.

[10] Report of an Expedition down the Zuñi and Colorado rivers; Washington, 1853.

Pueblo Grande or Kintiel, about 20 miles north of Navaho Springs. This large ruin, lying between the Cibolan and Tusayan groups, has been referred to both of these provinces, and would, if properly excavated, shed much light on the archeology of the two provinces.[11] Kinnazinde lies not far from Kintiel.

The ruins reported from Tonto Basin, of which little is known, may later be found to be connected with early migrations of those Hopi clans which claim southern origin. From what I can judge by the present appearance of ruins just north of the Mogollon mountains, in a direct line between Tonto Basin and the present Tusayan towns, there is nothing to show the age of these ruined villages, and it is quite likely that they may have been inhabited in the middle of the sixteenth century. While it is commonly agreed that the province of "Totonteac," which figures extensively in certain early Spanish narratives, was the same as Tusayan, the linguistic similarity of the word to "tonto" has been suggested by others. In the troublesome years between 1860 and 1870 the Hopi, decimated by disease and harried by nomads, sent delegates to Prescott asking to be removed to Tonto Basin, and it is not improbable that in making this reasonable request they simply wished to return to a place which they associated with their ancestors, who had been driven out by the Apache. Totonteac[12] is ordinarily thought to be the same as Tusayan, but it may have included some of the southern pueblos now in ruins west of Zuñi.

Having determined that the line of Verde ruins was continued into the Red-rock country, it was desirable to see how the latter compared with those nearer Tusayan. This necessitated reexamination of many ruins in Verde valley, which was my aim during the most of June. I followed this valley from the cavate dwellings near Squaw mountain past the great ruin in the neighborhood of Old Camp Verde, the unique Montezuma Well, to the base of the Red-rocks. Throughout this region I saw, as had been expected, no change in the character of the ruins great enough to indicate that they originally were inhabited by peoples racially different. Stopped from further advance by a barrier of rugged cliffs, I turned westward along their base until I found similar ruins, which were named Palatki and Hon-

[11] Smithsonian Report, 1883, Report of the Director of the Bureau of Ethnology, p. 62: "Pending the arrival of goods at Moki, Mr Cushing returned across the country to Zuñi for the purpose of observing more minutely than on former occasions the annual sun ceremonials. En route he discovered two ruins, apparently before unvisited. One of these was the outlying structure of K'n'-i-K'él, called by the Navajos Zïnni-jin'ne and by the Zuñis He'-sho'ta pathl-tãïe, both, according to Zuñi tradition, belonging to the Thlé-e-tâ-kwe, the name given to the traditional northwestern migration of the Bear, Crane, Frog, Deer, Yellow-wood, and other gentes of the ancestral pueblos."

[12] The reduplicated syllable recalls Hopi methods of forming their plural, but is not characteristic of them, and the word Totonteac has a Hopi sound. The supposed derivation of Tonto from Spanish *tonto*, "fool," is mentioned, elsewhere. The so-called Tonto Apache was probably an intruder, the cause of the desertion of the "basin" by the housebuilders. The question whether Totonteac is the same as Tusayan or Tuchano is yet to be satisfactorily answered. The map makers of the sixteenth century regarded them as different places, and notwithstanding Totonteac was reported to be "a hotte lake" in the middle of the previous century, it held its place on maps into the seventeenth century. It is always on or near a river flowing into the Gulf of California.

anki. Having satisfied myself that there was good evidence that the numbers of ancient people were as great here as at any point in the Verde valley and that their culture was similar, I continued the work with an examination of the ruins north of the Red-rocks, where there is substantial evidence that these were likewise of the same general character.

The last two months of the summer, July and August, 1895, were devoted to explorations of two Tusayan ruins, called Awatobi and Sikyatki. In this work, apparently unconnected with that already outlined, I still had in mind the light to be shed on the problem of Tusayan origin. The question which presented itself was: How are these ruins related to the modern pueblos? Awatobi was a historic ruin, destroyed in 1700, and therefore somewhat influenced by the Spaniards. Many of the survivors became amalgamated with pueblos still inhabited. Its kinship with the surviving villagers was clear. Sikyatki, however, was overthrown in prehistoric times, and at its destruction part of its people went to Awatobi. Its culture was prehistoric. The discovery of what these two ruins teach, by bringing prehistoric Tusayan culture down to the present time and comparing them with the ruins of Verde valley and southern Arizona, is of great archeological interest.

While engaged in preparing this report, having in fact written most of it, I received Mr Cosmos Mindeleff's valuable article on the Verde ruins,[13] in which special attention is given to the cavate lodges and villages of this interesting valley. This contribution anticipates many of my observations on these two groups of aboriginal habitations, and renders it unnecessary to describe them in the detailed manner I had planned. I shall therefore touch but briefly on these ruins, paying special attention to the cliff houses of Verde valley, situated in the Red-rock country. This variety of dwelling was overlooked in both Mearns' and Mindeleff's classifications, from the fact that it seems to be confined to the region of the valley characterized by the red-rock formation, which appears not to have been explored by them. The close resemblance of these cliff houses to those of the region north of Tusayan is instructive, in view of the ground, well taken, I believe, by Mr Mindeleff, that there is a close likeness between the Verde ruins and those farther north, especially in Tusayan.

---

[13] Thirteenth Annual Report of the Bureau of Ethnology.

RUINS IN VERDE VALLEY

CLASSIFICATION OF THE RUINS

The ruined habitations in the valley of the Rio Verde may be considered under three divisions or types, differing in form, but essentially the same in character. In adopting this classification, which is by no means restricted to this single valley, I do not claim originality, but follow that used by the best writers on this subject. My limitation of the types and general definitions may, however, be found to differ somewhat from those of my predecessors.

The three groups of ruins in our Southwest are the following:

I—Pueblos, or Independent habitations.
II—Cliff Houses } Dependent habitations.
III—Cavate Dwellings } Dependent habitations.

In the first group are placed those ancient or modern habitations which are isolated, on all sides, from cliffs. They may be situated in valleys or on elevations or mesas; they may be constructed of clay, adobe, or stone of various kinds, but are always isolated from cliffs. They are single or multiple chambered, circular or rectangular in shape, and may have been built either as permanent habitations or as temporary outlooks. Their main feature is freedom, on all sides except the foundation, from cliffs or walls of rock in place.

The second group includes those not isolated from natural cliffs, but with some part of their lateral walls formed by natural rock in situ, and are built ordinarily in caverns with overhanging roofs, which the highest courses of their walls do not join. Generally erected in caves, their front walls never close the entrances to those caverns. This kind of aboriginal buildings may, like the former, vary in structural material; but, so far as I know, they are not, for obvious reasons, made of adobe alone.

The third kind of pueblo dwellings are called cavate dwellings or lodges, a group which includes that peculiar kind of aboriginal dwelling where the rooms are excavated from the cliff wall, forming caves, where natural rock is a support or more often serves as the wall itself of the dwelling. The entrance may be partially closed by masonry, the floor laid with flat stones, and the sides plastered with clay; but never in this group is there a roof distinct from the top of the cave.

Naturally cavate dwellings grade into cliff houses, but neither of these types can be confounded with the first group, which affords us no difficulty in identification. All these kinds of dwellings were made by people of the same culture, the character of the habitation depending on geological environment.

BUREAU OF AMERICAN ETHNOLOGY — — SEVENTEENTH ANNUAL RE-
PORT PL. XCIa

Cavate Dwellings — Rio Verde

In Verde valley, villages, cliff houses, and cavate dwellings exist together, and were, I believe, contemporaneously inhabited by a people of the same culture.

These types of ancient habitations are not believed to stand in the relationship of sequence in development; nor is one simpler or less difficult of construction than the others. Cliff houses display no less skill and daring than do the villages in the plain, called pueblos. The cavate dwellings are likewise a form of habitation which shows considerable workmanship, and are far from caves like those inhabited by "cave men." These dwellings were laboriously excavated with rude implements; had floors, banquettes, windows, walled recesses, and the like. It is hardly proper to regard them, as less difficult to construct than pueblos or cliff houses.

Cavate dwellings, like villages or cliff houses, may be single or multiple, single or many chambered, and a cluster of these troglodytic dwellings was, in fact, as truly a village as a pueblo or cliff house. The same principle of seeking safety by crowding together held in all three instances; and this very naturally, for the culture of the inhabitants was identical. I shall consider only two of the three types of dwellings in Verde valley, namely, the second and third groups.

It has, I think, been conclusively shown by Mr Cosmos Mindeleff, so far as types of the first group of ruins on the Verde are concerned, that they practically do not differ from the modern Tusayan pueblos. The remaining types, when rightly interpreted, furnish evidence of no less important character. Notwithstanding Mindeleff's excellent descriptions of the cavate dwellings of this region, already cited, I have thought it well to bring into prominence certain features which seem to me to indicate that this form of aboriginal dwelling was high in its development, showing considerable skill in its construction, and was fashioned on the same general plan as the others. For this demonstration I have chosen one of the most striking clusters in Verde valley.

CAVATE DWELLINGS

The most accessible cavate dwellings in Verde valley (plate xci *a*) are situated on the left bank of the river, about eight miles southward from Camp Verde and three miles from the mouth of Clear creek. The general characteristics of this group have been well described by Mr Mindeleff in the Thirteenth Annual Report of the Bureau, so that I need but refer to a few additional observations made on these interesting habitations.[14]

These cavate lodges afford a fair idea of the best known of these prehistoric dwellings in this part of Arizona. Although Verde valley has many fine ranches, the land in immediate proximity to these ruins is uncultivated. The nearest habitation, however, is not far away, and it is not difficult to find guides to these caves, so well known are they to the inhabitants of this part of the valley. It did not take long to learn that any investigations which I might attempt there had been anticipated by other archeologists and laymen, for many of the rooms had been rifled of their contents and their walls thrown down, while it was also evident that some careful excavations had been made.

There is, however, abundant opportunity for more detailed scientific work than has yet been attempted on these ruins, and what has thus far been accomplished has been more in the nature of reconnoissance. The cemeteries and burial places of the prehistoric people of the cavate dwellings are yet to be discovered, and it is probable, judging from experience gained at other ruins, that when they are found and carefully investigated much light will be thrown on the character of ancient cave life.

The entrances to the cavate dwellings opposite Squaw mountain are visible from the road for quite a distance, appearing as rows of holes in the steep walls of the cliff on the opposite or left bank of the Rio Verde. Owing to their proximity to the river, from which the precipice in which they are situated rises almost vertically, we were unable to camp under them, but remained on the right bank of the river, where a level plain extends for some distance, bordering the river and stretching back to the distant cliffs. We pitched our camp on a bluff, about 30 feet

[14] Mr Mindeleff's descriptions deal with the same cluster of cavate ruins here described, but are more specially devoted to the more southern section of them, not considering, if I understand him, the northern row here described. I had also made extensive studies of the rooms figured by him previously to the publication of his article, but as my notes on these rooms are anticipated by his excellent memoir I have not considered the rooms described by him, but limited my account to brief mention of a neighboring row of chambers not described in his report.

above the river, in full sight of the cave entrances, near a small stone inclosure which bears quite a close resemblance to a Tusayan shrine.

Aboriginal people had evidently cultivated the plain where we camped, for there are many evidences of irrigating ditches and even walls of former houses. At present, however, this once highly cultivated field lies unused, and is destitute of any valuable plants save the scanty grass which served to eke out the fodder of our horses.

At the time of my visit the water of Rio Verde at this point was confined to a very narrow channel under the bluff near its right bank, but the appearance of its bed showed that in heavy freshets during the rainy season the water filled the interval between the base of the cliffs in which the cavate dwellings are situated and the bluffs which form the right bank.

In visits to the caves it was necessary, on account of the site of the camp, to ford the stream each time and to climb to their level over fallen stones, a task of no slight difficulty. The water in places was shallow and the current only moderately rapid. Considering the fact that it furnished potable liquid for ourselves and horses, and that the line of trees which skirted the bluff was available for firewood, our camp compared well with many which we subsequently made in our summer's explorations.

BUREAU OF AMERICAN ETHNOLOGY— — SEVENTEENTH ANNUAL REPORT PL. XCI[b]

Cavate Dwellings—Oak Creek

The section of the cliff which was examined embraced the northern series of these caves, extending from a promontory forming one side of a blind or box canyon to nearly opposite our camp. Adjacent to this series of rooms, but farther down the river, on the same side, there are two narrow side canyons, in both of which are also numerous caves, in all respects similar to the series we chose for examination. At several points on the summit of the cliffs, above the caves, large rectangular ruins, with fallen walls, were discovered; these ruins are, however, in no respect peculiar, but closely resemble those ordinarily found in a similar position throughout this region and elsewhere in Arizona and New Mexico. From their proximity to the caves it would seem that the cavate dwellings, and the pueblos on the summits of the mesas in which they are found, had been inhabited by one people; but better evidence that such is true is drawn from the character of the architecture and the nature of the art remains common to both.

Let us first consider the series of caves from a point opposite our camp to the promontory which forms a pinnacle at the mouth of the first of the two side caverns—a row of caves the entrances to which are shown in the accompanying illustration (plate xcii). I have lettered these rooms, as indicated by their entrances, *a* to *l*, beginning with the opening on the left.

The rock in which these caves have been hewn is very soft, and almost white in color, save for a slightly reddish brown stratum just below the line of entrances to the cavate chambers. Although, as a general thing, the wall of the cliff is almost perpendicular, and the caves at points inaccessible, entrance to the majority of them can be effected by mounting the heaps of small stones forming the débris, which has fallen even to the bed of the river at various places, and by following a ledge which connects the line of entrances. The easiest approach mounts a steep decline, not far from the promontory at the lower level of the line, which conducts to a ledge running along in front of the caves about 150 feet above the bed of the stream. Roughly speaking, this ledge is about 100 feet below the summit of the cliff. It was impossible to reach several of the rooms, and it is probable that when the caves were inhabited access to any one of them was even more difficult than at present.

Judging from the number of rooms, the cliffs on the left bank of the Verde must have had a considerable population when inhabited. These caverns, no doubt, swarmed with human beings, and their inaccessible position furnished the inhabitants with a safe refuge from enemies, or an advantageous outlook or observation shelter for their fields on the opposite side of the stream. The soft rock of which the mesa is formed is easily worked, and there are abundant evidences, from the marks of tools employed, that the greater part of each cave was pecked out by hand. Fragments of wood were very rarely seen in these cliff dugouts; and although there is much adobe plastering, only in a few instances were the mouths of the caves walled or a doorway of usual shape present. The last room at the southern end, near the promontory at the right of the entrance to a side canyon, has walls in front resembling those of true cliff houses and pueblos in the Red-rock country farther northward, as will be shown in subsequent pages.

This group of cavate dwellings, while a good example of the cavern type of ruins, is so closely associated, both in geographical position and in archeological remains, with other types in Verde valley, that we are justified in referring them to one and the same people. The number of these troglodytic dwelling places on the

Verde is very large; indeed the mesas may be said to be fairly honeycombed with subterranean habitations. Confined as a general thing to the softer strata of rock, which from its character was readily excavated, they lie side by side at the same general level, and are entered from a projecting ledge, formed by the top of the talus which follows the level of their entrances.

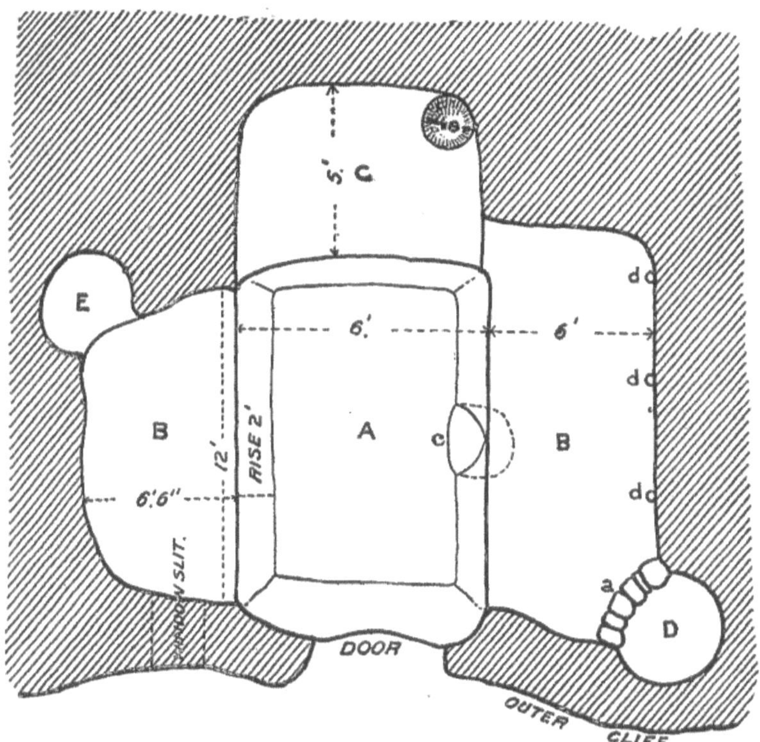

FIG. 245—PLAN OF CAVATE DWELLING ON RIO VERDE

This ledge is easily accessible in certain places from the river bed, where stones have fallen to the base of the cliff; but at most points no approach is possible, and in their impregnable position the inhabitants could easily defend themselves from hostile peoples.

BUREAU OF AMERICAN ETHNOLOGY—— SEVENTEENTH ANNUAL RE-
PORT PL. XCII

Entrances To Cavate Ruins

Whether the rock had recesses in it before the caves were enlarged would seem to be answered in the affirmative, for similar caves without evidences of habitations were observed. These, however, are as a rule small, and wherever available the larger caverns have been appropriated and enlarged by stone implements, as shown by the pecking on the walls. The enlargement of these caverns, however, would not be a difficult task, for the rock is very soft and easily worked.

Entering one of these cavate rooms the visitor finds himself in a dark chamber, as a rule with side openings or passageways into adjoining rooms. Broad lateral banquettes are prominent features in the most complicated caves, and there are many recesses and small closets or cists.

The ramifications formed by lateral rooms are often extensive, and the chambers communicate with others so dark that we can hardly regard them as once inhabited. In these dimly lighted rooms the walls were blackened with smoke, as if from former fires, and in many of the largest the position of fireplaces could plainly be discovered. As a type of one of the more complicated I have chosen that figured to illustrate the arrangement of these cavate dwellings (figure 245). Many are smaller, others have more lateral chambers, but one type is characteristic of all.

A main room (*a*, figure 245), or that first entered from outside, is roughly rectangular in shape, 12 feet long by 6 feet wide, and about 6 feet high. The floor, however, was covered with very dry débris which had blown in from the exterior or, in some instances, fallen from the roof. That part of the floor which was exposed shows that it was roughly plastered, sometimes paved or formed of solid rock.

On three sides of this room there is a step 2 feet high, to platforms, three in number, one in the rear and one on each side. These platforms are 5, 6, and 6 feet 6 inches wide, respectively, and of the same length as the corresponding sides of the central room. It would appear that these platforms are characteristic architectural features of these habitations, and we find them reproduced in some of the rooms of the cliff houses of the Red-rocks, while Nordenskiöld has described a kindred feature in the kivas of the Mesa Verde ruins. A somewhat similar elevation of the floor in modern Tusayan kivas forms what may be called the spectator's part, in front of the ladder as one descends, and the same feature is common to many older Hopi dwellings.[15]

Beginning with the lateral platforms (*b*, figure 245) we first note, as we step upon it at *c*, about midway of its length, a small circular depression in the floor of the central room extending slightly beneath the platform, as indicated by the dotted line. It is possible that this niche was a receptacle for important household objects, although it may have been a fireplace.

In a corner of the right platform a round cist, partially hewn out of the rock, was found, but its walls (*a*, figure 245) were badly broken down by some former explorer. The floor of this recess lies below that of the platform, while the cist itself (*d*) reminds one of the closed or walled structures, so commonly found in the Verde, attached to the side of the cliff. On the lateral wall of this chamber, at about the height of the head, a row of small holes had been drilled into the solid wall. These holes (*d, d, d*) are almost too small for the insertion of roof beams, and were probably made for pegs on which to rest a beam for hanging blankets and other textile fabrics when not in use. The roof of the cave was the natural rock, and showed over its whole surface marks of a pecking implement.

The left chamber is 6 feet 6 inches broad, and from one corner, opposite the doorway, a low passageway leads into a circular chamber, 6 feet in diameter, with its floor below the platform of the lateral room. Between the chamber, on the left of the entrance, and the open air, the wall of solid rock is broken by a slit-like crevice, which allows the light to enter, and no doubt served as a window. A recess, the floor of which is elevated, on a platform opposite the doorway, is 5 feet broad, and has a small circular depression in one corner. The floor and upraise of this recess is plastered with adobe, which in several places is smooth and well made.

In comparing the remaining cavate dwellings of this series with that described, we find every degree of complication in the arrangement of rooms, from a simple

---

[15] *Journal of American Ethnology and Archæology*, vol. ii, No. 1. All the Tusayan kivas with which I am familiar have this raised spectator's part at one end. The altars are always erected at the opposite end of the room, in which is likewise the hole in the floor called the *sipapû*, symbolic of the traditional opening through which races emerged to the earth's surface from an underworld. Banquettes exist in some Tusayan kivas; in others, however, they are wanting. The raised platform in dwelling rooms is commonly a sleeping place, above which blankets are hung and, in some instances, corn is stored. A small opening in the step often admits light to an otherwise dark granary below the floor. In no instance, however, are there more than one such platform, and that commonly partakes of the nature of another room, although seldom separated from the other chamber by a partition.

cave, or irregular hole in the side of the cliff, to squared chambers with lateral rooms. The room *I*,[16] for instance, is rectangular, 6 feet long by 3 feet wide, with an entrance the same width as that of the room itself.

In room *III*, however, the external opening is very small, and there is a low, narrow ledge, or platform, opposite the doorway. There is likewise in this room a small shelf in the left-hand wall. In *IV* there is a raised platform on two adjacent sides of the square room, and the doorway is an irregular orifice broken through the wall to the open air.

Room *IV* is a subterranean chamber, most of the floor of which is littered with large fragments of rock which have fallen from the roof. It has numerous small recesses in the wall resembling cubby-holes where household utensils of various kinds were undoubtedly formerly kept. This room is instructive, in that the entrance is partially closed by two walls of masonry, which do not join. The stones are laid in adobe in which fragments of pottery were detected. These unjoined walls leave a doorway which is thus flanked on each side by stone masonry, recalling in every particular the well-known walls of cliff houses. Here, in fact, we have so close a resemblance to the masonry of true cliff houses that we can hardly doubt that the excavators of the cavate dwellings were, in reality, people similar to those who built the cliff houses of Verde valley.

Room *VIII* is a simple cave hewn out of the rock, with a chamber behind it, entered by a passageway made of masonry, which partially fills a larger opening. The doorway through this masonry is small below, but broadens above in much the same manner as some of the doorways in Tusayan of today.

Continuing along the left bank of the river, from the row of cavate rooms, just described, on the first mesa, we round a promontory and enter a small canyon,[17] which is perforated on each side with numerous other cavate dwellings, large and small, all of the same general character as the type described. Here, likewise, are small external openings which evidently communicated with subterranean chambers, but many of them are so elevated that access to them from the floor of the canyon or from the cliff above is not possible. A marked feature of the whole series is the existence here and there of small, often inaccessible, stone cists of masonry plastered to the side of the rocky cliff like swallows' nests.

All of these cists which are accessible had been opened and plundered before my visit, but there yet remain a few which are still intact and would repay examination and study. Similar walled-up cists are likewise found, as we shall see later, in the cliff-houses of the Red-rock country, hence are not confined to the Verde system of ruins.

Cavate dwellings similar to those here described are reported to exist in the canyons of upper Salado, Gala, and Zuñi rivers, and we may with reason sus-

---

[16] Counting from the point of the cliff shown in plate xcia. The positions of the rooms are indicated by the row of entrances.

[17] It was from this region that the individual chambers, described by Mindeleff, were chosen.

pect that the distribution[18] of cavate dwellings is as wide as that of the pueblos themselves, the sole requisite being a soft tufaceous rock, capable of being easily worked by people with stone implements. In none of the different regions in which they exist is there any probability that these caves were made by people different in culture from pueblo or cliff dwellers. They are much more likely to have been permanent than temporary habitations of the same culture stock of Indians who availed themselves of rock shelters wherever the nature of the cliff permitted excavation in its walls.

That the cavate lodges are simple "horticultural outlooks" is an important suggestion, but one might question whether they were conveniently placed for that purpose. So far as overlooking the opposite plain (which had undoubtedly been cultivated in ancient times) is concerned, the position of some of them may be regarded good for that purpose, but certainly not so commanding as that of the hill or mesa above, where well-marked ruins still exist.

The position of the cavate dwellings is a disadvantageous one to reach any cultivated fields if defenders were necessary. When the Tusayan Indian today moves to his *kisi* or summer brush house shelter he practically camps in his corn or near it, in easy reach to drive away crows, or build wind-breaks to shelter the tender sprouts; but to go to their cornfields the inhabitants of the cavate dwellings I have described were forced to cross a river before the farm was reached. That these cavate dwellings were lookouts none can deny, but I incline to a belief that this does not tell the whole story if we limit them to such use. It is not wholly clear to me that they were not likewise an asylum for refuge, possibly not inhabited continuously, but a very welcome retreat when the agriculturist was sorely pressed by enemies. Following the analogy of a Hopi custom of building temporary booths near their fields, may we not suppose that the former inhabitants of Verde valley may have erected similar shelters in their cornfields during summer months, retiring to the cavate dwellings and the mesa tops in winter? All available evidence would indicate that the cavate dwellings were permanent habitations.[19]

There are several square ruins on top of the mesa above the cavate dwellings. The walls of these were massive, but they are now very much broken down, and the adobe plastering is so eroded from the masonry that I regard them of considerable antiquity. They do not differ from other similar ruins, so common elsewhere in New Mexico and Arizona, and are identical with others in the Verde region. I visited several of these ruins, but made no excavations in them, nor added any new data to our knowledge of this type of aboriginal buildings. The pottery picked up on the surface resembles that of the ruins of the Little Colorado and Gila.

---

[18] Mr Mindeleff, in his valuable memoir, has so completely described the cavate dwellings of the Rio Grande and San Juan regions that their discussion in this account would be superfluous.

[19] See Mindeleff, Cliff Ruins of Canyon de Chelly, *American Anthropologist*, April, 1895. The suggestion that cliff outlooks were farming shelters in some instances is doubtless true, but I should hesitate giving this use a predominance over outlooks for security. In times of danger, naturally the agriculturist seeks a high or commanding position for a wide outlook; but to watch his crops he must camp among them.

The dwellings which I have mentioned above are said[20] to be duplicated at many other points in the watershed of the Verde, and many undescribed ruins of this nature were reported to me by ranchmen. I do not regard them as older than the adjacent ruins on the mesa above or the plains below them, much less as productions of people of different stages of culture, for everything about them suggests contemporaneous occupancy.

From what little I saw of the village sites on the Verde I believe that Mindeleff is correct in considering that these ruins represent a comparatively late period of pueblo architecture. The character of the cliff houses of the Red-rocks shows no very great antiquity of occupancy. While it is not possible to give any approximate date when they were inhabited, their general appearance indicates that they are not more than two centuries old. There is, however, no reference to them in the early Spanish history of the Southwest.

BUREAU OF AMERICAN ETHNOLOGY — — SEVENTEENTH ANNUAL RE-
PORT PL. XCIII

Bowlder With Pictographs Near Wood's Ranch

Few pictographs were found in the immediate neighborhood of the cavate dwellings; indeed the rock in their vicinity is too soft to preserve for any considerable time any great number of these rock etchings. Examples of ancient paleography were, however, discovered a short distance higher up the river on malpais rock, which is harder and less rapidly eroded. A half-buried bowlder (plate xciii) near Wood's ranch was found to be covered with the well-known spirals with zigzag attachments, horned animals resembling antelopes, growing corn, rain clouds, and similar figures. These pictographs occur on a black, superficial layer of lava

[20] Ancient Dwellings of the Rio Verde Valley, Dr E. A. Mearns; *Popular Science Monthly*, vol. xxvii. Mindeleff, Aboriginal Remains in Verde Valley; Thirteenth Annual Report of the Bureau of Ethnology.

rock, or upon lighter stone with a malpais layer, which had been pecked through, showing a lighter color beneath. There is little doubt that many examples of aboriginal pictography exist in this neighborhood, which would reward exploration with interesting data. The Verde pictographs can not be distinguished, so far as designs are concerned, from many found elsewhere in Colorado, Utah, New Mexico, and Arizona.

An instructive pictograph, different from any which I have elsewhere seen, was discovered on the upturned side of a bowlder not far from Hance's ranch, near the road from Camp Verde to the cavate dwellings. The bowlder upon which they occur lies on top of a low hill, to the left of the road, near the river. It consists of a rectangular network of lines, with attached key extensions, crooks, and triangles, all pecked in the surface. This dædalus of lines arises from grooves, which originate in two small, rounded depressions in the rock, near which is depicted the figure of a mountain lion. The whole pictograph is 3-1/2 feet square, and legible in all its parts.

The intent of the ancient scribe is not wholly clear, but it has been suggested that he sought to represent the nexus of irrigating ditches in the plain below. It might have been intended as a chart of the neighboring fields of corn, and it is highly suggestive, if we adopt either of these explanations or interpretations, that a figure of the mountain lion is found near the depressions, which may provisionally be regarded as representing ancient reservoirs. Among the Tusayan Indians the mountain lion is looked on as a guardian of cultivated fields, which he is said to protect, and his stone image is sometimes placed there for the same purpose.

In the vicinity of the pictograph last described other bowlders, of which there are many, were found to be covered with smaller rock etchings in no respect characteristic, and there is a remnant of an ancient shrine a few yards away from the bowlder upon which they occur.

MONTEZUMA WELL

One of the most interesting sites of ancient habitation in Verde valley is known as Montezuma Well, and it is remarkable how little attention has been paid to it by archeologists.[21] Dr Mearns, in his article on the ancient dwellings of Verde valley, does not mention the well, and Mindeleff simply refers to the brief description by Dr Hoffman in 1877. These ruins are worthy of more study than I was able to give them, for like many other travelers I remained but a short time in the neighborhood. It is possible, however, that some of my hurried observations at this point may be worthy of record.

Montezuma Well (plate xciv) is an irregular, circular depression, closely resembling a volcanic crater, but evidently, as Dr Hoffman well points out, due to erosion rather than to volcanic agencies. As one approaches it from a neighboring

[21] Since the above lines were written Mr C. F. Lummis, who has made many well-known contributions to the ethnology and archeology of the Pueblo area, has published in *Land of Sunshine* (Los Angeles, 1895), a beautiful photographic illustration and an important description of this unique place.

ranch the road ascends a low elevation, and when on top the visitor finds that the crater occupies the whole interior of the hill. The exact dimensions I did not accurately determine, but the longest diameter of the excavation is estimated at about 400 feet; its depth possibly 70 feet. On the eastern side this depression is separated from Beaver creek by a precipitous wall which can not be scaled from that side. At the time of my visit there was considerable water in the "well," which was reported to be very deep, but did not cover the whole bottom. It is possible to descend to the water at one point on the eastern side, where a trail leads to the water's edge.

There appears to be a subterranean waterway under the eastern rim of the well, and the water from the spring rushes through this passage into Beaver creek. At the time of my visit this outflow was very considerable, and in the rainy season it must be much greater. The well is never dry, and is supplied by perennial subterranean springs rather than by surface drainage.

The geological agency which has been potent in giving the remarkable crater-like form to Montezuma Well was correctly recognized by Dr Hoffman[22] and others as the solvent or erosive power of the spring. There is no evidence of volcanic formation in the neighborhood, and the surrounding rocks are limestones and sandstones. Not far from Navaho springs there is a similar circular depression, called Jacob's Well, but which was dry when visited by me. This may later be found to have been formed in a similar way. At several places in Arizona there are formations of like geological character.

BUREAU OF AMERICAN ETHNOLOGY — — SEVENTEENTH ANNUAL REPORT PL. XCIV

Montezuma Well

[22] Miscellaneous Ethnographic Observations on Indians inhabiting Nevada, California, and Arizona, Tenth Annual Report of the Hayden Survey, p. 478; Washington, 1878.

The walls of Montezuma Well are so nearly perpendicular that descent to the edge of the water is difficult save by a single trail which follows the detritus to a cave on one side. In this cave, the roof of which is not much higher than the water level, there are fragments of masonry, as if structures of some kind had formerly been erected in it. I have regarded this cave rather as a place of religious rites than of former habitation, possibly a place of retreat for ancient priests when praying for rain or moisture, or a shrine for the deposit of prayer offerings to rain or water gods.

Several isolated cliff dwellings are built at different levels in the sides of the cliffs. One of the best of these is diametrically opposite the cave mentioned above, a few feet below the rim of the depression. While this house was entered with little difficulty, there were others which I did not venture to visit.

The accompanying illustration (plate xcv) gives an idea of the general appearance of one of these cliff houses of Montezuma Well. It is built under an overhanging archway of rock in a deep recess, with masonry on three sides. The openings are shown, one of which overlooks the spring; the other is an entrance at one side. The face of masonry on the front is not plastered, and if it was formerly rough cast the mud has been worn away, leaving the stones exposed. The side wall, which has been less exposed to the elements, still retains the plastering, which is likewise found on the inner walls where it is quite smooth in places.

The number of cliff rooms in the walls of the well is small and their capacity, if used as dwellings, very limited. There are, however, ruins of pueblos of some size on the edge of the well.

One of the largest of these, shown in the accompanying illustration (plate xcvi), is situated on the neck of land separating the well from the valley of Beaver creek. This pueblo was rectangular in form, of considerable size, built of stones, and although at present almost demolished, shows perfectly the walls of former rooms. Fragments of ancient pottery would seem to indicate that the people who once inhabited this pueblo were in no respect different from other sedentary occupants of Verde valley. From their housetops they had a wide view over the creek on one side and the spring on the other, defending, by the site of their village, the one trail by which descent to the well was possible.

The remarkable geological character of Montezuma Well, and the spring within it, would have profoundly impressed itself on the folklore of any people of agricultural bent who lived in its neighborhood after emigrating to more arid lands. About a month after my visit to this remarkable spring I described the place to some of the old priests at Walpi and showed them sketches of the ruins. These priests seemed to have legendary knowledge of a place somewhat like it where they said the Great Plumed Snake had one of his numerous houses. They reminded me of a legend they had formerly related to me of how the Snake arose from a great cavity or depression in the ground, and how, they had heard, water boiled out of that hole into a neighboring river. The Hopi have personal knowledge of Montezuma Well, for many of their number have visited Verde valley, and they claim the ruins there as the homes of their ancestors. It would not be strange, therefore, if this marvelous crater was regarded by them as a house of Palülükoñ, their mythic Plumed Serpent.

Practically little is known of the pictography of this part of the Verde valley people, although it has an important bearing on the distribution of the cliff dwellers of the Southwest. There is evidence of at least two kinds of petroglyphs, indicative of two distinct peoples. One of these was of the Apache Mohave; the other, the agriculturists who built the cliff homes and villages of the plain. Those of the latter are almost identical with the work of the Pueblo peoples in the cliff dweller stage, from southern Utah and Colorado to the Mexican boundary. It is not a difficult task to distinguish the pictography of these two peoples, wherever found. The pictographs of the latter are generally pecked into the rock with a sharpened implement, probably of stone, while those of the former are usually scratched or painted on the surface of the rocks. Their main differences, however, are found in the character of the designs and the objects represented. This difference can be described only by considering individual rock drawings, but the practiced eye may readily distinguish the two kinds at a glance. The pictographs which are pecked in the cliff are, as a rule, older than those which are drawn or scratched, and resemble more closely those widely spread in the Pueblo area, for if the cliff-house people ever made painted pictographs, as there is every reason to believe they did, time has long ago obliterated them.

The pictured rocks (plate xcvii) near Cliff's ranch, on Beaver creek, four miles from Montezuma Well, have a great variety of objects depicted upon them. These rocks, which rise from the left bank of the creek opposite Cliff's ranch, bear over a hundred different rock pictures, figures of which are seen in the accompanying illustration. The rock surface is a layer of black malpais, through which the totem signatures have been pecked, showing the light stone beneath, and thus rendering them very conspicuous. Among these pictographs many familiar forms are recognizable, among them being the crane or blue heron, bears' and badgers' paws, turtles, snakes, antelopes, earth symbols, spirals, and meanders.

Among these many totems there was an unusual pictograph in the form of the figure 8, above which was a bear's paw accompanied by a human figure so common in southwestern rock etchings. A square figure with interior parallel squares extending to the center is also found, as elsewhere, in cliff-dweller pictography.

BUREAU OF AMERICAN ETHNOLOGY — — SEVENTEENTH ANNUAL RE-
PORT PL. XCV

Cliff House, Montezuma Well

CLIFF HOUSES OF THE RED-ROCKS

After the road from old Camp Verde to Flagstaff passes a deserted cabin at Beaver Head, it winds up a steep hill of lava or malpais to the top of the Mogollones. If, instead of ascending this hill, one turns to the left, taking an obscure road across the river bed, which is full of rough lava blocks, and in June, when I traveled its course, was without water, he soon finds himself penetrating a rugged country with bright-red cliffs on his right (plate xcviii). Continuing through great parks and plains he finally descends to the well-wooded valley of Oak creek, an affluent of Rio Verde. Here he finds evidences of aboriginal occupancy on all sides — ruins of buildings, fortified hilltops, pictographs, and irrigating ditches — testifying that there was at one time a considerable population in this valley. The fields of the ancient inhabitants have now given place to many excellent ranches, one of the most flourishing of which is not far from a lofty butte of red rock called the Court-house, which from its great size is a conspicuous object for miles around. In many of these canyons there are evidences of a former population, but the country is as yet almost unexplored; there are many difficult places to pass, yet once near the base of the rocks a way can be picked from the mouth of one canyon to another. It does not take long to discover that this now uninhabited region contains, like that along the Verde and its tributaries, many ancient dwellings, for there is scarcely a single canyon leading into these red cliffs in which evidences of former human habitations are not found in the form of ruins. There is little doubt that these unfrequented canyons have many and extensive cliff houses, the existence of which has thus far escaped the explorer. The sandstone of which they are composed is much eroded into caves with overhanging roofs, forming admirable sites for cliff houses as distinguished from cavate dwellings like those we have described. They are the only described ruins of a type hitherto thought to be unrepresented in the valley of the Verde.[23]

In our excursion into the Red-rock country we were obliged to make our own wagon road, as no vehicle had ever penetrated the rugged canyons visited by us. It was necessary to carry our drinking water with us from Oak creek, which fact impeded our progress and limited the time available in our reconnoissance. There was, however, in the pool near the ruins of Honanki enough water for our horses, and at the time we were there a limited amount of grass for fodder was found. I was told that later in the season both forage and water are abundant, so that these prime necessities being met, there is no reason why successful archeological investigations may not be successfully conducted in this part of the Verde region.

The limited population of this portion of the country rendered it difficult to get laborers at the time I made my reconnoissance, so that it would be advisable for one who expects to excavate the ruins in this region to take with him workmen from the settled portions of the valley.

RUINS NEAR SCHÜRMANN'S RANCH

The valley of Oak creek, near Court-house butte, especially in the vicinity of Schürmann's ranch, is dotted with fortifications, mounds indicative of ruins, and like evidences of aboriginal occupancy. There is undoubted proof that the former occupants of this plain constructed elaborate irrigating ditches, and that the waters of Oak creek were diverted from the stream and conducted over the adjoining valleys. There are several fortified hills in this locality. One of the best of these defensive works crowned a symmetrical mountain near Schürmann's house. The top of this mesa is practically inaccessible from any but the southern side, and was found to have a flat surface covered with scattered cacti and scrub cedar, among which were walls of houses nowhere rising more than two feet. The summit is perhaps 200 feet above the valley, and the ground plan of the former habitations extends over an area 100 feet in length, practically occupying the whole of the summit. Although fragments of pottery are scarce, and other evidences of long habitation difficult to find, the house walls give every evidence of being extremely ancient, and most of the rooms are filled with red soil out of which grow trees of considerable age.

Descending from this ruin-capped mesa, I noticed on the first terrace the remains of a roundhouse, or lookout, in the middle of which a cedar tree had taken

[23] The cliff houses of Bloody Basin I have not examined, but I suspect they are of the same type as the so-called Montezuma Castle, or Casa Montezuma, on the right bank of Beaver creek. The latter is referred to the cliff-house class, but it differs considerably from the ruins of the Red-rocks, on account of the character of the cavern in which it is built (see figure 246).

root and was growing vigorously. Although the walls of this structure do not rise above the level of the ground, there is no doubt that they are the remains of either a lookout or circular tower formerly situated at this point.

Many similar ruins are found throughout this vicinity, yet but little more is known of them than that they antedate the advent of white men. The majority of them were defensive works, built by the house dwellers, and their frequency would indicate either considerable population or long occupancy. Although many of those on the hilltops differ somewhat from the habitations in the valleys, I think there is little doubt that both were built by the same people.[24] There are likewise many caves in this region, which seem to have been camping places, for their walls are covered with soot and their floors strewn with charred mescal, evidences, probably, of Apache occupancy. This whole section of country was a stronghold of this ferocious tribe within the last few decades, which may account for the modern appearance of many of the evidences of aboriginal habitation.

BUREAU OF AMERICAN ETHNOLOGY — — SEVENTEENTH ANNUAL RE-
PORT PL. XCVI

Ruin On The Brink Of Montezuma Well

There are some good pictographs on the foundation rocks of that great pinnacle of red rock, called the Court-house, not far from Schürmann's ranch.[25] Some

[24] Fortified hilltops occur in many places in Arizona and are likewise found in the Mexican states of Sonora and Chihuahua, where they are known as *trincheras*. They are regarded as places of refuge of former inhabitants of the country, contemporaneous with ancient pueblos and cliff houses.

[25] This pinnacle is visible for miles, and is one of many prominences in the surrounding country. Unfortunately this region is so imperfectly surveyed that only approximations

of these are Apache productions, and the neighboring caves evidently formed shelters for these nomads, as ash pit and half-burnt logs would seem to show. This whole land was a stronghold of the Apache up to a recent date, and from it they were dislodged, many of the Indians being killed or removed by authority of the Government.

From the geological character of the Red-rocks I was led to suspect that cavate dwellings were not to be expected. The stone is hard and not readily excavated by the rude implements with which the aborigines of the region were supplied. But the remarkable erosion shown in this rock elsewhere had formed many deep caverns or caves, with overreaching roofs, very favorable for the sites of cliff houses. My hurried examination confirmed my surmises, for we here found dwellings of this kind, so similar to the type best illustrated in Mancos canyon of southern Colorado. There were several smoke-blackened caves without walls of masonry, but with floors strewn with charred wood, showing Apache occupancy. No cavate dwellings were found in the section of the Red-rocks visited by our party.

The two largest of the Red-rock cliff houses to which I shall refer were named Honanki or Bear-house and Palatki or Red-house. The former of these, as I learned from the names scribbled on its walls, had previously been visited by white men, but so far as I know it has never been mentioned in archeological literature. My attention was called to it by Mr Schürmann, at whose hospitable ranch I outfitted for my reconnoissance into the Red-rock country. The smaller ruin, Palatki, we discovered by chance during our visit, and while it is possible that some vaquero in search of a wild steer may have visited the neighborhood before us, there is every reason to believe that the ruin had escaped even the notice of these persons, and, like Honanki, was unknown to the archeologist.

The two ruins, Honanki and Palatki, are not the only ones in the lone canyon where we encamped. Following the canyon a short distance from its entrance, there was found to open into it from the left a tributary, or so-called box canyon, the walls of which are very precipitous. Perched on ledges of the cliffs there are several rows of fortifications or walls of masonry extending for many yards. It was impossible for us to enter these works, even after we had clambered up the side of the precipice to their level, so inaccessible were they to our approach. These "forts" were probably for refuge, but they are ill adapted as points of observation on account of the configuration of the canyon. Their masonry, as examined at a distance with a field glass, resembles that of Palatki and Honanki.

I was impressed by the close resemblance between the large cliff houses of the Red-rocks, with their overhanging roof of rock, and those of the San Juan and its tributaries in northern New Mexico. While it is recognized that cliff houses have been reported from Verde valley, I find them nowhere described, and our lack of information about them, so far as they are concerned, may have justified Nordenskiöld's belief that "the basin of the Colorado actually contains almost all the cliff dwellings of the United States." As the Gila flows into the Colorado near its mouth, the Red-rock ruins may in a sense be included in the Colorado basin, but

of distances are possible in this account, and the maps known to me are too meager in detail to fairly illustrate the distribution of these buttes.

there are many and beautiful cliff houses higher up near the sources of the Gila and its tributary, the Salt. In calling attention to the characteristic cliff dwellings of the Red-rocks I am making known a new region of ruins closely related to those of Canyon de Tségi, or Chelly, the San Juan and its tributaries.

Although the cliff houses of Verde valley had been known for many years, and the ruins here described are of the same general character, anyone who examines Casa Montezuma, on Beaver creek, and compares it with Honanki, will note differences of an adaptive nature. The one feature common to Honanki and the "Cliff Palace" of Mancos canyon is the great overhanging roof of the cavern, which, in that form, we miss in Casa Montezuma (figure 246).[26]

FIG. 246—CASA MONTEZUMA ON BEAVER CREEK

We made two camps in the Red-rock country, one at the mouth of a wild canyon near an older camp where a well had been dug and the cellar of an American house was visible. This camp was fully six miles from Schürmann's ranch and was surrounded by some of the wildest scenery that I had ever witnessed. The accompanying view (plate xcviii) was taken from a small elevation near by, and gives a faint idea of the magnificent mountains by which we were surrounded. The colors of the rocks are variegated, so that the gorgeous cliffs appear to be banded, rising from 800 to 1,000 feet sheer on all sides. These rocks had weathered into fantastic

---

[26] In certain cavate houses on Oak creek we find these caverns in two tiers, one above the other, and the hill above is capped by a well-preserved building. In one of these we find the entrance to the cavern walled in, with the exception of a T-shape doorway and a small window. This chamber shows a connecting link between the type of true cavate dwellings and that of cliff-houses.

shapes suggestive of cathedrals, Greek temples, and sharp steeples of churches extending like giant needles into the sky. The scenery compares very favorably with that of the Garden of the Gods, and is much more extended. This place, I have no doubt, will sooner or later become popular with the sightseer, and I regard the discovery of these cliffs one of the most interesting of my summer's field work.

BUREAU OF AMERICAN ETHNOLOGY — — SEVENTEENTH ANNUAL RE-PORT PL. XCVII

Pictographs Near Cliff Ranch, Verde Valley

On the sides of these inaccessible cliffs we noticed several cliff houses, but so high were they perched above us that they were almost invisible. To reach them at their dizzy altitude was impossible, but we were able to enter some caves a few hundred feet above our camp, finding in them nothing but charred mescal and other evidences of Apache camps. Their walls and entrances are blackened with smoke, but no sign of masonry was detected.

We moved our camp westward from this canyon (which, from a great cliff resembling the Parthenon, I called Temple canyon), following the base of the precipitous mountains to a second canyon, equally beautiful but not so grand, and built our fire in a small grove of scrub oak and cottonwood. In this lonely place Lloyd had lived over a winter, watching his stock, and had dug a well and erected a corral. We adopted his name for this camp and called it Lloyd canyon. There was no water in the well, but a few rods beyond it there was a pool, from which we watered our horses. On the first evening at this camp we sighted a bear, which gave the name Honanki, "Bear-house," to the adjacent ruined dwellings.

The enormous precipice of red rock west of our camp at Lloyd's corral hid

Honanki from view at first, but we soon found a trail leading directly to it, and during our short stay in this neighborhood we remained camped near the cotton-woods at the entrance to the canyon, not far from the abandoned corral. Our studies of Honanki led to the discovery of Palatki (figure 247), which we investigated on our return to Temple canyon. I will, therefore, begin my description of the Red-rock cliff houses with those last discovered, which, up to the visit which I made, had never been studied by archeologists.

PALATKI

There are two neighboring ruins which I shall include in my consideration of Palatki, and these for convenience may be known as Ruin ı and Ruin ıı, the former situated a little eastward from the latter. They are but a short distance apart, and are in the same box canyon. Ruin ı (plate xcıx) is the better preserved, and is a fine type of the compact form of cliff dwellings in the Red-rock country.

This ruin is perched on the top of a talus which has fallen from the cliff above, and is visible for some distance above the trees, as one penetrates the canyon. It is built to the side of a perpendicular wall of rock which, high above its tallest walls, arches over it, sheltering the walls from rain or eroding influences. From the dry character of the earth on the floors I suspect that for years not a drop of water has penetrated the inclosures, although they are now roofless.

A highly characteristic feature of Ruin ı is the repetition of rounded or bow-shape front walls, occurring several times in their length, and arranged in such a way as to correspond roughly to the inclosures behind them. By this arrangement the size of the rooms was increased and possibly additional solidity given to the wall itself. This departure from a straight wall implies a degree of architectural skill, which, while not peculiar to the cliff dwellings of the Red-rocks, is rarely found in southern cliff houses. The total length of the front wall of the ruin, including the part which has fallen, is approximately 120 feet, and the altitude of the highest wall is not far from 30 feet.

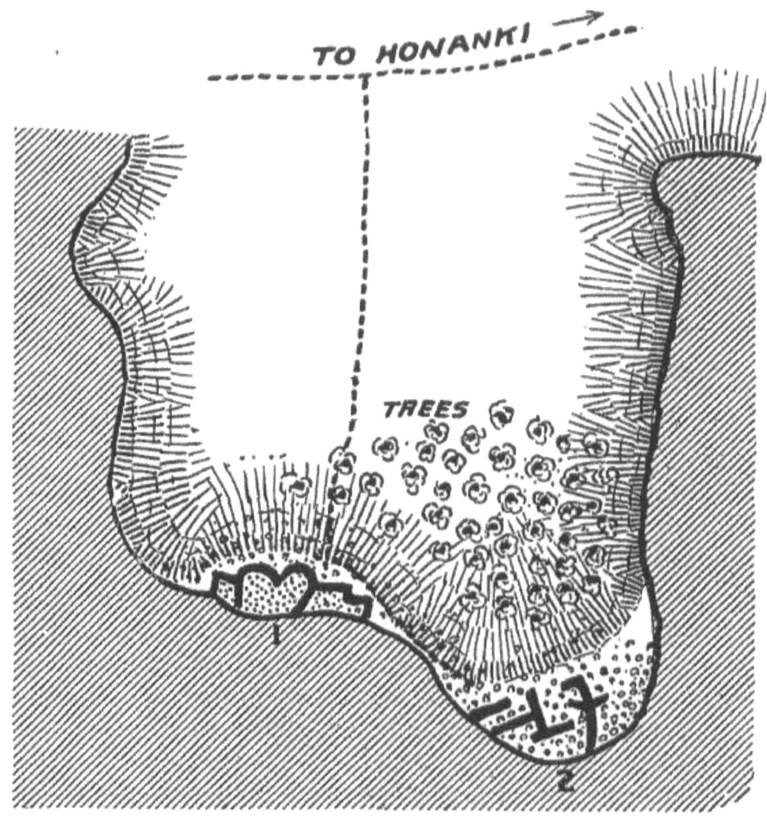

FIG. 247—GROUND PLAN OF PALATKI (RUINS I AND II)

From the arrangement of openings in the front wall at the highest part there is good evidence of the former existence of two stories. At several points the foundation of the wall is laid on massive bowlders, which contribute to the height of the wall itself. The masonry is made up of irregular or roughly squared blocks of red stone laid in red clay, both evidently gathered in the immediate neighborhood of the ruin. The building stones vary in size, but are as a rule flat, and show well directed fractures as if dressed by hammering. In several places there still remains a superficial plastering, which almost conceals the masonry. The blocks of stone in the lower courses are generally more massive than those higher up; this feature, however, whether considered as occurring here or in the cliff houses of Mesa Verde, as pointed out by Nordenskiöld, seems to me not to indicate different builders, but is due simply to convenience. There appears to be no regularity in the courses of component blocks of stone, and when necessity compelled, as in the courses laid on bowlders, which serve as a foundation, thin wedges of stone, or spalls, were inserted in the crevices. The walls are vertical, but the corners are sometimes far from perpendicular.

BUREAU OF AMERICAN ETHNOLOGY — — SEVENTEENTH ANNUAL RE-
PORT PL. XCVIII

The Red Rocks; Temple Canyon

The interior of the ruin is divided into a number of inclosures by partitions at right angles to the front wall, fastening it to the face of the cliff. This I have lettered, beginning at the extreme right inclosure with *A*. The inclosure has bounding walls, built on a bowlder somewhat more than six feet high. It has no external passageway, and probably the entrance was from the roof. This inclosure communicates by a doorway directly with the adjoining chamber, *B*. The corner of this room, or the angle made by the lateral with the front walls, is rounded, a constant feature in well-built cliff houses. No windows exist, and the upper edge of both front and lateral walls is but slightly broken.

The front wall of inclosure *B* bulges into bow-shape form, and was evidently at least two stories high. This wall is a finely laid section of masonry, composed of large, rough stones in the lower courses, upon which smaller, roughly hewn stones are built. It is probable, from the large amount of débris in the neighborhood, that formerly there were rows of single-story rooms in front of what are now the standing walls, but the character of their architecture is difficult to determine with certainty. Their foundations, although partially covered, are not wholly concealed.

The front wall of inclosure *B* is pierced by three openings, the largest of which is a square passageway into the adjoining room, and is situated in the middle of the curved wall. A wooden lintel, which had been well hewn with stone implements, still remains in place above this passageway, and under it the visitor passes through a low opening which has the appearance of having been once a doorway. Above this entrance, on each side, in the wall, is a square hole, which originally may have been the points of support of floor beams. Formerly, likewise, there was a large square opening above the middle passageway, but this has been closed with masonry, leaving in place the wooden beam which once supported the wall above. The upper edge of the front wall of inclosure *B* is level, and is but little broken except in two places, where there are notches, one above each of the square holes already mentioned. It is probable that these depressions were intended for the ends of the beams which once supported a combined roof and floor.

On the perpendicular wall which forms the rear of inclosure *B*, many feet above the top of the standing front walls, there are several pictographs of Apache origin. The height of these above the level of the former roof would appear to indicate the existence of a third story, for the hands which drew them must have been at least 15 feet above the present top of the standing wall.

The front of *C* is curved like that of inclosure *B*, and is much broken near the foundations, where there is a passageway. There is a small hole on each side of a middle line, as in *B*, situated at about the same level as the floor, indicating the former position of a beam. Within the ruin there is a well-made partition separating inclosures *B* and *C*.

The size of room *D* is much less than that of *B* or *C*, but, with the exception of a section at the left, the front wall has fallen. The part which remains upright, however, stands like a pinnacle, unconnected with the face of the cliff or with the second-story wall of inclosure *C*. It is about 20 feet in height, and possibly its altitude appears greater than it really is from the fact that its foundations rest upon a bowlder nearly six feet high (plate cx).

The foundations of rooms *E* and *F* (plate c) are built on a lower level than those of *B* and *C* or *D*, and their front walls, which are really low, are helped out by similar bowlders, which serve as foundations. The indications are that both these inclosures were originally one story in height, forming a wing to the central section of the ruin, which had an additional tier of rooms. There is an entrance to *F* at the extreme left, and the whole room was lower than the floor of the lower stories of *B*, *C*, and *D*.

The most conspicuous pictograph on the cliff above Ruin i of Palatki, is a circular white figure, seen in the accompanying illustration. This pictograph is situated directly above the first room on the right, *A*, and was apparently made with chalk, so elevated that at present it is far above the reach of a person standing on any of the walls. From its general character I am led to believe that it was made by the Apache and not by the builders of the pueblo.

There were no names of white visitors anywhere on the walls of Palatki, which, so far as it goes, affords substantial support of my belief that we were the first white men to visit this ruin. While it can not be positively asserted that we were the original discoverers of this interesting building, there is no doubt that I was the first to describe it and to call attention to its highly characteristic architectural plan.

The walls of Palatki are not so massive as those of the neighboring Honanki, and the number of rooms in both ruins which form Palatki is much smaller. Each of these components probably housed not more than a few families, while several phratries could readily be accommodated in Honanki.

BUREAU OF AMERICAN ETHNOLOGY— — SEVENTEENTH ANNUAL RE-PORT PL. XCIX

Palatki (Ruin I)

The second Palatki ruin is well preserved, and as a rule the rooms, especially those in front, have suffered more from vandalism and from the elements than have those of Ruin i. The arrangement of the rooms is somewhat different from that of the more exposed eastern ruin, to which it undoubtedly formerly belonged.

Ruin ii lies in a deep recess or cave, the roof of which forms a perfect arch above the walls. It is situated a few hundred feet to the west, and is easily approached by following the fallen débris at the foot of a perpendicular cliff. The front walls have all fallen, exposing the rear wall of what was formerly a row of rooms, as shown in the accompanying illustration (plate ci). There are evidences that this row of rooms was but a single story in height, while those behind it have indications of three stories. Ruin ii is more hidden by the trees and by its obscure position in a cavern than the former, but the masonry in both is of the same general character.

On approaching Ruin ii from Ruin i there is first observed a well-made though rough wall, as a rule intact, along which the line of roof and flooring can readily be traced (plate ci). In front of this upright wall are fragments of other walls, some standing in unconnected sections, others fallen, their fragments extending down the sides of the talus among the bushes. It was observed that this wall is broken by an entrance which passes into a chamber, which may be called *A*, and two square holes are visible, one on each side, above it. These holes were formerly filled by two logs, which once supported the floor of a second chamber, the line of which still remains on the upright wall. The small square orifice directly above the entrance is a peephole.

In examining the character of the wall it will be noticed that its masonry is in places rough cast, and that there was little attempt at regularity in the courses of the component stones, which are neither dressed nor aligned, although the wall is practically vertical.

At one point, in full view of the observer, a log is apparently inserted in the wall, and if the surrounding masonry be examined it will be found that an opening below it had been filled in after the wall was erected. It is evident, from its position relatively to the line indicating the roof, that this opening was originally a passageway from one room to another. Passing back of the standing wall an inclosure (room *A*) is entered, one side of which is the rock of the cliff, while the other three bounding walls are built of masonry, 20 feet high. This inclosure was formerly divided into an upper and a lower room by a partition, which served as the roof of the lower and the floor of the upper chambers. Two beams stretched across this inclosure about six feet above the débris of the present floor, and the openings in the walls, where these beams formerly rested, are readily observed. In the same way the beam-holes of the upper story may also be easily seen on the top of the wall. Between the rear wall of this inclosure and the perpendicular cliff there was a recess which appears to have been a dark chamber, probably designed for use as a storage room or granary. The configuration of the cliff, which forms the major part of the inclosing wall of this chamber, imparts to it an irregular or roughly triangular form.

The entire central portion of the ruin is very much broken down, and the floor is strewn to a considerable depth with the débris of fallen walls. On both sides there are nicely aligned, smoothly finished walls, with traces of beams on the level of former floors. Some of these bounding walls are curved; others are straight, and in places they rise 20 feet. Marks of fire are visible everywhere; most of the beams have been wrenched from their places, as a result of which the walls have been much mutilated, badly cracked, or thrown down.

There are no pictographs near this ruin, and no signs of former visits by white men.

Midway between Honanki and the second Palatki ruin a small ancient house of the same character as the latter was discovered. This ruin is very much exposed, and therefore the walls are considerably worn, but six well-marked inclosures, indicative of former rooms, were readily made out. No overarching rock shielded this ruin from the elements, and rubble from fallen walls covers the talus upon which it stands. The adobe mortar between the stones is much worn, and no fragment of plastering is traceable within or without. This evidence of the great weathering of the walls of the ruin is not considered indicative of greater age than the better preserved ruins in the neighborhood, but rather of exposure to the action of the elements. Not only are the walls in a very poor condition, but also the floors show, from the absence of dry soil upon them, that the whole ruin has suffered greatly from the same denudation. There are no fragments of pottery about it, and small objects indicating former habitation are also wanting. A cedar had taken root where the floor once was, and its present great size shows considerable age. If any pictographs formerly existed in the adjacent cliff they have disappeared. There is likewise no evidence that the Apache had ever sought it for shelter, or if they had, their occupancy occurred so long ago that time has effaced all evidence of their presence.

HONANKI

The largest ruin visited in the Red-rock country was called, following Hopi etymology, Honanki; but the nomenclature was adopted not because it was so called by the Hopi, but following the rule elsewhere suggested.

BUREAU OF AMERICAN ETHNOLOGY — — SEVENTEENTH ANNUAL RE-PORT PL. C

Palatki (Ruin I)

This ruin lies under a lofty buttress of rock westward from Lloyd's canyon, which presented the only available camping place in its neighborhood. At the time of my visit there was but scanty water in the canyon and that not potable except for stock. We carried with us all the water we used, and when this was exhausted were obliged to retrace our steps to Oak creek. There are groves of trees in the canyon and evidences that at some seasons there is an abundant water supply. A corral had been made and a well dug near its mouth, but with these exceptions there were no evidences of previous occupancy by white men. We had hardly pitched our camp before tracks of large game were noticed, and before we left we sighted a bear which had come down to the water to drink, but which beat a hasty retreat at our approach. As previously stated, the knowledge of this ruin was communicated to me by Mr Schürmann.

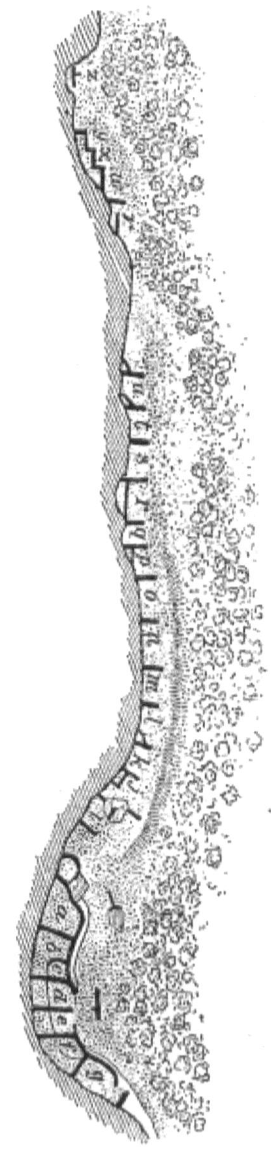

FIG. 248—GROUND PLAN OF HONANKI

The Honanki ruin (figure 248) extends along the base of the cliff for a considerable distance, and may for convenience of description be divided into two sections, which, although generally similar, differ somewhat in structural features. The former is lineal in its arrangement, and consists of a fringe of houses extending along the base of the cliff at a somewhat lower level than the other. The walls of this section were for the greater part broken, and at no place could anything more than the foundation of the front wall be detected, although fragments of masonry strewed the sides of the declivity near its base. The house walls which remain are well-built parallel spurs constructed at right angles to the cliff, which served as the rear of all the chambers. At the extreme right end of this row of rooms, situated deep in a large cavern with overhanging roof, portions of a rear wall of masonry are well preserved, and the lateral walls of one or two chambers in this portion of the ruin are still intact. Straggling along from that point, following the contour of the base of the cliff under which it lies, there extends a long row of rooms, all destitute of a front wall.

The first division (plate cii), beginning with the most easterly of the series, is quite hidden at one end in a deep cavern. At this point the builders, in order to obtain a good rear wall to their rooms, constructed a line of masonry parallel with the face of the cliff. At right angles to this construction, at the eastern extremity, there are remnants of a lateral wall, but the remainder had tumbled to the ground. The standing wall of z is not continuous with that of the next room, y, and apparently was simply the rear of a large room with the remains of a lateral wall at right angles to it. The other walls of this chamber had tumbled into a deep gorge, overgrown with bushes which conceal the fragments. This building is set back deeply in the cave, and is isolated from the remaining parts of the ruin, although at the level which may have been its roof there runs a kind of gallery formed by a ledge of rock, plastered with adobe, which formerly connected the roof with the rest of the pueblo. This ledge was a means of intercommunication, and a continuation of the same ledge, in rooms s, t, and u, supported the rafters of these chambers. At u there are evidences of two stories or two tiers of rooms, but those in front have fallen to the ground.

The standing wall at u is about five feet high, connected with the face of the cliff by masonry. The space between it and the cliff was not large enough for a habitable chamber, and was used probably as a storage place. In front of the standing wall of room u there was another chamber, the walls of which now strew the talus of the cliff.

The highest and best preserved room of the second series of chambers at Honanki is that designated p, at a point where the ruin reached an elevation of 20 feet. Here we have good evidence of rooms of two stories, as indicated by the points of insertion of the beams of a floor, at the usual levels above the ground. In fact, it is probable that the whole section of the ruin was two stories high throughout, the front walls having fallen along the entire length. From the last room on the left to the eastern extremity of the line of houses which leads to the main ruin of Honanki, no ground plans were detected at the base of the cliffs, but fallen rocks and scattered débris are strewn over the whole interval.

The eastern part of the main ruin of Honanki, however, lies but a short distance west of that described, and consists of many similar chambers, arranged side by side. These are lettered in the diagram *h* to *u*, beginning with *h*, which is irregularly circular in form, and ends with a high wall, the first to be seen as one approaches the ruin from Lloyd canyon. This range of houses is situated on a lower foundation and at a lower level than that of the main quarter of Honanki, and a trail runs along so close to the rooms that the whole series is easily visited without much climbing. No woodwork remains in any of these rooms, and the masonry is badly broken in places either by natural agencies or through vandalism.

Beginning with *h*, the round room, which adjoins the main quarter of Honanki, we find much in its shape to remind us of a kiva. The walls are in part built on foundations of large bowlders, one of which formed the greater part of the front wall. This circular room was found to be full of fallen débris, and could not be examined without considerable excavation. If it were a kiva, which I very much doubt, it is an exception among the Verde valley ruins, where no true kiva has yet been detected.[27]

BUREAU OF AMERICAN ETHNOLOGY— — SEVENTEENTH ANNUAL RE-PORT PL. CI

Front Wall Of Palatki (Ruin Ii)

---

[27] The absence of kivas in the ruins of the Verde has been commented on by Minde-leff, and has likewise been found to be characteristic of the cliff houses on the upper courses of the other tributaries of Gila and Salado rivers. The round kiva appears to be confined to the middle and eastern ruins of the pueblo area, and are very numerous in the ruins of San Juan valley.

Following *h* there is an inclosure which originally may have been a habitable room, as indicated by the well-constructed front wall, but it is so filled with large stones that it is difficult to examine its interior. On one side the wall, which is at right angles to the face of the cliff, is 10 feet high, and the front wall follows the surface of a huge bowlder which serves as its foundation.

Room *i* is clearly defined, and is in part inclosed by a large rock, on top of which there still remains a fragment of a portion of the front wall. A spur of masonry connects this bowlder with the face of the cliff, indicating all that remains of the former division between rooms *i* and *j*. An offshoot from this bowlder, in the form of a wall 10 feet high, formerly inclosed one side of a room. In the rear of chamber *j* there are found two receptacles or spaces left between the rear wall and the face of the cliff, while the remaining wall, which is 10 feet high, is a good specimen of pueblo masonry.

The two side walls of room *k* are well preserved, but the chamber resembles the others of the series in the absence of a front wall. In this room, however, there remains what may have been the fragment of a rear wall parallel with the face of the cliff. This room has also a small cist of masonry in one corner, which calls to mind certain sealed cavities in the cavate dwellings.

The two side walls of *m* and *n* are respectively eight and ten feet high. There is nothing exceptional in the standing walls of room *o*, one of which, five feet in altitude, still remains erect. Room *p* has a remnant of a rear wall plastered to the face of the cliff.

Room *r* (plate CIII) is a finely preserved chamber, with lateral walls 20 feet high, of well-constructed masonry, that in the rear, through which there is an opening leading into a dark chamber, occupying the space between it and the cliff. It is braced by connecting walls at right angles to the face of the solid rock.

At *s*, the face of the cliff forms a rear wall of the room, and one of the side walls is fully 20 feet high. The points of insertion of the flooring are well shown, about 10 feet from the ground, proving that the ruin at this point was at least two stories high.

Two walled inclosures, one within the other, characterize room *u*. On the cliff above it there is a series of simple pictographs, consisting of short parallel lines pecked into the rock, and are probably of Apache origin. This room closes the second series, along the whole length of which, in front of the lateral walls which mark different chambers, there are, at intervals, piles of débris, which enabled an approximate determination of the situation of the former front wall, fragments of the foundations of which are traceable in situ in several places.

The hand of man and the erosion of the elements have dealt harshly with this portion of Honanki, for not a fragment of timber now remains in its walls. This destruction, so far as human agency is concerned, could not have been due to white men, but probably to the Apache, or possibly to the cliff villagers themselves at the time of or shortly after the abandonment of the settlement.

From the second section of Honanki we pass to the third and best-preserved portion of the ruins (figure 249), indicated in the diagram from *a* to *g*. To this section I have referred as the "main ruin," for it was evidently the most populous quarter of the ancient cliff dwelling. It is better preserved than the remainder of Honanki, and is the only part in which all four walls of the chambers still remain erect. Built at a higher level than the series of rooms already considered, it must have towered above them, and possibly served as a place of retreat when danger beset the more exposed quarters of the village.

FIG. 249—THE MAIN RUIN OF HONANKI

Approaching the main ruin of Honanki (plate civ) from the east, or the parts already described, one passes between the buttress on which the front wall of the rounded room *h* is built and a fragment of masonry on the left, by a natural gateway through which the trail is very steep. On the right there towers above the visitor a well-preserved wall of masonry, the front of room *a*, and he soon passes abreast of the main portion of the ruin of Honanki. This section is built in a huge cavern, the overhanging roof of which, is formed by natural rock, arching far above the tops of the highest walls of the pueblo and suggesting the surroundings of the "Cliff Palace" of Mesa Verde, so well described by the late Baron G. Nordenskiöld in his valuable monograph on the ruins of that section of southern Colorado. The main ruin of Honanki is one of the largest and best preserved architectural monuments of the former people of Verde valley that has yet been described. Although somewhat resembling its rival, the well-known "Casa Montezuma" of Beaver creek, its architecture is dissimilar on account of the difference in the form of the cavern in which it is built and the geological character of the surrounding cliffs. Other Verde ruins may have accommodated more people, when inhabited, but none of its type south of Canyon de Chelly have yet been described which excel it in size and condition of preservation. I soon found that our party were not the first whites who had seen this lonely village, as the names scribbled on its walls attested; but so far as I know it had not previously been visited by archeologists.

BUREAU OF AMERICAN ETHNOLOGY — — SEVENTEENTH ANNUAL REPORT PL. CII

Honanki (Ruin Ii)

In the main portion of Honanki we found that the two ends of the crescentic row of united rooms which compose it are built on rocky elevations, with foundations considerably higher than those of the rooms in the middle portion of the ruins. The line of the front wall is, therefore, not exactly crescentic, but irregularly curved (figure 249), conforming to the rear of the cavern in which the houses are situated. About midway in the curve of the front walls two walls indicative of former rooms extend at an angle of about 25° to the main front wall. All the component rooms of the main part of Honanki can be entered, some by external passageways, others by doorways communicating with adjacent chambers. None of the inclosures have roofs or upper floors, although indications of the former existence of both these structural features may readily be seen in several places. Although wooden beams are invariably wanting, fragments of these still project from the walls, almost always showing on their free ends, inside the rooms, the effect of fire. I succeeded in adding to the collection a portion of one of these beams, the extremity of which had been battered off, evidently with a stone implement. In the alkaline dust which covered the floor several similar specimens were seen.

The stones which form the masonry of the wall (figure 250) were not, as a rule, dressed or squared before they were laid with adobe mortar, but were generally set in place in the rough condition in which they may still be obtained anywhere under the cliff.

All the mortar used was of adobe or the tenacious clay which serves so many purposes among the Pueblos. The walls of the rooms were plastered with a thick layer of the same material. The rear wall of each room is the natural rock of the cliff, which rises vertically and has a very smooth surface. The great natural archway which covers the whole pueblo protects it from wind and rain, and as a consequence, save on the front face, there are few signs of natural erosion. The hand of man, however, has dealt rudely with this venerable building, and many of the walls, especially of rooms which formerly stood before the central portion, lie prone upon the earth; but so securely were the component stones held together by the adobe that even after their fall sections of masonry still remain intact.

FIG. 250—STRUCTURE OF WALL OF HONANKI

There are seven walled inclosures in the main part of Honanki, and as each of these was formerly at least two stories high there is substantial evidence of the former existence of fourteen rooms in this part of the ruin. There can be little doubt that there were other rooms along the front of the central portion, and the fallen walls show them to have been of large size. It would likewise appear that the middle part was higher than the two wings, which would increase the number of chambers, so that with these additions it may safely be said that this part of Honanki alone contained not far from twenty rooms.

BUREAU OF AMERICAN ETHNOLOGY— — SEVENTEENTH ANNUAL RE-
PORT PL. CIII

Walls Of Honanki

The recess in the cliff in which the ruin is situated is lower in the middle than
at either side, where there are projecting ledges of rock which were utilized by the
builders in the construction of the foundations, the line of the front wall following
the inequalities of the ground. It thus results that rooms *g, a, b,* and a part of *c,* rise
from a foundation about breast high, or a little higher than the base of rooms *d, e,*
and *f.*

The front wall of *a* has for its foundation a spur or ledge of rock, which is continued under *b* and a part of *c.* The corner or angle of this wall, facing the round
chamber, is curved in the form of a tower, a considerable section of its masonry
being intact. Near the foundation and following the inequalities of the rock surface
the beginning of a wall at right angles to the face of the ruin at this point is seen. A
small embrasure, high above the base of the front wall, on the side by which one
approaches the ruin from the east, and two smaller openings on the same level,
looking out over the valley, suggest a floor and lookouts. The large square orifice
in the middle of the face of the wall has a wooden lintel, still in place; the opening
is large enough for use as a door or passageway. The upper edge of the front wall
is somewhat irregular, but a notch in it above the square opening is conspicuous.

The rear wall of room *a* was the face of the cliff, formed of solid rock without masonry and very much blackened by smoke from former fires. As, however, there is evidence that since its destruction or abandonment by its builders this ruin has been occupied as a camping place by the Apache, it is doubtful to which race we should ascribe this discoloration of the walls by soot.

On the ground floor there is a passageway into chamber *b*, which is considerably enlarged, although the position of the lintel is clearly indicated by notches in the wall. The beam which was formed there had been torn from its place and undoubtedly long ago used for firewood by nomadic visitors. The open passageway, measured externally, is about 15 feet above the foundation of the wall, through which it is broken, and about 8 feet below the upper edge of the wall.

Room *b* is an irregular, square chamber, two stories high, communicating with *a* and *c* by passages which are enlarged by breakage in the walls. A small hole in the front wall, about 6 feet from the floor, opens externally to the air. The walls are, in general, about 2 feet thick, and are composed of flat red stones laid in clay of the same color. The cliff forms the rear wall of the chamber. The clay at certain places in the walls, especially near the insertions of the beams and about the window openings, appears to have been mixed with a black pitch, which serves to harden the mixture.

Room *c* is the first of a series of chambers, with external passageways, but its walls are very much broken down, and the openings thereby enlarged. The front wall is almost straight and in one place stands 30 feet, the maximum height of the standing wall of the ruins. In one corner a considerable quantity of ashes and many evidences of fire, some of which may be ascribed to Apache occupants, was detected. A wooden beam, marking the line of the floor of a second story, was seen projecting from the front wall, and there are other evidences of a floor at this level. Large beams apparently extended from the front wall to the rear of the chamber, where they rested on a ledge in the cliff, and over these smaller sticks were laid side by side and at right angles to the beams. These in turn supported either flat stones or a layer of mud or clay. The method of construction of one of these roofs is typical of a Tusayan kiva, where ancient architectural forms are adhered to and best preserved.

The entrance to room *d* is very much enlarged by the disintegration of the wall, and apparently there was at this point a difference in level of the front wall, for there is evidence of rooms in advance of those connected with the chambers described, as shown by a line of masonry, still standing, parallel to the front face of inclosures *c* and *d*.

Room *e* communicates by a doorway with the chamber marked *f*, and there is a small window in the same partition. This room had a raised banquette on the side toward the cliff, recalling an arrangement of the floor similar to that in the cavate dwellings opposite Squaw mountain which I have described. This platform is raised about three feet above the remainder of the floor of *f*, and, like it, is strewn with large slabs of stone, which have fallen from the overhanging roof. In the main floor, at one corner, near the platform, there is a rectangular box-like structure made of thin slabs of stone set on edge, suggesting the grinding bins of the Pueblos. Room *f* communicates with *g* by a passageway which has a stone lintel. The holes in the walls, in which beams were once inserted, are seen in several places at different levels above the floor. The ends of several beams, one extremity of which is invariably charred, were found set in the masonry, and others were dug from the débris in the floor.

As a result of the curve in the front wall of the ruin at that point, the shape of room *f* is roughly quadrate, with banquettes on two sides. There are six large beam holes in the walls, and the position of the first floor is well shown on the face of the partition, separating *f* from *g*. The passageway from one of these rooms to the other is slightly arched.

Room *g* is elongated, without an external entrance, and communicates with *f* by a small opening, through which it is very difficult to crawl. Its longest dimension is almost at right angles to the front face of the remaining rooms, and it is raised above them by its foundation on an elevated rock like that of *a*, *b*, and *c*. There is a small, square, external opening which may have served as the position of a former beam or log. The upper level of the front wall is more or less broken down in places, and formerly may have been much higher. Beyond *g* a spur of masonry is built at right angles to the cliff, inclosing a rectangular chamber at the end of the ruin which could not be entered. Possibly in former times it was accessible by means of a ladder from the roof, whence communication with other portions of the structure was also had.

BUREAU OF AMERICAN ETHNOLOGY—— SEVENTEENTH ANNUAL REPORT PL. CIV

Approach To Main Part Of Honanki

A short distance beyond the westernmost rooms of Honanki, almost covered with bushes and adjoining the base of the cliff, there is a large ash heap in which are many fragments of pottery and the bones of various animals. It is probable that excavation in this quarter would reveal many interesting objects. In the cliffs above this ash heap, far beyond reach, there is a walled niche which has never been disturbed. This structure is similar to those near the cavate dwellings, and when opened will probably be found to contain buried mortuary objects of interesting character. I did not disturb this inclosure, inasmuch as I had no ladders or ropes with which to approach it.

It is very difficult to properly estimate, from the number of rooms in a cliff house, the former population, and as a general thing the tendency is rather to overstate than to fall short of the true total. In a pueblo like Hano, on the first or east mesa of Tusayan, for instance, there are many uninhabited rooms, and others serve as storage chambers, while in places the pueblo has so far fallen into ruin as to be uninhabitable. If a pueblo is very much concentrated the population varies at different seasons of the year. In summer it is sparsely inhabited; in winter it is rather densely populated. While Palatki and Honanki together had rooms sufficient to house 500 people, I doubt whether their aggregate population, ever exceeded 200. This estimate, of course, is based on the supposition that these villages were contemporaneously inhabited.

The evidences all point to a belief, however, that they were both permanent dwelling places and not temporary resorts at certain seasons of the year.

The pictographs on the face of the cliff above Honanki are for the greater part due to the former Apache occupants of the rooms, and are situated high above the tops of the walls of the ruin. They are, as a rule, drawn with white chalk, which shows very clearly on the red rock, and are particularly numerous above room *g*. The figure of a circle, with lines crossing one another diametrically and continued as rays beyond the periphery, possibly represent the sun. Many spiral figures, almost constant pictographs in cliff ruins, are found in several places. Another strange design, resembling some kind of insect, is very conspicuous.

A circle painted green and inclosed in a border of yellow is undoubtedly of Apache origin. There is at one point a row of small pits, arranged in line, suggesting a score or enumeration of some kind, and a series of short parallel lines of similar import was found not far away. This latter method of recording accounts is commonly used at the present time in Tusayan, both in houses and on cliffs; and one of the best of these, said to enumerate the number of Apache killed by the Hopi in a raid many years ago, may be seen above the trail by which the visitor enters the pueblo of Hano on the East Mesa. The names of several persons scratched on the face of the cliff indicate that Americans had visited Honanki before me.

The majority of the paleoglyphs at both Palatki and Honanki are of Apache origin, and are of comparatively modern date, as would naturally be expected. In some instances their colors are as fresh as if made a few years ago, and there is no doubt that they were drawn after the building was deserted by its original occupants. The positions of the pictographs on the cliffs imply that they were drawn before the roofs and flooring had been destroyed, thus showing how lately the ruin preserved its ancient form. In their sheltered position there seems to be no reason why the ancient pictographs should not have been preserved, and the fact that so few of the figures pecked in the cliff now remain is therefore instructive.

One of the first tendencies of man in visiting a ruin is to inscribe his name on its walls or on neighboring cliffs. This is shared by both Indians and whites, and the former generally makes his totem on the rock surface, or adds that of his gods, the sun, rain-cloud, or katcinas. Inscriptions recording events are less common, as they are more difficult to indicate with exactitude in this system of pictography. The majority of ancient pictographs in the Red-rock country, like those I have considered in other parts of Verde valley, are identical with picture writings now made in Tusayan, and are recognized and interpreted without hesitation by the Hopi Indians. In their legends, in which the migrations of their ancestors are recounted, the traditionists often mention the fact that their ancestors left their totem signatures at certain points in their wanderings. The Patki people say that you will find on the rocks of Palatkwabi, the "Red Land of the South" from which they came, totems of the rain-cloud, sun, crane, parrot, etc. If we find these markings in the direction which they are thus definitely declared to exist, and the Hopi say similar pictures were made by their ancestors, there seems no reason to question such circumstantial evidence that some of the Hopi clans once came from this region.[28]

One of the most interesting of the pictographs pecked in the rock is a figure which, variously modified, is a common decoration on cliff-dweller pottery from the Verde valley region to the ruins of the San Juan and its tributaries. This figure has the form of two concentric spirals, the ends of which do not join. As this design assumes many modifications, it may be well to consider a few forms which it assumes on the pottery of the cliff people and on that of their descendants, the Pueblos.

The so-called black-and-white ware, or white pottery decorated with black lines, which is so characteristic of the ceramics of the cliff-dwellers, is sometimes, as we shall see, found in ruins like Awatobi and Sikyatki; but it is so rare, as compared with other varieties, that it may be regarded as intrusive.

One of the simplest forms of the broken-line motive is a Greek fret, in which there is a break in the component square figures or where the line is noncontinuous. In the simplest form, which appears prominently on modern pottery, but which is rare or wanting on true black-and-white ware, we have two crescentic figures, the concavities of which face in different directions, but the horns overlap. This is a symbol which the participants in the dance called the Húmiskatcina still paint with pigments on their breasts, and which is used on shields and various religious paraphernalia.

A study of any large collection of decorated Pueblo ware, ancient or modern, will show many modifications of this broken line, a number of which I shall discuss more in detail when pottery ornamentation is considered. A design so dis-

---

[28] See "Tusayan Totemic Signatures," *American Anthropologist*, Washington, January, 1897.

tinctive and so widespread as this must certainly have a symbolic interpretation. The concentric spirals with a broken line, the Hopi say, are symbols of the whirlpool, and it is interesting to find in the beautiful plates of Chavero's *Antigüedades Mexicanas* that the water in the lagoon surrounding the ancient Aztec capital was indicated by the Nahuatl Indians with similar symbols.

OBJECTS FOUND AT PALATKI AND HONANKI

The isolation of these ruins and the impossibility of obtaining workmen, combined with the brief visit which I was able to make to them, rendered it impossible to collect very many specimens of ancient handiwork. The few excavations which were made were limited almost wholly to Honanki, and from their success I can readily predict a rich harvest for anyone who may attempt systematic work in this virgin field. We naturally chose the interior of the rooms for excavation, and I will say limited our work to these places. Every chamber was more or less filled with débris—fragments of overturned walls, detached rock from the cliff above, dry alkaline soil, drifted sand, dust, and animal excreta. In those places where digging was possible we found the dust and guano so dry and alkaline that it was next to impossible to work for any length of time in the rooms, for the air became so impure that the workmen could hardly breathe, especially where the inclosing walls prevented ventilation. Notwithstanding this obstacle, however, we removed the accumulated débris down to the floor in one or two chambers, and examined with care the various objects of aboriginal origin which were revealed.

In studying the specimens found in cliff-houses due attention has not always been given to the fact that occupants have oftentimes camped in them subsequently to their abandonment by the original builders. As a consequence of this temporary habitation objects owned by unrelated Indians have frequently been confused with those of the cliff-dwellers proper. We found evidences that both Honanki and Palatki had been occupied by Apache Mohave people for longer or shorter periods of time, and some of the specimens were probably left there by these inhabitants.

The ancient pottery found in the rooms, although fragmentary, is sufficiently complete to render a comparison with known ceramics from the Verde ruins. Had we discovered the cemeteries, for which we zealously searched in vain, no doubt entire vessels, deposited as mortuary offerings, would have been found; but the kind of ware of which they were made would undoubtedly have been the same as that of the fragments.

No pottery distinctively different from that which has already been reported from the Verde valley ruins was found, and the majority resembled so closely in texture and symbolism that of the cliff houses of the San Juan, in northern New Mexico and southern Utah, that they may be regarded as practically identical.

The following varieties of pottery were found at Honanki:

    I. Coiled ware.
    II. Indented ware.
    III. Smooth ware.
    IV. Smooth ware painted white, with black geometric figures.

V. Smooth red ware, with black decoration.

By far the largest number of fragments belong to the first division, and these, as a rule, are blackened by soot, as if used in cooking. The majority are parts of large open-mouth jars with flaring rims, corrugated or often indented with the thumb-nail or some hard substance, the coil becoming obscure on the lower surface. The inside of these jars is smooth, but never polished, and in one instance the potter used the corrugations of the coil as an ornamental motive. The paste of which this coiled ware was composed is coarse, with argillaceous grains scattered through it; but it was well fired and is still hard and durable. When taken in connection with its tenuity, these features show a highly developed potter's technique. A single fragment is ornamented with an S-shape coil of clay fastened to the corrugations in much the same way as in similar ware from the ruins near the Colorado Chiquito.

The fragments of smooth ware show that they, too, had been made originally in the same way as coiled ware, and that their outer as well as their inner surface had been rubbed smooth before firing. As a rule, however, they are coarse in texture and have little symmetry of form. Fragments identified as parts of bowls, vases, jars, and dippers are classed under this variety. As a rule they are badly or unevenly fired, although evidently submitted to great heat. There was seldom an effort made to smooth the outer surface to a polish, and no attempt at pictorial ornamentation was made.

The fragments represented in classes iv and v were made of a much finer clay, and the surface bears a gloss, almost a glaze. The ornamentation on the few fragments which were found is composed of geometric patterns, and is identical with the sherds from other ruins of Verde valley. A fragment each of a dipper and a ladle, portions of a red bowl, and a rim of a large vase of the same color were picked up near the ruin. Most of the fragments, however, belong to the first classes—the coiled and indented wares.

There was no evidence that the former inhabitants of these buildings were acquainted with metals. The ends of the beams had been hacked off evidently with blunt stone axes, aided by fire, and the lintels of the houses were of split logs which showed no evidence that any metal implement was used in fashioning them. We found, however, several stone tools, which exhibit considerable skill in the art of stone working. These include a single ax, blunt at one end, sharpened at the other, and girt by a single groove. The variety of stone from which the ax was made does not occur in the immediate vicinity of the ruin. There were one or two stone hammers, grooved for hafting, like the ax. A third stone maul, being grooveless, was evidently a hand tool for breaking other stones or for grinding pigments.

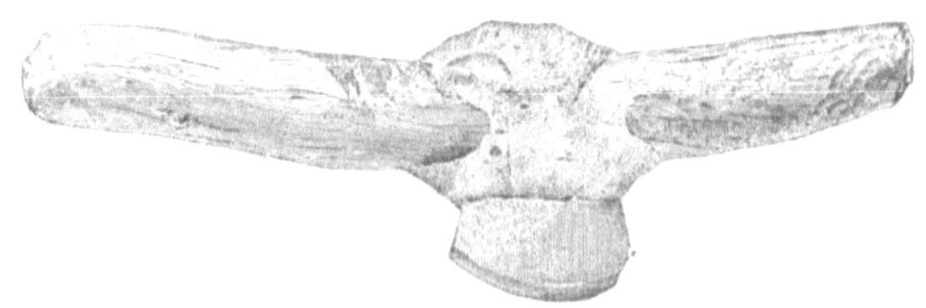

FIG. 251—STONE IMPLEMENT FROM HONANKI

Perhaps the most interesting stone implement which was found was uncovered in the excavation of one of the middle rooms of the western part of the ruin, about three feet below the surface. It consists of a wooden handle rounded at each end and slightly curved, with a sharpened stone inserted midway of its length and cemented to the wood with pitch or asphaltum. The stone of this implement would hardly bear rough usage, or sustain, without fracture, a heavy blow. The edge is tolerably sharp, and it therefore may have been used in skinning animals. Judging from the form of the handle, the implement is better suited for use as a scraper than for any other purpose which has occurred to me (figure 251).

The inhabitants of the two ruins of the Red-rocks used obsidian arrowpoints with shafts of reeds, and evidently highly regarded fragments of the former material for knives, spearheads, and one or two other purposes.

The stone metates from these ruins are in no respect characteristic, and several fine specimens were found in place on the floors of the rooms. One of these was a well-worn specimen of lava, which must have been brought from a considerable distance, since none of that material occurs in the neighborhood. The existence of these grinding stones implies the use of maize as food, and this evidence was much strengthened by the finding of corncobs, kernels of corn, and charred fragments at several points below the surface of the débris in the chambers of Honanki. One of these grinding stones was found set in the floor of one of the rooms in the same way that similar metates may be seen in Walpi today.

Of bone implements, our limited excavations revealed only a few fragments. Leg bones of the turkey were used for awls, bodkins, needles, and similar objects. In general character the implements of this kind which were found are almost identical in form with the bone implements from Awatobi and Sikyatki, which are later figured and described. Although the bone implements unearthed were not numerous, we were well repaid for our excavations by finding an ancient fireboard, identical with those now used at Tusayan in the ceremony of kindling "new fire," and probably universally used for that purpose in former times. The only shell was a fragment of a bracelet made from a *Pectunculus*, a Pacific coast mollusk highly esteemed in ancient times among prehistoric Pueblos. The majority of the wooden objects found showed marks of fire, which were especially evident on the ends of the roof and floor beams projecting from the walls.

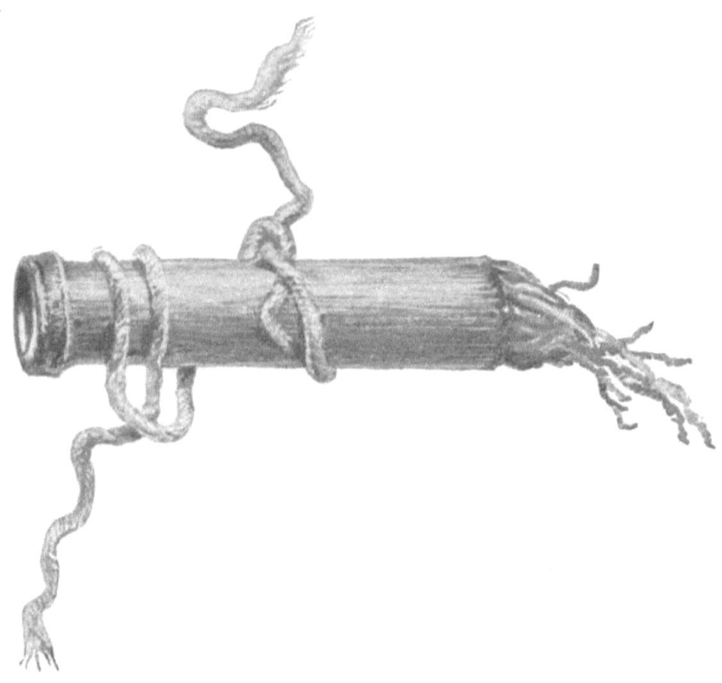

FIG. 252—TINDER TUBE FROM HONANKI

A considerable collection of objects made of wickerwork and woven vegetal fiber was found in the alkaline dust and ashes of the Red-rock cliff houses, and while there is some difficulty here as elsewhere, in deciding whether certain specimens belonged to the original builders or to later temporary occupants, there is little doubt that most of them were the property of the latter.

There were many specimens of basketry found on the surface of the rubbish of the floors which, from the position of their occurrence and from their resemblance to the wickerwork still used by the Apache, seem without doubt to have been left there by temporary occupants of the rooms. There were likewise many wisps of yucca fiber tied in knots which must probably be regarded as of identical origin. The *Yucca baccata* affords the favorite fiber used by the natives at the present time, and it appears to have been popular for that purpose among the ancients.

Several specimens of sandals, some of which are very much worn on the soles, were found buried at the floor level. These are all of the same kind, and are made of yucca leaves plaited in narrow strips. The mode of attachment to the foot was evidently by a loop passing over the toes. Hide and cloth sandals have as yet not been reported from the Red-rock ruins of Verde valley. These sandals belonged to the original occupants of the cliff houses.

Fabrics made of cotton are common in the ruins of the Red-rocks, and at times this fiber was combined with yucca. Some of the specimens of cotton cloth were finely woven and are still quite strong, although stained dark or almost black. Specimens of netting are also common, and an open-mesh legging, similar to the kind manufactured in ancient times by the Hopi and still worn by certain personators in their sacred dances, were taken from the western room of Honanki. There were also many fragments of rope, string, cord, and loosely twisted bands, resembling head bands for carrying burdens.

A reed (figure 252) in which was inserted a fragment of cotton fiber was unlike anything yet reported from cliff houses, and as the end of the cotton which projected beyond the cavity of the reed was charred, it possibly was used as a slow-match or tinder-box.

Several shell and turquois beads were found, but my limited studies of the cliff-houses revealed only a few other ornaments, among them being beads of turkey-bone and a single wristlet fashioned from a *Pectunculus*. One or two fragments of prayer-sticks were discovered in a rock inclosure in a cleft to the west of the ruin.

CONCLUSIONS REGARDING THE VERDE VALLEY RUINS

The ruins of the Verde region closely resemble those of Tusayan, and seem to support the claim of the Hopi that some of their ancestors formerly lived in that region. This is true more especially of the villages of the plains and mesa tops, for neither cave-houses nor cavate dwellings are found in the immediate vicinity of the inhabited Tusayan pueblos. The objects taken from the ruins are similar to those found universally over the pueblo area, and from them alone we can not say more than that they probably indicate the same substratum of culture as that from which modern pueblo life with its many modifications has sprung.

The symbolism of the decorations on the fragments of pottery found in the Verde ruins is the same as that of the ancient pueblos of the Colorado Chiquito, and it remains to be shown whether the ancestors of these were Hopi or Zuñi. I believe it will be found that they were both, or that when the villages along the Colorado Chiquito[29] were abandoned part of the inhabitants went to the mesas of Tusayan and others migrated farther up the river to the Zuñi villages.

Two centers of distribution of cliff houses occur in our Southwest: those of the upper tributaries of the Colorado in the north and the cliff houses of the affluents of the Salt and the Gila in the south. The watershed of the Rio Grande is, so far as is known, destitute of this kind of aboriginal dwellings. Between the two centers of distribution lie the pueblos of the Little Colorado and its tributaries, the home of the ancestors of the Hopi and the Zuñi. The many resemblances between the

---

[29] An exhaustive report on the ruins near Winslow, at the Sunset Crossing of the Little Colorado, will later be published. These ruins were the sites of my operations in the summer of 1896, and from them a very large collection of prehistoric objects was taken. The report will consider also the ruins at Chaves Pass, on the trail of migration used by the Hopi in prehistoric times in their visits, for barter and other purposes, to the Gila-Salado watershed.

cliff houses of the north and those of the south indicate that the stage of culture of both was uniform, and probably the same conditions of environment led both peoples to build similar dwellings. All those likenesses which can be found between the modern Zuñi and the Hopi to the former cliff peoples of the San Juan region in the north, apply equally to those of the upper Salado and the Gila and their tributaries to the south; and so far as arguments of a northern origin of either, built on architectural or technological resemblances, are concerned, they are not conclusive, since they are also applicable to the cliff peoples of the south. The one important difference between the northern and the southern tier of cliff houses is the occurrence of the circular kiva, which has never been reported south of the divide between the Little Colorado and the Gila-Salado drainage. If a kiva was a feature in southern cliff houses, which I doubt, it appears to have been a rectangular chamber similar to a dwelling room. The circular kiva exists in neither the modern Hopi nor the Zuñi pueblos, and it has not been found in adjacent Tusayan ruins; therefore, if these habitations were profoundly influenced by settlers from the north, it is strange that such a radical change in the form of this room resulted. The arguments advanced that one of the two component stocks of the Zuñi, and that the aboriginal, came from the cliff peoples of the San Juan, are not conclusive, although I have no doubt that the Zuñi may have received increment from that direction.

Cushing has, I believe, furnished good evidence that some of the ancestors of the Zuñi population came from the south and southwest; and that some of these came from pueblos now in ruins on the Little Colorado is indicated by the great similarity in the antiquities of ancient Zuñi and the Colorado Chiquito ruins. Part of the Patki people of the Hopi went to Zuñi and part to Tusayan, from the same abandoned pueblo, and the descendants of this family in Walpi still recognize this ancient kinship; but I do not know, and so far as can be seen there is no way of determining, the relative antiquity of the pueblos in Zuñi valley and those on the lower Colorado.

The approximate date of the immigration of the Patki people to Tusayan is as yet a matter of conjecture. It may have been in prehistoric times, or more likely at a comparatively late period in the history of the people. It seems well substantiated, however, that when this Water-house people joined the other Hopi, the latter inhabited pueblos and were to all intents a pueblo people. If this hypothesis be a correct one, the Snake, Horn, and Bear peoples, whom the southern colonists found in Tusayan, had a culture of their own similar to that of the people from the south. Whence that culture came must be determined by studies of the component clans of the Hopi before the arrival of the Patki people.[30]

The origin of the round shape of the estufa, according to Nordenskiöld (p.

---

[30] Possibly the Shoshonean elements in Hopi linguistics are due to the Snake peoples, the early colonists who came from the north, where they may have been in contact with Paiute or other divisions of the Shoshonean stock. The consanguinity of this phratry may have been close to that of the Shoshonean tribes, as that of the Patki was to the Piman, or the Asa to the Tanoan. The present Hopi are a composite people, and it is yet to be demonstrated which stock predominates in them.

168), is most easily explained on the hypothesis that it is a reminiscence of the cliff-dwellers' nomadic period. "There must be some very cogent reason for the employment of this shape," he says, "for the construction of a cylindrical chamber within a block of rectangular rooms involves no small amount of labor. We know how obstinately primitive nations cling to everything connected with their religious ideas. Then what is more natural than the retention, for the room where religious ceremonies were performed, of the round shape characteristic of the original dwelling place, the nomadic hut? This assumption is further corroborated by the situation of the hearth and the structure of the roof of the estufa, when we find points of analogy to the method employed by certain nomadic Indians in the erection of their huts." This theory of the origin of the round form of dwelling and its retention in the architecture of the kiva, advanced by Nordenskiöld in 1893, has much in its favor, but the rectangular form, which, so far as known, is the only shape of these sacred rooms in the Tusayan region, is still unexplained. From Castañeda's narrative of the Coronado expedition it appears that in the middle of the sixteenth century the eastern pueblos had both square and round estufas or kivas, and that these kivas belonged to the men while the rooms of the pueblo were in the possession of the women. The apparent reason why we find no round rooms or kivas in the southern cliff houses and in Tusayan may be due to several causes. Local conditions, including the character of the building sites on the Hopi mesa, made square rooms more practical, or the nomadic stage was so far removed that the form of the inclosure in which the ancients held their rites had not been preserved. Moreover, some of the most ancient and secret observances at Walpi, as the Flute ceremony, are not performed in special kivas, but take place in ordinary living rooms.

As in all the other ruins of Verde valley, circular kivas are absent in the Red-rock country, and this fact, which has attracted the attention of several observers, is, I believe, very significant. Although as yet our knowledge of the cliff houses of the upper Gila and Salado and their numerous tributaries is very fragmentary, and generalization on that account unsafe, it may be stated provisionally that no circular kivas have yet been found in any ruins of the Gila-Salado watershed. This form of kiva, however, is an essential feature of the cliff dwellings of Rio Colorado, especially of those along its affluents in southern Colorado and northern New Mexico. Roughly speaking, then, the circular kiva is characteristic of the ruins of this region and of certain others in the valley of the Rio Grande, where they still survive in inhabited pueblos.

Circular ruins likewise are limited in their distribution in the Southwest, and it is an interesting fact that the geographic distribution of ancient pueblos of this form is in a general way the same as that of circular kivas. There are, of course, many exceptions, but so far as I know these can readily be explained. No ruins of circular dwellings occur in the Gila-Salado drainage area, where likewise no circular kivas have been observed. Moreover, the circular form of dwelling and kiva is distinctively characteristic of prehistoric peoples east of Tusayan, and the few instances of their occurrence on its eastern border can readily be explained as extra-Hopi.

The explanation of these circular kivas advanced by Nordenskiöld and the Mindeleffs, that they are survivals of round habitations of nomads, has much to commend it; but whether sufficient or not, the geographic limitation of these structures tells in favor of the absence of any considerable migration of the prehistoric peoples of the upper Colorado and Rio Grande watersheds southward into the drainage area of the Gila-Salado. Had the migration been in that direction it may readily be believed that the round kiva and the circular form of dwelling would have been brought with it.

The round kiva has been regarded as a survival of the form of the original homes of the nomad, when he became a sedentary agriculturist by conquest and marriage.

The presence of rectangular kivas in the same areas in which round kivas occur does not necessarily militate against this theory, nor does it oblige us to offer an explanation of a necessarily radical change in architecture if we would derive it from a circular form. It would indeed be very unusual to find such a change in a structure devoted to religious purposes where conservatism is so strong. The rectangular kiva is the ancient form, or rather the original form; the round kiva is not a development from it, but an introduction from an alien people. It never penetrated southward of the Colorado and upper Rio Grande drainage areas because the element which introduced it in the north was never strong enough to influence the house builders of the Gila-Salado and tributary valleys.

RUINS IN TUSAYAN

GENERAL FEATURES

No region of our Southwest presents more instructive antiquities than the ancient province of Tusayan, more widely known as the Moki reservation. In the more limited use of the term, Tusayan is applied to the immediate surroundings of the Hopi pueblos, to which "province" it was given in the middle of the sixteenth century. In a broader sense the name would include an as yet unbounded country claimed by the component clans of this people as the homes of their ancestors.

The general character and distribution of Tusayan ruins (plate xvi) has been ably presented by Mr Victor Mindeleff in a previous report.[31] While this memoir is not regarded as exhaustive, it considers most of the large ruins in immediate proximity to the three mesas on which the pueblos inhabited by the Hopi are situated. It is not my purpose here to consider all Tusayan ruins, even if I were able to do so, but to supplement with additional data the observations already published on two of the most noteworthy pueblo settlements. Broadly speaking, I have attempted archeological excavations in order to obtain more light on the nature of prehistoric life in Tusayan. It may be advantageous, however, to refer briefly to some of the ruins thus far discovered in the Tusayan region as preliminary to more systematic descriptions of the two which I have chosen for special description.

The legends of the surviving Hopi contain constant references to former habitations of different clans in the country round about their present villages. These clans, which by consolidation make up the present population of the Hopi pueblos, are said to have originally entered Tusayan from regions as far eastward as the Rio Grande, and from the southern country included within the drainage of the Gila, the Salt, and their affluents. Other increments are reputed to have come from the northward and the westward, so that the people we now find in Tusayan are descendants from an aggregation of stocks from several directions, some of them having migrated from considerable distances. Natives of other regions have settled among the ancient Hopi, built pueblos, and later returned to their former homes; and the Hopi in turn have sent colonists into the eastern pueblo country.

These legends of former movements of the tribal clans of Tusayan are supplemented and supported by historical documents, and we know from this evidence that there has been a continual interchange between the people of Tusayan and almost every large pueblo of New Mexico and Arizona. Some of the ruins of this region were abandoned in historic times; others are prehistoric; many were simply

[31] A Study of Pueblo Architecture: Tusayan and Cibola; Eighth Annual Report of the Bureau of Ethnology, 1886-87.

temporary halting places in Hopi migrations, and were abandoned as the clans drifted together in friendship or destroyed as a result of internecine conflicts.

There is documentary evidence that in the years following the great rebellion of the Pueblo tribes in 1680, which were characterized by catastrophes of all kinds among the Rio Grande villagers, many Tanoan people fled to Tusayan to escape from their troubles. According to Niel, 4,000 Tanoan refugees, under Frasquillo, loaded with booty which they had looted from the churches, went to Oraibi by way of Zuñi, and there established a "kingdom," with their chief as ruler. How much reliance may be placed on this account is not clear to me, but there is no doubt that many Tanoan people joined the Hopi about this time, and among them were the Asa people, the ancestors of the present inhabitants of Hano pueblo, and probably the accolents of Payüpki. The ease with which two Franciscan fathers, in 1742, persuaded 441 of these to return to the Rio Grande, implies that they were not very hostile to Christianity, and it is possible that one reason they sought Tusayan in the years after the Spaniards were expelled may have been their friendship for the church party.

With the exception of Oraibi, not one of the present inhabited pueblos of Tusayan occupies the site on which it stood in the sixteenth century, and the majority of them do not antedate the beginning of the eighteenth century. The villages have shifted their positions but retained their names.

At the time of the advent of Tobar, in 1540, there was but one of the present three villages of East Mesa. This was Walpi, and at the period referred to it was situated on the terrace below the site of the present town, near the northwestern base of the mesa proper. Two well-defined ruins, called Kisakobi and Küchaptüvela, are now pointed out as the sites of Old Walpi. Of these Küchaptüvela is regarded as the older.

Judging by their ruins these towns were of considerable size. From their exposed situation they were open to the inroads of predatory tribes, and from these hostile raids their abandonment became necessary. From Küchaptüvela the ancient Walpians moved to a point higher on the mesa, nearer its western limit, and built Kisakobi, where the pueblo stood in the seventeenth century. There is evidence that a Spanish mission was erected at this point, and the place is sometimes called Nüshaki, a corruption of "Missa-ki," Mass-house. From this place the original nucleus of Walpians moved to the present site about the close of the seventeenth century. Later the original population was joined by other phratries, some of which, as the Asa, had lived in the cliff-houses of Tségi, or Canyon de Chelly, as late as the beginning of the eighteenth century. This, however, is not the place to trace the composition of the different modern villages.

Sichomovi was a colony from Walpi, founded about 1750, and Hano was built not earlier than 1700. The former was settled by the Badger people, later joined by a group of Tanoan clans called the Asa, from the Rio Grande, who were invited to Tusayan to aid the Hopi in resisting the invasions of northern nomads.

By the middle of the eighteenth century the population of the province of Tusayan was for the first time distributed in the seven pueblos now inhabited. No village has been deserted since that time, nor has any new site been occupied.

In order that the reader may have an idea of the Tusayan pueblos at the time mentioned, an account of them from a little-known description by Morfi in 1782 is introduced:[32]

Morfi's account of the Tusayan pueblos

Quarenta y seis leguas al Poniente de Zuñi, con alguna inclinacion al N. O. están los tres primeros pueblos de la provincia de Moqui, que en el dia en el corto distrito de 4-1/2 leguas (112 recto) tiene siete pueblos en tres mesas ó peñoles que corren linea recta de Oriente á Poniente.

Tanos[33]

En la punta occidental de la primera, y en la mas estrecho de su eminencia están situados tres de los quales el primero es el de Tanos (alli dicen Tegüas), cuyas moradores tienen idioma particular y distinto del Moquino. Es pueblo regular con un plaza en el centro, y un formacion de calles. Tendrá 110 familias.

El segundo[34] pueblo dista del precedente como un tiro de piedra, es de fundacion moderna, y se compondrá de mas 15 familias que se retiraron aqui de:

Gualpi

Gualpi que dista del anterior un tiro de fusil, es mas grande y populoso que los dos anteriores, puede tener hasta 200 familias. Estas tres pueblos tienen poco caballada, y algunas vacas; pero mucho ganado lanar.

Mosasnabi[35]

Al poniente de esta mesa, y á legua y media de distancia está la segunda, cuyo intermedio es un (112 v.) arenal, que ertrando un poco en ella la divide en dos brazas. En el septentrional, que es el mas inmediata á Gualpi hay dos anillos distantes entre si un tiro de piedra. En la cima del primero está situado el pueblo de Mosasnabi compuesto de 50 familias poco mas ó menos.

[32] This account was copied from a copy made by the eminent scholar, A. F. Bandelier, for the archives of the Hemenway Expedition, now at the Peabody Museum, in Cambridge, Massachusetts.

[33] Hano or "Tewa."

[34] Sichomovi. In the manuscript report by Don José Cortez, who wrote of the northern provinces of Mexico, where he lived in 1799, Sichomovi is mentioned as a nameless village between Tanos (Hano) and Gualpi (Walpi), settled by colonists from the latter pueblo. One of the first references to this village by name was in a report by Indian Agent Calhoun (1850), where it is called Chemovi.

[35] Mishoñinovi.

Xipaolabi[36]

En la cumbre del secundo cerrito se fundó el quinto pueblo llamado Xipaolabi, que tendrá solo 14 familias: está casi arruinado, porque sus vecinos se han trasladado al brazo austral de la mesa y formaron el sexto pueblo llamado:

Xongopabi[37]

Xongopabi goza mejor situacion que todos los demas, tienen tres quarteles mui bien dispuestos y en ellas unas 60 familias. Estos tres pueblos tienen mas caballada que los primeros y mucho ganado menor.

Oraybe

Dos y media leguas al Poniente de esta mesa, está la tercera, y en sucima el septimo pueblo que llaman Oraybe. Es como la capital de la provincia, el mayor y mas bien formado de toda ella, y acaso de todas las provincias internas. Tiene once quarteles ó manzanas bien largas y dispuestos con calles á cordel yá (113 r.) todos vientos, y puede llegar su poblacion á 800 familias. Tienen buena caballada, mucho ganado menor y algun vacuno. Aunque no gozan sino una pequeña fuente de buena agua, distante del pueblo mas de una milla al Norte, han construido para suplir esta escasez, en la misma mesa, y mui inmediato à las casas seis cisternas grandes donde recoger la agua de las lluvias y nieves.

The distribution of the population of Tusayan in the seven pueblos mentioned above remained practically the same during the century between 1782 and 1882. Summer settlements for farming purposes were inhabited by the Oraibi for brief periods. Between the years 1880 and 1890 a beginning of a new distribution of Hopi families began, when one or two of the less timid erected houses near Coyote spring, at the East Mesa. The Tewa, represented by Polaka and Jakwaina, took the lead in this movement. From 1890 to the present time a large number of Walpi, Sichomovi, and Hano families have built houses in the foothills of the East Mesa and in the plain beyond the "wash." A large schoolhouse has been erected at Sun spring and a considerable number of East Mesa villagers have abandoned their mesa dwellings. In this shifting of the population the isolated house is always adopted and the aboriginal method of roof building is abandoned. The indications are that in a few years the population of the East Mesa will be settled in unconnected farmhouses with little resemblance to the ancient communal pueblo.

This movement is shared to a less extent by the Middle Mesa and Oraibi people. On my first visit to the pueblos of these mesas, in 1890, there was not a single permanent dwelling save in the ancient pueblos; but now numerous small farmhouses have been erected at or near the springs in the foothills. I mention these

---

[36] Shipaulovi.
[37] Shuñopovi.

facts as a matter of record of progress in the life of these people in adapting themselves to the new conditions or influences by which they are surrounded. I believe that if this exodus of Hopi families from the old pueblo to the plain continues during the next two decades as it has in the last ten years, there are children now living in Walpi who will some day see it uninhabited.

This disintegration of the Hopi phratries, by which families are separated from one another, is, I believe, a return to the prehistoric distribution of the clans, and as Walpi grew into a pueblo by a union of kindred people, so now it is again being divided and distributed, still preserving family ties in new clusters or groupings. It is thus not impossible that the sites of certain old ruins, as Sikyatki, deserted for many years, will again be built upon if better suited for new modes of life. The settlement near Coyote spring, for instance, is not far from the old site of a former home of the Tanoan families, who went to Tusayan in the beginning of the eighteenth century, and the people who inhabit these new houses are all Tanoan descendants of the original contingent.

In order to become familiar with the general character of Tusayan ruins, I made a brief reconnoissance of those mentioned in the following list, from which I selected Awatobi and Sikyatki as places for a more exhaustive exploration. This list is followed by a brief mention of those which I believe would offer fair opportunities for a continuation of the work inaugurated. The ruins near Oraibi were not examined and are therefore omitted, not that they are regarded as less important, but because I was unable to undertake a study of them in the limited time at my disposal. There are also many ruins in Tusayan, north of the inhabited pueblos, which have never been described, and would well repay extended investigation. Some of these, as the ruins at the sacred spring called Kishuba, are of the utmost traditional importance.

I. *Middle Mesa ruins*—(1) Old Shuñopovi; (2) Old Mishoñi-novi; (3) Shitaumû; (4) Chukubi; (5) Payüpki.

II. *East Mesa ruins*—(1) Kisakobi; (2) Küchaptüvela; (3) Küküchomo; (4) Tukinobi; (5) Kachinba; (6) Sikyatki.

III. *Ruins in Keam's canyon.*

IV. *Jeditoh valley ruins*—(1) Bat-house; (2) Jeditoh, Kawaika; (3) Horn-house; (4) Awatobi; Smaller Awatobi.

This method of classification is purely geographical, and is adopted simply for convenience; but there are one or two facts worthy of mention in regard to the distribution of ruins in these four sections. The inhabited pueblos, like the ruins, are, as a rule, situated on the eastern side of their respective mesas, or on the cliffs or hills which border the adjacent plains on the west. This uniformity is thought to have resulted from a desire to occupy a sunny site for warmth and for other reasons.

The pueblos at or nearest the southern ends of the mesas were found to be best suited for habitation, consequently the present towns occupy those sites, or, as in the case of the Jeditoh series, the pueblo at that point was the last abandoned. The reason for this is thought to be an attempt to concentrate on the most inaccessible sites available, which implies inroads of hostile peoples. For the same reason, likewise, the tendency was to move from the foothills to the mesa tops when these invasions began.

Early settlers near East Mesa appeared to have chosen exposed sites for their pueblos. This would imply that they feared no invasion, and legendary history indicates that the first pueblos were erected before the hostile Ute, Apache, and Navaho appeared. The early settlements on Middle Mesa were also apparently not made with an absorbing idea of inaccessibility. All the Jeditoh villages, however, were on the mesa tops, these sites having been selected evidently with a view to protection, since they were not convenient to the farms.

For many reasons it would seem that the people who occupied the now ruined Jeditoh villages were later arrivals in Tusayan than those of East and Middle Mesas, and that, as a rule, they came from the eastward, while those of Middle Mesa arrived from the south. The first colonists of all, however, appear to have been the East Mesa clans, the Bear and Snake families. If this conjecture be true, we may believe that the oldest pueblos in Tusayan were probably the house groups of the Snake clan of East Mesa, for whom their traditionists claim a northern origin.

THE MIDDLE MESA RUINS

SHUÑOPOVI

The site of Old Shuñopovi (plate cv) at the advent of the first Spaniards, and for a century or more afterward, was at the foot of the mesa on which the present village stands. The site of the old pueblo is easily detected by the foundations of the ancient houses and their overturned walls, surrounded by mounds of soil filled with fragments of the finest pottery.

The old village was situated on a ridge of foothills east of the present town and near the spring, which is still used. On the highest point of the ridge there rise to a considerable height the massive walls of the old Spanish mission church, forming an inclosure, now used as a sheep corral. The cemeteries are near by, close to the outer walls, and among a clump of peach trees about half a mile east of the old houses. The pottery,[38] as shown by the fragments, is of the finest old Tusayan ware, cream and red being the predominating colors, while fragments of coiled and black-and-white ware are likewise common.

MISHOÑINOVI

The ruins of Old Mishoñinovi lie west of the present pueblo in the foothills, not far from the two rocky pinnacles at that point and adjacent to a spring. In strolling over the site of the old town I have noted its ground plan, and have picked up many sherds which indicate that the pottery made at that place was the fine cream-color ware for which Tusayan has always been famous. The site offers unusual opportunities for archeological studies, but excavation there is not practi-

[38] In 1896 I collected over a hundred beautiful specimens from this cemetery.

cable on account of the opposition of the chiefs.

Old Mishoñinovi was a pueblo of considerable size, and was probably inhabited up to the close of the seventeenth century. It was probably on this site that the early Spanish explorers found the largest pueblo of the Middle Mesa. The ruin of Shitaimovi, in the foothills near Mishoñinovi, mentioned by Mindeleff, was not visited by our party.

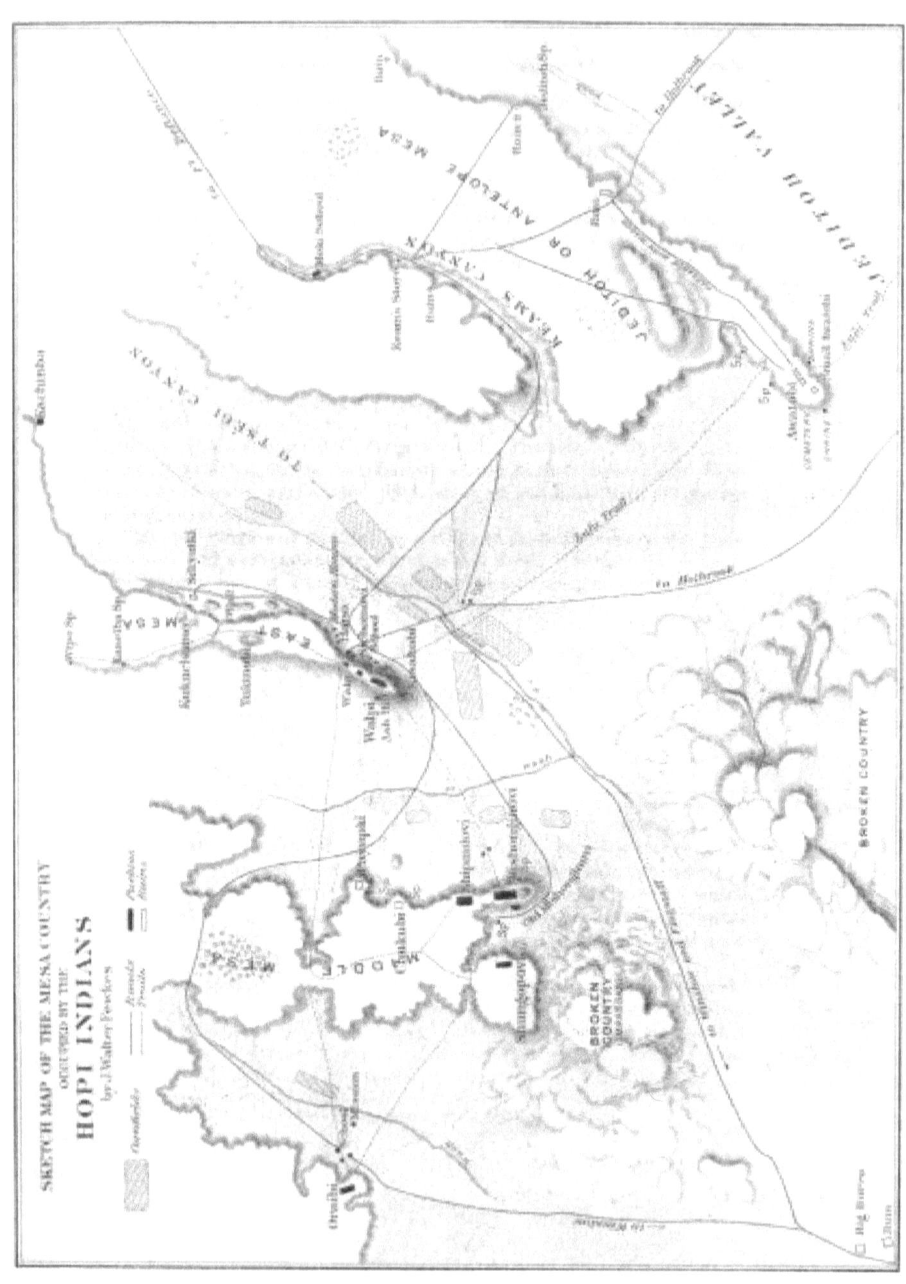

BUREAU OF AMERICAN ETHNOLOGY— — SEVENTEENTH ANNUAL RE-
PORT PL. CV.

Sketch Map Of The Mesa Country Occupied By The Hopi Indians

CHUKUBI

The ruin of Chukubi bears every evidence of antiquity. It is situated on one of the eastward projecting spurs of Middle Mesa, midway between Payüpki and Shipaulovi, near an excellent spring at the base of the mesa.

Chukubi was built in rectangular form, with a central plaza surrounded by rooms, two deep. There are many indications of outlying chambers, some of which are arranged in rows. The house walls are almost wholly demolished, and in far poorer state of preservation than those of the neighboring ruin of Payüpki. The evidence now obtainable indicates that it was an ancient habitation of a limited period of occupancy. It is said to have been settled by the Patuñ or Squash people, whose original home was far to the south, on Little Colorado river. A fair ground plan is given by Mindeleff in his memoir on Pueblo Architecture; but so far as known no studies of the pottery of this pueblo have ever been made.

PAYÜPKI

One of the best-preserved ruins on Middle Mesa is called Payüpki by the Hopi, and is interesting in connection with the traditions of the migration of peoples from the Rio Grande, which followed the troublesome years at the close of the seventeenth century. In the reconquest of New Mexico by the Spaniards we can hardly say that Tusayan was conquered; the province was visited and nominally subjugated after the great rebellion, but with the exception of repeated expeditions, which were often repulsed, the Hopi were practically independent and were so regarded. No adequate punishment was inflicted on the inhabitants of Walpi for the destruction of the town of Awatobi, and although there were a few military expeditious to Tusayan no effort at subjugation was seriously made.

Tusayan was regarded as an asylum for the discontented or apostate, and about the close of the seventeenth century many people from the Rio Grande fled there for refuge. Some of these refugees appear to have founded pueblos of their own; others were amalgamated with existing villages. Payüpki seems to have been founded about this period, for we find no account of it before this time, and it is not mentioned in connection with ancient migrations. In 1706 Holguin is said to have attacked the "Tanos" village between Walpi and Oraibi and forced the inhabitants to give hostages, but he was later set upon by the Tano and driven back to Zuñi. It would hardly seem possible that the pueblo mentioned could have been Hano, for this village does not lie between Oraibi and Walpi and could not have been surrounded in the way indicated in the account. Payüpki, however, not only lay on the trail between Walpi and Oraibi—about midway, as the chronicler states—but was so situated on a projecting promontory that it could easily have been surrounded and isolated from the other pueblos.

The Hopi legends definitely assert that the Payüpki people came from the "great river," the Rio Grande, and spoke a language allied to that of the people of Hano. They were probably apostates, who came from the east about 1680, but did not seem to agree well with the people of the Middle Mesa, and about 1750 returned to the river and were domiciled in Sandia, where their descendants still live. The name Payüpki is applied by the Hopi to the pueblo of Sandia as well as to the ruin on the Middle Mesa. The general appearance of the ruin of Payüpki indicates that it was not long inhabited, and that it was abandoned at a comparatively recent date. The general plan is not that common to ancient Tusayan ruins, but more like that of Hano and Sichomovi, which were erected about the time Payüpki was built. Many fragments of a kind of pottery which in general appearance is foreign to Tusayan, but which resembles the Rio Grande ware, were found on the mounds, and the walls are better preserved than those of the ancient Tusayan ruins.

A notable absence of fragments of obsidian, the presence of which in abundance is characteristic of ancient ruins, was observed on the site of Payüpki. All these evidences substantiate the Hopi legend that the Tanoan inhabitants of the village of Middle Mesa, above the trail from Walpi to Oraibi, made but a short stay in Tusayan.[39]

There is good documentary evidence that Sandia was settled by Tanoan people from Tusayan. Morfi in 1782 so states,[40] and in a copy of the acts of possession of the pueblo grants of 1748 we find still further proof of the settlement of "Moquinos" in Sandia.[41]

When Otermin returned to New Mexico in his attempted reconquest, in 1681, he reached Isleta on December 6, and on the 8th Dominguez encamped in sight of Sandia, but found the inhabitants had fled. The discord following this event drove the few surviving families of the Tiwa on their old range to Tusayan, for they were set upon by Keres and Jemez warriors on the plea that they received back the Spaniards. Possibly these families formed the nucleus of Payüpki. It was about this time, also, if we can believe Niel's story, that 4,000 Tanos went to Tusayan. It would thus appear that the Hopi Payüpki was settled in the decade 1680-1690.

THE EAST MESA RUINS

KÜCHAPTÜVELA AND KISAKOBI

The two ruins of Küchaptüvela and Kisakobi mark the sites of Walpi during

---

[39] There lived in Walpi, years ago, an old woman, who related to a priest, who repeated the story to the writer, that when a little girl she remembered seeing the Payüpki people pass along the valley under Walpi when they returned to the Rio Grande. Her story is quite probable, for the lives of two aged persons could readily bridge the interval between that event and our own time.

[40] "La Mission de N. Sra. de las Dolores de Zandia de Indios Teguas á Moqui."

[41] See J. F. Meline, Two Thousand Miles on Horseback, 1867. Sandia, according to Bancroft, is not mentioned by Menchero in 1744, but Bonilla gave it a population of 400 Indians in 1749. In 1742 two friars visited Tusayan, and, it is said, brought out 441 apostate Tiguas, who were later settled in the old pueblo of Sandia. Considering, then, that Sandia was resettled in 1748, six years after this visit, and that the numbers so closely coincide, we have good evidence that Payüpki, in Tusayan, was abandoned about 1742. It is probable, from known evidence, that this pueblo was built somewhere between 1680 and 1690; so that the whole period of its occupancy was not far from fifty years.

the period of Spanish exploration and occupancy between 1540 and 1700. The former was the older. In all probability the latter had a mission church and was inhabited at the time of the great rebellion in 1680, having been founded about fifty years previously.

The former or more ancient[42] pueblo was situated on the first or lowest terrace of East Mesa, below the present pueblo, on the northern and western sides. The name Küchaptüvela signifies "Ash-hill terrace," and probably the old settlement, like the modern, was known as Walpi, "Place-of-the-gap," referring to the gap or notch (*wala*) in the mesa east of Hano.

Old Walpi is said to have been abandoned because it was in the shade of the mesa, but doubtless the true cause of its removal was that the site was too much exposed, commanded as it was by the towering mesa above it, and easily approached on three sides. The Walpi which was contemporary with Sikyatki was built in an exposed location, for at that time the Hopi were comparatively secure from invaders. Later, however, Apache, Ute, and Navaho began to raid their fields, and the Spaniards came in their midst again and again, forcing them to work like slaves. A more protected site was necessary, and late in the seventeenth century the Walpians began to erect houses on the mesa, which formed the nucleus of the present town. The standing walls of Old Walpi are buried in the débris, but the plans of the rooms may readily be traced. Comparatively speaking, it was a large, compact, well-built pueblo, and, from the great piles of débris in the neighborhood, would seem to have been occupied during several generations.

The pottery found in the neighborhood is the fine, ancient Tusayan ware, like that of Sikyatki and Shuñopovi. Extended excavations would reveal, I am sure, many beautiful objects and shed considerable light on the obscure history of Walpi and its early population.

After moving from Old Walpi it seems that the people first built houses on the terrace above, or on the platform extending westward from the western limits of the summit of East Mesa. The whole top of that part of the mesa is covered with house walls, showing the former existence of a large pueblo. Here, no doubt, if we can trust tradition, the mission of Walpi was built, and I have found in the débris fragments of pottery similar to that used in Mexico, and very different from ancient or modern Pueblo ware. But even Kisakobi[43] was not a safe site for the

---

[42] Mindeleff mentions two other sites of Old Walpi—a mound near *Wala*, and one in the plain between Mishoñinovi and Walpi; but neither of these is large, although claimed as former sites of the early clans which later built the town on the terrace of East Mesa below Walpi. I have regarded Küchaptüvela as the ancient Walpi, but have no doubt that the Hopi emigrants had several temporary dwellings before they settled there.

[43] Sometimes called Nüsaki, a corruption of "Missa ki," Mass House, Mission. One of the beams of the old mission at Nüsaki or Kisakobi is in the roof of Pauwatiwa's house in the highest range of rooms of Walpi. This beam is nicely squared, and bears marks indicative of carving. There are also large planks in one of the kivas which were also probably from the church building, although no one has stated that they are. Pauwatiwa, however, declares that a legend has been handed down in his family that the above-mentioned rafter came from the mission.

Walpians to choose for their village, so after they destroyed the mission and killed the priest they moved up to their present site and abandoned both of their former villages.

It is said that with this removal of the villagers there were found to be no easy means of climbing the precipitous walls, and that the stairway trails were made as late as the beginning of the present century. In those early days there was a ladder near where the stairway trail is now situated, and some of the older men of Walpi have pointed out to me where this ladder formerly stood.

The present plan of Walpi shows marked differences from that made twenty years ago, and several houses between the stairway trail and the Wikwaliobi kiva, on the edge of the mesa, which have now fallen into ruin, were inhabited when I first visited Walpi in 1890. The buildings between the Snake kiva and the Nacab kiva are rapidly becoming unsafe for habitation, and most of these rooms will soon be deserted. As many Walpi families are building new houses on the plain, it needs no prophet to predict that the desertion of the present site of Walpi will progress rapidly in the next few years, and possibly by the end of our generation the pueblo may be wholly deserted—one more ruin added to the multitudes in the Southwest.

The site of Old Walpi, at Küchaptüvela, is the scene of an interesting rite in the New-fire ceremony at Walpi, for not far from it is a shrine dedicated to a supernatural being called Tüwapoñtumsi, "Earth-altar-woman." This shrine, or house, as it is called, is about 230 feet from the ruin, among the neighboring bowlders, and consists of four flat slabs set upright, forming an inclosure in which stands a log of fossil wood.

The ceremonials at Old Walpi in the New-fire rites are described in my account[44] of this observance, and from their nature I suspect that the essential part of this episode is the deposit of offerings at this shrine. The circuits about the old ruin are regarded as survivals of the rites which took place in former times at Old Walpi. The ruin was spoken of in the ceremony as the *Sipapüni*, the abode of the dead who had become *katcinas*, to whom the prayers said in the circuits were addressed.

KÜKÜCHOMO

The two conical mounds on the mesa above Sikyatki are often referred to that ancient pueblo, but from their style of architecture and from other considerations I am led to connect them with other phratries of Tusayan. From limited excavations made in these mounds in 1891, I was led to believe that they were round pueblos, similar to those east of Tusayan, and that they were temporary habitations, possibly vantage points, occupied for defense. Plate cvi illustrates their general appearance, while the rooms of which they are composed are shown in figure 253. At the place where the mesa narrows between these mounds and the pueblos to the west, a wall was built from one edge of the mesa to the other to defend the trail on this side. This wall appears to have had watch towers or houses at intervals, which are

[44] Proceedings of the Boston Society of Natural History, January 2, 1895, p. 441.

now in ruins, as shown in figure 254.

BUREAU OF AMERICAN ETHNOLOGY — — SEVENTEENTH ANNUAL RE-
PORT PL. CVI

The Ruins Of Küküchomo

FIG. 253—KÜKÜCHOMO

The legends concerning the ancient inhabitants of Küküchomo are conflicting. The late A. M. Stephen stated that tradition ascribes them to the Coyote and Pikya (Corn) peoples, with whom the denizens of Sikyatki made friendship, and whom the latter induced to settle there to protect them from the Walpians. He regarded them as the last arrivals of the Water-house phratry, while the Coyote people came from the north at nearly the same time. From his account it would appear that the twin mounds, Küküchomo, were abandoned before the destruction of Sikyatki. The Coyote people were, I believe, akin to the Kokop or Firewood phratry, and as the pueblo of Sikyatki was settled by the latter, it is highly probable that the inhabitants of the two villages were friendly and naturally combined against the Snake pueblo of Walpi. I believe, however, there is some doubt that any branch of the Patki people settled in Küküchomo, and the size of the town as indicated by the ruin was hardly large enough to accommodate more than one clan. Still, as there are two Küküchomo ruins, there may have been a different family in each of the two house clusters.

FIG. 254—DEFENSIVE WALL ON THE EAST MESA

It has been said that in ancient times, before the twin mounds of Küküchomo were erected, the people of Sikyatki were greatly harassed by the young slingers and archers of Walpi, who would come across to the edge of the high cliff and assail them with impunity. Anyone, however, who contemplates the great distance from Sikyatki to the edge of the mesa may well doubt whether it was possible for the Walpi bowmen to inflict much harm in that way.

Moreover, if the word "slingers" is advisedly chosen, it introduces a kind of warfare which is not mentioned in other Tusayan legends, although apparently throwing stones at their enemies was practiced among Pueblos of other stocks in early historic times.[45]

We may suppose, however, that the survivors of both Küküchomo and Sikyat-

[45] Thus in Castañeda's account we are told: "Farther off [near Cia?] was another large village where we found in the courtyards a great number of stone balls of the size of a leather bag, containing one arroba. They seem to have been cast with the aid of machines, and to have been employed in the destruction of the village." It is needless for me to say that I find no knowledge of such a machine in Tusayan!

ki sought refuge in Awatobi after the prehistoric destruction of their pueblos, for both were peopled by clans which came from the east, and naturally went to that village, the founders of which migrated from the same direction.

KACHINBA

The small ruin at Kachinba, the halting place of the Kachina people, seems to have escaped the attention of students of Tusayan archeology. It lies about six miles from Sikyatki, about east of Walpi, and is approached by following the trail at the foot of the same mesa upon which Küküchomo is situated. The ruin is located on a small foothill and has a few standing walls. It was evidently diminutive in size and only temporarily inhabited. The best wall found at this ruin lies at the base of the hill, where the spring formerly was. This spring is now filled in, but a circular wall of masonry indicates its great size in former times.

TUKINOBI

There are evidences that the large hill on top of East Mesa, not far from the twin mounds, was once the site of a pueblo of considerable size, but I have not been able to gather any definite legend about it. Near this ruin is the "Eagle shrine" in which round wooden imitations of eagle eggs are ceremonially deposited, and in the immediate vicinity of which is another shrine near which tracks are cut in the rock, and which were evidently considered by the Indian who pointed them out to me as having been made by some bird.[46] It is probably from these footprints, which are elsewhere numerous, that the two ruins called Küküchomo ("footprints mound") takes its name.

JEDITOH VALLEY RUINS

As one enters Antelope valley, following the Holbrook road, he finds himself in what was formerly a densely populated region of Tusayan. This valley in former times was regarded as a garden spot, and the plain was covered with patches of corn, beans, squashes, and chile. The former inhabitants lived in pueblos on the northern side, high up on the mesa which separates Jeditoh valley from Keam's canyon. All of these pueblos are now in ruins, and only a few Navaho and Hopi families cultivate small tracts in the once productive fields.

The majority of the series of ruins along the northern rim of Antelope valley resemble Awatobi, which is later described in detail. It is interesting to note that in the abandonment of villages the same law appears to have prevailed here as in the other Tusayan mesas, for in the shrinkage of the Hopi people they concentrated more and more to the points of the mesas. Thus, at East Mesa, Sikyatki, Kachinba, and Küküchomo were destroyed, while Walpi remained. At Middle Mesa, Chukubi and Payüpki became ruins, and in Antelope valley Awatobi was the last of the Jeditoh series to fall. There has thus been a gradual tendency to drift from readily

---

[46] The ceremonials attending to burial of the eagle, whose plumes are used in secret rites, have never been described, and nothing is known of the rites about the Eagle shrine at Tukinobi.

accessible locations to the most impregnable sites, which indicates how severely the Hopi must have been harassed by their foes. It is significant that some of the oldest pueblos were originally built in the most exposed positions, and it may rightly be conjectured that the pressure on the villagers came long after these sites were chosen. The ancient or original Hopi had a sense of security when they built their first houses, and they, therefore, did not find it necessary to seek the protection of cliffs. Many of them lived in the valley of the Colorado Chiquito, others at Kishuba. As time went on, however, they were forced, as were their kindred in other pueblos, to move to inaccessible mesas guarded by vertical cliffs.

Of the several ruins of Antelope valley, that on the mesa above Jeditoh or Antelope spring is one of the largest and most interesting. Stephen calls this ruin Mishiptonga, and a plan of the old house is given by Mindeleff.

The spring called Kawaika, situated near the former village of the same name, was evidently much used by the ancient accolents of Antelope valley. From this neighborhood there was excavated a few years ago a beautiful collection of ancient mortuary pottery objects, which was purchased by Mrs Mary Hemenway, of Boston, and is now in the Peabody Museum at Cambridge. These objects have never been adequately described, although a good illustration of some of the specimens, with a brief reference thereto, was published by James Mooney[47] a few years ago.

Among the most striking objects in this collection are clay models of houses, dishes, and small vases with rims pierced with holes, and rectangular vessels ornamented with pictures of birds. There are specimens of cream, yellow, red, and white pottery in the collection which, judging by the small size of most of the specimens, was apparently votive in character.

The ruins called by Stephen "Horn-house" and "Bat-house," as well as the smaller ruin between them, have been described by Mindeleff, who has likewise published plans of the first two. From their general appearance I should judge they were not occupied for so long a time as Awatobi, and by a population considerably smaller. If all these Jeditoh pueblos were built by peoples from the Rio Grande, it is possible that those around Jeditoh spring were the first founded and that Awatobi was of later construction; but from the data at hand the relative age of the ruins of this part of Tusayan can not be determined.

There are many ruins situated on the periphery of Tusayan which are connected traditionally with the Hopi, but are not here mentioned. Of these, the so-called "Fire-house" is said to have been the home of the ancestors of Sikyatki, and Kintiel of certain Zuñi people akin to the Hopi. Both of the ruins mentioned differ in their architectural features from characteristic prehistoric Tusayan ruins, for they are circular in form, as are many of the ruins in the middle zone of the pueblo area. With these exceptions there are no circular ruins within the area over which the Hopi lay claim, and it is probable that the accolents of Kintiel were more Zuñi than Hopi in kinship.

Many ruins north of Oraibi and in the neighborhood of the farming village of

[47] Recent Archeologic Find in Arizona, *American Anthropologist*, Washington, July, 1893.

Moenkopi are attributed to the Hopi by their traditionists. The ruins about Kishy-uba, connected with the Kachina people, also belong to Tusayan. These and many others doubtless offer most important contributions to an exact knowledge of the prehistoric migrations of this most interesting people.

Among the many Tusayan ruins which offer good facilities for archeological work, the two which I chose for that purpose are Awatobi and Sikyatki. My reasons for this choice may briefly be stated.

Awatobi is a historic pueblo of the Hopi, which was more or less under Spanish influence between the years 1540 and 1700. When properly investigated, in the light of archeology, it ought to present a good picture of Tusayan life before the beginning of the modifications which appear in the modern villages of that isolated province. While I expected to find evidences of Spanish occupancy, I also sought facts bearing on the character of Tusayan life in the seventeenth century.

Sikyatki, however, showed us the character of Tusayan life in the fifteenth century, or the unmodified aboriginal pueblo culture of this section of the Southwest. Here we expected to find Hopi culture unmodified by Spanish influence.

The three pueblos of Sikyatki, Awatobi, and Walpi, when properly studied, will show the condition of pueblo culture in three centuries—in Sikyatki, pure, unmodified pueblo culture; in Awatobi, pueblo life as slightly modified by the Spaniards, and in Walpi, those changes resulting from the advent of Americans superadded. While special attention has thus far been given by ethnologists mainly to the last-mentioned pueblo, a study of the ruins of the other two villages is of great value in showing how the modern life developed and what part of it is due to foreign influence.

A knowledge of the inner life of the inhabitants of Tusayan as it exists today is a necessary prerequisite to the interpretation of the ancient culture of that province; but we must always bear in mind the evolution of society and the influences of foreign origin which have been exerted on it. Many, possibly the majority, of modern customs at Walpi are inherited, but others are incorporated and still others, of ancient date, have become extinct.

As much stress is laid in this memoir on the claim that objects from Sikyatki indicate a culture uninfluenced by the Spaniards, it is well to present the evidence on which this assertion is based.

(1) Hopi legends all declare that Sikyatki was destroyed before the Spaniards, called the "long-gowned" and "iron-shirted" men, came to Tusayan. (2) Sikyatki is not mentioned by name in any documentary account of Tusayan, although the other villages are named and are readily identifiable with existing pueblos. (3) No fragment of glass, metal, or other object indicative of the contact of European civilization was found anywhere in the ruin. If we add to the above the general appearance of age in the mounds and the depth of the débris which has accumulated in the rooms and over the graves, we have the main facts on which I have relied to support my belief that Sikyatki is a prehistoric ruin.

AWATOBI

CHARACTERISTICS OF THE RUIN

No Tusayan ruin offers to the archeologist a better picture of the character of Hopi village life in the seventeenth century than that known as Awatobi (plate cvii).[48] It is peculiarly interesting as connecting the prehistoric culture of Sikyatki and modern Tusayan life, with which we have become well acquainted through recent research. Awatobi was one of the largest Tusayan pueblos in the middle of the sixteenth century, and continued to exist to the close of the seventeenth. It was therefore a historic pueblo. It had a mission, notices of which occur in historical documents of the period. From its preponderance in size, no less than from its position, we may suspect that it held relatively the same leadership among the other Antelope valley ruins that Walpi does today to Sichomovi and Hano.

The present condition of the ruins of Awatobi is in no respect peculiar or different from that of the remains of prehistoric structures, except that its mounds occupy a position on a mesa top commanding a wide outlook over a valley. On its east it is hemmed in by extensive sand dunes, which also stretch to the north and west, receding from the village all the way from a few hundred yards to a quarter of a mile. On the south the ruins overlook the plain, and the sands on the west separate it from a canyon in which there are several springs, some cornfields, and one or two modern Hopi houses. There is no water in the valley which stretches away from the mesa on which Awatobi is situated, and the foothills are only sparingly clothed with desert vegetation. The mounds of the ruin have numerous clumps of *sibibi* (*Rhus trilobata*), and are a favorite resort of Hopi women for the berries of this highly prized shrub. There is a solitary tree midway between the sand dunes west of the village and the western mounds, near which we found it convenient to camp. The only inhabitants of the Awatobi mesa are a Navaho family, who have appropriated, for the shade it affords, a dwarf cedar east of the old mission walls. No land is cultivated, save that in the canyons above mentioned, west of the sand hills; some fair harvests are, however, still gathered from Antelope valley by the Navaho, especially in the section higher up, near Jeditoh spring.

The ruin may be approached from the road between Holbrook and Keam's Canyon, turning to the left after climbing the mesa. This road, however, is not usually traveled, since it trends through the difficult sand hills. As Keam's Canyon is the only place in this region at which to provision an expedition, it is usual to approach Awatobi from that side, the road turning to the right shortly after one ascends the steep hill out of the canyon near Keam's trading post.

My archeological work at Awatobi began on July 6, 1895, and was continued for two weeks, being abandoned on account of the defection of my Hopi workmen, who left their work to attend the celebration of the *Niman* or "Farewell" *katcina*,[49] a July festival in which many of them participated. The ruin is conveniently

---

[48] For a previous description see the Preliminary Account, Smithsonian Report for 1895; also "Awatobi: An Archeological Verification of a Tusayan Legend," *American Anthropologist*, Washington, October, 1893.

[49] This important ceremony celebrates the departure from the pueblos of ancestral

situated for the best archeological results; it has a good spring near by, and is not far from Keam's Canyon, the base of supplies. The soil covering the rooms, however, is almost as hard as cement, and fragile objects, such as pottery, were often broken before their removal from the matrix. A considerable quantity of débris had to be removed before the floors were reached, and as this was firmly impacted great difficulty was encountered in successful excavations.

With a corps of trained workmen much better results than those we obtained might have been expected, and the experience which the Indians subsequently had at Sikyatki would have made my excavations at Awatobi, had they been carried on later in the season, more remunerative. While my archeological work at certain points in these interesting mounds of Awatobi was more or less superficial, it was in other places thorough, and revealed many new facts in regard to the culture of the inhabitants of this most important pueblo.

I found it inexpedient to dig in the burial places among the sand dunes, on account of the religious prejudices of my workmen. This fear they afterward overcame to a certain extent, but never completely outgrew, although the cemeteries at Sikyatki were quite thoroughly excavated, yielding some of the most striking results of the summer's exploration. The sand hills west of Sikyatki are often swept by violent gales, by which the surface is continually changing, and mortuary pottery is frequently exposed. This has always been a favorite place for the collector, and many a beautiful food bowl has been carried by the Indians from this cemetery to the trading store, for the natives do not seem to object to selling a vase or other object which they find on the surface, but rarely dig in the ground for the purpose of obtaining specimens.

NOMENCLATURE OF AWATOBI

The name Awatobi is evidently derived from *awata*, a bow (referring to the Bow clan, one of the strongest in the ancient pueblo), and *obi*, "high place of." A derivation from *owa*, rock, has also been suggested, but it seems hardly distinctive enough to be applicable, and is not accepted by the Hopi themselves.

While the different pueblos of Tusayan were not specially mentioned until forty years after they were first visited, the name Awatobi is readily recognized in the account of Espejo in 1583, where it is called Aguato,[50] which appears as Zaguato and Ahuato in Hakluyt.[51] In the time of Oñate (1598) the same name is written Aguatuybá.[52] Vetancurt,[53] about 1680, mentions the pueblo under the names Aguatobi and Ahuatobi, and in 1692, or twelve years after the great rebellion, Vargas visited "San Bernardo de Aguatuvi," ten leagues from Zuñi. The name appears on maps up to the middle of the eighteenth century, several years after its destruction. In more modern times various older spellings have been ad-

---

gods called *katcinas*, and is one of the most popular in the ritual.

[50] Pacheco-Cardenas, Colleccion de Documentos Inéditos, xv, 122, 182.

[51] Voyages, iii, pp. 463, 470, 1600; reprint 1810.

[52] Pacheco-Cardenas, Documentos Inéditos, op. cit., xvi, 139.

[53] Menologio Franciscano, 275; Teatro Mexicano, iii, 321.

opted or new ones introduced. Among these may be mentioned:

AGUATUVÍ. Buschmann, Neu-Mexico, 231, 1858.

AGUATUYA. Bandelier in Journal of American Ethnology and Archæology, III, 85, 1892 (misquoting Oñate).

AGUITOBI. Bandelier in Archæological Institute Papers, Am. series, III, pt. 1, 115, 1890.

AHUATU. Bandelier, ibid., 115, 135.

AHUATUYBA. Bandelier, ibid., 109.

AH-WAT-TENNA. Bourke, Snake Dance of the Moquis of Arizona, 195, 1884 (so called by a Tusayan Indian).

AQUATASI. Walch, Charte America, 1805.

AQUATUBI. Davis, Spanish Conquest of New Mexico, 368, 1869.

ATABI-HOGANDI. Bourke, op. cit., 84, 1884 (Navaho name).

AUA-TU-UI. Bandelier in Archæological Institute Papers, op. cit., IV, pt. 2, 368, 1892.

A-WA-TE-U. Cushing in Atlantic Monthly, 367, September, 1882.

AWATÚBI. Bourke, op. cit., 91, 1884.

Á WAT U I. Cushing in Fourth Report Bureau of Ethnology, 493, 1886 (or Aguatóbi).

ZAGNATO. Brackenridge, Early Spanish Discoveries, 19, 1857 (misprint of Hakluyt's Zaguato).

ZAGUATE. Prince, New Mexico, 34, 1883 (misquoting Hakluyt).

ZUGUATO. Hinton, Handbook to Arizona, 388, 1878 (misquoting Hakluyt).

The Navaho name of the ruin, as is well known, is Talla-hogan, ordinarily translated "Singing-house," and generally interpreted to refer to the mass said by the padres in the ancient church. It is probable, however, that kivas were used as chambers where songs were sung in ceremonials prior to the introduction of Christianity. Therefore why Awatobi should preeminently be designated as the "Singing-house" is not quite apparent.

The name of the mission, San Bernardino,[54] or San Bernardo, refers to its patron saint, and was first applied by Porras in honor of the natal day of this saint, on which day, in 1629, he and his companions arrived in Tusayan.

HISTORICAL KNOWLEDGE OF AWATOBI

The identification of Tusayan with the present country of the Hopi depends

---

[54] San Bernardino de Ahuatobi (Vetancurt, 1680); San Bernardo de Aguatuvi (Vargas, 1692). I find that the mission at Walpi was also mentioned by Vargas as dedicated to San Bernardino. The church at Oraibi was San Francisco de Oraybe and San Miguel. The mission at Shuñopovi was called San Bartolomé, San Bernardo, and San Bernabe.

in great measure on the correct determination of the situation of Cibola. I have regarded as conclusive Bandelier's argument that Cibola comprised the group of pueblos inhabited by the Zuñi in the sixteenth century.[55] Regarding this as proven, Tusayan corresponds with the Hopi villages, of which Awatobi was one of the largest. It lies in the same direction and about the same distance from Zuñi as stated in Castañeda's narrative. The fact that Cardenas passed through Tusayan when he went from Cibola to the Grand Canyon in 1540 is in perfect harmony with the identification of the Hopi villages with Tusayan, and Zuñi with Cibola. Tobar, in Tusayan, heard of the great river to the west, and when he returned to the headquarters of Coronado at Cibola the general dispatched Cardenas to investigate the truth of the report. Cardenas naturally went to Tusayan where Tobar had heard the news, and from there took guides who conducted him to the Grand Canyon. Had the general been in any Hopi town at the time he sent Tobar, and later Cardenas, it is quite impossible to find any cluster of ruins which we can identify as Tusayan in the direction indicated. There can be no doubt that Tusayan was the modern Hopi country, and with this in mind the question as to which Hopi pueblo was the one first visited by Tobar is worthy of investigation.

In order to shed what light is possible on this question, I have examined the account by Castañeda, the letter of Coronado to Mendoza, and the description in the "Relacion del Suceso," but find it difficult to determine that point definitely.

In Hakluyt's translation of Coronado's letter, it is stated that the houses of the "cities" which Tobar was sent to examine were "of earth," and the "chiefe" of these towns is called "Tucano." As this letter was written before Coronado had received word from Tobar concerning his discoveries, naturally we should not expect definite information concerning the new province. Capt. Juan Jaramillo's account speaks of "Tucayan" as a province composed of seven towns, and states that the houses are terraced.

In the "Relacion del Suceso" we likewise find the province called "Tuzan" (Tusayan), and the author notes the resemblance of the villages to Cibola, but he distinctly states that the inhabitants cultivated cotton.

Castañeda's account, which is the most detailed, is that on which I have relied in my identification of Awatobi as the first Hopi pueblo seen by the Spaniards.

It seems that Don Pedro de Tobar was dispatched by Coronado to explore a province called Tusayan which was reported to be twenty-five leagues from Cibola. He had in his command seventeen horsemen and one or two foot-soldiers, and was accompanied by Friar Juan de Padilla. They arrived in the new province after dark and concealed themselves under the edge of the mesa, so near that they heard the voices of the Indians in their houses. The natives, however, discovered them at daylight drawn up in order, and came out to meet them armed with wooden clubs, bow and arrows, and carrying shields. The chief drew a line of sacred meal across the trail, and in that way symbolized that the entrance to their pueblo

---

[55] This article was in type too early for a review of Dellenbaugh's identification of Cibola with a more southeasterly locality. His arguments bear some plausibility, but they are by no means decisive.

was closed to the intruders. During a parley, however, one of the men made a move to cross the line of meal, and an Indian struck his horse on the bridle. This opened hostilities, in which the Hopi were worsted, but apparently without loss of life. The vanquished brought presents of various kinds—cotton cloth, cornmeal, birds, skins, piñon nuts, and a few turquoises—and finding a good camping place near their pueblo, Tobar established headquarters and received homage from all the province. They allowed the Spaniards to enter their villages and traded with them.[56]

Espejo's reference to Awatobi in 1583 leaves no doubt that the pueblo was in existence in that year, and while, of course, we can not definitely say that it was not built between 1540 and 1583, the indications are that it was not. Hopi traditions assert that it was in existence when the Spaniards came, and the statement of the legendists whom I have consulted are definite that the survivors of Sikyatki went to Awatobi after the overthrow of the former pueblo. It would not appear, however, that Awatobi was founded prior to Sikyatki, nor is it stated that the refugees from Sikyatki built Awatobi, which is within the bounds of possibility, but it seems to be quite generally conceded that the Sikyatki tragedy antedated the arrival of the first Spaniards.

There can, I think, be no doubt that the Hopi pueblo first entered by Pedro de Tobar, in 1540, was Awatobi, and that the first conflict of Spanish soldiers and Hopi warriors, which occurred at that time, took place on the well-known Zuñi trail in Antelope valley, not far from Jeditoh or Antelope spring. This pueblo is the nearest village to Cibola (Zuñi), from which Tobar came, and as he took the Zuñi trail he would naturally first approach this village, even if the other pueblos on the rim of this valley were inhabited. It is interesting to consider a few lines from Castañeda, describing the event of that episode, to see how closely the site of Awatobi conforms to the narrative. In Castañeda's account of Tobar's visit we find that the latter with his command entered Tusayan so secretly that their presence was unknown to the inhabitants, and they traversed a cultivated plain without being seen, so that, we are told, they approached the village near enough to hear the voices of the Indians without being discovered. Moreover, the Indians, the narrative says, had a habit of descending to their cultivated fields, which implies that they lived on a mesa top. Awatobi was situated on a mesa, and the cultivated fields were in exactly the position indicated. The habit of retiring to their pueblo at night is still observed, or was to within a few years. Tobar arrived at the edge of Antelope valley after dark (otherwise he would have been discovered), crossed the cultivated fields under cover of night, and camped under the town at the base of the mesa. The soldiers from that point could readily hear the voices of the villagers above them. Even at the base of the lofty East Mesa I have often heard the Walpi people talking, while the words of the town crier are intelligible far out on the plain. From the configuration of the valley it would not, however, have been easier for Awatobians to have seen the approaching Spaniards than for the Walpians; still it was possible for the invaders to conceal their approach to Walpi in the same way.

---

[56] An exact translation by Winship of the copy of Castañeda in the Lenox Library was published in the Fourteenth Annual Report of the Bureau.

If, however, the first pueblo approached was Walpi, and Tobar followed the Zuñi trail, I think he would have been discovered by the Awatobi people before night-fall if he entered the cultivated fields early in the evening. It would be incredible to believe that he wandered from the trail; much more likely he went directly to Awatobi, the first village en route, and then encamped until the approach of day before entering the pueblo. At sunrise the inhabitants, early stirring, detected the presence of the intruders, and the warriors went down the mesa to meet them. They had already heard from Cibola of the strange beings, men mounted on animals which were said to devour enemies.

It may seem strange that the departure of an expedition against Tusayan was unknown to the Hopi, but the narrative leads us to believe that such was the fact. The warriors descended to the plain, and their chief drew a line of sacred meal across the trail to symbolize that the way to their pueblo was closed; whoever crossed it was an enemy, and punishment should be meted out to him. This custom is still preserved in several ceremonials at the present day, as, for instance, in the New-fire rites[57] in November and in the Flute observance in July.[58] The priests say that in former times whoever crossed a line of meal drawn on the trail at that festival was killed, and even now they insist that no one is allowed to pass a closed trail. The Awatobi warriors probably warned Tobar and his comrades not to advance, but the symbolic barrier was not understood by them. The Spaniards were not there to parley long, and it is probable that their purpose was to engage in a quarrel with the Indians. Urged on by the priest, Juan de Padilla, "who had been a soldier in his youth," they charged the Indians and overthrew a number, driving the others before them. The immediate provocation for this, according to the historian, was that an Indian struck one of the horses on the bridle, at which the holy father, losing patience, exclaimed to his captain, "Why are we here?" which was interpreted as a sign for the assault.

It must, however, be confessed that if the pueblo of Walpi was the first discovered an approach by stealth without being seen would have been easier for Tobar if the village referred to was Walpi then situated on the Ash-hill terrace, with the East Mesa between it and the Zuñi trail. To offset this probability, however, is the

[57] "At evening the chiefs asked that notices be written for them warning all white people to keep away from the mesa tomorrow, and these were set up by the night patrols in cleft wands on all the principal trails. At daybreak on the following morning the principal trails leading from the four cardinal points were 'closed' by sprinkling meal across them and laying on each a whitened elk horn. Anawita told the observer that in former times if any reckless person had the temerity to venture within this proscribed limit the Kwak-wantû inevitably put him to death by decapitation and dismemberment." ("Naacnaiya," *Journal of American Folk-lore*, vol. v, p. 201.) This appears to be the same way in which the Awatobians "closed" the trail to Tobar.

[58] When the Flute people approach Walpi, as is biennially dramatized at the present time, "an assemblage of people there (at the entrance to the village) meet them, and just back of a line of meal drawn across the trail stood Winuta and Hoñyi," also two girls and a boy. After these Flute people are challenged and sing their songs the trail is opened, viz: "Alosaka drew the end of his *moñkohu* along the line of meal, and Winuta rubbed off the remainder from the trail with his foot." "Walpi Flute Observance," *Journal of American Folk-lore*, vol. vii, p. 19.

fact that the Zuñi trail now runs through Awatobi, or in full view of it and there is hardly a possibility that Tobar left that trail to avoid Awatobi. He would naturally visit the first village, and not go out of his way seven miles beyond it, seeking a more distant pueblo.

The effect of this onslaught on men armed with spears, clubs, and leather shields can be imagined, and the encounter seems to have discouraged the Awatobi warriors from renewed resistance. They fled, but shortly afterward brought presents as a sign of submission, when Tobar called off his men. Thus was the entry of the Spaniards into Tusayan marked with bloodshed for a trifling offense. Shortly afterward Tobar entered the village and received the complete submission of the people.

The names of the Tusayan pueblos visited by Tobar in this first entrance are nowhere mentioned in the several accounts which have come down to us. Forty years later, however, the Spaniards returned and found the friendly feeling of Awatobi to the visitors had not lapsed. When Espejo approached the town in 1583, over the same Zuñi trail, the multitudes with their caciques met him with great joy and poured maize (sacred meal?) on the ground for the horses to walk upon. This was symbolic of welcome; they "made" the trail, a ceremony which is still kept up when entrance to the pueblo is formally offered.[59]

The people, considering their poverty, were generous, and gave Espejo "hand towels with tassels" at the corners. These were probably dance kilts and ceremonial blankets, which then, as now, the Hopi made of cotton.

The pueblo, called "Aguato" in the account of that visit, was without doubt Awatobi. The name Aguatuybá, mentioned by Oñate, is also doubtless the same, although, as pointed out to me by Mr Hodge, "through an error probably of the copyist or printer, the name Aguatuybá is inadvertently given by Oñate among his list of Hopi chiefs, while Esperiez is mentioned among the pueblos." In Oñate's list we recognize Oraibi in "Naybi," and Shuñopovi in "Xumupamí" and "Comupaví," the most westerly town of the Middle Mesa. "Cuanrabi" and "Esperiez" are not recognizable as pueblos.

Espejo, therefore, appears to have been the first to mention Awatobi as "Aguato," which is metamorphosed in Hakluyt into "Zaguato or "Ahuzto,"[60] although evidently Oñate's "Aguatuybá" was intended as a name of a pueblo.

I have not been able to determine satisfactorily the date of the erection of the

[59] This custom of sprinkling the trail with sacred meal is one of the most common in the Tusayan ritual. The gods approach and leave the pueblos along such lines, and no doubt the Awatobians regarded the horses of Espejo as supernatural beings and threw meal on the trail before them with the same thought in mind that they now sprinkle the trails with meal in all the great ceremonials in which personators of the gods approach the villages.

[60] According to the reprint of 1891. In the reprint of 1810 it appears as "Ahuato." I would suggest that possibly the error in giving the name of a pueblo to a chief may have arisen not from the copyist or printer, but from inability of the Spaniards and Hopi to understand each other. If you ask a Hopi Indian his name, nine times out of ten he will not tell you, and an interlocutor for a party of natives will almost invariably name the pueblos from which his comrades came.

mission building of San Bernardino at Awatobi, but the name is mentioned as early as 1629. In that year three friars went to Tusayan and began active efforts to convert the Hopi.[61]

It is recorded[62] that Padre Porras, with Andres Gutierrez, Cristoval de la Concepcion, and ten soldiers, arrived in Tusayan, "dia del glorioso San Bernardo (que és el apellido que aora tiene aquel pueblo)," which leaves no doubt why the mission at Awatobi was so named. Although an apostate Indian had spread the report, previously to the advent of these priests in Tusayan, that the Spaniards were coming among them to burn their pueblos, rob their homes, and devour[63] their children, the zealous missionaries in 1629 converted many of the chiefs and baptized their children. The cacique, Don Augustin, who appears to have been baptized at Awatobi, apparently lived in Walpi or at the Middle Mesa, and returning to his pueblo, prepared the way for a continuation of the apostolic work in the villages of the other mesas.

But the missionary labors of Porras came to an untimely end. It is written that by 1633 he had made great progress in converting the Hopi, but in that year, probably at Awatobi, he was poisoned. Of the fate of his two companions and the success of their work little is known, but it is recorded that the succession of padres was not broken up to the great rebellion in 1680. Figueroa, who was massacred at Awatobi in that year, went to Tusayan in 1674 with Aug. Sta. Marie. Between the death of Porras and the arrival of Figueroa there was an interval of eleven years, during which time the two comrades of Porras or Espeleta, who went to Tusayan in 1650, took charge of the spiritual welfare of the Hopi. Espeleta and Aug. Sta. Marie were killed in 1680 at San Francisco de Oraibi and Walpi, respectively, and José Trujillo probably lost his life at Old Shuñopovi at the same time. As there is no good reason to suppose that Awatobi, one of the most populous Tusayan pueblos, was neglected by the Spanish missionaries after the death of Porras in 1633, and as it was the first pueblo encountered on the trail from Zuñi, doubtless San Bernardino was one of the earliest missions erected in Tusayan. From 1680 until 1692, the period of independence resulting from the great Pueblo revolt, there was no priest in Tusayan, nor, indeed, in all New Mexico. Possibly the mission was repaired between 1692 and 1700, but it is probable that it was built as early as the time Porras lived in Awatobi. It is explicitly stated that in the destruction of Awatobi in 1700 no missionaries were killed, although it is recorded that early in that year Padre Garaycoechea made it a visit.

The disputes between the Jesuits and Franciscans to obtain the Hopi field for missionary work during the eighteenth century naturally falls in another chapter of Spanish-Tusayan history. Aside from sporadic visits to the pueblos, nothing tangible appears to have resulted from the attempts at conversion in this epoch. True,

[61] This was possibly the expedition which P. Fr. Antonio (Alonzo?) made among the Hopi in 1628; however that may be, there is good evidence that Porras, after many difficulties, baptized several chiefs in 1629.

[62] *Segunda Relacion de la grandiosa conversion que ha avido en el Nuevo Mexico. Embiada por el Padre Estevã de Perea*, etc, 1633.

[63] An earlier rumor was that the horses were anthropophagous.

many apostates were induced to return to their old homes on the Rio Grande and some of the Hopi frequently asked for resident priests, making plausible offers to protect them; but the people as a whole were hostile, and the mission churches were never rebuilt, nor did the fathers again live in this isolated province.

In 1692 Awatobi was visited by Don Diego de Vargas, the reconquerer of New Mexico, who appears to have had no difficulty bringing to terms the pueblos of Awatobi, Walpi, Mishoñinovi, and Shuñopovi.[64] He found, however, that Awatobi was "fortified," and the entrance so narrow that but one man could enter at a time. The description leads us to conclude that the fortification was the wall at the eastern end, and the entrance the gateway, the sides of which are still to be seen. The plaza in which the cross was erected was probably just north of the walls of the mission.

There would seem to be no doubt that a mission building was standing at Awatobi before 1680, for Vetancurt, writing about the year named, states that in the uprising it was burned.[65] At the time of the visit of Garaycoechea, in the spring of 1700, he found that the mission had been rebuilt. In this connection it is instructive, as bearing on the probable cause of the destruction of Awatobi, to find that while the inhabitants of this pueblo desired to have the mission rehabilitated, the other Tusayan pueblos were so hostile that the friends of the priest in Awatobi persuaded him not to attempt to visit the other villages. This warning was no doubt well advised, and the tragic fate which befell Awatobi before the close of the year shows that the trouble was brewing when the padre was there, and possibly Garaycoechea's visit hastened the catastrophe or intensified the hatred of the other pueblos.

At the time of Garaycoechea's visit he baptized, it is said, 73 persons. This rite was particularly obnoxious[66] to the Hopi, as indeed to the other Pueblo Indians, notwithstanding they performed practically the same ceremony in initiations into their own secret societies. The Awatobians, however, or at least some of them, allowed this rite of the Christians, thus intensifying the hatred of the more conservative of their own village and of the neighboring pueblos. These and other facts seem to indicate that the real cause of the destruction of Awatobi was the reception of Christianity by its inhabitants, which the other villagers regarded as sorcery. The conservative party, led by Tapolo, opened the gate of the town to the warriors of Walpi and Mishoñinovi, who slaughtered the liberals, thus effectually rooting out the new faith from Tusayan, for after that time it never again obtained

[64] As Vargas appears not to have entered Oraibi at this time he may have found it too hostile. Whether Frasquillo had yet arrived with his Tanos people and their booty is doubtful. The story of the migration to Tusayan of the Tanos under Frasquillo, the assassin of Fray Simón de Jesus, and the establishment there of a "kingdom" over which he ruled as king for thirty years, is a most interesting episode in Tusayan history. Many Tanos people arrived in several bands among the Hopi about 1700, but which of them were led by Frasquillo is not known to me.

[65] "El templo acabo en llamas." At this time Awatobi was said to have 800 inhabitants.

[66] At the present time one of the most bitter complaints which the Hopi have against the Spaniards is that they forcibly baptized the children of their people during the detested occupancy by the conquerors.

a foothold.

The visit of Padre Juan Garaycoechea to Tusayan was at the invitation of Espeleta, chief of Oraibi, but he went no farther than Awatobi, where he baptized the 73 Hopi. He then returned to the "governor," and arrived at Zuñi in June. According to Bancroft (p. 222), "In the 'Moqui Noticias' ms., 669, it is stated that the other Moquis, angry that Aguatuvi had received the padres, came and attacked the pueblo, killed all the men, and carried off all the women and children, leaving the place for many years deserted." Although I have not been able to consult the document quoted, this conclusion corresponds so closely with Hopi tradition that I believe it is practically true, although Bancroft unfortunately closes the quotation I have made from his account with the words, "I think this must be an error." Espeleta, the Oraibi chief, and 20 companions were in Santa Fé in October, 1700, and proposed a peace in which the Hopi asked for religious toleration, which Governor Cubero refused. As a final appeal he desired that the fathers should not permanently reside with them, but should visit one pueblo each year for six years; but this request was also rejected. Espeleta returned to Oraibi, and immediately on his appearance an unsuccessful attempt was made to destroy Awatobi, followed, as recounted in the legend, by a union with Walpi and Mishoñinovi, by which the liberal-minded villagers of the Antelope mesa were overthrown. Documentary and legendary accounts are thus in strict accord regarding the cause of the destruction.

The meager fragmentary historical evidence that can be adduced shows that the destruction of Awatobi occurred in the autumn or early winter of 1700. In May of that year we have the account of the visiting padre, and in the summer when Espeleta was at Santa Fé, the pueblo was flourishing. The month of November would have been a favorable one for the destruction of the town for the reason that during this time the warriors would all be engaged in secret kiva rites. The legend relates that the overthrow of the pueblo was at the *Naacnaiya*,[67] which now takes place in November.

For many years after its destruction the name of Awatobi was still retained on maps including the Tusayan province, and there exist several published references to the place as if still inhabited; but these appear to be compilations, as no traveler visited the site subsequently to 1700. It is never referred to in writings of the eighteenth or first half of the nineteenth centuries, and its site attracted no attention. The ruins remained unidentified until about 1884, when the late Captain J. G. Bourke published his book on the "Snake Dance of the Moquis," in which he showed that the ruin called by the Navaho Tally-hogan was the old Awatobi which played such a prominent part in early Tusayan history.

The ruin was described and figured a few years later by Mr Victor Mindeleff in his valuable memoir on Cibola and Tusayan architecture. Bourke's reference is very brief and Mindeleff's plan deficient, as it includes only a portion of the ruin, namely, the conspicuous mission walls and adjacent buildings, overlooking

---

[67] *Naacnaiya* and *Wüwütcimti* are the elaborate and abbreviated New-fire ceremonies now observed by four religious warrior societies, known as the *Tataukyamû*, *Wüwütcimtû*, *Aaltû* and *Kwakwantû*. Both of these ceremonials, as now observed at Walpi, have elsewhere been described.

entirely the older or western mounds, which are the most characteristic. In 1892 I published the first complete ground-plan of the ruins of Awatobi, including both eastern and western sections. As Mindeleff's plan is defective, his characterization of the architectural features of the pueblo is consequently faulty. He says: "The plan suggests that the original pueblo was built about three sides of a rectangular court, the fourth or southeast side, later occupied by the mission buildings, being left open or protected by a low wall." While the eastern portion undoubtedly supports this conclusion, had he examined the western or main section he would doubtless have qualified his conclusion (plate cvii). This portion was compact, without a rectangular court, and was of pyramidal form. The eastern section was probably of later construction, and the mission was originally built outside the main pueblo, although probably a row of rooms of very ancient date extended along the northern side opposite the church. As it was customary in Tusayan to isolate the kivas, these rooms in Awatobi were probably extramural and may have been situated in this eastern court, but the majority of the people lived in the western section. The architecture of the mission and adjacent rooms shows well-marked Spanish influence, which is wholly absent in the buildings forming the western mounds.

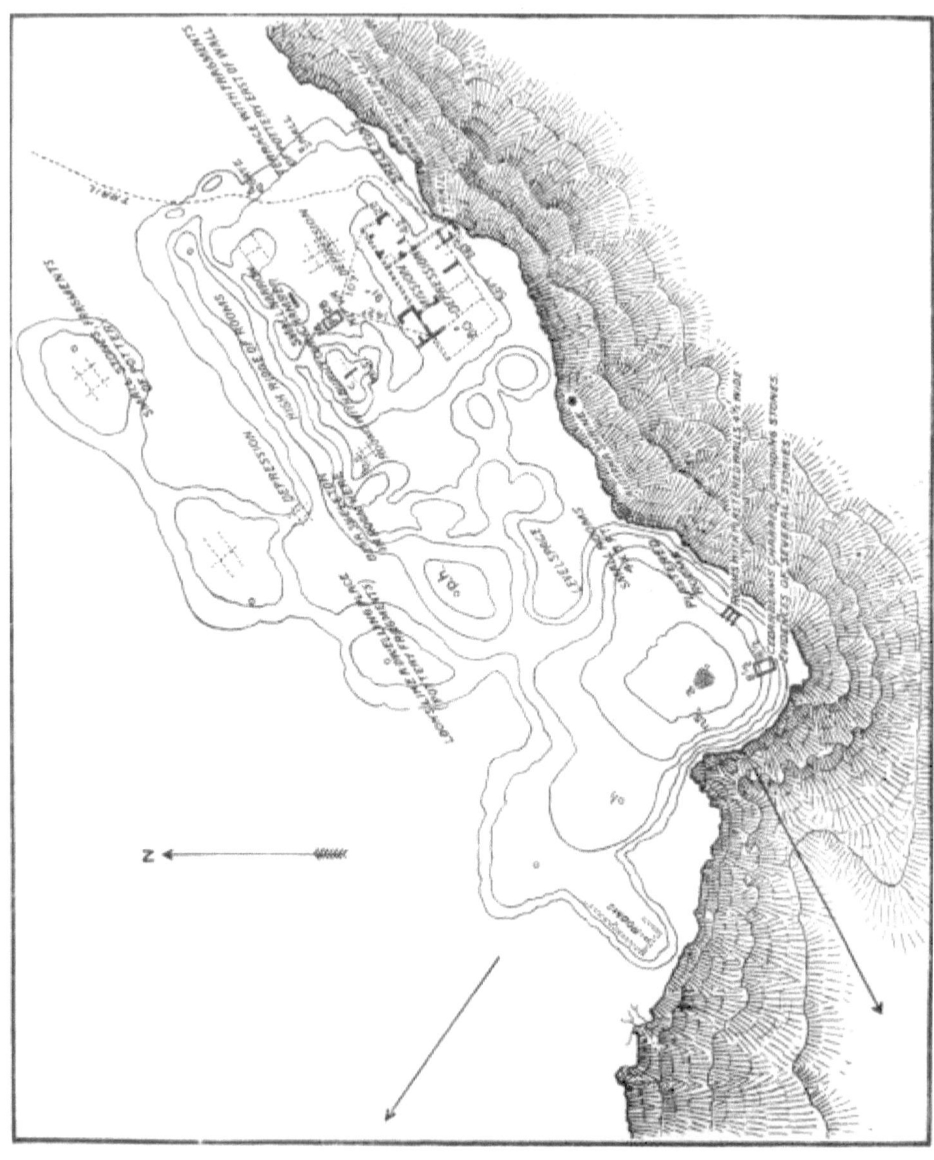

BUREAU OF AMERICAN ETHNOLOGY — — SEVENTEENTH ANNUAL RE-
PORT PL. CVII

Ground Plan Of Awatobi

LEGEND OF THE DESTRUCTION OF AWATOBI

The legend of the overthrow of Awatobi is preserved in detail among the
living villagers of Tusayan, and like all stories which have been transmitted for
several generations exist in several variants, differing in episodes, but coinciding

in general outlines. In the absence of contemporary documentary history, which some time may possibly be brought to light, the legends are the only available data regarding an event of great importance in the modern history of Tusayan.

I have obtained the legends from Supela, Shimo,[68] Masiumptiwa, and Saliko, and the most complete appears to be that of the last mentioned. The others dilated more on the atrocities which were committed on the bodies of the unfortunate captives, and the tortures endured before they were killed. All show traces of modification, incorporation, and modern invention.

Destruction of Awatobi as related by Saliko[69]

"The chiefs Wiki and Shimo, and others, have told you their stories, and surely their ancestors were living here at Walpi when Awatobi was occupied. It was a large village, and many people lived there, and the village chief was called Tapolo, but he was not at peace with his people, and there were quarreling and trouble. Owing to this conflict only a little rain fell, but the land was fertile and fair harvests were still gathered. The Awatobi men were bad (*powako*, sorcerers). Sometimes they went in small bands among the fields of the other villagers and cudgeled any solitary worker they found. If they overtook any woman they ravished her, and they waylaid hunting parties, taking the game, after beating and sometimes killing the hunters. There was considerable trouble in Awatobi, and Tapolo sent to the Oraibi chief asking him to bring his people and kill the evil Awatobians. The Oraibi came and fought with them, and many were killed on both sides, but the Oraibi were not strong enough to enter the village, and were compelled to withdraw. On his way back the Oraibi chief stopped at Walpi and talked with the chiefs there. Said he, 'I can not tell why Tapolo wants the Oraibi to kill his folks, but we have tried and have not succeeded very well. Even if we did succeed, what benefit would come to us who live too far away to occupy the land? You Walpi people live close to them and have suffered most at their hands; it is for you to try.' While they were talking Tapolo had also come, and it was then decided that other chiefs of all the villages should convene at Walpi to consult. Couriers were sent out, and when all the chiefs had arrived Tapolo declared that his people had become sorcerers (Christians), and hence should all be destroyed.

"It was then arranged that in four days large bands from all the other villages should prepare themselves, and assemble at a spring not far from Awatobi. A long while before this, when the Spaniards lived there, they had built a wall on the side of the village that needed protection, and in this wall was a great, strong

[68] Obiit 1892. Shimo was chief of the Flute Society and "Governor" of Walpi.

[69] Oldest woman of the Snake clan; mother of Kopeli, the Snake chief of Walpi; chief priestess of the Mamzráuti ceremony.

door. Tapolo proposed that the assailants should come before dawn, and he would be at this door ready to admit them, and under this compact he returned to his village. During the fourth night after this, as agreed upon, the various bands assembled at the deep gulch spring, and every man carried, besides his weapons, a cedar-bark torch and a bundle of greasewood. Just before dawn they moved silently up to the mesa summit, and, going directly to the east side of the village, they entered the gate, which opened as they approached. In one of the courts was a large kiva, and in it were a number of men engaged in sorcerer's rites. The assailants at once made for the kiva, and plucking up the ladder, they stood around the hatchway, shooting arrows down among the entrapped occupants. In the numerous cooking pits fire had been maintained through the night for the preparation of food for a feast on the appointed morning, and from these they lighted their torches. Great numbers of these and the bundles of greasewood being set on fire, they were cast down the hatchway, and firewood from stacks upon the house terraces were also thrown into the kiva. The red peppers for which Awatobi was famous were hanging in thick clusters along the fronts of the houses, and these they crushed in their hands and flung upon the blazing fire in the kiva to further torment their burning occupants. After this, all who were capable of moving were compelled to travel or drag themselves until they came to the sand-hills of Mishoñinovi, and there the final disposition of the prisoners was made.

"My maternal ancestor had recognized a woman chief (*Mamzrau moñwi*), and saved her at the place of massacre called Maski, and now he asked her whether she would be willing to initiate the woman of Walpi in the rites of the *Mamzrau*. She complied, and thus the observance of the ceremonial called the Mamzráuti came to Walpi. I can not tell how it came to the other villages. This Mamzrau-moñwi had no children, and hence my maternal ancestor's sister became chief, and her *tiponi* (badge of office) came to me. Some of the other Awatobi women knew how to bring rain, and such of them as were willing to teach their songs were spared and went to different villages. The Oraibi chief saved a man who knew how to cause peaches to grow, and that is why Oraibi has such an abundance of peaches now. The Mishoñinovi chief saved a prisoner who knew how to make the sweet, small-ear corn grow, and that is why it is more abundant there than elsewhere. All the women who knew song prayers and were willing to teach them were spared, and no children were designedly killed, but were divided among the villages, most of them going to Mishoñinovi. The remainder of the prisoners, men and women, were again tortured and dismembered and left to die on the sand hills, and there their bones are, and that is the reason the place is called *Maschomo* (Death-mound). This is the story of Awatobi told by my old people."

All variants of the legend are in harmony in this particular, that Awatobi was destroyed by the other Tusayan pueblos, and that Mishoñinovi, Walpi, and probably Oraibi and Shuñopovi participated in the deed. A grievance that would unite the other villagers against Awatobi must have been a great one, indeed, and not a mere dispute about water or lands. The more I study the real cause, hidden in the term *powako*, "wizard" or "sorcerer," the more I am convinced that the progress Christianity was making in Awatobi, after the reconquest of the Pueblos in 1692, explains the hostility of the other villagers. The party favoring the Catholic fathers in Awatobi was increasing, and the other Tusayan pueblos watched its growth with alarm. They foresaw that it heralded the return of the hated domination of the priests, associated in their minds with practical slavery, and they decided on the tragedy, which was carried out with all the savagery of which their natures were capable.

They greatly feared the return of the Spanish soldiers, as the epoch of Spanish rule, mild though it may have been, was held in universal detestation. Moreover, after the reconquest of the Rio Grande pueblos, many apostates fled to Tusayan and fanned the fires of hatred against the priests. Walpi received these malcontents, who came in numbers a few years later. Among these arrivals were Tanoan warriors and their families, part of whom were ancestors of the present inhabitants of Hano.

It was no doubt hoped that the destruction of Awatobi would effectually root out the growing Christian influence, which it in fact did; and for fifty years afterward Tusayan successfully resisted all efforts to convert it. Franciscans from the east and Jesuits from the Gila in the south strove to get a new hold, but they never succeeded in rebuilding the missions in this isolated province, which was generally regarded as independent.

From the scanty data I have been able to collect from historical and legendary sources, it seems probable that Awatobi was always more affected by the padres than were the other Tusayan pueblos. This was the village which was said to have been "converted" by Padre Porras, whose work, after his death by poison in 1633, was no doubt continued by his associates and successors. About 1680, as we learn from documentary accounts, the population of Awatobi was 800,[70] and it was probably not much smaller in 1700, the time of its destruction.

EVIDENCES OF FIRE IN THE DESTRUCTION

Wherever excavations were conducted in the eastern section of Awatobi, we

[70] Vetancurt, Chronica, says that Aguatobi (Awatobi) had 800 inhabitants and was converted by Padre Francisco de Porras. In 1630 Benavides speaks of the Mokis as being rapidly converted. It would appear, if we rely on Vetancurt's figures, that Awatobi was not one of the largest villages of Tusayan in early times, for he ascribes 1,200 to Walpi and 14,000 to Oraibi. The estimate of the population of Awatobi was doubtless nearer the truth than that of the other pueblos, and I greatly doubt if Oraibi ever had 14,000 people. Probably 1,400 would be more nearly correct.

could not penetrate far below the surface without encountering unmistakable evidences of a great conflagration. The effect of the fire was particularly disastrous in the rooms of the eastern section, or that part of the pueblo contiguous to the mission. Hardly a single object was removed from this part of Awatobi that had not been charred. Many of the beams were completely burned; others were charred only on their surfaces. The rooms were filled with ashes and scoriæ, while the walls had been cracked as if by intense heat.

Perhaps the most significant fact in regard to the burning of Awatobi was seen in some of the houses where the fire seems to have been less intense. In many chambers of the eastern section, which evidently were used as granaries, the corn was stacked in piles just as it is today under many of the living rooms at Walpi, a fact which tends to show that there was no attempt to pillage the pueblo before its destruction. The ears of corn in these store-rooms were simply charred, but so well preserved that entire ears of maize were collected in great numbers. It may here be mentioned that upon one of the stacks of corn I found during my excavations for the Hemenway Expedition in 1892, a rusty iron knife-blade, showing that the owner of the room was acquainted with objects of Spanish manufacture. This blade is now deposited with the Hemenway collection in the Peabody Museum at Cambridge.

THE RUINS OF THE MISSION

The mission church of San Bernardino de Awatobi was erected very early in the history of the Spanish occupancy, and its ruined walls are the only ones now standing above the surface. This building was constructed by the padres on a mesa top, while the churches at Walpi and Shuñopovi were built in the foothills near those pueblos. The mission at Oraibi likewise stood on a mesa top, so that we must qualify Mindeleff's statement[71] that "at Tusayan there is no evidence that a church or mission house ever formed part of the villages on the mesa summits.... These summits have been extensively occupied only in comparatively recent time, although one or more churches may have been built here at an early date as outlooks over the fields in the valley below."

At the time of the Spanish invasion three of the Hopi villages stood on the foothills or lower terraces of the mesas on which they now stand, and the other two, Awatobi and Oraibi, occupied the same sites as today, on the summits of the mesas.

---

[71] Architecture of Cibola and Tusayan, p. 225.

BUREAU OF AMERICAN ETHNOLOGY — — SEVENTEENTH ANNUAL RE-
PORT PL. CVIII

Ruins Of San Bernardino De Awatobi

I believe that at the time of the Spanish discovery of Tusayan by Pedro de Tobar in 1540, there were only five Tusayan towns — Walpi, Awatobi, Shuñopovi, Mishoñinovi, and Oraibi. Later, Awatobi was destroyed, and shortly after 1680 Walpi, the only East Mesa town, together with Mishoñinovi and Shuñopovi, on the Middle Mesa, were moved to the elevated sites they now occupy. Oraibi, there-fore, is probably the only Tusayan pueblo, at present inhabited, which occupies practically the same site that it did in 1540.

In their excavations for the foundations of new houses the present inhabitants of Oraibi often find, as I am informed by Mr H. R. Voth, the missionary at that place, vessels or potsherds of ancient Tusayan ware closely resembling that which is found in the ruins of Sikyatki and Awatobi.

The mission building at Awatobi, known in the church history of New Mexico and Arizona as San Bernardo or San Bernardino, was reputed to be the largest in Tusayan, and its walls are still the best preserved of any mission structure in that province. This, however, does not imply that the church structures of Tusayan are well preserved, for the mission buildings at Walpi have wholly disappeared, while at Oraibi little more than a pile of stones remains. Of the Shuñopovi mission of San Bernabe there are no standing walls save at one end, which are now used as a sheep corral.

The mission of San Bernardino de Awatobi was built on the southern side of the eastern part of the pueblo on the edge of the cliff, and its walls are the only ones of Awatobi now standing above ground. From the situation of these walls, as compared with the oldest part of Awatobi—the western mounds—I believe that San Bernardino mission was, when erected, beyond the limits of the pueblo proper—a custom almost universally followed in erecting pueblo mission churches— necessary in this instance, since from the compactness of the village there was no other available site. The same was true of the missions of Oraibi and Shuñopovi, and probably of Old Walpi. As time passed additional buildings were erected near it, this eastward extension altering the original plan of the town, but in no way affecting the configuration of the older portion.

From its commanding position on the edge of the mesa the mission walls must have presented an imposing appearance from the plain below, rising as they did almost continuously with the side of the cliff, making a conspicuous structure for miles across Antelope valley, from which its crumbling walls are still visible (plate CVIII).

When compared with the masonry of unmodified pueblo ruins the walls of the mission may be designated massive, and excavation at their foundations was very difficult on account of the great amount of débris which had fallen about them. With the limited force of laborers at my command the excavations could not be conducted with a great degree of thoroughness.

In the middle of what I supposed to have been the main church there was much sand, evidently drift, and in it I sank a trench 10 feet below the surface without reaching anything which I considered a floor. We found in excavations at the foundation of the church walls fragments of glass, several copper nails, a much-corroded iron hook, a copper bell pivot, and fragments of Spanish pottery. From the character of these objects alone there is no doubt in my mind of the former existence of Spanish influence, and the method of construction of the mission walls and the addition constructed of adobe containing chopped straw, substantiate this conclusion. Supposing, from the architecture and orientation of other New Mexican missions, that the altar was at the western end, opposite the entrance to the church, I sank a trench along the foundation of the wall on that side, but encountered such a mass of fallen stone at that point that I found it impossible to make much progress, and the fact that the floor was more than 10 feet below the surface of the central depression led me to abandon, as impossible with my little band of native excavators, the laying bare of the floor of the church.

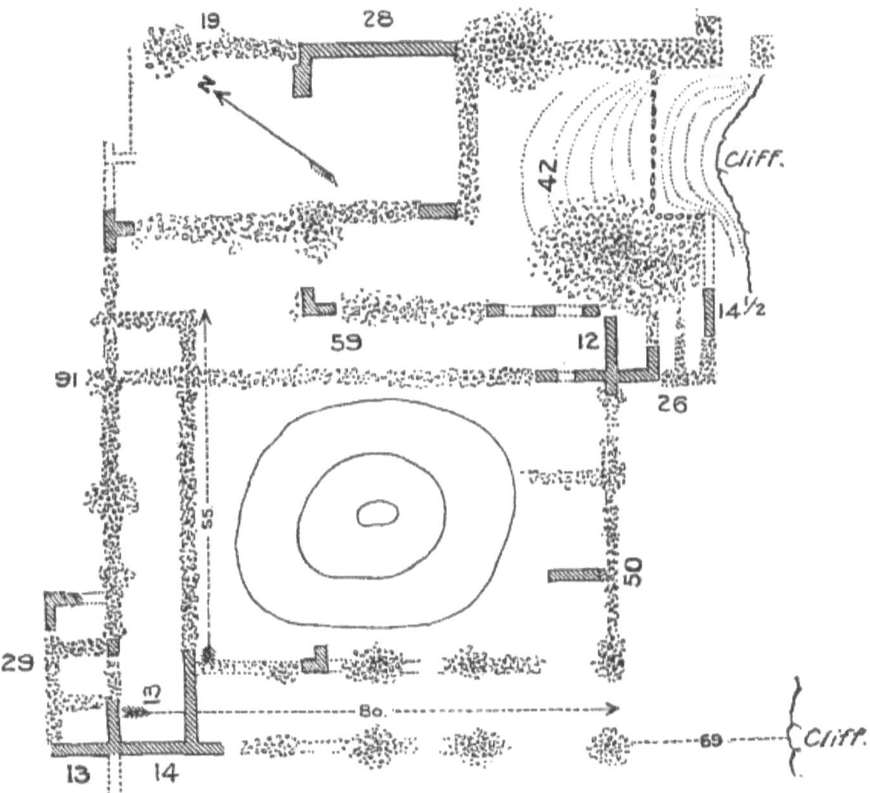

FIG. 255—GROUND PLAN OF SAN BERNARDINO DE AWATOBI

The ground plan (figure 255) of the mission resembles that of the Zuñi church, and is not unlike the plans of the churches in the Rio Grande pueblos. The tall buttresses, which rise 15 or 20 feet above the trail up the mesa on the southern corner, are, I believe, remnants of towers which formerly supported a balcony. During a previous visit to Tusayan I obtained fragments[72] of the ancient bell, which are now on exhibition in the Hemenway section of the Peabody Museum at Cambridge.

The stone walls of the mission were rarely dressed or carefully fitted, the interstices being filled in with loose rubble laid in adobe. There was apparently a gallery over the entrance to the building overlooking many smaller buildings, which evidently were the quarters of the resident priest. The construction of the walls was apparently a laborious task, as many of the stones are large and must have been brought a considerable distance. These stones were laid in adobe, and apparently were plastered without and within, although little evidence of the former plastering may now be seen. At the northwestern corner, however, there still

[72] There are two fragments, one of which is large enough to show the size of the bell, which was made either in Mexico or in Spain. The smaller fragment was used for many years as a paint-grinder by a Walpi Indian priest.

remain well-made adobe walls, the clay having been intermixed with straw. From the general appearance of these walls I regard them as of late construction, probably long after the destruction of the mission.

An examination of the plan of the mission building shows that it was oriented about north and south, with the entrance toward the latter direction. Compared with many other pueblo missions, this would seem to be an exceptional position. In my excavations I naturally sought the probable position of the entrance and, opposite it, the recess for the altar. It is evident, from the form of the standing walls, that an entrance from the east would be blocked by standing walls, and the axis of the building is north and south. The theory that the door was at the south has much in its favor, but there are several almost fatal objections to this conclusion.

If, however, we suppose that the entrance was in the south wall, the high walls still standing above the trail up the mesa would then recall the façades of other missions. The rooms east of the largest inclosure, by this interpretation, would be outbuildings—residence rooms for the padres—one side of which forms the eastern walls of the church edifice. The form of the Awatobi church, as indicated by the walls still standing, is very similar to that of Zuñi, notwithstanding the orientation appears to be somewhat different.

Excavations failed to reveal any sign of the altar recess at either the northern or the western end, which is not surprising, since the walls are so poorly preserved in both these directions. It was, moreover, very difficult to make a satisfactory examination of the foundations of the walls at any point on account of the fallen stories, which encumbered the floor at their bases.

From the appearance of antiquity it seems probable that long before the mission buildings were erected a ridge of many-storied houses extended eastward from the pueblo on the northern side of a level space or court, in which there were, either then or later, ceremonial chambers or kivas. The southern side of this open space was the site of the mission, but was then unoccupied. This open space recalls the large court at Walpi, where the Snake dance occurs, but it was considerably broader, one side being formed by the structures which rose from the edge of the mesa. In course of time, however, the mission buildings were erected on this site, and a wall connecting the ridge of houses on the north and the outhouses of the mission was made, thus inclosing the court on all four sides. It was into this inclosure, through a gateway, the buttresses of which still remain, that the assailants passed on that eventful night when Awatobi was destroyed.

There is good evidence that a massacre of Awatobians occurred in the southeastern angle of the eastern part of the pueblo, just east of the mission. If so, it is probable that many of the unfortunates sought refuge in the outbuildings of the church. Suspecting that such was the case, I excavated a considerable space of ground at these places and found many human skulls and other bones thrown together in confusion. The earth was literally filled with bones, evidently hastily placed there or left where the dead fell. These bodies were not buried with pious care, for there were no fragments of mortuary pottery or other indication of burial objects. Many of the skulls were broken, some pierced with sharp implements.

While it is true that possibly this may have been a potter's field, or, from its position east of the mission, a Christian burial place, as at Zuñi, the evidence from the appearance of the bodies points to a different conclusion. According to the legends, the hostiles entered the pueblo through the adjacent gateway; their anger led them especially against those of the inhabitants who were regarded as *powako* or sorcerers, and their first acts of violence would naturally have been toward those who sought refuge in the buildings adjacent the church. Near this hated "Singing-house" the slaughter began, soon extending to the kivas and the whole of the eastern section of the village. There was no evidence of murderous deeds in the rooms of the western section of the old pueblo, and the legends agree in relating that most of the men were in kivas, not far from the mission, when the village was overthrown. There is no legendary evidence that there were any Spanish priests in the mission at the time of its destruction, and there is no record extant of any Spaniards losing their lives at Awatobi at the time of its destruction, although the fact of the occurrence, according to Bandelier,[73] was recorded.

The traditional clans which inhabited Awatobi were the Awata (Bow), Honani (Badger), Piba (Tobacco), and Buli (Butterfly). The Bow people appear to have been the most important of these, since their name was applied to the village. Their totemic signatures, in pictographic form, may still be seen on the sides of the cliff under Awatobi, and in the ruins was found a fine arrowshaft polisher on which was an incised drawing of a bow and an arrow, suggesting that the owner was a member of the Bow phratry. Saliko, the chief of the woman's society known as the Mamzrautû, insists that this priesthood was strong in the fated pueblo, and that a knowledge of its mysteries was brought to Walpi by one of the women who was saved.

It is claimed by the folklorists of the Tataukyamû, a priesthood which, controls the New-fire ceremonies at Walpi, and is prominent in the Soyaluña, or the rites of the winter solstice, that the Piba or Tobacco phratry brought the fetishes of that society to Walpi, and there are many obscurely known resemblances between the Mamzrauti and the Wüwütcimti celebrations in Walpi which appear to support that claim. The Piba phratry is likewise said to have come to Walpi comparatively late in the history of the village, which fact points the same way.

Undoubtedly Awatobi received additions to its population from the south when the pueblos on the Little Colorado were abandoned, and there are obscure legends which support that belief; but the largest numbers were recruited from the pueblos in the eastern section of the country.[74]

THE KIVAS OF AWATOBI

A pueblo of the size of Awatobi, with so many evidences of long occupancy, would no doubt have several ceremonial chambers or kivas, but as yet no one has definitely indicated their positions. I have already called attention to evidences

[73] See his Final Report, p. 372.

[74] The only Awatobi name I know is that of a chief, Tapolo, which is not borne by any Hopi of my acquaintance (see page 603).

that if they existed they were probably to be looked for in the open court east of the western mounds and in the space north of the mission. In all the inhabited Tusayan pueblos the kivas are separated from the house clusters and are surrounded by courts or dance plazas. No open spaces existed in the main or western mounds of Awatobi, and there was no place there for kivas unless the pueblo was exceptional in having such structures built among the dwellings, as at Zuñi. A tradition has survived that Awatobi had regular kivas, partially subterranean, of rectangular shape, and that they were situated in open courts. This would indicate that the space east of the oldest part of the ruin may have been the sites of these chambers. The old priests whom I have consulted in regard to the probable positions of Awatobi kivas have invariably pointed out the mounds north of the mission walls in the eastern section of the ruin as the location of the kivas, and in 1892 I proved to my satisfaction that these directions were correct.

There is no reason to suppose that the kiva was a necessity in the ancient performance of the Tusayan ritual, and there are still performed many ceremonials as secret and as sacred as any others which occur in rooms used as dwellings or for the storage of corn. Thus, the Flute ceremony, one of the most complicated in Tusayan, is not, and according to legends never was, performed in a kiva. On the contrary, the secret rites of the Flute society are performed in the ancestral Flute chamber or home of the oldest woman of the Flute clan. Originally, I believe, the same was true in the case of other ceremonials, and that the kiva was of comparatively recent introduction into Tusayan.[75]

Speaking of the sacred rooms of Awatobi, Mindeleff says: "No traces of kivas were visible at the time the ruin was surveyed," but Stephen is quoted in a legend that "the people of Walpi had partly cleaned out one of these chambers and used it as a depository for ceremonial plume-sticks, but the Navaho carried off their sacred deposits, tempted probably by their market value as ethnologic specimens." It is true that while from a superficial examination of the Awatobi mounds the position of the kivas is difficult to locate, a little excavation brings their walls to light. It is likewise quite probable that the legend reported by Stephen has a basis in fact, and that the people at Walpi may have used old shrines in Awatobi, after its destruction, as the priests of Mishoñinovi do at the present time; but I very much doubt if the Navaho sold any of the sacred prayer emblems from these fanes. It is hardly characteristic of these people to barter such objects among one another, and no specimens from the shrines appear to have made their way into the numerous collections of traders known to me. There is, however, archeological evidence revealed by excavations that the room centrally placed in the court north of the mission contained a shrine in its floor on the night Awatobi fell.

In 1892, while removing the soil from a depression about the middle of the eastern court of Awatobi, about 100 feet north of the northern wall of the mission, I laid bare a room 28 by 14 feet, in which were found a skull and many other human bones which, from their disposition, had not been buried with care. The

---

[75] This explains the fact that the ruins in Tusayan, as a rule, have no signs of kivas, and the same appears to be true of the ruins of the pueblos on the Little Colorado and the Verde, in Tonto Basin, and other more southerly regions.

discovery of these skeletons accorded with the Hopi traditions that this was one of the rooms in which the men of Awatobi were gathered on the fatal night, and the inclosure where many died. I was deterred from further excavation at that place by the horror of my workmen at the desecration of the chamber. In 1895, however, I determined to continue my earlier excavations and to trace the course of the walls of adjacent rooms. The results obtained in this work led to a new phase of the question, which sheds more light on the character of the rooms in the middle of the eastern court of Awatobi. Instead of a single room at this point, there are three rectangular chambers side by side, all of about the same size (plate cviii). In the center of the floor of the middle room, 6 feet below the surface, I came upon a cist or stone shrine. As the workmen approached the floor they encountered a stone slab, horizontally placed in the pavement of the room. This slab was removed, and below it was another flat stone which was perforated by a rectangular hole just large enough to admit the hand and forearm. This second slab was found to cover a stone box, the sides of which were formed of stone slabs about 2-1/2 feet square. On the inner faces of the upright slabs rain-cloud symbols were painted. These symbols were of terrace form, in different colors outlined with black lines. One of the stones bore a yellow figure, another a red, and a third white. The color of the fourth was not determinable, but evidently, from its position relatively to the others, was once green. This arrangement corresponds with the present ceremonial assignment of colors to the cardinal points, or at least the north and south, as at the present time, were yellow and red, respectively, and presumably the white and green were on the east and west sides of the cist. The colors are still fairly bright and may be seen in the restoration of this shrine now in the National Museum.

There was no stone floor to this shrine, but within it were found fragments of prayer-plumes or pahos painted green, but so decayed that, when exposed to sunlight, some of them fell into dust. There were likewise fragments of green carbonate of copper and kaolin, a yellow ocher, and considerable vegetal matter mixed with the sand. All these facts tend to the belief that this crypt was an ancient shrine in the floor of a chamber which may have been a kiva.

The position of this room with a shrine in the middle of the court is interesting in comparison with that of similar shrines in some of the modern Hopi pueblos. Shrines occupy the same relative position in Sichomovi, Hano, Shipaulovi, and elsewhere, and within them sacred prayer-offerings are still deposited on ceremonial occasions. At Walpi, in the middle of the plaza, there is a subterranean crypt in which offerings are often placed, as I have elsewhere described in treating of certain ceremonies. This shrine is not visible, for a slab of stone which is placed over it lies on a level with the plaza, and is securely luted in place with adobe. There are similar subterranean prayer crypts in other Tusayan villages. They represent the traditional opening, or *sipapu*, through which, in Pueblo cosmogony, races crawled to the surface of the earth from an underworld. In Awatobi also there is a similar shrine, for the deposit of prayer-offerings, almost in the middle of a plaza bounded on three sides by the mission, the spur of many-storied houses, and the wall with a gateway, while the remaining side was formed by the great communal houses of the western part of the pueblo.

While we were taking from their ancient resting places the slabs of stone which formed this Awatobi shrine, the workmen reminded me how closely it resembled the *pahoki* used by the *katcinas,* and when, a month later, I witnessed the *Nimán-kat-cina* ceremony at Walpi, and accompanied the chief, Intiwa, when he deposited the prayer-sticks in that shrine,[76] I was again impressed by the similarity of the two, one in a ruin deserted two centuries ago, the other still used in the performance of ancient rites, no doubt much older than the overthrow of the great pueblo of Antelope mesa.

OLD AWATOBI

The western mounds of Awatobi afford satisfactory evidence that they cover the older rooms of the pueblo, and show by their compact form that the ancient village in architectural plan was similar to modern Walpi. They indicate that Awatobi was of pyramidal form, was symmetrical, three or four stories high,[77] without a central plaza, but probably penetrated by narrow courts or passages. No great ceremonial dance could have taken place in the heart of the pueblo, since there was not sufficient space for its celebration, but it must have occurred outside the village, probably in the open space to the east, near where the ruined walls of the mission now stand.

From the nature of the western mounds I found it advantageous to begin the work of excavation in the steep decline on the southern side, and to penetrate the mound on the level of its base or the rock formation which forms its foundation. In this way all the débris could advantageously be moved and thrown over the side of the mesa. We began to open the mounds, therefore, on the southern side, making converging trenches at intervals, working toward their center. We found that these trenches followed continuous walls connected by cross partitions, forming rooms, and that these were continued as far as we penetrated. The evidence is good that these rooms are followed by others which extend into the deepest part of the mound. We likewise excavated at intervals over the whole surface of the western area of Awatobi, and wherever we dug, walls of former rooms, which diminished in altitude on the northern side, were found. From these excavations I concluded that if any part of the western mound was higher than the remainder, it was on the southern side just above the edge of the mesa, and from that highest point the pueblo diminished in altitude to the north, in which direction it was continued for some distance in low, single-story rooms.

ROOMS OF THE WESTERN MOUND

The older or western portion of Awatobi is thus believed to be made up of a number of high mounds which rise steeply, and for a considerable height from the southern edge of the cliff, from which it slopes more gradually to the north and west. On account of this steep declivity we were able to examine, in vertical section, the arrangement of the rooms, one above the other (figure 256). By beginning excavations on the rocky foundation and working into the mound, parallel

[76] See Journal of American Ethnology and Archæology, vol. ii.

[77] "Las casas son de tres altos" — *Segunda Relacion,* p. 580.

walls were encountered at intervals as far as we penetrated. From the edge of the cliff there seemed to extend a series of these parallel walls, which were united by cross partitions, forming a series of rooms, one back of another. The deeper we penetrated the mound the higher the walls were found to be, and this was true of the excavations along the whole southern side of the elevation (plate cix). If, as I suspect, these parallel walls extend to the heart of the mounds, the greatest elevation of the former buildings must have been four stories. It would likewise seem probable that the town was more or less pyramidal, with the highest point somewhat back from the one- or two-story walls at the edge of the cliff, a style of architecture still preserved in Walpi. The loftiest wall, which was followed down to the floor, was 15 feet high, but as that was measured over 20 feet below the apex of the mound, it would seem that, from a distance, there would be a wall 30 feet high in the center of the mound. Even counting 7 feet as the height of each story we would have four stories above the foundation, and this, I believe, was the height of the old pueblo. But probably the wall did not rise to this height at the edge of the mesa, where it could not have been more than one or two stories high. There is no evidence of the former existence of an inclosed court of any considerable size between the buildings and the cliff, although a passage probably skirted the brink of the precipice, and house ladders may have been placed on that side for ready access to upper rooms. By a series of platforms or terraces, which were in fact the roofs of the houses, one mounted to the upper stories which formed the apex of the pueblo.

BUREAU OF AMERICAN ETHNOLOGY — — SEVENTEENTH ANNUAL RE-
PORT PL. CIX

Excavations In The Western Mound Of Awatobi

FIG. 256—STRUCTURE OF HOUSE WALL OF AWATOBI

On the western, northern, and eastern sides the slope is more gradual, and while there are many obscurely marked house plans visible over the surface, even quite near the top of the elevation, they are doubtless the remains of single-story structures. This leads me to suspect that when Awatobi was built it was reared on a mound of soil or sand, and not on the solid rock surface of the mesa. The configuration, then, shows that the pueblo sloped by easy decline to the plain to the north, but rose more abruptly from the south and west. There are low extramural mounds to the north, showing that on this side the dwellings were composed of straggling chambers. The general character of the rooms on the level slope at the western side of old Awatobi is shown in the accompanying illustration (plate cx). The peculiarity of these rooms appears by a comparison with the many-story chambers of the southern declivity of the ruin. Extending the excavations four feet below the surface we encountered a floor which rested on solid earth, and there were no signs of walls beneath it. This was without doubt a single-story house, the roof of which had disappeared. The surrounding surface of the ground is level, but the tops of adjoining walls of rooms may readily be traced near by.

The room was rectangular, twice as long as wide, and without passageways into adjoining chambers. The northern, eastern, and western walls were unbroken, and there was nothing peculiar in the floor of these sections; but we found a well-preserved, elevated settle at the southern side, extending two-thirds of the length of the main wall to a small side wall, inclosing a square recess, the object of which is unknown to me.

All walls were smoothly plastered, and the floor was paved with flat stones set in adobe. The singular inclosure at the southern corner could not be regarded as a fireplace, for there was no trace of soot upon its walls. I incline to the belief that it may have served as a closet, or possibly as a granary. Its arrangement is not unlike that in certain modern rooms at Walpi.

An examination of the masonry of the rooms of the western mounds of Awatobi shows that the component stones were in a measure dressed into shape, which was, as a rule, cubical. In this respect they differ from the larger stones of which the mission walls were built, for in this masonry the natural cleavage is utilized for the face of the wall.

The differences between the masonry of the mission and that of the room in which we found a chief buried were very marked. In the former, elongated slabs of stone, without pecking or dressing, were universal, while in the latter the squared stones were laid in courses and neatly fitted together. The partitions likewise are narrower, being not more than 6 inches thick.

BUREAU OF AMERICAN ETHNOLOGY— — SEVENTEENTH ANNUAL RE-
PORT PL. CX

Excavated Room In The Western Mound Of Awatobi

SMALLER AWATOBI

About an eighth of a mile west of the great mounds of Awatobi there is a small rectangular ruin, the ground plan of which is well marked, and in which individual houses are easy to trace. Like its larger neighbor, it stands on the very edge of the mesa. None of its walls rise above the surface of the mounds, which, however, are considerably elevated and readily distinguished for some distance. The pueblo was built in the form of a rectangle of single-story houses surrounding a plaza. There was an opening or entrance on the southern side, near which is a mound, possibly the remains of a kiva. A trail now passes directly through the ruin and down the mesa side to Jeditoh valley, probably the pathway by which the ancient inhabitants ascended the cliff. The Hopi Indians employed by me in excavating Awatobi had no name for this ruin and were not familiar with its existence before I pointed it out to them. For want of a better interpretation I have regarded it as a colony of old Awatobi, possibly of later construction.

Excavations in its mounds revealed no objects of interest, although fragments of beautiful pottery, related to that found at Awatobi and Sikyatki, show that it must have been made by people of the older or best epoch[78] of Tusayan ceramics.

MORTUARY REMAINS

Although it is well known that the ancient inhabitants of the great houses of the Gila-Salado drainage buried some of their dead within their dwellings, or in other rooms, and that the same mortuary practice was observed in ancient Zuñi-Cibola, up to the time of my excavations this form of burial had never been found in Tusayan. I am now able to record that the same custom was practiced at Awatobi.

Excavation made in the southeastern declivity of the western mounds led to a burial chamber in which we found the well-preserved skeleton of an old man, apparently a priest. The body was laid on the floor, at full length, and at his head, which pointed southward, had been placed, not mortuary offerings of food in bowls, but insignia of his priestly office. Eight small objects of pottery were found on his left side (plate cxii, *a, b, d, e*). Among these was a symmetrical vase of beautiful red ware (plate cxi, *a*) richly decorated with geometric patterns, and four globular paint pots, each full of pigment of characteristic color. These paint pots were of black-and-white ware, and contained, respectively, yellow ocher, sesquioxide of iron, green copper carbonate, and micaceous hematite (plate cxiii, *a, d, e*) such as is now called *yayala* and used by the Snake priests in the decoration of their faces. There were also many arrowpoints in an earthen colander, and a ladle was luted over the mouth of the red vase. My native excavators pronounced this the grave of a warrior priest. The passageways into this chamber of death had all been closed,

---

[78] So far as our limited knowledge of the older ruins of Tusayan goes, we find that their inhabitants must have been as far removed from rude Shohonean nomads as their descendants are today. The settlement at the early site of Walpi is reported to have been made in very early times, some legends stating that it occurred at a period when the people were limited to one family—the Snake. The fragments of pottery which I have found in the mounds of that ancient habitation are as fine and as characteristic of Tusayan as that of Sikyatki or Awatobi. It is inferior to none in the whole pueblo area, and betrays long sedentary life of its makers before it was manufactured.

and there were no other mortuary objects in the room. This was the only instance of intramural interment which I discovered in the excavations at Awatobi, but a human bone was found on the floor of another chamber. So far as known the Awatobi people buried most of their dead outside the town, either in the foothills at the base of the mesa, or in the adjacent sand-dunes.

The work of excavating the graves at the foot of the mesa was desultory, as I found no single place where many interments had been made. Several food vessels were dug up at a grave opened by Kópeli, the Snake chief. I was not with him when he found the grave, but he called me to see it soon after its discovery. We took from this excavation a sandstone fetish of a mountain-lion, a fragment of the bottom of a basin perforated with holes as if used as a colander. Deposited in this fragment were many stone arrowheads, several fragments of green paint, a flat green paho ornamented with figures of dragon-flies in black. In addition to a single complete prayer-stick there were fragments of many others too much broken to be identified. One of these was declared by Kópeli to be a chief's paho. The grave in which these objects were found was situated about halfway down the side of the mesa to the southward of the highest mounds of the western division of the pueblo.

Here and there along the base of all the foothills south of Awatobi are evidences of former burials, and complete bowls, dippers, and vases were unearthed (plate cxiii, *b, c*). The soil is covered with fragments of pottery, and in places, where the water has washed through them, exposing a vertical section of the ground, it was found that the fragments of pottery extended through the soil sometimes to a depth of fifty feet below the surface. There was evidence, however, that this soil had been transported more or less by rain water, which often courses down the sides of the mesa in impetuous torrents.

Human bones and mortuary vessels were found south of the mission near the trail, at the foot of the mesa. In a single grave, a foot below the surface, there were two piles of food bowls, each pile containing six vessels, all broken.

The cemetery northwest of Awatobi, where the soil is sandy and easy to excavate, had been searched by others, and many beautiful objects of pottery taken from it. This burial place yielded many bowls (plates clxvii, clxviii) and jars, as well as several interesting pahos similar to those from Sikyatki, which I shall later describe but which have never before been reported from Awatobi. It was found that one of these prayer-sticks was laid over the heart of the deceased, and as the skeleton was in a sitting posture, with the hand on the breast, the prayer-stick may thus have been held at the time of burial. Our success in finding places of interment on all sides of Sikyatki, irrespective of direction, leads me to suspect that further investigation of the sand-dunes north of Awatobi will reveal graves at that point.

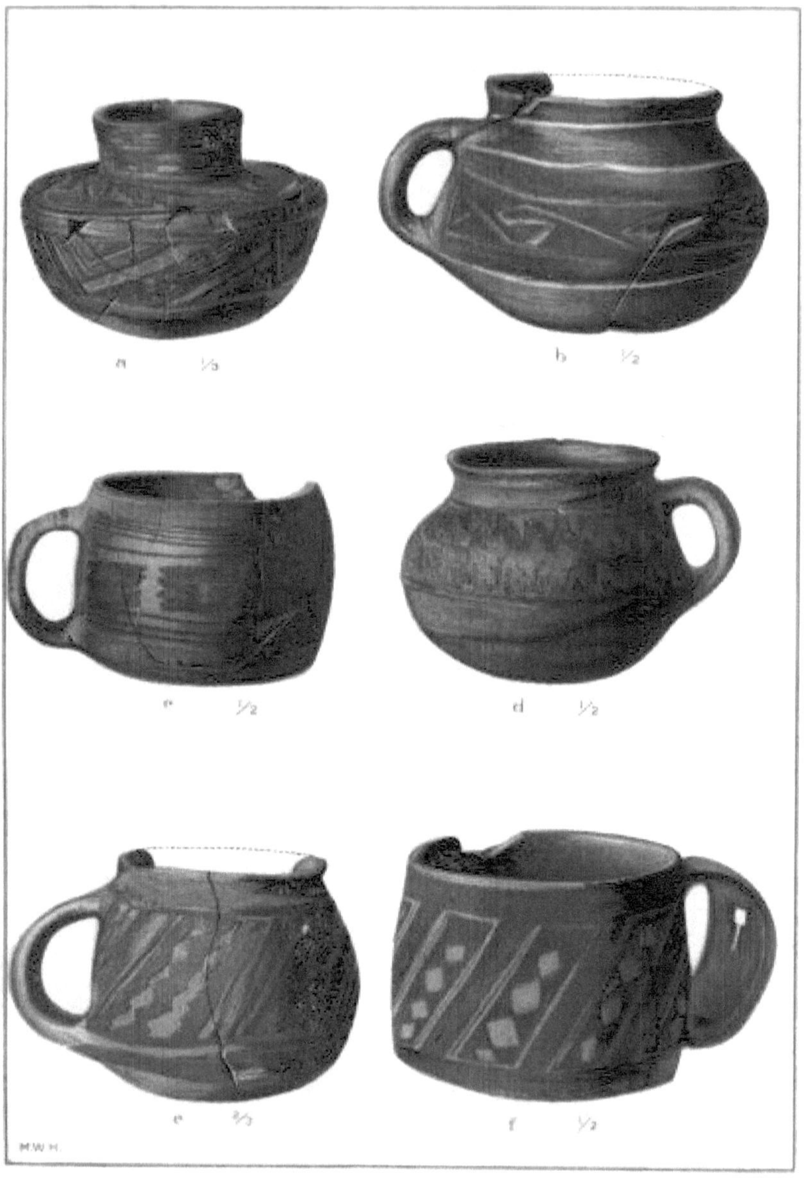

BUREAU OF AMERICAN ETHNOLOGY—— SEVENTEENTH ANNUAL RE-
PORT PL. CXI

Vase And Mugs From The Western Mounds Of Awatobi

I have already called attention to the great abundance of charred corn found in
the rooms north of the mission. Renewed work in this quarter revealed still greater
quantities of this corn stacked in piles, sometimes filling the entire side of a room.
Evidently, as I have elsewhere shown, the row of rooms at this part of the ruin

were burned with all their contents. The corn was not removed from the granaries, as it would have been if the place had been gradually abandoned. When an Indian burns stored corn in such quantities as were found at Awatobi we can not believe he was bent on pillage, and it is an instructive fact that thus far no stacked corn has been found in the western or most ancient section of Awatobi.

SHRINES

Although Awatobi was destroyed almost two centuries ago, the shrines of the old pueblo were used for many years afterward, and are even now frequented by some of the Mishoñinovi priests. In one of these ancient depositories two wooden figurines sat in state up to within a few years ago.

This shrine lies below the ruins of the mission, among the bowlders on the side of the cliff, about fifty feet from the edge of the mesa, and is formed in an eroded cavity in the side of a bowlder of unusual size. A rude wall had been built before this recess, which opened to the east, and apparently the orifice was closed with logs, which have now fallen in. The present appearance of this shrine is shown in the accompanying illustration (figure 257).

In former times two wooden idols, called the *Alosaka*, were kept in this crypt, in much the same manner as the Dawn Maid is now sealed up by the Walpians, when not used in the New-fire ceremony, as I have described in my account of *Naacnaiya*.[79] Mr Thomas V. Keam, not knowing that the Awatobi idols were still used in the Mishoñinovi ritual, had removed them to his residence, but when this was known a large number of priests begged him to return them, saying that they were still used in religious exercises. With that consideration which he has always shown to the Indians, Mr Keam allowed the priests to take the images of *Alosaka*. The figurines were this time carried to Mishoñinovi, the priests sprinkling a line of meal along the trail over which they carried them. The two idols[80] have not been seen by white people since that time, and are now, no doubt, in some hidden crypt near the Mishoñinovi village.

There is a shrine of simple character, near the ruins of smaller Awatobi, which bears evidence of antiquity (figure 258). It consisted, in 1892, of a circle of small stones in which were two large water-worn stones and a fragment of petrified wood. There was no evidence that it had lately been used.

---

[79] Journal of American Folk-lore, vol. v, No. xviii, 1892.

[80] There is a rude sketch of these two idols of *Alosaka* in the archives of the Hemenway Expedition. They represent figurines about 4 feet tall, with two horns on the head not unlike those of the Tewan clowns or gluttons called Paiakyamû. As so little is known of the Mishoñinovi ritual, the rites in which they are used are at present inexplicable.

FIG. 257—ALOSAKA SHRINE AT AWATOBI

On the extreme western point of the mesa, at the very edge of the cliff, there was also a simple shrine (figure 259). Judging from its general appearance, this, likewise, had not been used in modern times, but there were several old prayer-sticks not far away.

BUREAU OF AMERICAN ETHNOLOGY — — SEVENTEENTH ANNUAL RE-
PORT PL. CXII

Paint Pots, Bowl, And Dipper From Awatobi

At the foot of the mesa, below the point last mentioned, however, there is a
shrine (figure 260), the earth of which contained hundreds of prayer-sticks, in all
stages of decay, while some of them had been placed there only a few days before
my visit. This shrine, I was told, is still used by the Mishoñinovi priests in their

sacred observances. Among other forms of prayer offerings there were many small wooden cylinders with radiating sticks connected with yarn, the symbolic prayer offering for squashes.[81] In former times Antelope valley was the garden spot of Tusayan, and from what we know of the antiquity of the cultivation of squashes in the Southwest, there is little doubt that they were cultivated by the Awatobians, and that similar offerings were made by the ancient farmers for a good crop of these vegetables.

FIG. 258—SHRINE AT AWATOBI

FIG. 259—SHRINE AT AWATOBI

---

[81] See the ear-ornament of the mask shown in plate cviii, of the Fifteenth Annual Report.

POTTERY

The mounds of Awatobi are entirely covered with fragments of pottery of all the various kinds and colors known to ancient Tusayan. There were found coiled and indented ware, coarse undecorated vessels, fine yellow and smooth ware with black-and-white and red decorations. There is no special kind of pottery peculiar to Awatobi, but it shares with the other Tusayan ruins all types, save a few fragments of black glazed ware, which occur elsewhere.

FIG. 260—SHRINE AT AWATOBI

It is highly probable that the few specimens of black-and-white ware found in this ruin were not manufactured in the village, and the red ware probably came from settlements to the south, on the Little Colorado. These colors are in part due to the character of the paste which was used, and the clay most often selected by Awatobi potters made a fine yellow vessel. The material from which most of the vessels were manufactured came, no doubt, from a bank near the ruin, where there is good evidence that it was formerly quarried.

Three coarse clay objects, such as might have been used for roof drains, were found. The use of these objects, possibly indicated by their resemblance, is not, however, perfectly clear. Their capacity would not be equal to the torrents of rain which, no doubt, often fell on the housetops of Awatobi, and they can hardly be identified as spouts of large bowls, since they are attached to a circular disk with smooth edges. In want of a satisfactory explanation I have provisionally regarded them as water spouts, but whether they are from ancient vessels or from the roofs of houses I am in much doubt.[82]

One of the most instructive fragments of pottery taken from the ruins is that of a coarse clay vessel, evidently a part of a flat basin or saucer. The rim of this vessel is punctured with numerous holes, the intervals between which are not greater than the diameter of the perforations.

Several platter-like vessels with similar holes about their rims have been taken from other ruins of Jeditoh valley and mesa, the holes being regarded as having been made as a means of suspension. Near a sacred spring called Kawaika,[83] not far from Jeditoh, near Awatobi, a large number of beautiful vessels with similar holes in their rims were excavated by Mr T. V. Keam, and later passed into the collections of the Hemenway Expedition, now installed at Cambridge. They are of all kinds of ware, widely different in shape, the number of marginal perforations varying greatly. As they were found in large numbers near a spring they are regarded as sacrificial vessels, in which food or sacred meal was deposited as an offering to some water deity. The handle of a mug (plate cxi, *f*) from Awatobi, so closely resembles the handles of certain drinking cups taken from the cliff-houses of San Juan valley that it should be specially mentioned. There is in the handle of this mug a T-shape opening quite similar in form to the peculiar doorways of certain cliff-dwellings. The mug is made of the finest white ware, decorated with black lines arranged in geometric patterns. So close is its likeness in form and texture to cliff-house pottery that the two may be regarded as identical. Moreover, it is not impossible that the object may have been brought to Tusayan from Tségi canyon, in the cliff-houses of which Hopi clans[84] lived while Awatobi was in its prime, and, indeed, possibly after the tragedy of 1700. The few fragments of Tségi canyon pottery known to me have strong resemblances to ancient Hopi ware, although the black-and-white variety predominates.

---

[82] Similar "spouts" were found by Mindeleff at Awatobi, and a like use of them is suggested in his valuable memoir.

[83] The Keresan people are called by the same name, Kawaika, which, as hitherto explained, is specially applied to the modern pueblo of Laguna.

[84] The Asa people who came to Tusayan from the Rio Grande claim to have lived for a few generations in Tubka or Tségi (Chelly) canyon.

Pottery From Intramural Burial At Awatobi

The collection of pottery from Awatobi is, comparatively speaking, small, but it shows many interesting forms. Awatobi pottery may be classed under the same groups as other old Tusayan ceramics, but most of the specimens collected belong to the yellow, black-and-white, and red varieties. It resembles that of Sikyatki, but bears little likeness to modern ware in texture or symbolism. One is impressed by the close resemblance between the Awatobi pottery and that from the ruins of the Little Colorado and Zuñi,[85] which no doubt is explained, in part, by the identity in the constituents of the potter's clay near Awatobi with that in more southerly regions.

Evidences of Spanish influence may be traced on certain objects of pottery from Awatobi, especially on those obtained from the eastern mounds of the ruin. In most essentials, however, the Awatobi ware resembles that of the neighboring ruins, and is characteristically Tusayan.

The differentiation in modern Cibolan and Tusayan symbolism is much greater than that of the ancient pottery from the same provinces, a fact which is believed to point to a similarity, possibly identity, of culture in ancient times. With this thought in mind, it would be highly instructive to study the ancient ruins of the Rio Grande region, as unfortunately no large collections of archeological objects from that part of the Southwest have been made.[86]

The majority of the bowls from Awatobi are decorated in geometric patterns and a few have animal or human figures. The symbols, as well as the pottery itself, can not be distinguished from those of Sikyatki. Fragments of glazed ware are not unknown at Awatobi, but so far as recorded, entire specimens have never been obtained from the latter ruin.

In order that the character of the geometric designs on Awatobi pottery may be better understood, two plates are introduced to illustrate their modifications in connection with my discussion of the geometric forms figured on Sikyatki ware. The figures on these bowls (plates CLXVI, CLXVII), with one or two exceptions, need no special description in addition to what is said of Sikyatki geometric designs, which they closely resemble.

The cross-shape figure (plate CLXVI, *b*) may profitably be studied in connection with the account of the modification of Sikyatki sun symbols. Evidences of the use of a white pigment as a slip were found on one or two fragments of fine pottery from Awatobi, but no decoration of this kind was observed on the Sikyatki vessels. The red ware is the same as that found in ancient Cibola, while one or two fragments of glossy black recall the type common to modern Santa Clara.

Two bird-shape vessels, one made of black-and-white ware, the other red with black-and-white decoration, were found at Awatobi. Large masses of clay suited to the potter's art were not uncommonly found in the corners of the rooms or in the niches in their walls. Some of these masses are of fine paste, the others coarse with grains of sand. The former variety was used in making the finest Tusayan ceramics; the latter was employed in modeling cooking pots and other vessels of

[85] The pottery of ancient Cibola is practically identical with that of the ruined pueblos of the Colorado Chiquito, near Winslow, Arizona.

[86] The specimens labeled "New Mexico" and "Arizona" are too vaguely classified to be of any service in this consideration. It is suggested that collectors carefully label their specimens with the exact locality in which they are found, giving care to their association and, when mortuary, to their position in the graves in relation to the skeletons.

ruder finish.

Several flute-shape objects of clay, with flaring extremities, were found on the surface of the mounds of Awatobi, and one was taken from a Sikyatki grave. The use of these objects is unknown to me.

Among the fragments of dippers from Awatobi are several with perforations in the bottom, irregularly arranged or in geometric form, as that of a cross. These colanders were rare at Sikyatki, but I find nothing in them to betray Spanish influence.[87] Handled dippers or mugs have been found so often by me in the prehistoric ruins of our Southwest that I can not accept the dictum that the mug form was not prehistoric, and the conclusion is legitimate that the Tusayan Indians were familiar with mugs when the Spaniards came among them. The handles of the dippers or ladles are single or double, solid or hollow, simply turned up at one end or terminating with the head of an animal. The upper side of the ladle handle may be grooved or convex. No ladle handle decorated with an image of a "mud-head" or clown priest, so common on modern ladles, was found either at Awatobi or Sikyatki.

Rudely made imitations in miniature of all kinds of pottery, especially of ladles, were common. These are regarded as votive offerings, from the fact that they were found usually in the graves of children, and were apparently used as playthings before they were buried.

A common decoration on the handles of ladles is a series of short parallel lines arranged in alternating longitudinal and transverse zones. This form of decoration of ladle handles I have observed on similar vessels from the Casas Grandes of Chihuahua, and it reappears on pottery in all the ruins I have studied between Mexico and Tusayan. In the exhibit of the Mexican Government at Madrid in 1892-93 a fine collection of ancient pottery from Oaxaca was shown, and I have drawings of one of these ladles with the same parallel marks on the handle that are found on Pueblo ware from the Gila-Salado, the Cibola, and the Tusayan regions.

The only fragment of pottery from Awatobi or Sikyatki with designs which could be identified with any modern picture of a *katcina* was found, as might be expected, in the former ruin. This small fragment is instructive, in that it indicates the existence of the *katcina* cult in Tusayan before 1700; but the rarity of the figures of these supernatural beings is very suggestive. The fragment in question is of ancient ware, resembling the so-called orange type of pottery, and is apparently a part of the neck of a vase. The figure represents Wupamo, the Great-cloud *katcina*, and is marked like the doll of the same as it appears in the *Powamû* or February celebration at Walpi.[88]

The associates of the *katcinas* are the so-called "mud-heads" or clowns, an or-

[87] I am informed by Mr F. W. Hodge that similar fragments were found by the Hemenway Expedition in 1888 in the prehistoric ruins of the Salado.

[88] The head is round, with lateral appendages. The face is divided into two quadrants above, with chin blackened, and marked with zigzag lines, which are lacking in modern pictures. In the left hand the figure holds a rattle. The body is wanting, but the breast is decorated with rectangles.

der of priests as widely distributed as the Pueblo area. In Tusayan villages they are called the Tcukuwympkia, and are variously personated. As they belong especially to the *katcina* cult, which is naturally supposed to have been in vogue at Awatobi, I was greatly interested in the finding of a fragment representing a grotesque head which reminded me of a glutton of the division of the Tcukuwympkia called Tcuckutû. While there may be some doubt of the validity of my identification, yet, taken in connection with the fragment of a vase with the face of Wupamo, I think there is no doubt that the *katcina* cult was practiced at Awatobi.

STONE IMPLEMENTS

Comparatively few stone implements, such as mauls, hammers, axes, and spearpoints, were found; but some of those unearthed from the mounds are finely finished, being regular in form and highly polished. There were many spherical stones, resembling those still sometimes used in Tusayan on important occasions as badges of authority. These stones were tied in a buckskin bag, which was attached to a stick and used as a warclub. Many of the axes were grooved for hafting; one of the specimens was doubly grooved and had two cutting edges. By far the largest number were blunt at one pole and sharpened at the opposite end. A single highly polished specimen (plate CLXXI, *f*) resembles a type very common in the Gila Salado ruins.

Arrowheads, some of finely chipped obsidian, were common, being frequently found in numbers in certain mortuary bowls. Three or four specimens of other kinds of implements fashioned from this volcanic glass were picked up on the surface of the mounds.

Metates, or flat stones for grinding corn, were dug up in several houses; they were in some instances much worn, and were eagerly sought by the Indian women who visited our camp. These specimens differ in no respect from similar mealing stones still used at Walpi and other modern Tusayan pueblos. Many were made of very coarse stone[89] for use in hulling corn preparatory to grinding; others were of finer texture, and both kinds were accompanied by the corresponding mano or muller held in the hand in grinding meal.

The modern Hopi often use as seats in their kivas cubical blocks of stone with depressions in two opposite sides which serve as handholds by which they are carried from place to place. Two of these stones, about a cubic foot in size, were taken out of the chamber which I have supposed to be the Awatobi kiva. In modern Tusayan these seats are commonly made of soft sandstone, and are so few in number that we can hardly regard them as common. They are often used to support the uprights of altars when they are erected, and I have seen priests grind pigments in the depressions. Incidentally, it may be said that I have never seen priests use chairs in any kiva celebration; nor do they have boxes to sit upon. During the droning of the tedious songs they have nothing under them except a folded blanket or sheepskin.

[89] A single metate of lava or malpais was excavated at Awatobi. This object must have had a long journey before it reached the village, since none of the material from which it was made is found within many miles of the ruin.

Excavations in the Awatobi rooms revealed several interesting shallow mortars used for grinding pigments, but no one of these is comparable in finish with that shown in the accompanying illustration (plate CLXXII, *a*). This object is made of a hard stone in the form of a perfect parallelopipedon with slightly rounded faces. The depression is shallow, and when found there was a discoloration of pigment upon its surface.

In almost every house that bore evidence of former occupancy, beautifully made mullers and metates were exhumed. These were ordinarily in place in the corner of the chamber, and were much worn, as if by constant use. In one grave there was found a metate reversed over a skeleton, probably that of a woman— although the bones were so disintegrated that the determination of the sex of the individual was impossible. Several of these metates were taken by Indian women, who prized them so highly that they loaded the stones on burros and carried them ten miles to Walpi, where they are now applied to the same purpose for which they were used over two centuries ago.

On the surface of the mesa, beyond the extension of the ground plan of the ruin, there are many depressions worn in the rocks where the Awatobi women formerly whetted their grinding stones, doubtless in the manner practiced by the modern villagers of Tusayan. These depressions are especially numerous near the edge of the cliff, between the eastern and western sections of the ruin.[90]

---

[90] There are many fine pictographs, some of which are evidently ancient, on the cliffs of the Awatobi mesa. These are in no respect characteristic, and among them I have seen the *awata* (bow), *honani* (badger's paw), *tcüa* (snake), and *omowûh* (rain-cloud). On the side of the precipitous wall of the mesa south of the western mounds there is a row of small hemispherical depressions or pits, with a groove or line on one side. There is likewise, not far from this point, a realistic figure of a vulva, not very unlike the *asha* symbols on Thunder mountain, near Zuñi.

BUREAU OF AMERICAN ETHNOLOGY — — SEVENTEENTH ANNUAL RE-
PORT PL. CXIV

Bone Implements From Awatobi And Sikyatki

BONE OBJECTS

A large and varied collection of bone implements was gathered at Awatobi, and a few additional specimens were exhumed from Sikyatki. It is worthy of note that, as a rule, bone implements are more common in houses than in graves; and since the Awatobi excavations were conducted mostly in living rooms, while those at Sikyatki were largely in the cemeteries, the bone implements from the former pueblo far outnumber those from the latter.

The collection consists of awls, bodkins, needles, whistles, and tubes made of the bones of birds and quadrupeds. The two animals which contributed more than others to these objects were the turkey and the rabbit, although there were fragments of the horns and shin-bones of the antelope or deer. Several of these specimens were blackened by fire, and one was stained with green pigment. There was also evidence of an attempt at ornamenting the implements by incised lines, while one was bound with string. Bones of animals which had served for food were very common in all the excavations at Awatobi, especially near the floors of the houses. With the exception of a number of large bones of a bear, found in one of the houses in the northern range of the eastern section, these bones were not carefully collected.

Plate cxiv gives a general idea of some of the forms of worked bone which were obtained. Figure *a* shows an awl, for the handle of which one of the trochanters was used, the point at the opposite end being very sharp; *b* and *c* are similar objects, but slighter, and more carefully worked; *d* is a flattened bone implement perforated with two holes, and may have been used as a needle. There are similar implements in the collection, but with a single terminal perforation. Other forms of bone awls are shown in *e, f, g,* and *j*.

There are a number of bone objects the use of which is problematical. One of the best of these is a section of the tibia of a bird, cut longitudinally, convex on the side represented in plate cxiv, *h*, and concave on the opposite side. When found this bone fragment was tied to a second similar section by a string (remnants of which can be seen in the figure), thus forming a short tube. The use of this object is not known to me, nor were any satisfactory suggestions made by the Indians whom I consulted in relation to it. This does not apply, however, to the object illustrated in plate cxiv, *i*, which was declared by several Hopi to be a bird whistle, similar to that used in ceremonials connected with medicine making.

The manner in which a bone whistle is used in imitation of a bird's call has been noticed by me in the accounts of several ceremonials, and I will therefore quote the description of its use in the *Nimankatcina* at Walpi.[91]

> Then followed an interval of song and accompanying rattle, at the termination of which Intiwa's associate took the bird whistle (*tatükpi*) and blew three times into the liquid, making a noise not unlike that produced by a toy bird whistle. This was repeated four times, accompanied by song and rattle. He first inserted the bone whistle on the north side, then on the other cardinal points in turn. The monotonous song and rattle then ceased, and Intiwa sprinkled corn pollen on the ears of corn in the water, and upon the line of pahos.

The object of the whistle is to call the summer birds which are associated with planting and harvesting. The whistle figures in many rites, especially in those connected with the making of medicine or charm liquid.

MISCELLANEOUS OBJECTS

ORNAMENTS IN THE FORM OF BIRDS AND SHELLS

In the excavations, as well as on the surface of the mounds at Awatobi, were found many imitations of marine shells made of clay, often painted red and ranging from the size of half a dollar to that of the thumb nail (plate clxxiii, *j-m*). On the convex surface of these objects parallel lines are etched, and they are pierced at the valves for suspension. I have never found them suspended from the neck of a skeleton, although their general appearance indicates that they were used as ornaments. Similarly made clay images of birds (plate clxxiii, *g, h, i*) with extended wings were also found, and of these there are several different forms in the collection. A small perforated knob at the breast served for attachment. In the absence of any better explanation of these objects, I have regarded them as gorgets, or pendants, for personal decoration.

[91] *Journal of American Ethnology and Archæology*, vol. ii, No. 1, p. 77.

In the Awatobi collections there are several small disks made apparently of pipe clay, which also were probably used as ornaments. These are very smooth and wonderfully regular in shape—in one case with a perforation near the rim. Turquois and shell beads were found in considerable numbers in the excavations at Awatobi, but, as they are similar to those from Sikyatki, I have reserved a discussion of them for following pages. A few fragments of shell armlets and wristlets were also exhumed. These were made generally of the Pacific coast *Pectunculus*, so common in the ruins of the Little Colorado.[92]

CLAY BELL

Copper bells are said to be used in the secret ceremonials of the modern Tusayan villages, and in certain of the ceremonial foot races metal bells of great age and antique pattern are sometimes tied about the waists of the runners. Small copper hawk bells,[93] found in southern Arizonian ruins, are identical in form and make with those used by the ancient Nahuatl people. So far as the study of the antiquities of the ruins of Tusayan immediately about the inhabited towns has gone, we have no record of the finding of copper bells of any great age. It was, therefore, with considerable interest that I exhumed from one of the rooms of the westernmost or oldest section of Awatobi a clay bell (figure 261) made in exact imitation of one of the copper bells that have been reported from several southern ruins (plate CLXXIII, *a*). While it may be said that it would be more decisive evidence of the prehistoric character of this object if Awatobi had not been under Spanish influence for over a century, still, from the position where it was dug up and its resemblance to metal bells which are undoubtedly prehistoric, there seems to be little reason to question its age. As with the imitation of marine shells in clay, it is probable that in this bell we have a facsimile of a metal bell with which the ancient Tusayan people were undoubtedly familiar.[94]

---

[92] In the expedition of 1896 there were found a large number of shell ornaments, which will be described in a forthcoming report of the operations during that year. See the preliminary account in the article "Pacific Coast Shells in Tusayan Ruins," *American Anthropologist*, December, 1896.

[93] One of these bells was found in a grave at Chaves Pass during the field work of 1896.

[94] Bells made of clay are not rare in modern Tusayan villages, and while their form is different from that of the Awatobi specimen, and the size larger, there seems no reason to doubt the antiquity of the specimen from the ruin of Antelope mesa.

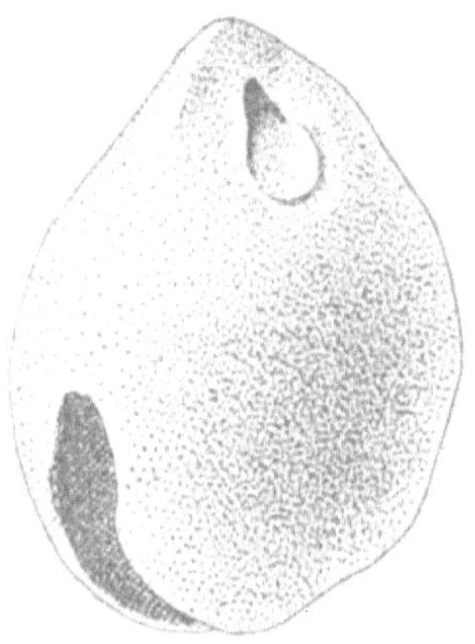

FIG. 261—CLAY BELL FROM AWATOBI (NATURAL SIZE)

TEXTILE FABRICS

In the very earliest accounts which we have of Tusayan the Hopi are said to raise cotton and to weave it into mantles. These mantles, or "towels" as they were styled by Espejo, were, according to Castañeda, ornamented with embroidery, and had tassels at the corners. In early times garments were made of the fiber of the maguey, and of feathers and rabbit skins. Fabrics made of animal fiber are mentioned by Friar Marcos de Niza, and he was told that the inhabitants of Totonteac obtained the material from which they were made from animals as large as the greyhounds which the father had with him. The historical references which can be mentioned to prove that the Tusayan people, when they were first visited, knew how to spin and weave are numerous, and need not be quoted here. That the people of Awatobi made cotton fabrics there is no doubt, for it is distinctly stated by early visitors that they were acquainted with the art of weaving, and some of the presents made to the first Spanish explorers were of native cotton.

The archeological evidence supports the historical in this particular, and several fragments of cloth were found in our excavations in the western mounds of the village. These fragments were of cotton and agave fiber, of cotton alone, and in one instance of the hair of some unknown animal. No signs of the famous rabbit-skin blankets were seen, and from the perishable nature of the material of which they were made it would be strange if any traces had been discovered. At Sikyatki a small textile fragment made of feathers was found in one of the burial vases, but no feather garments or even fragments of the same were unearthed at Awatobi.

A woven rope of agave fiber and many charred strings of the same material were found in a niche in the wall of a house in the eastern section, and from the same room there was taken a string, over a yard long, made of human hair. It was suggested to me by one of the Hopi that this string was part of the coiffure of an Awatobi maid, and that it was probably used to tie up her hair in whorls above the ears, as is still the Hopi custom.

The whole number of specimens of textile fabrics found at Awatobi was small, and their character disappointing for study, for the conditions of burial in the soil are not so good for their preservation as in the dry caves or cliff houses, from which beautifully preserved cloth, made at a contemporary period, has been taken.

PRAYER-STICKS—PIGMENTS

Among the most significant mortuary objects used by the ancient Tusayan people may be mentioned the so-called prayer-sticks or pahos. These were found in several graves, placed on the breast, in the hand, or at the side of the person interred, and have a variety of form, as shown in the accompanying illustrations (plates CLXXIV, CLXXV). As I shall discuss the forms and meaning of prayer-sticks in my account of Sikyatki, where a much larger number were found, I will simply mention a few of the more striking varieties from Awatobi.

One of the most instructive of these objects is flat in shape, painted green, and decorated with figures of a dragon-fly. As this insect is a symbol of rain, its occurrence on mortuary objects is in harmony with the Hopi conception of the dead which will later be explained.

Pahos, in the form of flat slats with a notched extension at one end were common, but generally were poorly preserved. The prayer-sticks from the shrine in the middle of the rooms in the plaza of the eastern section crumbled into fragments when exposed to the air, but they were apparently small, painted green, and decorated with black spots. On several of the prayer-sticks the impressions of the string and feathers that were formerly attached are still readily seen. It is probable that the solution of a carbonate of copper, with which the green pahos were so colored, contributed to the preservation of the wood of which they had been manufactured.

The only pigments detected on the prayer-sticks are black, red, and green, and traces of red are found also on the inner surface of a stone implement from a grave at the base of the mesa. All the pigments used by the modern Tusayan Indians were found in the intramural burial already described. My Hopi workmen urged me to give them small fragments of these paints, regarding them efficacious in their ceremonials.

OBJECTS SHOWING SPANISH INFLUENCE

We would naturally expect to find many objects of Caucasian origin in the ruins of a pueblo which had been under Spanish influence for a century. I have already spoken of certain architectural features in the eastern part of Awatobi which may be traced to the influence of the Spanish missionaries, and of small objects there were several different kinds which show the same thing. The old iron knife-blade already mentioned as having been found among the corn in a storage chamber in the northern row of houses was not the only metallic object found. Not far from the mission there were unearthed many corroded iron nails, a small hook of the same metal, a piece of cast copper, and a fragment of what appeared to be a portion of a bell. There were several pieces of glass, the surfaces of which had become ground by the sand which had beaten upon them during the years in which they had been exposed. There was found also a fragment of a green glazed cup, which was undoubtedly of Spanish or Mexican make, and sherds of white china similar to that sold today by the traders. These latter specimens were, as a rule, found on the surface of the ground.

It will therefore appear that the archeology of Awatobi supports the documentary evidence that the pueblo was under Spanish influence for some time, and the fact that all the above-mentioned objects were taken on or in the eastern mounds emphasizes the conclusion that this section of the town was the part directly under Spanish influences. Nothing of Spanish manufacture was found in the rooms of the western mounds, but from this negative evidence there is no reason to suspect that this section of Awatobi was not inhabited contemporaneously with that in the vicinity of the mission.

THE RUINS OF SIKYATKI

TRADITIONAL KNOWLEDGE OF THE PUEBLO

Very vague ideas are current regarding the character of Hopi culture prior to Tobar's visit to Tusayan in 1540, and with the exception of the most meager information nothing concerning it has come down to us from early historical references in the sixteenth century. It is therefore interesting to record all possible information in regard to these people prior to the period mentioned, and this must be done mainly through archeology.

Although there are many Tusayan ruins which we have every reason to believe are older than the time of Coronado, no archeologist has gathered from them the evidences bearing on prehistoric Tusayan culture which they will undoubtedly yield. Large and beautiful collections of pottery ascribed to Tusayan ruins have shown the excellent artistic taste of the ancient potters of this region, indicating that in the ceramic art they were far in advance of their descendants. But these collections have failed to teach, the lesson they might have taught, from the fact that data concerning the objects composing them are so indefinite. Very little care had been taken to label these collections accurately or to collect any specimens but those which were strikingly beautiful or commercially valuable. It was therefore with the hope of giving a more precise and comprehensive character to our knowledge of Tusayan antiquities that I wished to excavate one of the ruins of this province which was undoubtedly prehistoric. Conditions were favorable for success at the mounds called by the Indians Sikyatki.[95] These ruins are situated near the modern Tusayan pueblos of East Mesa, from which I could hire workmen, and not far from Keam's Canyon, which could be made a base of supplies. The existing legends bearing on these ruins, although obscure, are sufficiently definite for all

[95] Many of the specimens in the well-known Keam collection, now in the Tusayan room of the Peabody Museum at Cambridge, are undoubtedly from Sikyatki, and still more are from Awatobi. Since the beginning of my excavations at Sikyatki it has come to be a custom for the Hopi potters to dispose of, as Sikyatki ware, to unsuspecting white visitors, some of their modern objects of pottery. These fraudulent pieces are often very cleverly made.

practical purposes.

I find no mention of Sikyatki in early historical documents, nor can the name be even remotely identified with any which has been given to a Tusayan pueblo. My knowledge of the mounds which mark the site of this ancient village dates back to 1892, when I visited them with one of the old men of Walpi, who then and there narrated the legend of its destruction by the Walpians previously to the advent of the Spaniards. I was at that time impressed by the extent of the mounds, and prepared a rough sketch of the ground plan of the former houses, but from lack of means was unable to conduct any systematic excavation of the ruin.

Comparatively nothing concerning the ruin of Sikyatki has been published, although its existence had been known for several years previously to my visit. In his brief account Mr Victor Mindeleff[96] speaks of it as two prominent knolls, "about 400 yards apart," the summits of which are covered with house walls. He also found portions of walls on intervening hummocks, but gives no plan of the ruin. The name, Sikyatki, is referred to the color of the sandstone of which the walls were built. He found some of the rooms were constructed of small stones, dressed by rubbing, and laid in mud. The largest chamber was stated to be 9-1/2 by 4-1/2 feet, and it was considered that many of the houses were "built in excavated places around the rocky summits of the knolls."[97] Mr Mindeleff identified the former inhabitants with the ancestors of the Kokop people, and mentioned the more important details of their legend concerning the destruction of the village.

We can rely on the statement that Sikyatki was inhabited by the Kokop or Firewood people of Tusayan, who were so named because they obtained fire from wood by the use of drills. These people are represented today at Walpi by Katci, whose totem is a picture of Masauwû, the God of Fire. It is said that the home of the Firewood people before they built Sikyatki was at Tebuñki, or Fire-house, a round ruin northeastward from Keam's canyon. They were late arrivals in Tusayan, coming at least after the Flute people, and probably before the Honani or Badger people, who brought, I believe, the *katcina* cult. Although we can not definitely assert that this cultus was unknown at Sikyatki, it is significant that in the ruins no ornamental vessel was found with a figure of a *katcina* mask, although these figures occur on modern bowls. The original home of the Kokop people is not known, but indefinite legends ascribe their origin to Rio Grande valley. They are reputed to have had kindred in Antelope valley and at the Fire-house, above alluded to, near Eighteen-mile spring.

The ruin of Fire-house, one of the pueblos where the Kokop people are reputed to have lived before they built Sikyatki, is situated on the periphery of Tusayan. It is built of massive stones and differs from all other ruins in that province in that it is circular in form. The round type of ruin is, however, to be seen in the two conical mounds on the mesa above Sikyatki, which was connected in some way with

[96] Architecture of Tusayan and Cibola, op. cit., pp. 20, 21.

[97] These rooms I failed to find. One of the rocky knolls may be that called by me the "acropolis." The second knoll I cannot identify, unless it is the elevation in continuation of the same side toward the east. Possibly he confounded the ruin of Küküchomo with that of Sikyatki.

the inhabitants who formerly lived at its base.

The reason the Kokop people left Fire-house is not certain, but it is said that they came in conflict with Bear clans who were entering the province from the east. Certain it is that if the Kokop people once inhabited Fire-house they must have been joined by other clans when they lived at Sikyatki, for the mounds of this pueblo indicate a village much larger than the round ruin on the brink of the mesa northeast of Keam's canyon. The general ground plan of the ruin indicates an inclosed court with surrounding tiers of houses, suggesting the eastern type of pueblo architecture.

The traditional knowledge of the destruction of Sikyatki is very limited among the present Hopi, but the best folklorists all claim that it was destroyed by warriors from Walpi and possibly from Middle Mesa. Awatobi seems not to have taken part in the tragedy, while Hano and Sichomovi did not exist when the catastrophe took place.

The cause of the destruction of Sikyatki is not clearly known, and probably was hardly commensurate with the result. Its proximity to Walpi may have led to disputes over the boundaries of fields or the ownership of the scanty water supply. The people who lived there were intruders and belonged to clans not represented in Walpi, which in all probability kept hostility alive. The early Tusayan peoples did not readily assimilate, but quarreled with one another even when sorely oppressed by common enemies.

There is current in Walpi a romantic story connected with the overthrow of Sikyatki. It is said that a son of a prominent chief, disguised as a *katcina*, offered a prayer-stick to a maiden, and as she received it he cut her throat with a stone knife. He is said to have escaped to the mesa top and to have made his way along its edge to his own town, taunting his pursuers. It is also related that the Walpians fell upon the village of Sikyatki to avenge this bloody deed, but it is much more likely that there was ill feeling between the two villages for other reasons, probably disputes about farm limits or the control of the water supply, inflamed by other difficulties. The inhabitants of the two pueblos came into Tusayan from different directions, and as they may have spoken different languages and thus have failed to understand each other, they may have been mutually regarded as interlopers. Petty quarrels no doubt ripened into altercations, which probably led to bloodshed. The forays of the Apache from the south and the Ute from the north, which began at a later period, should naturally have led to a defensive alliance; but in those early days confederation was not dreamed of and the feeling between the two pueblos culminated in the destruction of Sikyatki. This was apparently the result of a quarrel between two pueblos of East Mesa, or at least there is no intimation that the other pueblos took prominent part in it. It is said that after the destruction some of those who escaped fled to Oraibi, which would imply that the Walpi and Oraibi peoples, even at that early date, were not on very friendly terms. If, however, the statement that Oraibi was then a distinct pueblo be true, it in a way affords a suggestion of the approximate age[98] of this village.

[98] The legends of the origin of Oraibi are imperfectly known, but it has been stated that the pueblo was founded by people from Old Shuñopovi. It seems much more likely,

There was apparently a more or less intimate connection between the inhabitants of old Sikyatki and those of Awatobi, but whether or not it indicates that the latter was founded by the refugees from the former I have not been able definitely to make out. All my informants agree that on the destruction of Sikyatki some of its people fled to Awatobi, but no one has yet stated that the Kokop people were represented in the latter pueblo. The distinctive clans of the pueblo of Antelope mesa are not mentioned as living in Sikyatki, and yet the two pueblos are said to have been kindred. The indications are that the inhabitants of both came from the east—possibly were intruders, which may have been the cause of the hostility entertained by both toward the Walpians. The problem is too complex to be solved with our present limited knowledge in this direction, and archeology seems not to afford very satisfactory evidence one way or the other. We may never know whether the Sikyatki refugees founded Awatobi or simply fled to that pueblo for protection.

There appears to be no good evidence that Sikyatki was destroyed by fire, nor would it seem that it was gradually abandoned. The larger beams of the houses have disappeared from many rooms, evidently having been appropriated in building or enlarging other pueblos.

There is nothing to show that any considerable massacre of the people took place when the village was destroyed, in which respect it differs considerably from Awatobi. There is little doubt that many Sikyatki women were appropriated by the Walpians, and in support of this it is stated that the Kokop people of the present Walpi are the descendants of the people of that clan who dwelt at Sikyatki. This conclusion is further substantiated by the statements of one of the oldest members of the Kokop phratry who frequently visited me while the excavations were in progress.

The destruction of Sikyatki and its consequent abandonment doubtless occurred before the Spaniards obtained a foothold in the country. The aged Hopi folklorists insist that such is the case, and the excavations did not reveal any evidence to the contrary. If we add to the negative testimony that Sikyatki is not mentioned in any of the early writings, and that no fragment of metal, glass, or Spanish glazed pottery has been taken from it, we appear to have substantial proof of its prehistoric character.

In the early times when Sikyatki was a flourishing pueblo, Walpi was still a small settlement on the terrace of the mesa just below the present town that bears its name. Two ruins are pointed out as the sites of Old Walpi, one to the northward of the modern town, and a second more to the westward. The former is called at present the Ash-heap house or pueblo, the latter Kisakobi. It is said that the people whose ancestors formed the nucleus of the more northerly town moved from there to Kisakobi on account of the cold weather, for it was too much in the shadow of the mesa. Its general appearance would indicate it to be older than the more westerly ruin, higher up on the mesa. It was a pueblo of some size, and was situated on

however, that our knowledge is too incomplete to accept this conclusion without more extended observations. The composition of the present inhabitants indicates amalgamation from several quarters, and neighboring ruins should be studied with this thought in mind.

the edge of the terrace. The refuse from the settlement was thrown over the edge of the decline, where it accumulated in great quantities. This débris contains many fragments of characteristic pottery, similar to that from Sikyatki, and would well repay systematic investigation. No walls of the old town rise more than a few feet above the surface, for most of the stones have long ago been used in rebuilding the pueblo on other sites. Kisakobi was situated higher up on the mesa, and bears every appearance of being more modern than the ruin below. Its site may readily be seen from the road to Keam's canyon, on the terrace-like prolongation of the mesa. Some of the walls are still erect, and the house visible for a great distance is part of the old pueblo. This, I believe, was the site of Walpi at the time the Spaniards visited Tusayan, and I have found here a fragment of pottery which I believe is of Spanish origin. The ancient pueblo crowned the ridge of the terrace which narrows here to 30 or 40 feet, so that ancient Walpi was an elongated pueblo, with narrow passageways and no rectangular court. I should judge, however, that the pueblo was not inhabited for a great period, but was moved to its present site after a few generations of occupancy. The Ash-hill village was inhabited contemporaneously with Sikyatki, but Kisakobi was of later construction. Neither Sichomovi nor Hano was in existence when Sikyatki was in its prime, nor, indeed, at the time of its abandonment. In 1782 Morfi spoke of Sichomovi as a pueblo recently founded, with but fifteen families. Hano, although older, was certainly not established before 1700.[99]

The assertions of all Hopi traditionists that Sikyatki is a prehistoric ruin, as well as the scientific evidence looking the same way, are most important facts in considering the weight of deductions in regard to the character of prehistoric Tusayan culture.

Although we have no means of knowing how long a period has elapsed since the occupancy and abandonment of Sikyatki, we are reasonably sure that objects taken from it are purely aboriginal in character and antedate the inception of European influence. It is certain, however, that the Sikyatki people lived long enough in that pueblo to develop a ceramic art essentially peculiar to Tusayan.

NOMENCLATURE

The commonly accepted definition of Sikyatki is "yellow house" (*sikya*, yellow; *ki*, house). One of the most reliable chiefs of Walpi, however, called my attention to the fact that the hills in the locality were more or less parallel, and that there might be a relationship between the parallel valleys and the name. The application of the term "yellow" would not seem to be very appropriate so far as it is distinctive of the general color of the pueblo. The neighboring spring, however, contains water

---

[99] It is distinctly stated that the Tanoan families whose descendants now inhabit Hano were not in Tusayan when Awatobi fell. To be sure they may have been sojourning in some valley east of the province, which, however, is not likely, since they were "invited" to East Mesa for the specific purpose of aiding the Hopi against northern nomads. Much probability attaches to a suggestion that they belonged to the emigrants mentioned by contemporary historians as leaving the Rio Grande on account of the unsettled condition of the country after the great rebellion of 1680.

which after standing some time has a yellowish tinge, and it was not unusual to name pueblos from the color of the adjacent water or from some peculiarity of the spring, which was one of the most potent factors in the determination of the site of a village. Although the name may also refer to a cardinal point, a method of nomenclature followed in some regions of the Southwest, if such were the case in regard to Sikyatki it would be exceptional in Tusayan.

BUREAU OF AMERICAN ETHNOLOGY — — SEVENTEENTH ANNUAL RE-PORT PL. CXV

Sikyatki Mounds From The Kanelba Trail

FORMER INHABITANTS OF SIKYATKI

The origin of the pueblo settlement at Sikyatki is doubtful, but as I have shown in my enumeration of the clans of Walpi, the Kokop (Firewood) and the Isauûh (Coyote) phratries which lived there are supposed to have come into Tusayan from the far east or the valley of the Rio Grande. The former phratry is not regarded as one of the earliest arrivals in Tusayan, for when its members arrived at Walpi they found living there the Flute, Snake, and Water-house phratries. It is highly probable that the Firewood, or as they are sometimes called the Fire, people, once lived in the round pueblo known as Fire-house, and as the form of this ruin is exceptional in Tusayan, and highly characteristic of the region east of this province, there is archeological evidence of the eastern origin of the Fire people. Perhaps the most intelligent folklorist of the Kokop people was Nasyuñweve, who died a few years ago—unfortunately before I had been able to record all the traditions which he knew concerning his ancestors. At the present day Katci, his successor[100] in these sacerdotal duties in the Antelope-Snake mysteries, claims that his people

[100] The succession of priests is through the clan of the mother, so that commonly, as in the case of Katci, the nephew takes the place of the uncle at his death. Some instances,

formerly occupied Sikyatki, and indeed the contiguous fields are still cultivated by members of that phratry.

It is hardly possible to do more than estimate the population of Sikyatki when in its prime, but I do not believe that it was more than 500;[101] probably 300 inhabitants would be a closer estimate if we judge from the relative population to the size of the pueblo of Walpi at the present time. On the basis of population given, the evidences from the size of the Sikyatki cemeteries would not point to an occupancy of the village for several centuries, although, of course, the strict confines of these burial places may not have been determined by our excavations. The comparatively great depth at which some of the human remains were found does not necessarily mean great antiquity, for the drifting sands of the region may cover or uncover the soil or rocks in a very short time, and the depth at which an object is found below the surface is a very uncertain medium for estimating the antiquity of buried remains.

GENERAL FEATURES

The ruin of Sikyatki (plates cxv, cxvi) lies about three miles east of the recent settlement of Tanoan families at Isba or Coyote spring, near the beginning of the trail to Hano. Its site is in full view from the road extending from the last-mentioned settlement to Keam's canyon, and lies among the hills just below the two pyramidal elevations called Küküchomo, which are visible for a much greater distance. When seen from this road the mounds of Sikyatki are observed to be elevated at least 300 feet above the adjacent cultivated plain, but at the ruin itself this elevation is scarcely appreciable, so gradual is the southerly decline to the arroyo which drains the plain. The ruin is situated among foothills a few hundred yards from the base of the mesa, and in the depression between it and the mesa there is a stretch of sand in which grow peach trees and a few stunted cedars. At this point, likewise, there is a spring, now feeble in its flow from the gradually drifting sand, yet sufficient to afford a trickling stream by means of which an enterprising native, named Tcino, irrigates a small garden of melons and onions. On all sides of the ruin there are barren stretches of sand relieved in some places by stunted trees and scanty vegetation similar to that of the adjacent plains. The soil in the plaza of the ruin is cultivated, yielding a fair crop of squashes, but is useless for corn or beans.

Here and there about the ruins stand great jagged bowlders, relieving what would otherwise be a monotonous waste of sand. One of these stony outcrops forms what I have called the "acropolis" of Sikyatki, which will presently be described. On the eastern side the drifting sand has so filled in around the elevation on which the ruin stands that the ascent is gradual, and the same drift extends to

---

however, have come to my knowledge where, the clan having become extinct, a son has been elevated to the position made vacant by the death of a priest. The Kokop people at Walpi are vigorous, numbering 21 members if we include the Coyote and Wolf clans, the last mentioned of which may be descendants of the former inhabitants of Küküchomo, the twin ruins on the mesa above Sikyatki.

[101] In this census I have used also the apparently conservative statement of Vetancurt that there were 800 people in Awatobi at the end of the seventeenth century.

the rim of the mesa, affording access to the summit that otherwise would necessitate difficult climbing. Along the ridge of this great drift there runs a trail which passes over the mesa top to a beautiful spring, on the other side, called Kanelba.[102]

The highest point of the ruin as seen from the plain is the rocky eminence rising at the western edge, familiarly known among the members of my party as the "acropolis." As one approaches the ruin from a deep gulch on the west, the acropolis appears quite lofty, and a visitor would hardly suspect that it marks the culminating point of a ruin, so similar does it appear to surrounding hills of like geologic character where no vestiges of former house-walls appear.

The spring from which the inhabitants of the old pueblo obtained their water supply lies between the ruin and the foot of the mesa, nearer the latter. The water is yellow in color, especially after it has remained undisturbed for some time, and the quantity is very limited. It trickles out of a bed of clay in several places and forms a pool from which it is drawn to irrigate a small garden and a grove of peach trees. It is said that when Sikyatki was in its prime this spring was larger than at present, and I am sure that a little labor spent in digging out the accumulation of sand would make the water more wholesome and probably sufficiently abundant for the needs of a considerable population.

The nearest spring of potable water available for our excavation camp at Sikyatki was Kanelba, or Sheep spring, one of the best sources of water supply in Tusayan. The word Kanelba, containing a Spanish element, must have replaced a Hopi name, for it is hardly to be supposed that this spring was not known before sheep were brought into the country. There is a legend that formerly the site of this spring was dry, when an ancient priest, who had deposited his *tiponi*, or chieftain's badge, at the place, caused the water to flow from the ground; at present however the water rushes from a hole as large as the arm in the face of the rock, as well as from several minor openings. It is situated on the opposite side of the mesa from Sikyatki, a couple of miles northeastward from the ruin.

---

[102] *Kanel* = Spanish *carnero*, sheep; *ba* = water, spring.

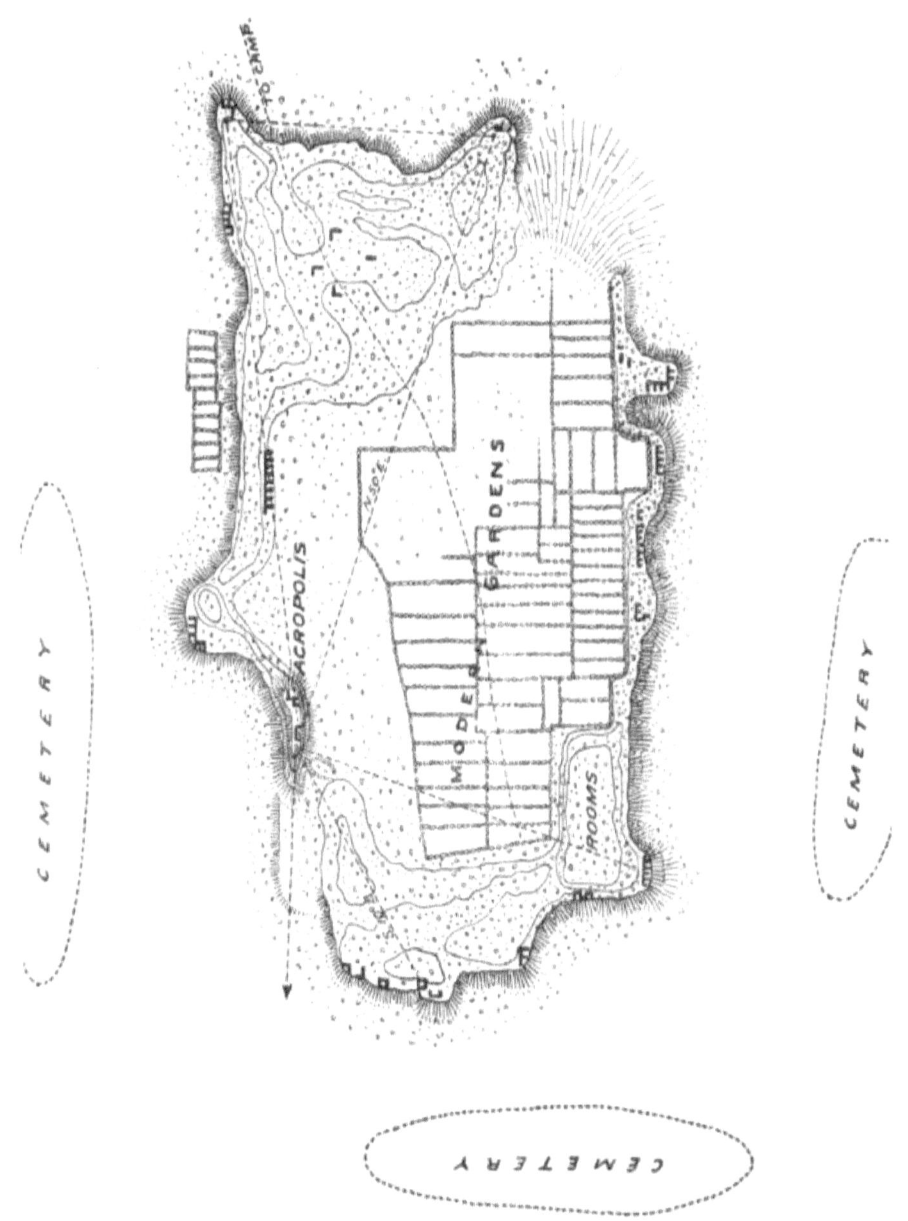

BUREAU OF AMERICAN ETHNOLOGY — — SEVENTEENTH ANNUAL RE-
PORT PL. CXVI

Ground Plan Of Sikyatki

Half-way up the side of the mesa, about opposite Sikyatki, there is a large reservoir, used as a watering place for sheep. The splash of the water, as it falls into this reservoir, is an unusual sound in this arid region, and is worth a tramp of many miles. There are many evidences that this spring was a popular one in former times. As it is approached from the top of the mesa, a brief inspection of the surroundings shows that for about a quarter of a mile, on either side, there are signs of ancient terraced gardens, walled in with rows of stones. These gardens have today greatly diminished in size, as compared with the ancient outlines, and only that portion which is occupied by a grove of peach trees is now under cultivation, although there is plenty of water for the successful irrigation of a much larger tract of land than the gardens now cover.[103] Judging from their size, many of the peach trees are very old, although they still bear their annual crop of fruit. Everything indicates, as the legends relate, that these Kanelba gardens, the walls of which now form sheep corrals, were long ago abandoned.

The terraces south of the Kanelba peach grove resemble the lower terraces of Wipo. About 100 rods farther south, along the foot of the mesa, on the same level, are a number of unused fields, and a cluster of house remains. The whole of this terrace is of a type which shows greater action of the weather than the others, but the boundaries of the fields are still marked with rows of stones. The adjacent foothills contain piles of ashes in several places, as if the sites of ancient pottery kilns, and very old stone inclosures occur on the top of the mesa above Kanelba. All indications seem to point to the ancient occupancy of the region about Kanelba by many more farmers than today. Possibly the inhabitants of Sikyatki, which is only two or three miles away, frequented this place and cultivated these ancient gardens. Kanelba is regarded as a sacred spring by several Hopi religious societies of East Mesa. The Snake priests of Walpi always celebrate a feast there on the day of the snake hunt to the east in odd years,[104] while in the alternate years it is visited by the Flute men.

The present appearance of Sikyatki (plate cxv) is very desolate, and when visited by our party previously to the initiation of the work, seemed to promise little in the way of archeological results. No walls were standing above ground, and the outlines of the rooms were very indistinct. All we saw at that time was a series of mounds, irregularly rectangular in shape, of varying altitude, with here and there faint traces of walls. Prominent above all these mounds, however, was the pinnacle of rock on the northwestern corner, rising abruptly from the remainder of the ruin, easily approached from the west and sloping more gradually to the south. This rocky elevation, which we styled the acropolis, was doubtless once covered with houses.

[103] Wipo spring, a few miles northward from the eastern end of the mesa, would be an excellent site for a Government school. It is sufficiently convenient to the pueblos, has an abundant supply of potable water at all seasons, and cultivable fields in the neighborhood.

[104] The boy who brought our drinking water from Kanelba could not be prevailed upon to visit it on the day of the snake hunt to the east in 1895, on the ground that no one not a member of the society should be seen there or take water from it at that time. This is probably a phase of the taboo of all work in the world-quarter in which the snake hunts occur, when the Snake priests are engaged in capturing these reptilian "elder brothers."

On the western edge of the ruin a solitary farmhouse, used during the summer season, had been constructed of materials from the old walls, and was inhabited by an Indian named Lelo and his family during our excavations. He is the recognized owner of the farm land about Sikyatki and the cultivator of the soil in the old plaza of the ruins. Jakwaina, an enterprising Tewan who lives not far from Isba, the spring near the trail to Hano, has also erected a modern house near the Sikyatki spring, but it had not been completed at the time of our stay. Probably never since its destruction in prehistoric times have so many people as there were in our party lived for so long a time at this desolate place.

The disposition of the mounds show that the ground plan of Sikyatki (plate cxvi) was rectangular in shape, the houses inclosing a court in which are several mounds that may be the remains of kivas. The highest range of rooms, and we may suppose the most populous part of the ancient pueblo, was on the same side as the acropolis, where a large number of walled chambers in several series were traced.

The surface of what was formerly the plaza is crossed by rows of stones regularly arranged to form gardens, in which several kinds of gourds are cultivated. In the sands north of the ruin there are many peach trees, small and stunted, but yearly furnishing a fair crop. These are owned by Tcino,[105] and of course were planted long after the destruction of the pueblo.

In order to obtain legends of the former occupancy and destruction of Sikyatki, I consulted Nasyuñweve, the former head of the Kokop people, and while the results were not very satisfactory, I learned that the land about Sikyatki is still claimed by that phratry. Nasyuñweve,[106] Katci, and other prominent Kokop people occupy and cultivate the land about Sikyatki on the ground of inheritance from their ancestors who once inhabited the place.

---

[105] Tcino lives at Sichomovi, and in the Snake dance at Walpi formerly took the part of the old man who calls out the words, *"Awahaia,"* etc. at the kisi, before the reptiles are carried about the plaza. These words are Keresan, and Tcino performed this part on account of his kinship. He owns the grove of peach trees because they are on land of his ancestors, a fact confirmatory of the belief that the people of Sikyatki came from the Rio Grande.

[106] Nasyuñweve, who died a few years ago, formerly made the prayer-stick to Masauwûh, the Fire or Death god. This he did as one of the senior members of the Kokop or Firewood people, otherwise known as the Fire people, because they made fire with the fire-drill. On his death his place in the kiva was taken by Katci. Nasyuñweve was Intiwa's chief assistant in the Walpi *katcinas,* and wore the mask of Eototo in the ceremonials of the *Niman.* All this is significant, and coincides with the theory that *katcinas* are incorporated in the Tusayan ritual, that Eototo is their form of Masauwûh, and that he is a god of fire, growth, and death, like his dreaded equivalent.

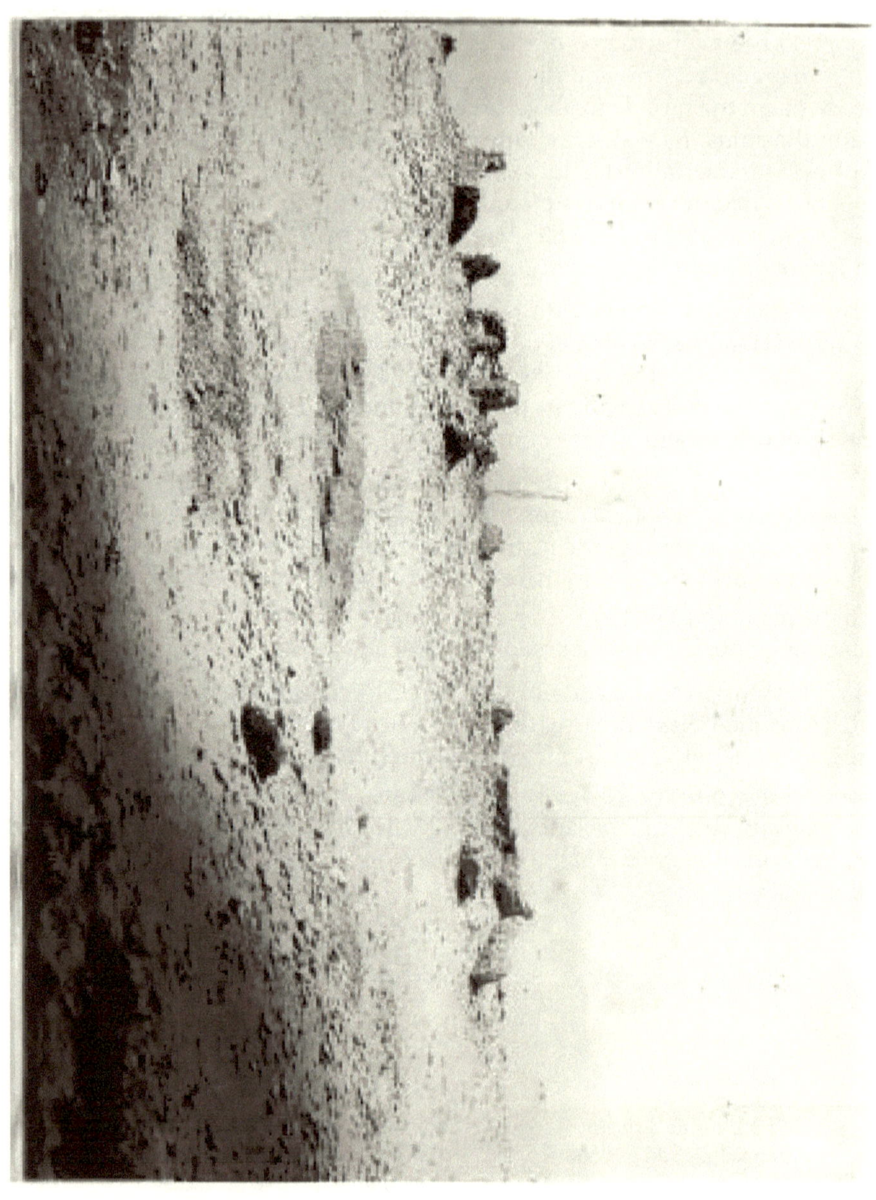

Awatobi

Teva

Trail to Mispo

Red Rocks

Awatobi

Nimá Katcina Dance

Tewa boy + girl

Pictographs - Beaver Creek

Montezuma Well, Beaver Creek

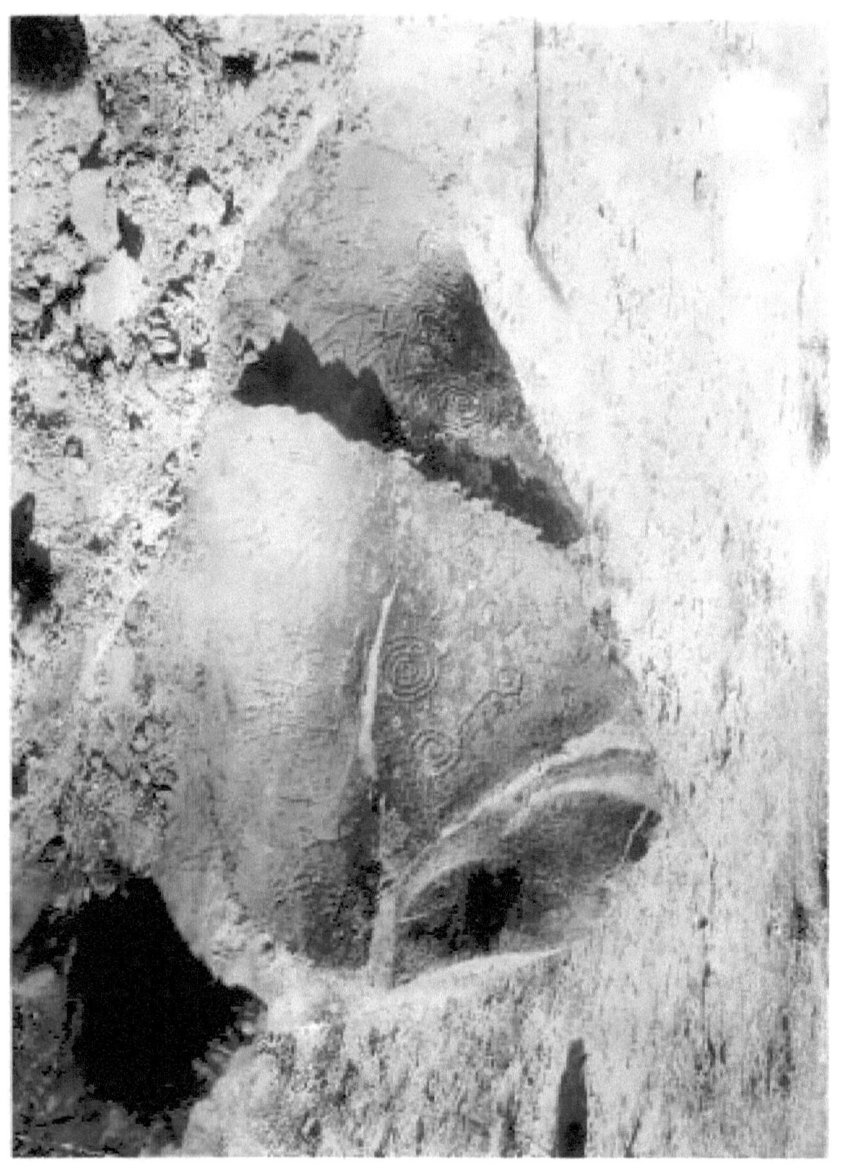

Pictograph - Lower Verde

Red Rocks

Sikyatki Ruins in Mesa

Sikyatki Camp

Red Rocks

Awatobi

Red Rocks

Sikyatki

Sikyatki
Ruins on Acropolis

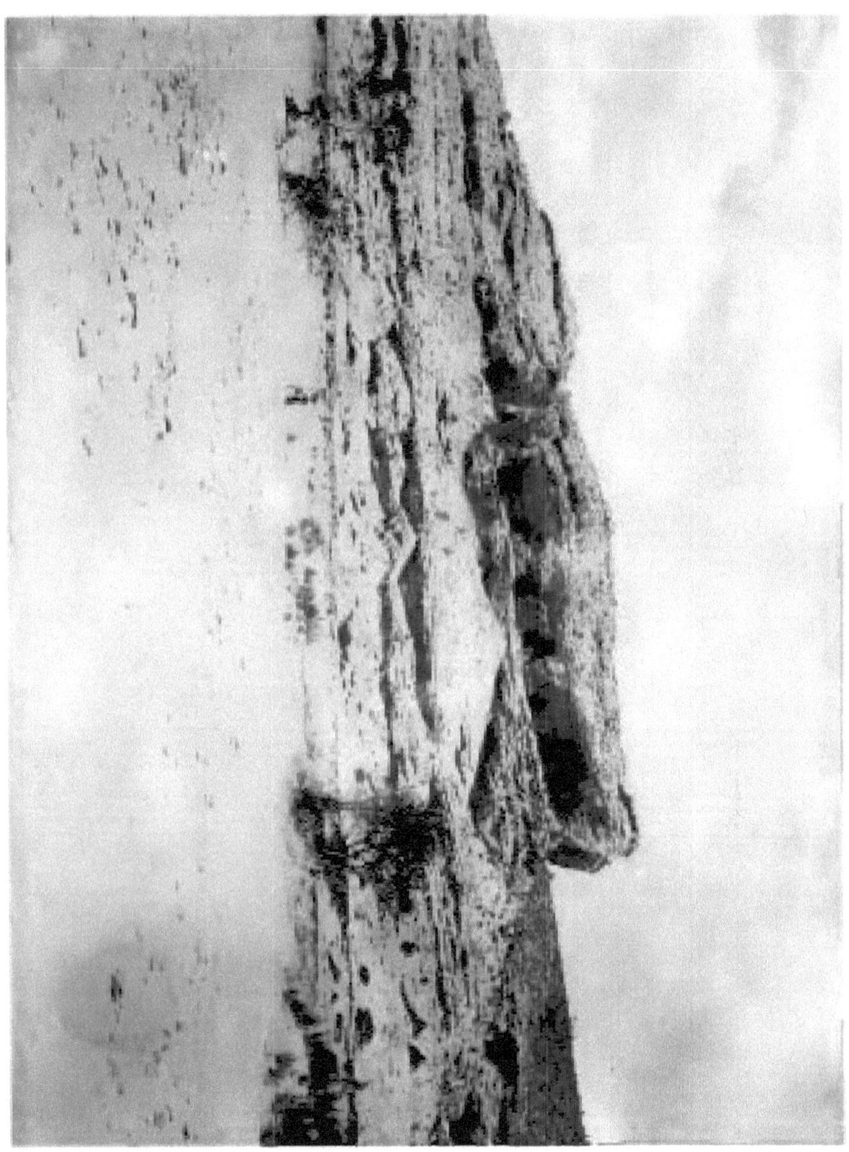

Caves on Lower Verde

Caves on Lower Verde

Red Rocks

Red Rocks

Red Rocks

Red Rocks

Red Rocks

Ruins near Montezuma Well

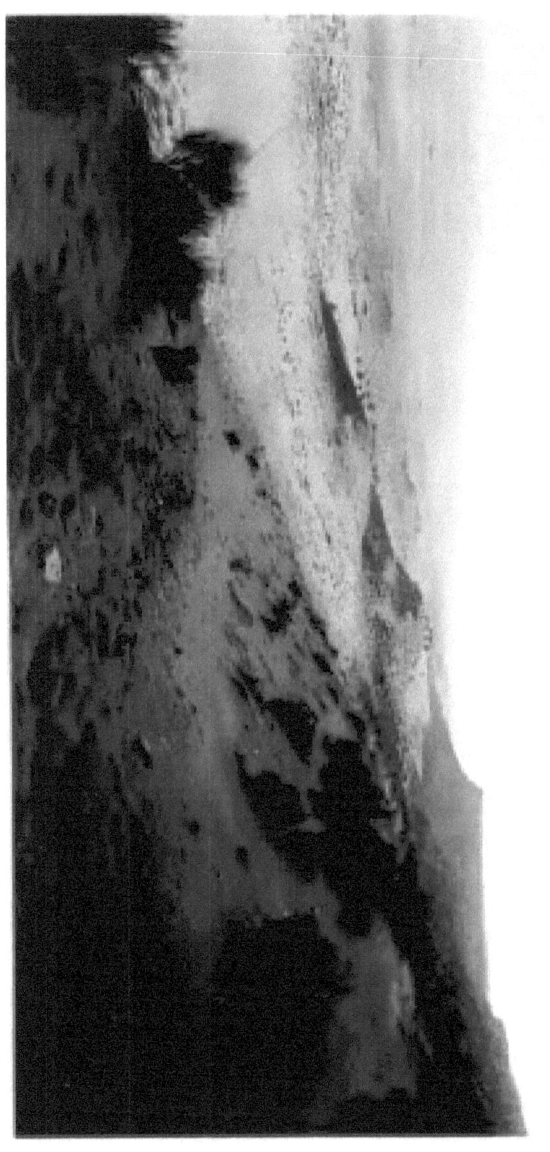

Sikyatki

Sikyatki Ruins in Mesa

Walpi

Sikiatki

Ruins on Acropolis

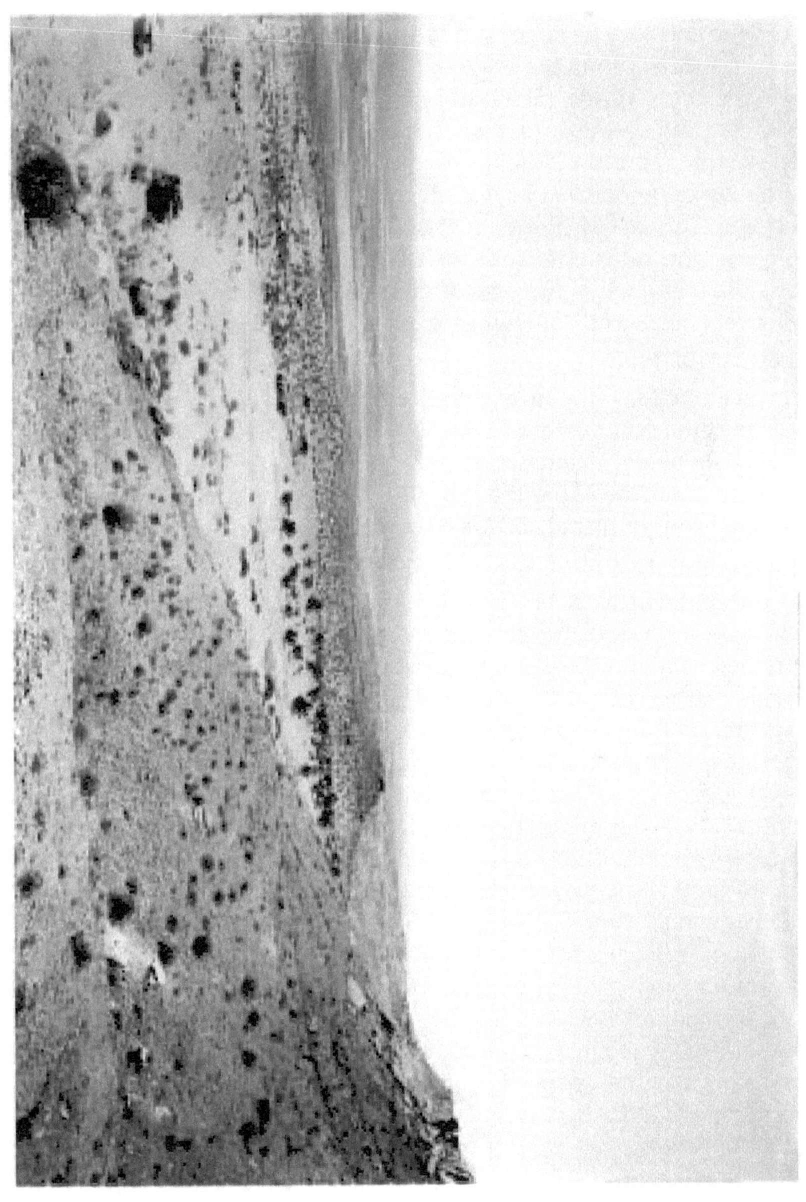

Sikiatki
General View

Two routes were taken to approach Sikyatki—one directly across the sandy plain from the entrance to Keam's canyon, following for some distance the road to East Mesa; the other along the edge of the mesa, on the first terrace, to the cluster of houses at Coyote spring. The trail to the pueblos of East Mesa ascends the cliff just above Sikyatki spring, and joins that to Kanelba or Sheep spring, not far from Küküchomo, the twin mounds. By keeping along the first terrace a well-traveled trail, with interesting views of the plain and the ruin, joins the old wagon road to *Wala*, the "gap" of East Mesa, at a higher level than the cluster of Tewan houses at Isba. In going and returning from their homes our Hopi workmen preferred the trail along the mesa, which we also often used; but the climb to the mesa top from the ruin is very steep and somewhat tiresome.

We prosecuted our excavations at Sikyatki for a few days over three weeks, choosing as a site for our camp a small depression to the east of the ruin near a dwarf cedar at the point where the trail to Kanelba passes the ruin. The place was advantageously near the cemeteries, and not too far from water. For purposes other than cooking and drinking the Sikyatki spring was used, the remainder of the supply being brought from Kanelba by means of a burro.

I employed Indian workmen at the ruin, and found them, as a rule, efficient helpers. The zeal which they manifested at the beginning of the work did not flag, but it must be confessed that toward the close of the excavations it became necessary to incite their enthusiasm by prizes, and, to them, extraordinary offers of overalls and calico. They at first objected to working in the cemeteries, regarding it as a desecration of the dead, but several of their number overcame their scruples, even handling skulls and other parts of skeletons. The Snake chief, Kopeli, however, never worked with the others, desiring not to dig in the graves. Respecting his feelings, I allotted him the special task of excavating the rooms of the acropolis, which he performed with much care, showing great interest in the results. At the close of our daily work prayer-offerings were placed in the trenches by the Indian workmen, as conciliatory sacrifices to Masauwûh, the dread God of Death, to offset any malign influence which might result from our desecration of his domain. A superstitious feeling that this god was not congenial to the work which was going on, seemed always to haunt the minds of the laborers, and once or twice I was admonished by old men, visitors from Walpi, not to persist in my excavations. The excavators, at times, paused in their work and called my attention to strange voices echoing from the cliffs, which they ascribed, half in earnest, to Masauwûh.

The Indians faithfully delivered to me all objects which they found in their digging, with the exception of turquoises, many of which, I have good reason to suspect, they concealed while our backs were turned and, in a few instances, even before our eyes.

The accompanying plan of Sikyatki (plate cxvi) shows that it was a rectangular ruin with an inclosed plaza. It is evident that the ancient pueblo was built on a number of low hills and that the eastern portion was the highest. In this respect it resembled Awatobi, but apparently differed from the latter pueblo in having the inclosed plaza. In the same way it was unlike Walpi or the ancient and modern pueblos of Middle Mesa and Oraibi. In fact, there is no Tusayan ruin which resembles it in ground plan, except Payüpki, a Tanoan town of much later construction. The typical Tusayan form of architecture is the pyramidal, especially in the most ancient pueblos. The ground plan of Sikyatki is of a type more common in the eastern pueblo region and in those towns of Tusayan which were built by emigrants from the Rio Grande region. Sikyatki and some of the villages overlooking Antelope valley are of this type.

In studying the ground plans of the three modern villages on East Mesa, the fact is noted that both Sichomovi and Hano differ architecturally from Walpi. The forms of the former smaller pueblos are primarily rectangular with an inclosed plaza in which is situated the kiva; Walpi, on the other hand, although furnished with a small plaza at the western end, has kivas located peripherally rather than in an open space between the highest house clusters. Sichomovi is considered by the Hopi as like Zuñi, and is sometimes called by the Hano people, Sionimone, "Zuñi court," because to the Tewan mind it resembles Zuñi; but the term is never applied to Walpi.[107] The distinction thus recognized is, I believe, architecturally valid. The inclosed court or plaza in Tusayan is an intrusion from the east, and as eastern colonists built both Hano and Sichomovi, they preserved the form to which they were accustomed. The Sikyatki builders drew their architectural inspiration likewise from the east, hence the inclosed court in the ruins of that village.

The two most considerable house clusters of Sikyatki are at each end of a longer axis, connected by a narrow row of houses on the other sides. The western rows of houses face the plain, and were of one story, with a gateway at one point. The opposite row was more elevated, no doubt overlooking cultivated fields beyond the confines of the ruin. No kivas were discovered, but if such exist they ought to be found in the mass of houses at the southern end. I thought we had found circular rooms in that region, but cursory excavations did not demonstrate their existence. As there is no reason to suspect the existence of circular kivas in ancient Tusayan, it would be difficult to decide whether or not any one of the large rectangular rooms was used for ceremonial purposes, for it is an interesting fact that some of the oldest secret rites in the Hopi villages occur, not in kivas, but in ordinary dwelling rooms in the village. It has yet to be shown that there were special kivas in prehistoric Tusayan.

[107] The Hano people call the Hopi *Koco* or *Koso*; the Santa Clara (also Tewa) people call them *Khoso*, according to Hodge.

BUREAU OF AMERICAN ETHNOLOGY— — SEVENTEENTH ANNUAL RE-PORT PL. CXVII

Excavated Rooms On The Acropolis Of Sikyatki

The longer axis of the ruin is about north and south; the greatest elevation is approximately 50 feet. Rocks outcrop only at one place, the remainder of the ruin being covered with rubble, sand, stones, and fragments of pottery. The mounds are not devoid of vegetation, for sagebrush, cacti, and other desert genera grow quite profusely over their surface; but they are wholly barren of trees or large bushes, and except in the plaza the ruin area is uncultivated. As previously stated, Sikyatki is situated about 250 or 300 feet above the plain, and when approached from Keam's canyon appears to be about halfway up the mesa height. On several adjacent elevations evidences of former fires, or places where pottery was burned, were found, and one has not to go far to discover narrow seams of an impure lignite. Here and there are considerable deposits of selenite, which, as pointed out by Sitgreaves in his report on the exploration of the Little Colorado, looks like frost exuding from the ground in early spring.

THE ACROPOLIS

During the limited time devoted to the excavation of Sikyatki it was impossible, in a ruin so large, to remove the soil covering any considerable number of rooms. The excavations at different points over such a considerable area as that covered by the mounds would have been more or less desultory and unsatisfactory, but a limited section carefully opened would be much more instructive and typical. While, therefore, the majority of the Indian workmen were kept employed at the cemeteries, Kopeli, the Snake chief, a man in whom I have great confidence, was assigned to the excavation of a series of rooms at the highest point of the ruin, previously referred to as the acropolis (figure 262). Although his work in these chambers did not yield such rich results as the others, so far as the number of objects was concerned, he succeeded in uncovering a number of rooms to their floors, and unearthed many interesting objects of clay and stone. A brief description of these excavations will show the nature of the work at that point.

The acropolis, or highest point of Sikyatki, is a prominent rocky elevation at the western angle, and overlooks the entire ruin. On the side toward the western cemetery it rises quite abruptly, but the ascent is more gradual from the other sides. The surface of this elevation, on which the houses stood, is of rock, and originally was as destitute of soil as the plaza of Walpi. This surface supported a double series of rooms, and the highest point is a bare, rocky projection.

From the rooms of the acropolis there was a series of chambers, probably terraced, sloping to the modern gardens now occupying the old plaza, and the broken walls of these rooms still protrude from the surface in many places (plate cxviii). When the excavations on the acropolis were begun, no traces of the biserial rows of rooms were detected, although the remains of the walls were traceable. The surface was strewn with fragments of pottery and other evidences of former occupancy.

On leveling the ground and throwing off the surface stones, it was found that the narrow ridge which formed the top of the acropolis was occupied by a double line of well-built chambers which show every evidence of having been living rooms. The walls were constructed of squared stones set in adobe, with the inner surface neatly plastered. Many of the rooms communicated by means of passageways with adjacent chambers, some of them being provided with niches and shelves. The average height of the standing walls revealed by excavation, as indicated by the distance of the floor below the surface of the soil, was about 5 feet.

FIG. 262—THE ACROPOLIS OF SIKYATKI

The accompanying illustration (plate cxviii) shows a ground plan of nine of these rooms, which, for purposes of reference, are lettered *a* to *l*. A description of each, it is hoped, will give an idea of a typical room of Sikyatki. Room *a* is rectangular in shape, 5 feet 3 inches by 6 feet 8 inches, and is 5 feet 8 inches deep. It has two depressions in the floor at the southeastern corner, and there is a small niche in the side wall above them. Some good specimens of mural plastering, much blackened by soot, are found on the eastern wall. Room *a* has no passageway into room *b*, but it opens into the adjoining room *c* by an opening in the wall 3 feet 4 inches wide, with a threshold 9 inches high.

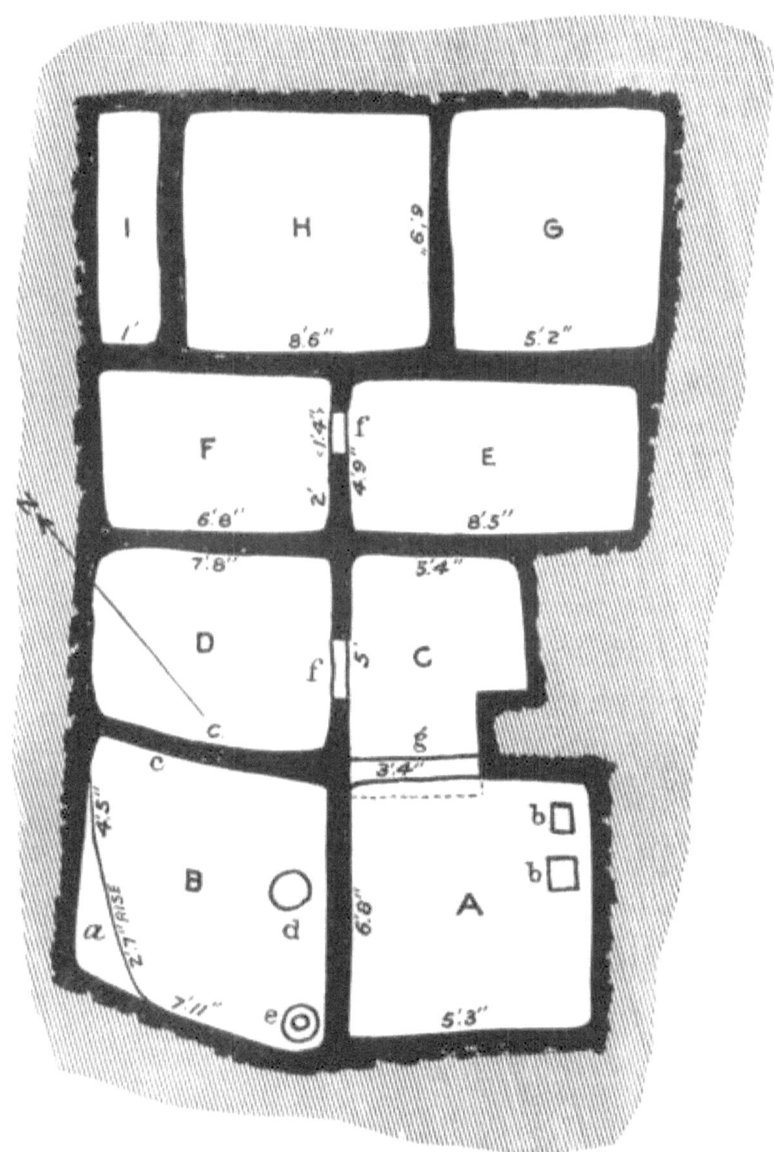

BUREAU OF AMERICAN ETHNOLOGY — — SEVENTEENTH ANNUAL RE-
PORT PL. CXVIII

Plan Of Excavated Rooms On The Acropolis Of Sikyatki

(Dimensions in feet and inches)

The shape of room *b* is more irregular. It is 8 feet 1 inch long by 4 feet 5 inches wide, and the floor is 5 feet 2 inches below the surface. In one corner there is
a raised triangular platform 2 feet 7 inches above the floor. A large cooking pot,

blackened with soot, was found in one corner of this room, and near it was a circular depression in the floor 17 inches in diameter, evidently a fireplace.

Room *c* is smaller than either of the preceding, and is the only one with two passageways into adjoining chambers. Remains of wooden beams in a fair state of preservation were found on the floors of rooms *c* and *b*, but they were not charred, as is so often the case, nor were there any ashes except in the supposed fireplace.

Room *d* is larger than those already mentioned, being 7 feet 8 inches by 5 feet, and connects with room *c* by means of a passageway. Rooms *e* and *f* communicate with each other by an opening 16 inches wide. We found the floors of these rooms 4 feet below the surface. The length of room *e* is 8 feet.

Room *f* is 6 feet 8 inches long and of the same width as *e*. The three chambers *g*, *h*, and *i* are each 6 feet 9 inches wide, but of varying width. Room *g* is 5 feet 2 inches, *h* is 8 feet 6 inches, and *i*, the smallest of all, only a foot wide. These three rooms have no intercommunication.

The evidence of former fires in some of these rooms, afforded by soot on the walls and ashes in the depressions identified as old fireplaces, is most important. In one or two places I broke off a fragment of the plastering and found it to be composed of many strata of alternating black and adobe color, indicating successive plasterings of the room. Apparently when the surface wall became blackened by smoke it was renewed by a fresh layer or wash of adobe in the manner followed in renovating the kiva walls today.[108]

An examination of the dimensions of the rooms of the acropolis will show that, while small, they are about the average size of the chambers in most other southwestern ruins. They are, however, much smaller than the rooms of the modern pueblo of Walpi or those of the cliff ruins in the Red-rock region, elsewhere described. Evidently the roof was 2 or 3 feet higher than the top of the present walls, and the absence of external passageways would seem to indicate that entrance was through the roof. The narrow chamber, *i*, is no smaller than some of those which were excavated at Awatobi, but unless it was a storage bin or dark closet for ceremonial paraphernalia its function is not known to me. The mural plastering was especially well done in rooms *g* and *h*, a section thereof showing many successive thin strata of soot and clay, implying long occupancy. No chimneys were found, the smoke, as is the case with that from kiva fires today, doubtless finding an exit through the hatchway in the roof.

MODERN GARDENS

The whole surface of the ancient plaza of Sikyatki is occupied by rectangular gardens outlined by rows of stones. These are of modern construction and are cultivated by an enterprising Hopi who, as previously mentioned, has erected a

[108] The replastering of kivas at Walpi takes place during the *Powamu*, an elaborate *katcina* celebration. I have noticed that in this renovation of the kivas one corner, as a rule, is left unplastered, but have elicited no satisfactory explanation of this apparent oversight, which, no doubt, has significance. Someone, perhaps overimaginative, suggested to me that the unplastered corner was the same as the break in encircling lines on ancient pottery.

habitable dwelling on one of the western mounds from the stones of the old ruin. These gardens are planted yearly with melons and squashes, and stones forming the outlines serve as wind-breaks to protect the growing plants from drifting sand. The plotting of the plan of these gardens was made in 1891, when a somewhat larger part of the plaza was under cultivation than in 1895.[109]

There is a grove of dwarf peach trees in the sands between the northern side of the ruin and the mesa along the run through which sometimes trickles a little stream from the spring. These trees belong to an inhabitant of Sichomovi named Tcino, who, it is claimed, is a descendant of the ancient Sikyatkians. The trees were of course planted there since the fall of the village, on land claimed by the Kokop phratry by virtue of their descent from the same phratral organization of the ancient pueblo.[110] The spring shows no evidence of having been walled up, but apparently has been filled in by drifting sand since the time that it formed the sole water supply of the neighboring pueblo. It still preserves the yellow color mentioned in traditions of the place.

THE CEMETERIES

By far the largest number of objects found at Sikyatki were gathered from the cemeteries outside the ruin, and were therefore mortuary in character. It would seem that the people buried their dead a short distance beyond the walls, at the three cardinal points. The first of these cemeteries was found in the dune between the ruin and the peach trees below the spring, and from its relative position from the pueblo has been designated the northern cemetery. The cemetery proper lies on the edge of the sandy tract, and was first detected by the finding of the long-bones of a human skeleton projecting from the soil. The position of individual graves was indicated usually by small, oblong piles of stones; but, as this was not an invariable sign, it was deemed advisable to extend long trenches across the lower part of the dune. As a rule, the deeper the excavations the more numerous and elaborate were the objects revealed. Most of the skeletons were in a poor state of preservation, but several could have been saved had we the proper means at our disposal to care for them.

No evidence of cremation of the dead was found, either at Awatobi or Sikyatki, nor have I yet detected any reference to this custom among the modern Hopi Indians. They have, however, a strange concept of the purification of the breath-body, or shade of the dead, by fire, which, although I have always regarded it as due to the teaching of Christian missionaries, may be aboriginal in character. This account of the judgment of the dead is as follows:

There are two roads from the grave to the Below. One of these is a straight way connected with the path of the sun into the Underworld. There is a branch

[109] I was aided in making this plan by the late J. G. Owens, my former assistant in the field work of the Hemenway Expedition. It was prepared with a few simple instruments, and is not claimed to be accurate in all particulars.

[110] The existence of these peach trees near Sikyatki suggests, of course, an abandonment of the neighboring pueblo in historic times, but I hardly think it outweighs other stronger proofs of antiquity.

trail which divides from this straight way, passing from fires to a lake or ocean (*patübha*). At the fork of the road sits Tokonaka, and when the breath-body comes to this place this chief looks it over and, if satisfied, he says "*Üm-pac lo-la-mai, ta ai,*" "You are very good; go on." Then the breath-body passes along the straight way to the far west, to the early *Sipapû*, the Underworld from which it came, the home of Müiyinwû. Another breath-body comes to the fork in the road, and the chief says, "You are bad," and he conducts it along the crooked path to the place of the first fire pit, where sits a second chief, Tokonaka, who throws the bad breath-body into the fire, and after a time it emerges purified, for it was not wholly bad. The chief says, "You are good now," and carries it back to the first chief, who accepts the breath-body and sends it along the straight road to the west.

If, on emerging from the first fire, the soul is still unpurified, or not sufficiently so to be accepted, it is taken to the second fire pit and cast into it. If it emerges from this thoroughly purified, in the opinion of the judge, it is immediately transformed into a *ho-ho-ya-üh*, or prayer-beetle. All the beetles we now see in the valleys or among the mesas were once evil Hopi. If, on coming out of the second fire pit, the breath-body is still considered bad by the chief, he takes it to the third fire, and, if there be no evil in it when it emerges from this pit, it is metamorphosed into an ant, but if unpurified by these three fires—that is, if the chief still finds evil left in the breath-body—he takes it to a fourth fire and again casts it into the flames, where it is utterly consumed, the only residue being soot on the side of the pit.

I have not recorded this as a universal or an aboriginal belief among the Hopi, but rather to show certain current ideas which may have been brought to Tusayan by missionaries or others. The details of the purification of the evil soul are characteristic.

The western cemetery of Sikyatki is situated among the hillocks covered with surface rubble below a house occupied in summer by a Hopi and his family. From the nature of the soil the excavation of this cemetery was very difficult, although the mortuary objects were more numerous. Repeated attempts to make the Indians work in a systematic manner failed, partly on account of the hard soil and partly from other reasons. Although the lower we went the more numerous and beautiful were the objects exhumed, the Indians soon tired of deep digging, preferring to confine their work to within two or three feet of the surface. At many places we found graves under and between the huge bowlders, which are numerous in this cemetery.

The southern cemetery lies between the outer edge of the ruin on that side and the decline to the plain, a few hundred feet from the southern row of houses. Two conspicuous bowlders mark the site of most of the excavations in that direction. The mortuary objects from this cemetery are not inferior in character or number to those from the other burial places. All attempts to discover a cemetery on the eastern side of the pueblo failed, although a single food basin was brought to the camp by an Indian who claimed he had dug it out of the deep sand on the eastern side of the ruins. Another bowl was found in the sand drift near the trail over the mesa to Kanelba, but careful investigation failed to reveal any systematic deposit of mortuary vessels east of the ruin.[111]

The method of excavation pursued in the cemeteries was not so scientific as I had wished, but it was the only practicable one to be followed with native workmen. Having found the location of the graves by means of small prospecting holes sunk at random, the workmen were aligned and directed to excavate a single long, deep trench, removing all the earth as they advanced. It was with great difficulty that the Indians were taught the importance of excavating to a sufficient depth, and even to the end of the work they refused to be taught not to burrow. In their enthusiasm to get the buried treasures they worked very well so long as objects were found, but became at once discouraged when relics were not so readily forthcoming and went off prospecting in other places when our backs were turned. A shout that anyone had discovered a new grave in the trench was a signal for the others to stop work, gather around the place, light cigarettes, and watch me or my collaborators dig out the specimens with knives. This we always insisted on doing, for the reason that in their haste the Indians at first often broke fragile pottery after they had discovered it, and in spite of all precautions several fine jars and bowls were thus badly damaged by them. It is therefore not too much to say that most of the vessels which are now entire were dug out of the impacted sand by Mr Hodge or myself.

No rule could be formulated in regard to the place where the pottery would occur, and often the first indication of its presence was the stroke of a shovel on the fragile edge of a vase or bowl. Having once found a skeleton, or discolored sand which indicated the former presence of human remains, the probability that burial objects were near by was almost a certainty, although in several instances even these signs failed.

A considerable number of the pottery objects had been broken when the soil and stones were thrown on the corpse at interment. So many were entire, however, that I do not believe any considerable number were purposely broken at that time, and none were found with holes made in them to "kill" or otherwise destroy their utility.

No evidences of cremation—no charred bones of man or animal in or near the mortuary vessels—were found. From the character of the objects obtained from neighboring graves, rich and poor were apparently buried side by side in the same soil. Absolutely no evidence of Spanish influence was encountered in all the excavations at Sikyatki—no trace of metal, glass, or other object of Caucasian manufacture such as I have mentioned as having been taken from the ruins of Awatobi—thus confirming the native tradition that the catastrophe of Sikyatki antedated the middle of the sixteenth century, when the first Spaniards entered the country.

It is remarkable that in Sikyatki we found no fragments of basketry or cloth, the fame of which among the Pueblo Indians was known to Coronado before he left

[111] The position of the cemeteries in ancient Tusayan ruins is by no means uniform. They are rarely situated far from the houses, and are sometimes just outside the walls. While the dead were seldom carried far from the village, a sandy locality was generally chosen and a grave excavated a few feet deep. Usually a few stones were placed on the surface of the ground over the burial place, evidently to protect the remains from prowling beasts.

Mexico. That the people of Sikyatki wore cotton kilts no one can doubt, but these fabrics, if they were buried with the dead, had long since decayed. Specimens of strings and ropes of yucca, which were comparatively abundant at Awatobi, were not found at Sikyatki; yet their absence by no means proves that they were not used, for the marks of the strings used to bind feathers to the mortuary pahos, on the green paint with which the wood was covered, may still be readily seen.

The insight into ancient beliefs and practices afforded by the numerous objects found at Sikyatki is very instructive, and while it shows the antiquity of some of the modern symbols, it betrays a still more important group of conventionalized figures, the meaning of which may always remain in doubt. This is particularly true of the decoration on many specimens of the large collection of highly ornamented pottery found in the Sikyatki cemeteries.

If we consider the typical designs on modern Hopi pottery and compare them with the ancient, as illustrated by the collections from Awatobi and Sikyatki, it is noted, in the first place, how different they are, and secondly, how much better executed the ancient objects are than the modern. Nor is it always clear how the modern symbols are derived from the ancient, so widely do they depart from them in all their essential characters.

POTTERY

CHARACTERISTICS—MORTUARY POTTERY

The pottery exhumed from the burial places of Sikyatki falls in the divisions known as—

I—Coiled and indented ware.
II—Smooth undecorated ware.
III—Polished decorated ware.

    a. Yellow.
    b. Red.
    c. Black-and-white.

By far the largest number of ancient pottery objects from this locality belong to the yellow-ware group in the above classification. This is the characteristic pottery of Tusayan, although coiled and indented ware is well represented in the collection. The few pieces of red ware are different from that found in the ruins of the Little Colorado, while the black-and-white pottery closely resembles the archaic ware of northern cliff houses. Although the Sikyatki pottery bears resemblance to that of Awatobi, it can be distinguished from it without difficulty. The paste of both is of the finest character and was most carefully prepared. Some of the ancient specimens are much superior to those at present made, and are acknowledged by the finest potters of East Mesa to be beyond their power of ceramic production. The coloration is generally in red, brown, yellow, and black. Decorative treatment by spattering is common in the food basins, and this was no doubt performed, Chinese fashion, by means of the mouth. The same method is still employed by the Hopi priests in painting their masks.

The Sikyatki collection of pottery shows little or no duplication in decorative design, and every ornamented food basin bears practically different symbols. The decoration of the food basins is mainly on the interior, but there is almost invariably a geometrical design of some kind on the outside, near the rim. The ladles, likewise, are ornamented on their interior, and their handles also are generally decorated. When the specimens were removed from the graves their colors, as a rule, were apparently as well preserved as at the time of their burial; nor, indeed, do they appear to have faded since their deposit in the National Museum.

The best examples of ceramic art from the graves of Sikyatki, in texture, finish, and decoration, are, in my judgment, superior to any pottery made by ancient or modern Indians north of Mexico. Indeed, in these respects the old Tusayan pottery will bear favorable comparison even with Central American ware. It is far superior to the rude pottery of the eastern pueblos, and is also considerably better than that of the great villages of the Gila and Salado. Among the Hopi themselves the ceramic art has degenerated, as the few remaining potters confess. These objects can hardly be looked upon as products of a savage people destitute of artistic feeling, but of a race which has developed in this line of work, through the plane of savagery, to a high stage of barbarism. While, as a whole, we can hardly regard the modern Hopi as a degenerate people with a more cultured ancestry, certainly the entire Pueblo culture in the Southwest, judged by the character of their pottery manufacture, has greatly deteriorated since the middle of the sixteenth century.

BUREAU OF AMERICAN ETHNOLOGY — — SEVENTEENTH ANNUAL RE-
PORT PL. CXIX

Coiled And Indented Pottery From Sikyatki

COILED AND INDENTED WARE

The rudest type of pottery from Sikyatki has been classed as coiled and indented ware. It is coarse in texture, not polished, and usually not decorated. Although
the outer surface of the pottery of this class is rough, the general form of the ware
is not less symmetrical than that of the finer vessels. The objects belonging to this
group are mostly jars and moccasin-shape vessels, there being no bowls of this
type. As a rule, the vessels are blackened with soot, although some of the speci-

mens are light-brown in color. The former variety were undoubtedly once used in cooking; the latter apparently for containing water or food. In the accompanying illustration (plate CXIX, *a*) is shown one of the best specimens of indented ware, the pits forming an equatorial zone about the vessel. All traces of the coil of clay with which the jar was built up have been obliterated save on the bottom. The vessel is symmetrical and the indentations regular, as if made with a pointed stone, bone, or stick.

In another form of coarse pottery (plate CXIX, *b*) the rim merges into two ears or rudimentary handles on opposite sides. Traces of the original coiling are readily observable on the sides of this vessel.

Another illustration (plate CXIX, *c*) shows an amphora or jar with diametrically opposite handles extending from the rim to the side of the bowl. The surface of this rude jar is rough and without decoration, but the form is regular and symmetrical. In another amphora (plate CXIX, *d*) the opposite handles appear below the neck of the vessel; they are broader and apparently more serviceable.

The jar shown in plate CXIX, *e*, has two ear-like extensions or projections from the neck of the jar, which are perforated for suspension. This vessel is decorated with an incised zigzag line, which surrounds it just above its equator. This is a fair example of ornamented rough ware.

Several of the vessels made of coarse clay mixed with sand, the grains of which make the surface very rough, are of slipper or moccasin shape. These are covered with soot or blackened by fire, indicating their former use as cooking pots. By adopting this form the ancients were practically enabled to use the principle of the dutch-oven, the coals being piled about the vessels containing the food to be cooked much more advantageously than in the vase-like forms.

The variations in slipper-shape cooking pots are few and simple. The blind end is sometimes of globular form, as in the example illustrated in plate CXX, *a*, and sometimes pointed as in figures *b* and *c* of the same plate. One of the specimens of this type has a handle on the rim and another has a flaring lip. Slipper-form vessels are always of coarse ware for the obvious reason that, being somewhat more porous, they are more readily heated than polished utensils. They are not decorated for equally obvious reasons.

SMOOTH UNDECORATED WARE

There are many specimens of undecorated ware of all shapes and sizes, a type of which is shown in plate CXX, *d*. These include food bowls, saucers, ladles, and jars, and were taken from many graves. These utensils differ from the coarse-ware vessels not only in the character of the clay from which they are made, but also in their superficial polish, which, in some instances, is as fine as that of vessels with painted designs. Several very good spoons of half-gourd shape were found, and there are many undecorated food bowls and vases. The first attempts at ornamentation appear to have been a simple spattering of the surface with liquid pigment or a drawing of simple encircling bands. In one instance (plate CXX, *d*) a blackening of the surface by exposure to smoke was detected, but no superficial gloss, as in the Santa Clara ware, was noted.

POLISHED DECORATED WARE

By far the greater number of specimens of mortuary pottery from Sikyatki are highly polished and decorated with more or less complicated designs. Of these there are at least three different groups, based on the color of the ware. Most of the vessels are light yellow or of cream color; the next group in point of color is the red ware, the few remaining specimens being white with black decorations in geometric patterns. These types naturally fall into divisions consisting of vases, jars, bowls, square boxes, cups, ladles, and spoons.

In the group called vases (plates cxxi, cxxii) many varieties are found; some of these are double, with an equatorial constriction; others are rounded below, flat above, with an elevated neck and a recurved lip. It is noteworthy that these jars or vases are destitute of handles, and that their decoration is always confined to the equatorial and upper sections about the opening. In the specimens of this group which were found at Sikyatki there is no basal rim and no depression on the pole opposite the opening. No decoration is found on the interior of the vases, although in several instances the inside of the lip bears lines or markings of various kinds. The opening is always circular, sometimes small, often large; the neck of a vessel is occasionally missing, although the specimens bear evidence of use after having been thus broken. In one or two instances the equatorial constriction is so deep that the jar is practically double; in other cases the constriction is so shallow that it is hardly perceptible (plate cxxvi, *a, b*). The size varies from a simple globular vessel not larger than a walnut to a jar of considerable size. Many show marks of previous use; others are as fresh as if made but yesterday.

BUREAU OF AMERICAN ETHNOLOGY — — SEVENTEENTH ANNUAL RE-
PORT PL. CXX

Saucers And Slipper Bowls From Sikyatki

One of the most fragile of all the globular vessels is a specimen of very thin
black-and-white ware, perforated near the rim for suspension (plate cxxxii). This

form, although rare at Sikyatki, is represented by several specimens, and in mode of decoration is very similar to the cliff-house pottery. From its scarcity in Tusayan I am inclined to believe that this and related specimens were not made of clay found in the immediate vicinity of Sikyatki, but that the vessels were brought to the ancient pueblo from distant places. As at least some of the cliff houses were doubtless inhabited contemporaneously with and long after the destruction of Sikyatki, I do not hesitate to say that the potters of that pueblo were familiar with the cliff-dweller type of pottery and acquainted with the technic which gave the black-and-white ware its distinctive colors.

By far the largest number of specimens of smooth decorated pottery from Sikyatki graves are food bowls or basins, evidently the dishes in which food was placed on the floor before the members of a family at their meals. As the mortuary offerings were intended as food for the deceased it is quite natural that this form of pottery should far outnumber any and all the others. In no instance do the food bowls exhibit marks of smoke blackening, an indication that they had not been used in the cooking of food, but merely as receptacles of the same.

The beautiful decoration of these vessels speaks highly for the artistic taste of the Sikyatki women, and a feast in which they were used must have been a delight to the native eye so far as dishes were concerned. When filled with food, however, much of the decoration of the bowls must have been concealed, a condition avoided in the mode of ornamentation adopted by modern Tusayan potters; but there is no doubt that when not in use the decoration of the vessels was effectually exhibited in their arrangement on the floor or convenient shelves.

The forms of these food bowls are hemispherical, gracefully rounded below, and always without an attached ring of clay on which to stand to prevent rocking. Their rims are seldom flaring, but sometimes have a slight constriction, and while the rims of the majority are perfectly circular, oblong variations are not wanting. Many of the bowls are of saucer shape, with almost vertical sides and flat bases; several are double, with rounded or flat base.

The surface, inside and out, is polished to a fine gloss, and when exteriorly decorated, the design is generally limited to one side just below the rim, which is often ornamented with double or triple parallel lines, drawn in equidistant, quaternary, and other forms. Most of the bowls show signs of former use, either wear on the inner surface or on the base where they rested on the floor in former feasts.

These mortuary vessels were discovered generally at one side of the chest or neck of the person whose remains they were intended to accompany, and a single specimen was found inverted over the head of the deceased. The number of vessels in each grave was not constant, and as many as ten were found with one skeleton, while in other graves only one or two were found. In one instance a nest of six of these basins, one inside another, was exhumed. While many of these mortuary offerings were broken and others chipped, there were still a large number as perfect as when made. Some of the bowls had been mended before burial, as holes drilled on each side of a crack clearly indicate. Fragments of various vessels, which evidently had been broken before they were thrown into the graves, were common.

There is a general similarity in the artistic decoration of bowls found in the same grave, as if they were made by the same potter; and persons of distinction, as shown by other mortuary objects, were, as a rule, more honored than some of their kindred in the character and number of pottery objects deposited with their remains. There were also a number of skeletons without ceramic offerings of any kind.

In one or two interments two or more small jars were found placed inside of a food bowl, and in many instances votive offerings, like turquois, beads, stones, and arrowpoints, had been deposited with the dead. The bowls likewise contained, in some instances, prayer-sticks and other objects, which will later be described.

One of the most interesting modifications in the form of the rim of one of these food bowls is shown in plate cxx, *e*, which illustrates a variation from the circular shape, forming a kind of handle or support for the thumb in lifting the vessel. The utility of this projection in handling a bowl of hot food is apparent. This form of vessel is very rare, it being the only one of its kind in the collection.

A considerable number of cups were found at Sikyatki; these vary in size and shape from a flat-bottom saucer like specimen to a mug-shape variety, always with a single handle (plate cxxv). Many of these resemble small bowls with rounded sides, but there are others in which the sides are vertical, and still others the sides of which incline at an angle to the flattened base.

The handles of these cups are generally smooth, and in one instance adorned with a figure in relief. The rims of these dippers are never flaring, either inward or outward. As a rule they are decorated on the exterior; indeed there is only one instance of interior decoration. The handles of the dippers are generally attached at both ends, but sometimes the handle is free at the end near the body of the utensil and attached at the tip. These handles are usually flat, but sometimes they are round, and often are decorated. Traces of imitations of the braiding of two coils of clay are seen in a single specimen.[112]

---

[112] The excavations at Homolobi in 1896 revealed two beautiful cups with braided handles and one where the clay strands are twisted.

Decorated Pottery From Sikyatki

Decorated Pottery From Sikyatki

Small and large ladles, with long handles, occurred in large numbers in Sikyatki graves, but there was little variation among them except in the forms of their
handles. Many of these utensils were much worn by use, especially on the rim

opposite the attachment of the handle, and in some specimens the handle itself had evidently been broken and the end rounded off by rubbing long before it was placed in the grave. From the comparatively solid character of the bowls of these dippers they were rarely fractured, and were commonly found to contain smaller mortuary objects, such as paint, arrowheads, or polishing stones.

The ladles, unlike most of the cups, are generally decorated on the interior as well as on the exterior. Their handles vary in size and shape, are usually hollow, and sometimes are perforated at the end. In certain specimens the extremity is pro-longed into a pointed, recurved tip, and sometimes is coiled in a spiral. A groove in the upper surface of one example is an unusual variation, and a right-angle bend of the tip is a unique feature of another specimen. The Sikyatki potters, like their modern descendants,[113] sometimes ornamented the tip of a single handle with the head of an animal and painted the upper surface of the shaft with alternate parallel bars, zigzags, terraces, and frets.

Several spoons or scoops of earthenware, which evidently had been used in much the same way as similar objects in the modern pueblos, were found. Some of these have the shape of a half gourd—a natural object which no doubt furnished the pattern. These spoons, as a rule, were not decorated, but on a single specimen bars and parallel lines may be detected. In the innovations of modern times pewter spoons serve the same purpose, and their form is sometimes imitated in earthenware. More often, in modern and probably also in ancient usage, a roll of paper-bread or *piki* served the same purpose, being dipped into the stew and then eaten with the fingers. Possibly the Sikyatkian drank from the hollow handle of a gourd ladle, as is frequently done in Walpi today, but he generally slaked his thirst by means of a clay substitute.[114]

Several box-like articles of pottery of both cream and red ware were found in the Sikyatki graves, some of them having handles, others being without them (plate cxxv). They are ornamented on the exterior and on the rim, and the handle, when not lacking, is attached to the longer side of the rectangular vessel. Not a single bowl was found with a terraced rim, a feature so common in the medicine bowls of Tusayan at the present time.[115]

In addition to the various forms of pottery which have been mentioned, there

-----

[113] The modern potters commonly adorn the ends of ladle handles with heads of different mythologic beings in their pantheon. The knob-head priest-clowns are favorite personages to represent, although even the Corn-maid and different *katcinas* are also sometimes chosen for this purpose. The heads of various animals are likewise frequently found, some in artistic positions, others less so.

[114] The clay ladles with perforated handles with which the modern Hopi sometimes drink are believed to be of late origin in Tusayan.

[115] The oldest medicine bowls now in use ordinarily have handles and a terraced rim, but there are one or two important exceptions. In this connection it may be mentioned that, unlike the Zuñi, the Hopi never use a clay bowl with a basket-like handle for sacred meal, but always carry the meal in basket trays. This the priests claim is a very old practice, and so far as my observations go is confirmed by archeological evidence. The bowl with a basket-form handle is not found either in ancient or modern Tusayan.

are also pieces made in the form of birds, one of the most typical of which is figured in plate cxii, *c*. In these objects the wings are represented by elevations in the form of ridges on the sides, and the tail and head by prolongations, which unfortunately were broken off.

Toys or miniature reproductions of all the above-mentioned ceramic specimens occurred in several graves. These are often very roughly made, and in some cases contained pigments of different colors. The finding of a few fragments of clay in the form of animal heads, and one or two rude images of quadrupeds, would seem to indicate that sometimes such objects were likewise deposited with the dead. A clay object resembling the flaring end of a flageolet and ornamented with a zigzag decoration is unique in the collections from Sikyatki, although in the western cemetery there was found a fragment of an earthenware tube, possibly a part of a flute.

In order to show more clearly the association of mortuary objects in single graves a few examples of the grouping of these deposits will be given.

In a grave in the western cemetery the following specimens were found: 1, ladle; 2, paint grinder; 3, paint slab; 4, arrowpoints; 5, fragments of a marine shell (*Pectunculus*); 6, pipe, with fragments of a second pipe, and 7, red paint (sesquioxide of iron).

In the grave which contained the square medicine bowl shown in plate cxxviii, *a*, a ladle containing food was also unearthed.

The bowl decorated with a picture of a girl's head was associated with fragments of another bowl and four ladles.

Another single grave contained four large and small cooking pots and a broken metate.

In a grave 8 feet below the surface in the western cemetery we found: 1, decorated food vessel; 2, black shoe-shape cooking pot resting in a food bowl and containing a small rude ladle; 3, coarse undecorated basin.

A typical assemblage of mortuary objects comprised: 1, small decorated bowl containing polishing stones; 2, miniature cooking pot blackened by soot; 3, two small food bowls.

In modern Hopi burials the food bowls with the food for the dead are not buried with the deceased, but are placed on the mound of soil and stones which covers the remains. From the position of the mortuary pottery as regards the skeletons in the Sikyatki interments, it is probable that this custom is of modern origin. Whether in former times food bowls were placed on the burial mounds as well as in the grave I am not able to say. The number of food bowls in ancient graves exceeds those placed on modern burials.

The Sikyatki dead were apparently wrapped in coarse fabrics, possibly matting.

BUREAU OF AMERICAN ETHNOLOGY— — SEVENTEENTH ANNUAL RE-
PORT PL. CXXIII

Decorated Pottery From Sikyatki

PALEOGRAPHY OF THE POTTERY

GENERAL FEATURES

The pottery from Sikyatki is especially rich in picture writing, and imperfect as these designs are as a means of transmitting a knowledge of manners, customs, and religious conceptions, they can be interpreted with good results.

One of the most important lessons drawn from the pottery is to be had from a study of the symbols used in its decoration, as indicative of current beliefs and practices when it was made. The ancient inhabitants of Sikyatki have left no writ- ten records, for, unlike the more cultured people of Central America, they had no codices; but they have left on their old mortuary pottery a large body of picture writings or paleography which reveals many instructive phases of their former culture. The decipherment of these symbols is in part made possible by the aid of a knowledge of modern survivals, and when interpreted rightly they open a view of ancient Tusayan myths, and in some cases of prehistoric practices.[116]

Students of Pueblo mythology and ritual are accumulating a considerable

---

[116] Symbolism rather than realism was the controlling element of archaic decoration. Thus, while objects of beauty, like flowers and leaves, were rarely depicted, and human forms are most absurd caricatures, most careful attention was given to minute details of symbolism, or idealized animals unknown to the naturalist.

body of literature bearing on modern beliefs and practices. This is believed to be the right method of determining their aboriginal status, and is therefore necessary as a basis of our knowledge of their customs and beliefs. It is reasonable to suppose that what is now practiced in Pueblo ritual contains more or less of what has survived from prehistoric times, but from Taos to Tusayan there is no pueblo which does not show modifications in mythology and ritual due to European contact. Modern Pueblo life resembles the ancient, but is not a facsimile of it, and until we have rightly measured the effects of incorporated elements, we are more or less inexact in our estimation of the character of prehistoric culture. The vein of similarity in the old and the new can be used in an interpretation of ancient paleography, but we overstep natural limitations if by so doing we ascribe to prehistoric culture every concept which we find current among the modern survivors. To show how much the paleography of Tusayan has changed since Sikyatki was destroyed, I need only say that most of the characteristic figures of deities which are used today in the decoration of pottery are not found on the Sikyatki ware. Perhaps the most common figures on modern food bowls is the head of a mythologic being, the Corn-maid, *Calako-mana*, but this picture, or any which resembles it, is not found on the bowls from Sikyatki. A knowledge of the cult of the Corn-maid possibly came into Tusayan, through foreign influences, after the fall of Sikyatki, and there is no doubt that the picture decoration of modern Tusayan pottery, made within a league of Sikyatki, is so different from the ancient that it indicates a modification of the culture of the Hopi in historic times, and implies how deceptive it may be to present modern beliefs and practices as facsimiles of ancient culture.

The main subjects chosen by the native women for the decoration of their pottery are symbolic, and the most abundant objects which bear these decorations are food bowls and water vases. Many mythic concepts are depicted, among which may be mentioned the Plumed Snake, various birds, reptiles, frogs, tadpoles, and insects. Plants or leaves are seldom employed as decorative motives, but the flower is sometimes used. The feather was perhaps the most common object utilized, and it may likewise be said the most highly conventionalized.

An examination of the decorations of modern food basins used in the villages of East Mesa shows that the mythologic personages most commonly chosen for the ornamentation of their interiors are the Corn or Germ goddesses.[117] These assume a number of forms, yet all are reducible to one type, although known by very different names, as Hewüqti, "Old Woman," Kokle, and the like.

Figures of reptiles, birds, the antelope, and like animals do not occur on any of the food bowls from the large collection of modern Tusayan pottery which I have studied, and as these figures are well represented in the decorations on Sikyatki food bowls, we may suppose their use has been abandoned or replaced by figures

[117] Certainly no more appropriate design could be chosen for the decoration of the inside of a food vessel than the head of the Corn-maid, and from our ideas of taste none less so than that of a lizard or bird. The freshness and absence of wear of many of the specimens of Sikyatki mortuary pottery raises the question whether they were ever in domestic use. Many evidently were thus employed, as the evidences of wear plainly indicate, but possibly some of the vessels were made for mortuary purposes, either at the time of the decease of a relative or at an earlier period.

of the Corn-maids.[118] This fact, like so many others drawn from a study of the Tusayan ritual, indicates that the cult of the Corn-maids is more vigorous today than it was when Sikyatki was in its prime.

Many pictures of masks on modern Tusayan bowls are identified as *Tacab* or Navaho *katcinas*.[119] Their symbolism is well characterized by chevrons on the cheeks or curved markings for eyes. None of these figures, however, have yet been found on ancient Tusayan ceramics. Taken in connection with facts adduced by Hodge indicative of a recent advent of this vigorous Athapascan tribe into Tusayan, it would seem that the use of the *Tacab katcina* pictures was of recent date, and is therefore not to be expected on the prehistoric pottery of the age of that found in Sikyatki.

In the decoration of ancient pottery I find no trace of figures of the clown-priests, or *tcukuwympkiya*, who are so prominent in modern Tusayan *katcina* celebrations. These personages, especially the Tatcukti, often called by a corruption of the Zuñi name Kóyimse (Kóyomäshi), are very common on modern bowls, especially at the extremities of ladles or smaller objects of pottery.

Many handles of ladles made at Hano in late times are modeled in the form of the Paiakyamu,[120] a glutton priesthood peculiar to that Tanoan pueblo. From the data at hand we may legitimately conclude that the conception of the clown-priest is modern in Tusayan, so far as the ornamentation of pottery is concerned.

The large collections of so-called modern Hopi pottery in our museums is modified Tanoan ware, made in Tusayan. Most of the component specimens were made by Hano potters, who painted upon them figures of *katcinas*, a cult which they and their kindred introduced.

Several of the food bowls had evidently cracked during their firing or while in use, and had been mended before they were buried in the graves. This repairing was accomplished either by filling the crack with gum or by boring a hole on each side of the fracture for tying. In one specimen of black-and-white ware a perfectly round hole was made in the bottom, as if purposely to destroy the usefulness of the bowl before burial. This hole had been covered inside with a rounded disk of old pottery, neatly ground on the edge. It was not observed that any considerable number of mortuary pottery objects were "killed" before burial, although a large number were chipped on the edges. It is a great wonder that any of these fragile objects were found entire, the stones and soil covering the corpse evidently having

---

[118] The figure shown in plate cxxix, *a*, was probably intended to represent the Corn-maid, or an Earth goddess of the Sikyatki pantheon. Although it differs widely in drawing from figures of Calako-mana on modern bowls, it bears a startling resemblance to the figure of the Germ goddess which appears on certain Tusayan altars.

[119] Hopi legends recount how certain clans, especially those of Tanoan origin, lived in Tségi canyon and intermarried with the Navaho so extensively that it is said they temporarily forgot their own language. From this source may have sprung the numerous so-called Navaho *katcinas*, and the reciprocal influence on the Navaho cults was even greater.

[120] These priests wear a close-fitting skullcap, with two long, banded horns made of leather, to the end of which corn husks are tied. For an extended description see *Journal of American Ethnology and Archæology*, vol. ii, No. 1, page 11.

been thrown into the grave without regard to care.

The majority of the ancient symbols are incomprehensible to the present Hopi priests whom I have been able to consult, although they are ready to suggest many interpretations, sometimes widely divergent. The only reasonable method that can be pursued in determining the meaning of the conventional signs with which the modern Tusayan Indians are unfamiliar seems, therefore, to be a comparative one. This method I have attempted to follow so far as possible.

There is a closer similarity between the symbolism of the Sikyatki pottery and that of the Awatobi ware than there is between the ceramics of either of these two pueblos and that of Walpi, and the same likewise may be said of the other Tusayan ruins so far as known. It is desirable, however, that excavations be made at the site of Old Walpi in order to determine, if possible, how widely different the ceramics of that village are from the towns whose ruins were studied in 1895. There are certain practical difficulties in regard to work at Old Walpi, one of the greatest of which is its proximity to modern burial places and shrines still used. Moreover, it is probable—indeed, quite certain—that most of the portable objects were carried from the abandoned pueblo to the present village when the latter was founded; but the old cemeteries of Walpi contain many ancient mortuary bowls which, when exhumed, will doubtless contribute a most interesting chapter to the history of modern Tusayan decorative art.

One of the largest, and, so far as form goes, one of the most unique vessels, is shown in plate cxxvi, *b*. This was not exhumed from Sikyatki, but was said to have been found in the vicinity of that ruin. While the ware is very old, I do not believe it is ancient, and it is introduced in order to show how cleverly ancient patterns maybe simulated by more modern potters. The sole way in which modern imitations of ancient vessels may be distinguished is by the peculiar crackled or crazed surface which the former always has. This is due, I believe, to the method of firing and the unequal contraction or expansion of the slip employed. All modern imitations are covered with a white slip which, after firing, becomes crackled, a characteristic unknown to ancient ware. The most expert modern potter at East Mesa is Nampéo, a Tanoan woman who is a thorough artist in her line of work. Finding a better market for ancient than for modern ware, she cleverly copies old decorations, and imitates the Sikyatki ware almost perfectly. She knows where the Sikyatki potters obtained their clay, and uses it in her work. Almost any Hopi who has a bowl to sell will say that it is ancient, and care must always be exercised in accepting such claims.

An examination of the ornamentation of the jar above referred to shows a series of birds drawn in the fashion common to early pottery decoration. This has led me to place this large vessel among the old ware, although the character of the pottery is different from that of the best examples found at Sikyatki. I believe this vessel was exhumed from a ruin of more modern date than Sikyatki. The woman who sold it to me has farming interests near Awatobi, which leads me to conjecture that she or possibly one of her ancestors found it at or near that ruin. She admitted that it had been in the possession of her family for some time, but that the story she had heard concerning it attributed its origin to Sikyatki.

HUMAN FIGURES

Very few figures of men or women are found on the pottery, and these are confined to the interior of food basins (plate cxxix).[121] They are ordinarily very roughly drawn, apparently with less care and with much less detail than are the figures of animals. From their character I am led to the belief that the drawing of human figures on pottery was a late development in Tusayan art, and postdates the use of animal figures on their earthenware. There are, however, a few decorations in which human figures appear, and these afford an interesting although meager contribution to our knowledge of ancient Tusayan art and custom.

---

[121] The rarity of human figures on such kinds of pottery as are found in the oldest ruins would appear to indicate that decorations of this kind were a late development. No specimen of black-and-white ware on which pictures of human beings are present has yet been figured. The sequence of evolution in designs is believed to be (1) geometrical figures, (2) birds, (3) other animals, (4) human beings.

BUREAU OF AMERICAN ETHNOLOGY — — SEVENTEENTH ANNUAL RE-
PORT PL. CXXIV

Decorated Pottery From Sikyatki

As is well known, the Hopi maidens wear their hair in two whorls, one over each ear, and that on their marriage it is tied in two coils falling on the breast. The whorl is arranged on a U-shape stick called a *gñela*; it is commonly done up by a sister, the mother, or some friend of the maiden, and is stiffened with an oil pressed from squash seeds. The curved stick is then withdrawn and the two puffs held in place by a string tightly wound between them and the head. The habit of dressing the hair in whorls is adopted after certain puberty ceremonials, which have elsewhere been described. When on betrothal a Hopi maid takes her gifts of finely ground cornmeal to the house of her future mother-in-law, her hair is dressed in this fashion for the last time, because on her return she is attacked by the women of the pueblo, drawn hither and thither, her hair torn down, and her body smeared with dirt. If her gifts are accepted she immediately becomes the wife of her lover, and her hair is thenceforth dressed in the fashion common to matrons.

The symbolic meaning of the whorls of hair worn by the maidens is said to be the squash-flower, or, perhaps more accurately speaking, the potential power of fructification. There is legendary and other evidence that this custom is very ancient among the Tusayan Indians, and the data obtainable from their ritual point the same way. In the personification of ancestral "breath-bodies," or spirits by men, called *katcinas*, the female performers are termed *katcina-manas* (katcina-virgins), and it is their custom to wear the hair in the characteristic coiffure of maidens. In the personification of the Corn-maid by symbolic figures, such as graven images,[122] pictures, and the like, in secret rites, the style of coiffure worn by the maidens is common, as I have elsewhere shown in the descriptions of the ceremonials known as the Flute, *Lalakonti*, *Mamzrauti*, *Palülükoñti*, and others. The same symbol is found in images used as dolls of Calako-mana, the equivalent, as the others, of the same Corn-maid. From the nature of these images there can hardly be a doubt of the great antiquity of this practice, and that it has been brought down, through their ritual, to the present day. This style of hair dressing was mentioned by the early Spanish explorers, and is represented in pictographs of ancient date; but if all these evidences of its antiquity are insufficient the testimony afforded by the pictures on certain food-basins from Sikyatki leaves no doubt on this point.[123]

Plate cxxix, *b*, represents a food-basin, on the inside of which is drawn, in brown, the head and shoulders of a woman. On either side the hair is done up in coils which bear some likeness to the whorls worn by the present Hopi maidens. It must be borne in mind, however, that similar coils are sometimes made after ceremonial head-washing, and certain other rites, when the hair is tied with corn husks. The face is painted reddish, and the ears have square pendants similar to the turquois mosaics worn by Hopi women at the present day. Although there is other evidence than this of the use of square ear-pendants, set with mosaic, among the ancient people—and traditions point the same way—this figure of the head of a woman from Sikyatki leaves no doubt of the existence of this form of ornament in that ancient pueblo.

However indecisive the last-mentioned picture may be in regard to the coiffure of the ancient Sikyatki women, plate cxxix, *a*, affords still more conclusive

[122] In some of the figurines used in connection with modern Hopi altars these whorls are represented by small wheels made of sticks radiating from a common juncture and connected by woolen yarn.

[123] The natives of Cibola, according to Castañeda, "gather their hair over the two ears, making a frame which looks like an old-fashioned headdress." The Tusayan Pueblo maidens are the only Indians who now dress their hair in this way, although the custom is still kept up by men in certain sacred dances at Zuñi. The country women in Salamanca, Spain, do their hair up in two flat coils, one on each side of the forehead, a custom which Castañeda may have had in mind when he compared the Pueblo coiffure to an "old-fashioned headdress."

evidence. This picture represents a woman of remarkable form which, from likenesses to figures at present made in sand on an altar in the *Lalakonti* ceremony,[124] I have no hesitation in ascribing to the Corn-maid. The head has the two whorls of hair very similar to those made in that rite on the picture of the Goddess of Germs, and the square body is likewise paralleled in the same figure. The peculiar form is employed to represent the outstretched blanket, a style of art which is common in Mayan codices.[125] On each lower corner representations of feathered strings, called in the modern ritual *nakwákwoci*,[126] are appended. The figure is represented as kneeling, and the four parallel lines are possibly comparable with the prayer-sticks placed in the belt of the Germ goddess on the *Lalakonti* altar. In her left hand (which, among the Hopi, is the ceremonial hand or that in which sacred objects are always carried) she holds an ear of corn, symbolic of germs, of which she is the deity. The many coincidences between this figure and that used in the ceremonials of the September moon, called Lalakonti, would seem to show that in both instances it was intended to represent the same mythic being.

There is, however, another aspect of this question which is of interest. In modern times there is a survival among the Hopi of the custom of decorating the inside of a food basin with a figure of the Corn-maid, and this is, therefore, a direct inheritance of ancient methods represented by the specimen under consideration. A large majority of modern food bowls are ornamented with an elaborate figure of Calako-mana, the Corn-maid, very elaborately worked out, but still retaining the essential symbolism figured in the Sikyatki bowl.[127]

---

[124] *American Anthropologist*, April, 1892.

[125] Troano and Cortesiano codices.

[126] A *nakwákwoci* is an individual prayer-string, and consists of one or more prescribed feathers tied to a cotton string. These prayer emblems are made in great numbers in every Tusayan ceremony.

[127] The evidence afforded by this bowl would seem to show that the cult of the Corn-maid was a part of the mythology and ritual of Sikyatki. The elaborate figures of the rain-cloud, which are so prominent in representations of the Corn-maid on modern plaques, bowls, and dolls, are not found in the Sikyatki picture.

BUREAU OF AMERICAN ETHNOLOGY — — SEVENTEENTH ANNUAL RE-
PORT PL. CXXV

Flat Dippers And Medicine Box From Sikyatki

While one of the two figures shown in plate cxxix, *e*, is valuable as affording additional and corroborative evidence of the character of the ancient coiffure
of the women, its main interest is of a somewhat different kind. Two figures are
rudely drawn on the inside of the basin, one of which represents a woman, the
other, judging from the character of the posterior extremity of the body, a reptilian
conception in which a single foreleg is depicted, and the tail is articulated at the

end, recalling a rattlesnake. Upon the head is a single feather;[128] the two eyes are represented on one side of the head, and the line of the alimentary tract is roughly drawn. The figure is represented as standing before that of the woman.

With these few lines the potter no doubt intended to depict one of those many legends, still current, of the cultus hero and heroine of her particular family or priesthood. Supposing the reptilian figure to be a totemic one, our minds naturally recall the legend of the Snake-hero and the Corn-mist-maid[129] whom he brought from a mythic land to dwell with his people.

The peculiar hairdress is likewise represented in the figures on the food basin illustrated in plate cxxix, *c*, which represent a man and a woman. Although the figures are partly obliterated, it can easily be deciphered that the latter figure wears a garment similar to the *kwaca* or dark-blue blanket for which Tusayan is still famous, and that this blanket was bound by a girdle, the ends of which hang from the woman's left hip. While the figure of the man is likewise indistinct (the vessel evidently having been long in use), the nature of the act in which he is engaged is not left in doubt.[130]

Among the numerous deities of the modern Hopi Olympus there is one called Kokopeli,[131] often represented in wooden dolls and clay images. From the obscurity of the symbolism, these dolls are never figured in works on Tusayan images. The figure in plate cxxix, *d*, bears a resemblance to Kokopeli. It represents a man with arms raised in the act of dancing, and the head is destitute of hair as if covered by one of the peculiar helmets, used by the clowns in modern ceremonials. As many of the acts of these priests may be regarded as obscene from our point of view, it is not improbable that this figure may represent an ancient member of this archaic priesthood.

The three human figures on the food basin illustrated in plate cxxix, *f*, are highly instructive as showing the antiquity of a curious and revolting practice almost extinct in Tusayan.

As an accompaniment of certain religious ceremonials among the Pueblo and the Navaho Indians, it was customary for certain priests to insert sticks into the

---

[128] The reason for my belief that this is a breath feather will be shown under the discussion of feather and bird pictures.

[129] For the outline of this legend see *Journal of American Ethnology and Archæology*, vol. IV. The maid is there called the Tcüa-mana or Snake-maid, a sacerdotal society name for the Germ goddess. The same personage is alluded to under many different names, depending on the society, but they are all believed to refer to the same mythic concept.

[130] The attitude of the male and female here depicted was not regarded as obscene; on the contrary, to the ancient Sikyatki mind the picture had a deep religious meaning. In Hopi ideas the male is a symbol of active generative power, the female of passive reproduction, and representations of these two form essential elements of the ancient pictorial and graven art of that people.

[131] The doll of Kokopeli has along, bird-like beak, generally a rosette on the side of the head, a hump on the back, and an enormous penis. It is a phallic deity, and appears in certain ceremonials which need not here be described. During the excavations at Sikyatki one of the Indians called my attention to a large Dipteran insect which he called "Kokopeli."

esophagus. These sticks are still used to some extent and may be obtained by the collector. The ceremony of stick-swallowing has led to serious results, so that now in the decline of this cult a deceptive method is often adopted.

In Tusayan the stick-swallowing ceremony has been practically abandoned at the East Mesa, but I have been informed by reliable persons that it has not wholly been given up at Oraibi. The illustration above referred to indicates its former existence in Sikyatki. The middle figure represents the stick-swallower forcing the stick down his esophagus, while a second figure holds before him an unknown object. The principal performer is held by a third figure, an attendant, who stands behind him. This instructive pictograph thus illustrates the antiquity of this custom in Tusayan, and would seem to indicate that it was once a part of the Pueblo ritual.[132] It is possible that the Navaho, who have a similar practice, derived it from the Pueblos, but there are not enough data at hand to demonstrate this beyond question.

Regarding the pose of the three figures in this picture, I have been reminded by Dr Walter Hough of the performers who carry the wad of cornstalks in the Antelope dance. In this interpretation we have the "carrier," "hugger," and possibly an Antelope priest with the unknown object in his hand. This interpretation appears more likely to be a correct one than that which I have suggested; and yet Kopeli, the Snake chief, declares that the Snake family was not represented at Sikyatki. Possibly a dance similar to the Antelope performance on the eighth day of the Snake dance may have been celebrated at that pueblo, and the discovery of a rattlesnake's rattle in a Sikyatki grave is yet to be explained.

One of the most prominent of all the deities in the modern Tusayan Olympus is the cultus-hero called Püükoñhoya, the Little War God. Hopi mythology teems with legends of this god and his deeds in killing monsters and aiding the people in many ways. He is reputed to have been one of twins, children of the Sun and a maid by parthenogenetic conception. His adventures are told with many variants and he reappears with many aliases.

---

[132] The practice still exists at Zuñi, I am told, and there is no sign of its becoming extinct. It is said that old Naiutci, the chief of the Priesthood of the Bow, was permanently injured during one of these performances. (Since the above lines were written I have excavated from one of the ruins on the Little Colorado a specimen of one of these objects used by ancient stick-swallowers. It is made of bone, and its use was explained to me by a reliable informant familiar with the practices of Oraibi and other villagers. It is my intention to figure and describe this ancient object in the account of the explorations of 1896.)

BUREAU OF AMERICAN ETHNOLOGY — — SEVENTEENTH ANNUAL RE-
PORT PL. CXXVI

Double-Lobe Vases From Ṣikyatki

The symbolism of Püükoñhoya at the present day consists of parallel marks on
the face or body, and when personated by a man the figure is always represented
as carrying weapons of war, such as a bow and arrows. Images of the same hero
are used in ceremonies, and are sometimes found as household gods or penates,
which are fed as if human beings. A fragment of pottery represented in the accompanying illustration (figure 263), shows enough of the head of a personage to
indicate that Püükoñhoya was intended, for it bears on the cheek the two parallel
marks symbolic of that deity, while in his hands he holds a bow and a jointed ar-

row as if shooting an unknown animal. All of these features are in harmony with the identification of the figure with that of the cultus-hero mentioned, and seem to indicate the truth of the current legend that as a mythologic conception he is of great antiquity in Tusayan.

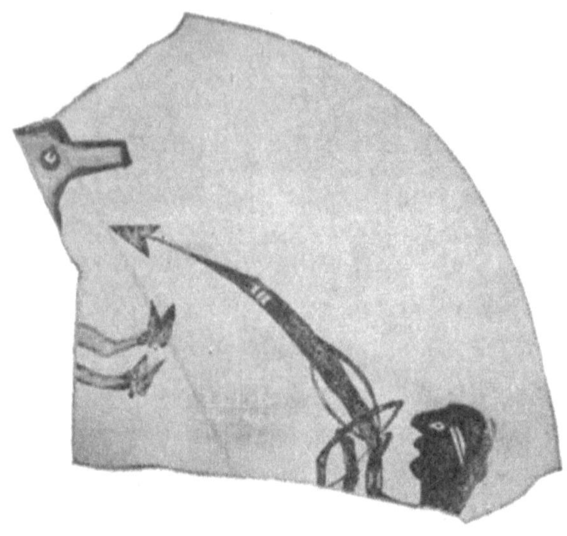

FIG. 263—WAR GOD SHOOTING AN ANIMAL. (FRAGMENT OF FOOD BOWL.)

In this connection it may be instructive to call attention to two figures on a food bowl collected by Mr H. R. Voth from a ruin near Oraibi. It represents a man and a woman, the former with two horns, a crescent on the forehead, and holding in his outstretched hand a staff. The woman has a curious gorget, similar to some which I have found in ruins near Tusayan, and a belt like those still worn by Pueblo Indians. This smaller figure likewise has a crescent on its face and three strange appendages on each side of the head.

Another food basin in Mr Voth's collection is also instructive, and is different in its decoration from any which I have found. The character of the ware is ancient, but the figure is decidedly modern. If, however, it should prove to be an ancient vessel it would carry back to the time of its manufacture the existence of the *katcina* cult in Tusayan, no actual proof of the existence of which, at a time when Sikyatki was in its prime, has yet been discovered.

The three figures represent Hahaiwüqti, Hewüqti, and Natacka exactly as these supernatural beings are now personated at Walpi in the *Powamû*, as described and figured in a former memoir.[133]

---

[133] "Tusayan Katcinas," Fifteenth Annual Report of the Bureau of Ethnology, 1893-94, Washington, 1897. Hewüqti is also called Soyokmana, a Keresan-Hopi name meaning the Natacka-maid. The Keresan (Sia) Skoyo are cannibal giants, according to Mrs Stevenson, an admirable definition of the Hopi Natackas.

It is unfortunate that the antiquity of this specimen, suggestive as it is, must be regarded as doubtful, for it was not exhumed from the ruin by an archeologist, and the exact locality in which it was found is not known.

THE HUMAN HAND

Excepting the figure of the maid's head above described, the human hand, for some unknown reason, is the only part of the body chosen by the ancient Hopi for representation in the decoration of their pottery. Among the present Tusayan Indians the human hand is rarely used, but oftentimes the beams of the kivas are marked by the girls who have plastered them with impressions of their muddy hands, and there is a *katcina* mask which has a hand painted in white on the face. As in the case of the decoration of all similar sacred paraphernalia, there is a legend which accounts for the origin of the *katcina* with the imprint of the hand on its mask. The following tale, collected by the late A. M. Stephen, from whose manuscript I quote, is interesting in this connection:

"The figure of a hand with extended fingers is very common, in the vicinity of ruins, as a rock etching, and is also frequently seen daubed on the rocks with colored pigments or white clay. These are vestiges of a test formerly practiced by the young men who aspired for admission to the fraternity of the Calako. The Calako is a trinity of two women and a man from whom the Hopi obtained the first corn, and of whom the following legend is told:

"In the early days, before houses were built, the earth was devastated by a whirlwind. There was then neither springs nor streams, although water was so near the surface that it could be found by pulling up a tuft of grass. The people had but little food, however, and they besought Masauwûh to help them, but he could not.

"There came a little old man, a dwarf, who said that he had two sisters who were the wives of Calako, and it might be well to petition them. So they prepared an altar, every man making a *paho*, and these were set in the ground so as to encircle a sand hillock, for this occurred before houses were known.

"Masauwûh's brother came and told them that when Calako came to the earth's surface wherever he placed his foot a deep chasm was made; then they brought to the altar a huge rock, on which Calako might stand, and they set it between the two pahos placed for his wives.

"Then the people got their rattles and stood around the altar, each man in front of his own paho; but they stood in silence, for they knew no song with which to invoke this strange god. They stood there for a long while, for they were afraid to begin the ceremonies until a young lad, selecting the largest rattle, began to shake it and sing. Presently a sound like rushing water was heard, but no water was seen; a sound also like great winds, but the air was perfectly still, and it was seen that the rock was pierced with a great hole through the center. The people were frightened and ran away, all save the young lad who had sung the invocation.

BUREAU OF AMERICAN ETHNOLOGY — — SEVENTEENTH ANNUAL RE-PORT PL. CXXVII

Unusual Forms Of Vases From Sikyatki

"The lad soon afterward rejoined them, and they saw that his back was cut and bleeding and covered with splinters of yucca and willow. The flagellation, he told them, had been administered by Calako, who told him that he must endure this laceration before he could look upon the beings he had invoked; that only to those who passed through his ordeals could Calako become visible;

and, as the lad had braved the test so well, he should thenceforth be chief of the Calako altar. The lad could not describe Calako, but said that his two wives were exceedingly beautiful and arrayed with all manner of fine garments. They wore great headdresses of clouds and every kind of corn which they were to give to the Hopi to plant for food. There were white, red, yellow, blue, black, blue-and-white speckled, and red-and-yellow speckled corn, and a seeded grass (*kwapi*).

"The lad returned to the altar and shook his rattle over the hole in the rock, and from its interior Calako conversed with him and gave him instructions. In accordance with these he gathered all the Hopi youths and brought them to the rock, that Calako might select certain of them to be his priests. The first test was that of putting their hands in the mud and impressing them upon the rock. Only those were chosen as novices the imprints of whose hands had dried on the instant.

"The selected youths then moved within the altar and underwent the test of flagellation. Calako lashed them with yucca and willow. Those who made no outcry were told to remain in the altar, to abstain from salt and flesh for ten days, when Calako would return and instruct them concerning the rites to be performed when they sought his aid.

"Calako and his two wives appeared at the appointed time, and after many ceremonials gave to each of the initiated five grains of each of the different kinds of corn. The Hopi women had been instructed to place baskets woven of grass at the foot of the rock, and in these Calako's wives placed the seeds of squashes, melons, beans, and all the other vegetables which the Hopi have since possessed.

"Calako and his wives, after announcing that they would again return, took off their masks and garments, and laying them on the rock disappeared within it.

"Some time after this, when the initiated were assembled in the altar, the Great Plumed Snake appeared to them and said that Calako could not return unless one of them was brave enough to take the mask and garments down into the hole and give them to him. They were all afraid, but the oldest man of the Hopi took them down and was deputed to return and represent Calako.

"Shortly afterward Masauwûh stole the paraphernalia, and with his two brothers masqueraded as Calako and his wives. This led the Hopi into great trouble, and they incurred the wrath of Muiyinwûh, who withered all their grain and corn.

"One of the Hopi finally discovered that the supposed Calako carried a cedar bough in his hand, when it should have been willow; then they knew that it was Masauwûh who had been misleading them.

"The boy hero one day found Masauwûh asleep, and so regained possession of the mask. Muiyinwûh then withdrew his punishments and sent Palülükoñ (the Plumed Snake) to tell the Hopi that Calako would never return to them, but that the boy hero should wear his mask and represent him, and his festival should be celebrated when they had a proper number of novices to be initiated."[134]

Several food basins from Sikyatki have a human hand depicted upon them, and in one of these both hands are represented. On the most perfect of these hand figures (plate cxxxvii, *c*) a wristlet is well represented, with two triangular figures, which impart to it an unusual form. From between the index and second finger there arises a triangular appendage, which joins a graceful curve, extending on one side to the base of the thumb and continued on the other side to the arm. The whole inside of the basin, except the figure of the hand and its appendage, is decorated with spattering,[135] and on the outside there is a second figure, evidently a hand or the paw of some animal. This external decoration also has a triangular figure in which are two terraces, recalling rain-cloud symbols.

One of the most interesting representations of the human hand (figure 354) is found on the exterior of a beautiful bowl. The four fingers and the thumb are shown with representations of nails, a unique feature in such decorations. From between the index finger and the next, or rather from the tip of the former, arises an appendage comparable with that before mentioned, but of much simpler form. The palm of the hand is crossed by a number of parallel lines, which recall a custom of using the palm lines in measuring ceremonial prayer sticks, as I have described in a memoir on the Snake dance. In place of the arm this hand has many parallel lines, the three medial ones being continued far beyond the others, as shown in the figure.

QUADRUPEDS

Figures of quadrupeds are sparingly used in the decoration of food bowls or basins, but the collection shows several fine specimens on which appear some of the mammalia with which the Hopi are familiar. Most of these are so well drawn that there appears to be no question as to their identification.

One of the most instructive of these figures is shown in plate cxxx, *a*, which is much worn, and indistinct in detail, although from what can be traced it was probably intended to represent a mythic creature known as the Giant Elk. The head

[134] The celebration occurs in the modern Tusayan pueblos in the *Powamû* where the representative of Calako flogs the children. Calako's picture is found on the *Powamû* altars of several of the villages of the Hopi.

[135] Figures of the human hand have been found on the walls of cliff houses. These were apparently made in somewhat the same way as that on the above bowl, the hand being placed on the surface and pigment spattered about it. See "The Cliff Ruins of Canyon de Chelly," by Cosmos Mindeleff; Sixteenth Annual Report, 1894-95.

bears two branched horns, drawn without perspective, and the neck has a number of short parallel marks similar to those occurring on the figure of an antelope on the walls of one of the kivas at Walpi. The hoofs are bifid, and from a short stunted tail there arises a curved line which encircles the whole figure, connecting a series of round spots and terminating in a triangular figure with three parallel lines representing feathers. Perhaps the strangest of all appendages to this animal is at the tail, which is forked, recalling the tail of certain birds. Its meaning is unknown to me.

Medicine Box And Pigment Pots From Sikyatki

There can be no doubt that the delineator sought to represent in this figure one of the numerous horned *Cervidæ* with which the ancient Hopi were familiar, but the drawing is so incomplete that to choose between the antelope, deer, and elk seems impossible. It may be mentioned, however, that the Horn people are reputed to have been early arrivals in Tusayan, and it is not improbable that representatives of the Horn clans lived in Sikyatki previous to its overthrow.

Two faintly drawn animals, evidently intended for quadrupeds, appear on the interior of the food bowl shown in plate cxxx, *b*. These are interesting from the method in which they were drawn. They are not outlined with defined lines, but are of the original color of the bowl, and appear as two ghost-like figures surrounded by a dense spattering of red spots, similar in technic to the figure of the human hand. I am unable to identify these animals, but provisionally refer them to the rabbit. They have no distinctive symbolism, however, and are destitute of the characteristic spots which members of the Rabbit clan now invariably place on their totemic signatures.

FIG. 264—MOUNTAIN SHEEP

The animal design on the bowl illustrated in plate cxxx, *c*, probably represents a rabbit or hare, quite well drawn in profile, with a feathered appendage from the head. Behind it is the ordinary symbol of the dragon-fly. Several crosses are found in an opposite hemisphere, separated from that occupied by the two animal pictures by a series of geometric figures ornamented with crooks and other designs.

The interior of the food bowl shown in plate cxxx, *d*, as well as the inner sides of the two ladles represented in plate cxxxi, *b*, *d*, are decorated with peculiar figures which suggest the porcupine. The body is crescentic and covered with spines, and only a single leg, with claws, is represented. It is worthy of mention that so many of these animal forms have only one leg, representative, no doubt, of a single pair, and that many of these have plantigrade paws like those of the bear and badger. The appendages to the head in this figure remind one of those of certain forms regarded as reptiles, with which this may be identical.

FIG. 265—MOUNTAIN LION

In another decoration we have what is apparently the same animal furnished with both fore and hind legs, the tail curving upward like that of a cottontail rabbit, which it resembles in other particulars as well. This figure also hangs by a band from a geometric design formed of two crescents and bearing four parallel marks representing feathers. The single crescent depicted on the inside of the ladle shown in plate cxxxi, *b*, is believed to represent the same conception, or the moon; and in this connection the very close phonetic resemblance between the Hopi name for moon[136] and that for the mammal may be mentioned. In the decoration last

[136] Mu'yi, mole or gopher; mu'iyawû, moon. There maybe some Hopi legend con-

described the same crescentic figure is elaborated into its zoömorphic equivalent.

BUREAU OF AMERICAN ETHNOLOGY SEVENTEENTH ANNUAL REPORT
PL. CXXIX

Designs On Food Bowls From Sikyatki

An enumeration of the pictographic representations of mammalia includes

necting the gopher with the moon, but thus far it has eluded my studies, and I can at present do no more than call attention to what appears to be an interesting etymological coincidence.

the beautiful food bowl shown in plate cxxx, *e*, which is made of fine clay spattered with brown pigment. This design (reproduced in figure 264) represents probably some ruminant, as the mountain sheep or possibly the antelope, both of which gave names to clans said to have resided at Sikyatki. The hoofs are characteristic, and the markings on the back suggest a fawn or spotted deer. There is a close similarity between the design below this animal and that of the exterior decorations of certain vases and square medicine bowls.

Among the pictures of quadrupedal animals depicted on ancient food bowls there is none more striking than that illustrated in plate cxxx, *f*, which has been identified as the mountain lion. While this identification is more or less problematical, it is highly possible. The claws of the forelegs (figure 265) are evidently those of one of the carnivora of the cat family, of which the mountain lion is the most prominent in Tusayan. The anterior part of the body is spotted; the posterior and the hind legs are black. The snout bears little resemblance to that of the puma.

The entire inner surface of the bowl, save a central circle in which the head, fore-limbs, and anterior part of the body are represented, is decorated by spattering. Within this spattered area there are highly interesting figures, prominent among which is a squatting figure of a man, with the hand raised to the mouth and holding a ceremonial cigarette, as if engaged in smoking. The seven patches in black might well be regarded as either footprints or leaves, four of which appear to be attached to the band inclosing the central area. In the intervals between three of these there are branched bodies representing plants or bushes.

REPTILES

Snakes and other reptilian forms were represented by the ancient potters in the decoration of food bowls, and it is remarkable how closely some of these correspond in symbolism with conceptions still current in Tusayan. Of all reptilian monsters the worship of which forms a prominent element in Hopi ritual, that of the Great Plumed Snake is perhaps the most important. Effigies of this monster exist in all the larger Hopi villages, and they are used in at least two great rites—the *Soyaluña* in December and the *Palülükonti* in March, as I have already described. The symbolic markings and appendages of the Plumed Snake effigy are distinctive, and are found in all modern representations of this mystic being. While several pictographs of snakes are found on Sikyatki pottery, there is not a single instance in which these modern markings appear; consequently there is considerable doubt in regard to the identification of many of the Sikyatki serpents with modern mythologic representatives.

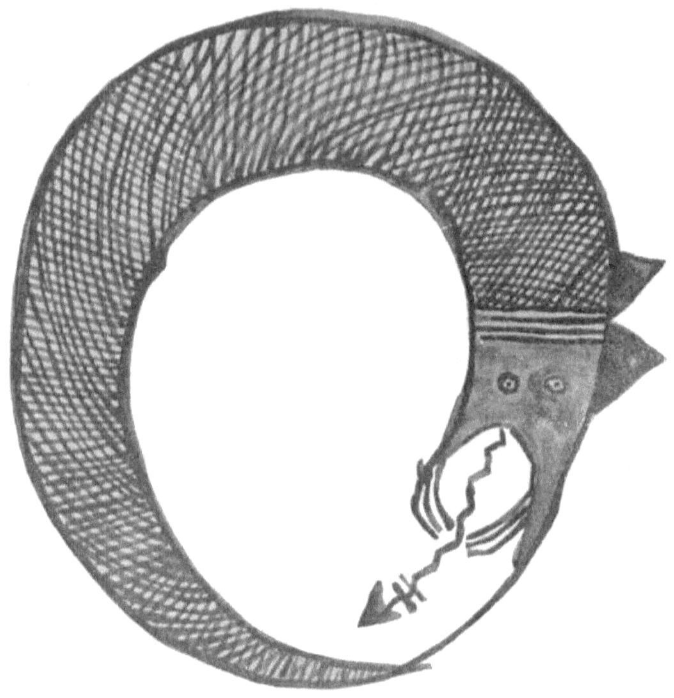

FIG. 266—PLUMED SERPENT

In questioning the priests in regard to the derivation of the Plumed Serpent cult in Tusayan, I have found that they declare that this cultus was brought into Tusayan from a mythic land in the south, called Palatkwabi, and that the effigies and fetiches pertaining to it were introduced by the Patki or Water-house people. From good evidence, I suspect that the arrival of this phratry was comparatively late in Tusayan history, and it is possible that Sikyatki was destroyed before their advent, for in all the legends which I have been able to gather no one ascribes to Sikyatki any clan belonging to the phratries which are said to have migrated from the far south. I believe we must look toward the east, whence the ancestors of the Kokop or Firewood people are reputed to have come, for the origin of the symbolic markings of the snakes represented on Sikyatki ceramics. Figures of apodal reptiles, with feathers represented on their heads, occur in Sikyatki pictography, although there is no resemblance in the markings of their bodies to those of modern pictures. One of the most striking of these occurs on the inside of the food basin shown in plate cxxxii, *a*. It represents a serpent with curved body, the tail being connected with the head, like an ancient symbol of eternity. The body (figure 266) is destitute of any distinctive markings, but is covered with a crosshatching of black lines. The head bears two triangular markings, which are regarded as feather symbols. The position of the eyes would seem to indicate that the top of the head is represented, but this conclusion is not borne out by comparative studies, for it was often the custom of ancient Tusayan potters, like other primitive artists, to represent both eyes on one side of the head.

Food Bowls With Figures Of Quadrupeds From Sikyatki

The zigzag line occupying the position of the tongue and terminating in a triangle is a lightning symbol, with which the serpent is still associated. While striving not to strain the symbolism of this figure, it is suggested that the three curved marks on the lower and upper jaws represent fangs. It is highly probable that conceptions not greatly unlike those which cluster about the Great Plumed Serpent were associated with this mythic snake, the figure of which is devoid of some of the most essential elements of modern symbolism.

While from the worn character of the middle of the food bowl illustrated in plate cxxxii, *b*, it is not possible to discover whether the animal was apodal or not from the crosshatching of the body and the resemblance of the appendages of the head to those of the figure last considered, it appears probable that this pictograph likewise was intended to represent a snake of mystic character. Like the previous figure, this also is coiled, with the tail near the head, its body crosshatched, and with two triangular appendages to the head. There is, however, but one eye, and the two jaws are elongated and provided with teeth,[137] as in the case of certain reptiles.

The similarity of the head and its appendages to the snake figure last described would lead me to regard the figure shown in plate cxxxii, *c*, as representing a like animal, but the latter picture is more elaborately worked out in details, and one of the legs is well represented. I have shown in the discussion of a former figure how the decorator, recognizing the existence of two eyes, represented them both on one side of the head of a profile figure, although only one is visible, and we see in this picture (figure 267) a somewhat similar tendency, which is very common in modern Tusayan figures of animals. The breath line is drawn from the extremity of the snout halfway down the length of the body. In modern pictography a representation of the heart is often depicted at the blind extremity of this line, as if, in fact, there was a connection with this organ and the tubes through which the breath passes. In the Sikyatki pottery, however, I find only this one specimen of drawing in which an attempt to represent internal organs is made.

The tail of this singular picture of a reptile is highly conventionalized, bearing appendages of unknown import, but recalling feathers, while on the back are other appendages which might be compared with wings. Both of these we might expect, considering the association of bird and serpent in the Hopi conception of the Plumed Snake.

Exact identifications of these pictures with the animals by which the Hopi are or were surrounded, is, of course, impossible, for they are not realistic representations, but symbolic figures of mythic beings unknown save to the imagination of the primitive mythologist.

---

[137] This form of mouth I have found in pictures of quadrupeds, birds, and insects, and is believed to be conventionalized. Of a somewhat similar structure are the mouths of the *Natacka* monsters which appear in the Walpi *Powamû* ceremony. See the memoir on "Tusayan Katcinas," in the Fifteenth Annual Report.

FIG. 267—UNKNOWN REPTILE

BUREAU OF AMERICAN ETHNOLOGY— — SEVENTEENTH ANNUAL RE-
PORT PL. CXXXI

Ornamented Ladles From Sikyatki

FIG. 268—UNKNOWN REPTILE

A similar reptile is pictured on the food bowl shown in plate cxxxii, *d*, in which design, however, there are important modifications, the most striking of which are: (1) The animal (figure 268) has both fore and hind legs represented; (2) the head is round; (3) the mouth is provided with teeth; and (4) there are four instead of two feather appendages on the head, two of which are much longer than the others. Were it not that ears are not represented in reptiles, one would be tempted to regard the smaller appendages as representations of these organs. Their similarity to the row of spines on the back and the existence of spines on the head of the "horned toad" suggests this reptile, with which both ancient and modern Hopi are very familiar. On a fragment of a vessel found at Awatobi there is depicted the head of a reptile evidently identical with this, since the drawing is an almost perfect reproduction. There is a like figure, also from Sikyatki, in the collection of pottery made at that ruin by Dr Miller, of Prescott, the year following my work there. The most elaborate of all the pictures of reptiles found on ancient Tusayan pottery is shown in plate cxxxii, *e*, in which the symbolism is complicated and the details carefully worked out. A few of these symbols I am able to decipher; others elude present analysis. There is no doubt as to the meaning of the appendage to the head (figure 269), for it well portrays an elaborate feathered headdress on which the markings that distinguish tail-feathers, three in number, are prominent. The extension of the snout is without homologue elsewhere in Hopi pictography, and, while decorative in part, is likewise highly conventionalized. On the body semicircular rain cloud symbols and markings similar to those of the bodies of certain birds are distinguishable. The feet likewise are more avian than reptilian, but of a form quite unusual in structure. It is interesting to note the similarity in the carved line with six sets of parallel bars to the band surrounding the figure of the human hand shown in plate cxxxvii, *c*. In attempting to identify the pictograph on the bowl reproduced in plate cxxxiv, *a*, there is little to guide me, and the nearest I can come to its significance is to ascribe it to a reptile of some kind. Highly symbolic, greatly conventionalized as this figure is, there is practically nothing on which to base the absolute identification of the figure save the serrated appendage to the body and the leg, which resembles that of the lizard as it is sometimes drawn. The two eyes indicate that the enlargement in which these were placed is the head, and the extended curved snout a beak. All else is incomprehensible to me, and my identification is therefore provisional and largely speculative.

FIG. 269—UNKNOWN REPTILE

I wish, however, in leaving the description of this beautiful bowl, to invite attention to the brilliancy and the characteristics of the coloring, which differ from the majority of the decorated ware from Sikyatki.

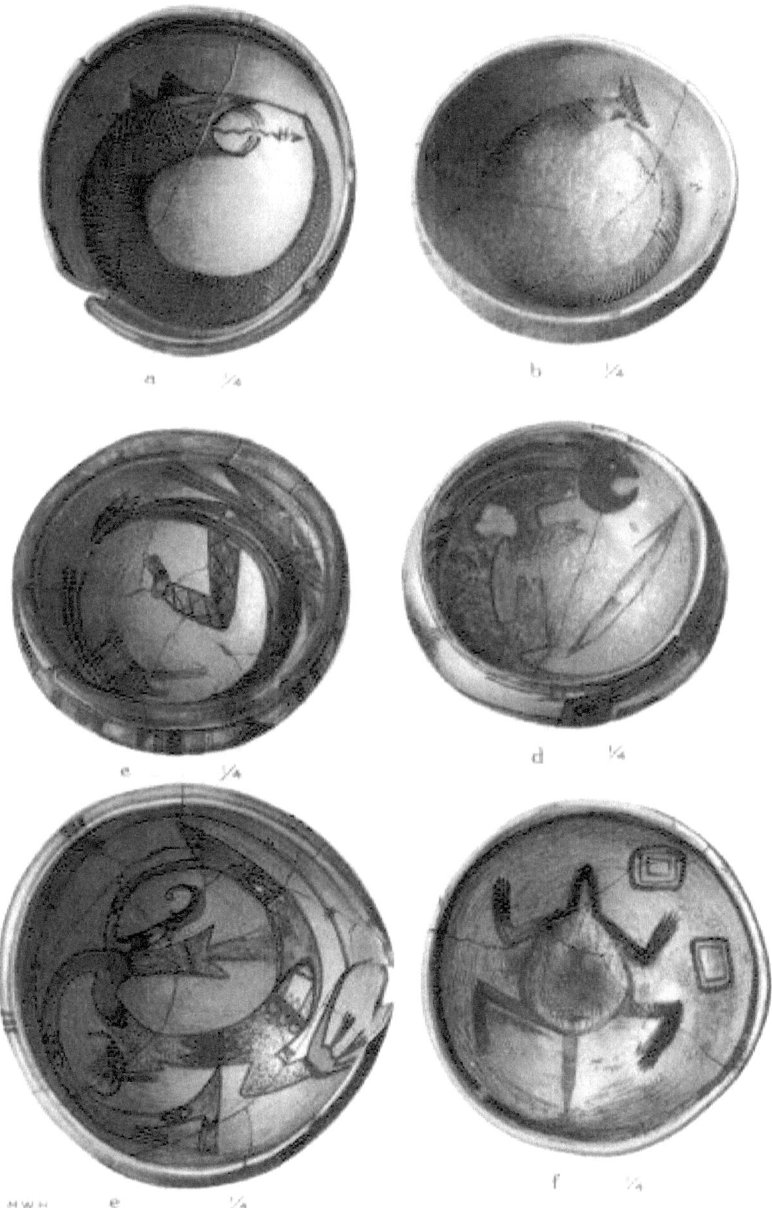

BUREAU OF AMERICAN ETHNOLOGY—— SEVENTEENTH ANNUAL RE-
PORT PL. CXXXII

Food Bowls With Figures Of Reptiles From Sikyatki

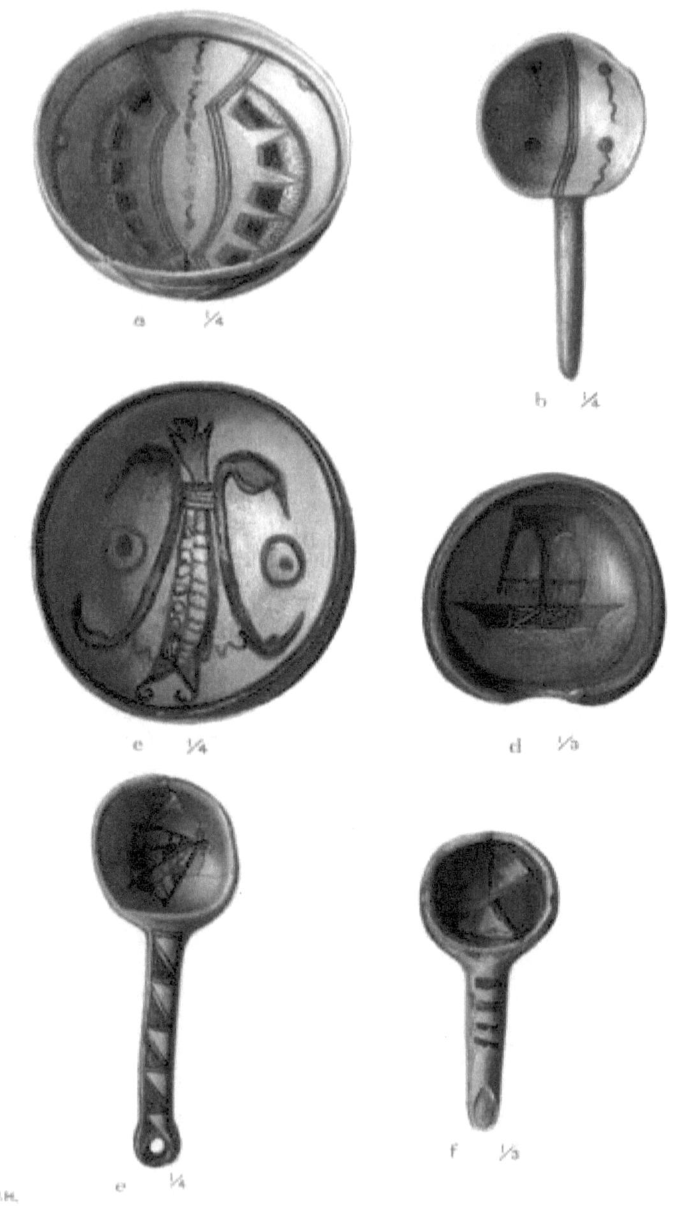

Bowls And Dippers With Figures Of Tadpoles, Birds, Etc. From Sikyatki

BUREAU OF AMERICAN ETHNOLOGY — — SEVENTEENTH ANNUAL RE-
PORT PL. CXXXIV

Food Bowls With Figures Of Sun, Butterfly, And Flower From Sikyatki

Among the fragments of pottery found in the Sikyatki graves there was one which, had it been entire, would doubtless have thrown considerable light on ancient pictography. This fragment has depicted upon it portions of the body and the whole head and neck of a reptilian animal. We find on that part of the body which is represented, three parallel marks which recall those on the modern pictures of the Great Plumed Serpent. On the back there were apparently the representations of wings, a feather of which is shown above the head. The head likewise bears a crest of three feathers, and there are three reptilian like toes. Whether this represents a reptile or a bird it is impossible for me to say, but enough has already been recorded to indicate how close the symbolism of these two groups sometimes is in ancient pictography. It would almost appear as if the profound anatomical discovery of the close kinship of birds and reptiles was unconsciously recognized by a people destitute of the rudiments of the knowledge of morphology.

TADPOLES

Among the inhabitants of an arid region, where rain-making forms a dominant element in their ritual, water animals are eagerly adopted as symbols. Among these the tadpole occupies a foremost position. The figures of this batrachian are very simple, and are among the most common of those used on ceremonial paraphernalia in Tusayan at the present time. In none of these is anything more than a globular head and a zigzag tail represented, and, as in nature, these are colored black. The tadpole appears on several pieces of painted pottery from Sikyatki, one of the best of which is the food bowl illustrated in plate cxxxiii, *a*. The design represents a number of these aquatic animals drawn in line across the diameter of the inner surface of the bowl, while on each side there is a row of rectangular blocks representing rain clouds. These blocks are separated from the tadpole figures by crescentic lines, and above them are short parallel lines recalling the symbol of falling rain.

One of the most beautiful forms of ladles from Sikyatki is figured in plate cxxxiii, *b*, a specimen in which the art of decoration by spattering is effectively displayed. The interior of the bowl of this dipper is divided by parallel lines into two zones, in each of which two tadpoles are represented. The handle is pointed at the end and is decorated. This specimen is considered one of the best from Sikyatki.

The rudely drawn picture on the bowl figured in plate cxxxii, *f*, would be identified as a frog, save for the presence of a tail which would seem to refer it to the lizard kind. But in the evolution of the tadpole into the frog a tailed stage persists in the metamorphosis after the legs develop. In modern pictures[138] of the frog with which I am familiar, this batrachian is always represented dorsally or ventrally with the legs outstretched, while in the lizards, as we have seen, a lateral view is always adopted. As the sole picture found on ancient pottery where the former method is employed, this fact may be of value in the identification of this rude outline as a frog rather than as a true reptile.

BUTTERFLIES OR MOTHS

One of the most characteristic modern decorations employed by the Hopi, especially as a symbol of fecundity, is the butterfly or moth. It is a constant device on the beautiful white or cotton blankets woven by the men as wedding gifts, where it is embroidered on the margin in the forms of triangles or even in more realistic patterns. This symbol is a simple triangle, which becomes quite realistic

[138] Figures of the tadpole and frog are often found on modern medicine bowls in Tusayan. The snake, so common on Zuñi ceremonial pottery, has not been seen by me on a single object of earthenware in use in modern Hopi ritual.

when a line is drawn bisecting one of the angles. This double triangle is not only a constant symbol on wedding blankets, but also is found on the dadoes of houses, resembling in design the arrangement of tiles in the Alhambra and other Moorish buildings. This custom of decorating the walls of a building with triangles placed at intervals on the upper edge of a dado is a feature of cliff-house kivas, as shown in Nordenskiöld's beautiful memoir on the cliff villages of Mesa Verde. While an isosceles triangle represents the simplest form of the butterfly symbol, and is common on ancient pottery, a few vessels from Sikyatki show a much more realistic figure. In plate cxxxiv, *f*, is shown a moth with extended proboscis and articulated antennæ, and in *d* of the same plate another form, with the proboscis inserted in a flower, is given. As an associate with summer, the butterfly is regarded as a beneficent being aside from its fecundity, and one of the ancient Hopi clans regarded it as their totem. Perhaps the most striking, and I may say the most inexplicable, use of the symbol of the butterfly is the so-called *Hokona* or Butterfly virgin slab used in the Antelope ceremonies of the Snake dance at Walpi, where it is associated with the tadpole water symbol.

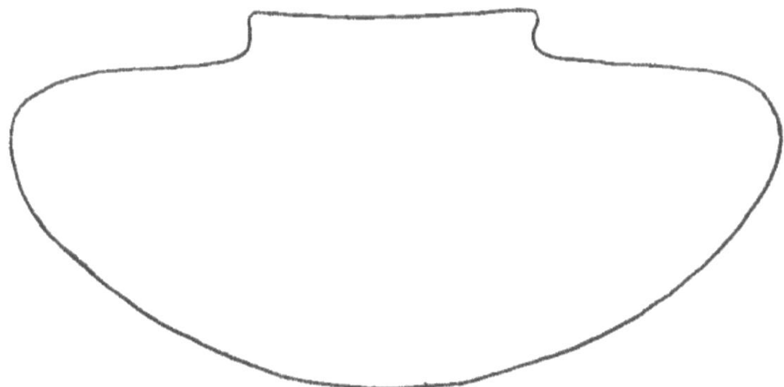

FIG. 270—OUTLINE OF PLATE CXXXV, B

The most beautiful of all the butterfly designs are the six figures on the vase reproduced in plate cxxxv, *b*. From the number of these pictures it would seem that they bore some relationship to the six world-quarters—north, west, south, east, zenith, and nadir. The vase has a flattened shoulder, and the six butterfly figures are represented as flying toward the orifice. These insect figures closely resemble one another, and are divided into two groups readily distinguished by the symbolism of the heads. Three have each a cross with a single dot in each quadrant, and each of the other three has a dotted head without the cross. These two kinds alternate with each other, and the former probably indicate females, since the same symbols on the heads of the snakes in the sand picture of the Antelope altar in the Snake dance are used to designate the female.[139]

---

[139] *Journal of American Ethnology and Archæology*, vol. iv.

BUREAU OF AMERICAN ETHNOLOGY— — SEVENTEENTH ANNUAL RE-
PORT PL. CXXXV

Vases With Figures Of Butterflies From Sikyatki

Vases With Figures Of Birds And Feathers From Sikyatki

Two antennæ and a double curved proboscis are indicated in all the figures of butterflies on the vase under consideration. The zones above and below are both cut by a "line of life," the opening through which is situated on opposite equatorial poles in the upper and under rim.

FIG. 271—BUTTERFLY DESIGN ON UPPER SURFACE OF PLATE CXXXV, B

The rectangular figures associated with the butterflies on this elaborately decorated vase are of two patterns alternating with each other. The rectangles forming one of these patterns incloses three vertical feathers, with a triangle on the right side and a crook on the left. The remaining three rectangles also have three feathers, but they are arranged longitudinally on the surface of the vase.

The elaborate decoration of the zone outside the six butterflies is made up of feathers arranged in three clusters of three each, alternating with key patterns, crosshatched crooks, triangles, and frets. The wealth of ornament on this part of the vase is noteworthy, and its interpretation very baffling. This vase may well be considered the most elaborately decorated in the whole collection from Sikyatki.

There are several figures of butterflies, like those shown in plate cxxxi, *a*, in which the modifications of wings and body have proceeded still further, and the only features which refer them to insects are the jointed antennæ. The passage from this highly conventionalized design into a triangular figure is not very great. There are still others where the head, with attached appendages, arises not from an angle of a triangle, but from the middle of one side. This gives us a very common form of butterfly symbol, which is found, variously modified, on many ancient vessels. In such designs there is commonly a row of dots on each side, which may be represented by a sinuous line, a series of triangles, bars, or parallel bars.

The design reproduced in plate cxxxiv, *d*, represents a moth or butterfly associated with a flower, and several star symbols. It is evidently similar to that figured in *a* of the same plate, and has representations of antennæ and extended proboscis, the latter organ placed as if extracting honey from the flower. The conventional flower is likewise shown in *e* of this plate. The two crescentic designs in plate cxxxv, *a*, are regarded as butterflies.

The jar illustrated in plate cxlv, *b*, is ornamented with highly conventionalized figures on four sides, and is the only one taken from the Sikyatki cemeteries in which the designs are limited to the equatorial surface. The most striking figure, which is likewise found on the base of the paint saucer shown in plate cxlvi, *f*, is a diamond-shape design with a triangle at each corner (figure 276). The pictures drawn on alternating quadrants have very different forms, which are difficult to classify, and I have therefore provisionally associated this beautiful vessel with those bearing the butterfly and the triangle. The form of this vessel closely approaches that of the graceful cooking pots made of coiled and coarse indented ware, but the vessel was evidently not used for cooking purposes, as it bears no marks of soot.[140]

DRAGON-FLIES

Among the most constant designs used in the decoration of Sikyatki pottery are figures of the dragon-fly. These decorations consist of a line, sometimes enlarged into a bulb at one end, with two parallel bars drawn at right angles across the end, below the enlargement. Like the tadpole, the dragon-fly is a symbol of water, and with it are associated many legends connected with the miraculous sprouting of corn in early times. It is a constant symbol on modern ceremonial paraphernalia, as masks, tablets, and pahos, and it occurs also on several ancient vessels (plates cxl, *b*; clxiii, *a*), where it always has the same simple linear form, with few essential modifications.

---

[140] Although made of beautiful yellow ware, it shows at one point marks of having been overheated in firing, as is often the case with larger vases and jars.

Vessels With Figures Of Human Hand, Birds, Turtle, Etc. From Sikyatki

The symbols of four dragon-flies are well shown on the rim of the square box represented in plate cxxviii, *a*. This box, which was probably for charm liquid, or possibly for feathers used in ceremonials, is unique in form and is one of the most beautiful specimens from the Sikyatki cemeteries. It is elaborately decorated on the four sides with rain-cloud and other symbols, and is painted in colors which retain their original brilliancy. The interior is not decorated.

The four dragon-flies on the rim of this object are placed in such a way as to represent insects flying about the box in a dextral circuit, or with the heads turned to the right. This position indicates a ceremonial circuit, which is exceptional among the Tusayan people, although common in Navaho ceremonies. In the sand picture of the Snake society, for instance, where four snakes are represented in a border surrounding a mountain lion, these reptiles are represented as crawling about the picture from right to left. This sequence is prescribed in Tusayan ceremonials, and has elsewhere been designated by me as the sinistral circuit, or a circuit with the center on the left hand. The circuit used by the decorator of this box is dextral or sunwise.

Several rectangular receptacles of earthenware, some with handles and others without them, were obtained in the excavations at Sikyatki. The variations in their forms may be seen in plates cxxviii, *a, c,* and cxxv, *f.* These are regarded as medicine bowls, and are supposed to have been used in ancient ceremonials where asperging was performed. In many Tusayan ceremonials square medicine bowls, some of them without handles, are still used,[141] but a more common and evidently more modern variety are round and have handles. The rim of these modern sacred vessels commonly bears, in its four quadrants, terraced elevations representing rain-clouds of the cardinal points, and the outer surface of the bowl is decorated with the same symbols, accompanied with tadpole or dragon-fly designs.

One of the best figures of the dragon-fly is seen on the saucer shown in plate cxx, *f.* The exterior of this vessel is decorated with four rectangular terraced rain-cloud symbols, one in each quadrant, and within each there are three well-drawn figures of the dragon-fly. The curved line below represents a rainbow. The terrace form of rain-cloud symbol is very ancient in Tusayan and antedates the well-known semicircular symbol which was introduced into the country by the Patki people. It is still preserved in the form of tablets[142] worn on the head and in sand paintings and various other decorations on altars and religious paraphernalia.

BIRDS

The bird and the feather far exceed all other motives in the decoration of ancient Tusayan pottery, and the former design was probably the first animal figure employed for that purpose when the art passed out of the stage where simple geometric designs were used exclusively. A somewhat similar predominance is found in the part which the bird and the feather play in the modern Hopi ceremonial sys-

[141] One of the best examples of the rectangular or ancient type of medicine bowl is used in the celebration of the Snake dance at Oraibi, where it stands on the rear margin of the altar of the Antelope priesthood of that pueblo.

[142] One of the best of these is that of the Humis-katcina, but good examples occur on the dolls of the Calakomanas. The Lakone maid, however, wears a coronet of circular rain-cloud symbols, which corresponds with traditions which recount that this form was introduced by the southern clans or the Patki people.

tem. As one of the oldest elements in the decoration of Tusayan ceramics, figures of birds have in many instances become highly conventionalized; so much so, in fact, that their avian form has been lost, and it is one of the most instructive problems in the study of Hopi decoration to trace the modifications of these designs from the realistic to the more conventionalized. The large series of food bowls from Sikyatki afford abundant material for that purpose, and it may incidentally be said that by this study I have been able to interpret the meaning of certain decorations on Sikyatki bowls of which the best Hopi traditionalists are ignorant.[143] In order to show the method of reasoning in this case I have taken a series illustrating the general form of an unknown bird.

There can be no reasonable doubt that the decoration of the food basin shown in plate cxxxvii, *a*, represents a bird, and analogy would indicate that it is the picture of some mythologic personage. It has a round head (figure 272), to which is attached a headdress, which we shall later show is a highly modified feather ornament. On each side of the body from the region of the neck there arise organs which are undoubtedly wings, with feathers continued into arrowpoints. The details of these wings are very carefully and, I may add, prescriptively worked out, so that almost every line, curve, or zigzag is important. The tail is composed of three large feathers, which project beyond two triangular extensions, marking the end of the body.

The technic of this figure is exceedingly complicated and the colors very beautiful. Although this bowl was quite badly broken when exhumed, it has been so cleverly mended by Mr Henry Walther that no part of the symbolism is lost.

While it is quite apparent that this figure represents a bird, and while this identification is confirmed by Hopi testimony, it is far from a realistic picture of any known bird with which the ancients could have been familiar. It is highly conventionalized and idealized with significant symbolism, which is highly suggestive.

---

[143] In the evolution of ornament among the Hopi, as among most primitive peoples where new designs have replaced the old, the meaning of the ancient symbols has been lost. Consequently we are forced to adopt comparative methods to decipher them. If, for instance, on a fragment of ancient pottery we find the figure of a bird in which the wing or tail feathers have a certain characteristic symbol form, we are justified, when we find the same symbolic design on another fragment where the rest of the bird is wanting, in considering the figure that of a wing or tail feather. So when the prescribed figure of the feather has been replaced by another form it is not surprising to find it incomprehensible to modern shamans. The comparative ethnologist may in this way learn the meanings of symbols to which the modern Hopi priest can furnish no clue.

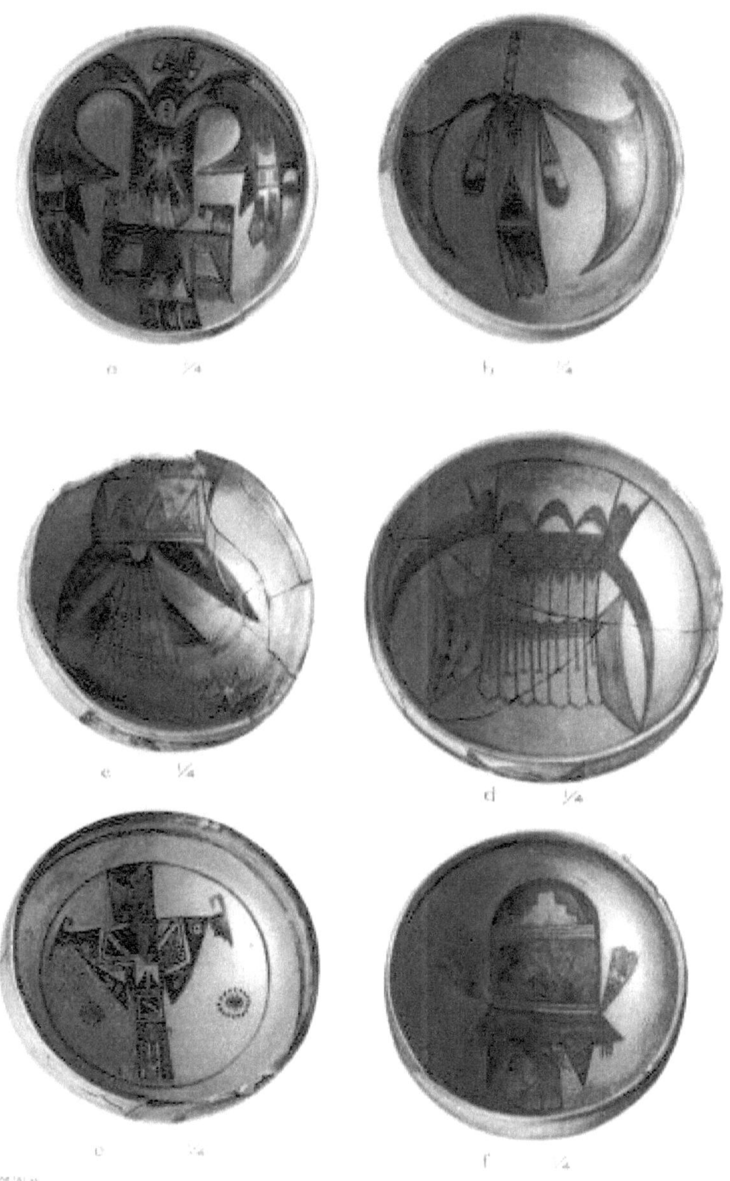

Food Bowls With Figures Of Birds From Sikyatki

Bearing in mind the picture of this bird, we pass to a second form (plate cxxxviii, *a*), in which we can trace the same parts without difficulty. On a round head

is placed a feathered headdress. The different parts of the outstretched wings are readily homologized even in details in the two figures. There are, for instance, two terminal wing feathers in each wing; the appendages to the shoulder exist in both, and the lateral spurs, exteriorly and interiorly, are represented with slight modifications.

FIG. 272—MAN-EAGLE

The body is ornamented in the same way in both figures. It is continued posteriorly on each side into triangular extensions, and the same is true of its anterior, which in one figure has three curved lines, and in the other a simple crook. There are three tail-feathers in each figure. I believe there can be no doubt that both these designs represent the same idea, and that a mythologic bird was intended in each instance.

The step in conventionalism from the last-mentioned figure of a bird to the next (plate CXLVII, *a*) is even greater than in the former. The head in this picture is square or rectangular, and the wings likewise simple, ending in three incurved triangles without appendages. The tail has five feathers instead of three, in which, however, the same symbolic markings which distinguish tail-feathers are indicated.

The conventionalized wings of this figure are repeated again and again in ancient Tusayan pottery decorations, as one may see by an examination of the various birds shown in the plates. In many instances, however, all the other parts of the bird are lost and nothing but the triangular feathers remain; but as these have the same form, whatever organs are missing, the presumption is that their meaning has not changed.

In passing to the figure of the bird shown in plate cxxxviii, *b*, we find features homologous with those already considered, but also detect considerable modification. The head is elongated, tipped with three parallel lines, but decorated with markings similar to those of the preceding figure. The outstretched wings have a crescentic form, on the anterior horn of which are round spots with parallel lines arising from them. This is a favorite figure in pottery decoration, and is found very abundantly on the exterior of food bowls; it represents highly conventionalized feathers, and should be so interpreted wherever found. The figure of the body of the bird depicted is simple, and the tail is continued into three tail-feathers, as is ordinarily the case in highly conventionalized bird figures.

The most instructive of all the appendages to the body are the club-shape bodies, one on each side, rising from the point of union of the wings and the breast. These are spatulate in form, with a terraced terminal marking. They, like other appendages, represent feathers, but that peculiar kind which is found under the wing is called the breath feather.[144] This feather is still used in certain ceremonials, and is tied to certain prayer offerings. Its ancient symbolism is very clearly indicated in this picture, and is markedly different from that of either the wing or tail feathers, which have a totally different ceremonial use at the present time.

For convenience of comparison, a number of pictures which undoubtedly refer to different birds in ancient interpretations will be grouped in a single series.

Plate cxxxviii, *d*, represents a figure of a bird showing great relative modification of organs when compared with those previously discussed. The head is very much broadened, but the semicircular markings, which occur also on the heads of previously described bird figures, are well drawn. The wings are mere curved appendages, destitute of feather symbols, but are provided with lateral spurs and have knobs at their bases. The body is rectangular; the tail-feathers are numerous, with well-marked symbolism. Perhaps the most striking appendages to the body are the two well-defined extensions of parts of the body itself, which, although represented in other pictures of birds, nowhere reach such relatively large size.

---

[144] In an examination of many figures of ancient vessels where this peculiar design occurs it will be found that in all instances they represent feathers, although the remainder of the bird is not to be found. The same may also be said of the design which represents the tail-feathers. This way of representing feathers is not without modern survival, for it may still be seen in many dolls of mystic personages who are reputed to have worn feathered garments.

BUREAU OF AMERICAN ETHNOLOGY — — SEVENTEENTH ANNUAL RE-
PORT PL. CXXXIX

Food Bowls With Figures Of Birds From Sikyatki

The figure of a bird shown in plate cxxxviii, *c*, is similar in many respects
to that last described. The semicircular markings on the head of the former are

here replaced by triangles, but both are symbolic of rain-clouds. The wings are curved projections, without any suggestion of feathers or basal spurs and knobs. The tail-feathers show nothing exceptional, and the body is bounded posteriorly by triangular extensions, as in figures of birds already described.

The representation of the bird in plate cxxxviii, *e*, has a triangular body continued into two points on the posterior end, between which the tail-feathers are situated. The body is covered with terraced and triangular designs, and the head is rectangular in form. On each side of the bird figure there is a symbol of a flower, possibly the sunflower or an aster.

In the figures of birds already considered the relative sizes of the heads and bodies are not overdrawn, but in the picture of a bird on the food bowl shown in plate cxxxviii, *f*, the head is very much enlarged. It bears a well-marked terraced rain-cloud symbol above triangles of the same meaning. The wings are represented as diminutive appendages, each consisting of two feathers. The body has a triangular extension on each side, and the tail is composed of two comparatively short rectangular feathers. The figure itself could hardly be identified as a representation of a bird were it not for the correspondence, part for part, with figures which are undoubtedly those of birds or flying animals.

A more highly conventionalized figure of a bird than any thus far described is painted on the food bowl reproduced in plate cxl, *b*. The head is represented by a terraced figure similar to those which appear as decorations on some of the other vessels; the wings are simply extended crescents, the tips of which are connected by a band which encircles the body and tail; the body is continued at the posterior end into two triangular appendages, between which is a tail, the feathers of which are not differentiated. On each side of the body, in the space inclosed by the band connecting the tips of the wings, a figure of a dragon-fly appears.

The figure on the food bowl illustrated in plate cxxxix, *c*, may also be reduced to a conventionalized bird symbol. The two pointed objects on the lower rim represent tail-feathers, and the triangular appendages, one on each side above them, the body, as in the designs which have already been described. Above the triangles is a rectangular figure with terraced rain-cloud emblems, a constant feature on the body and head of the bird, and on each side, near the rim of the bowl, occur the primary feathers of the wings. The cross, so frequently associated with designs representing birds, is replaced by the triple intersecting lines in the remaining area. The resemblance of this figure to those already considered is clearly evident after a little study.

The decoration on the food basin presented in plate cxxxix, *a*, is interesting in the study of the evolution of bird designs into conventional forms. In this figure those parts which are identified as homologues of the wings extend wholly across the interior of the food bowl, and have the forms of triangles with smaller triangular spurs at their bases. The wings are extended at right angles to the axis of the body, and taper uniformly to the rim of the bowl. The smaller spurs near the union of the wings and body represent the posterior part of the latter, and between them are the tail-feathers, their number being indicated by three triangles.

There is no representation of a head, although the terraced rain-cloud figure is drawn on the anterior of the body between the wings.

The reduction of the triangular wings of the last figure to a simple band drawn diametrically across the inner surface of the bowl is accomplished in the design shown in plate cxxxix, *b*. At intervals along this line there are arranged groups of blocks, three in each group, representing stars, as will later be shown. The semicircular head has lost all appendages and is reduced to a rain-cloud symbol. The posterior angles of the body are much prolonged, and the tail still bears the markings representing three tail-feathers.

The association of a cross with the bird figure is both appropriate and common; its modified form in this decoration is not exceptional, but why it is appended to the wings is not wholly clear. We shall see its reappearance on other bowls decorated with more highly conventionalized bird figures.

In the peculiar decoration used in the treatment of the food bowl shown in plate cxxxix, *c*, we have almost a return to geometric figures in a conventional representation of a bird. In this case the semblance to wings is wholly lost in the line drawn diametrically across the interior of the bowl. On one side of it there are many crosses representing stars, and on the other the body and tail of a bird. The posterior triangular extensions of the former are continued to a bounding line of the bowl, and no attempt is made to represent feathers in the tail. The rectangular figure, with serrated lower edge and inclosed terraced figures, finds, however, a homologue in the heads and bodies of most of the representations of birds which have been described.

This gradual reduction in semblance to a bird has gone still further in the figure represented in plate cxxxix, *d*, where the posterior end of the body is represented by two spurs, and the tail by three feathers, the triangular rain-clouds still persisting in the rectangular body. In fact, it can hardly be seen how a more conventionalized figure of a bird were possible did we not find in *e* of the same plate this reduction still greater. Here the tail is represented by three parallel lines, the posterior of the body by two dentate appendages, and the body itself by a square.

BUREAU OF AMERICAN ETHNOLOGY — — SEVENTEENTH ANNUAL RE-
PORT PL. CXL

Figures Of Birds From Sikyatki

In plate CXL, *c*, we have a similar conventional bird symbol where two birds, instead of one, are represented. In both these instances it would appear that the diametric band, originally homologous to wings, had lost its former significance.

It must also be pointed out that there is a close likeness between some of these so-called conventionalized figures of birds and those of moths or butterflies. If, for instance, they are compared with the figures of the six designs of the upper surface of the vase shown in plate cxxxv, *b*, we note especially this resemblance. While, therefore, it can hardly be said there is absolute proof that these highly conventionalized figures always represent birds, we may, I think, be sure that either the bird or the moth or butterfly is generally intended.

There are several modifications of these highly conventionalized figures of birds which may be mentioned, one of the most interesting of which is figured in plate cxxxix, *f*. In this representation the two posterior triangular extensions of the body are modified into graceful curves, and the tail-feathers are simply parallel lines. The figure in this instance is little more than a trifid appendage to a broad band across the inner surface of the food bowl. In addition to this highly conventionalized bird figure, however, there are two crosses which represent stars. In this decoration all resemblance to a bird is lost, and it is only by following the reduction of parts that one is able to identify this geometric design with the more elaborate pictures of mythic birds. When questioned in regard to the meaning of this symbol, the best informed Hopi priests had no suggestion to offer.

In all the figures of birds thus far considered, the head, with one or two exceptions, is represented or indicated by symbolic markings. In that which decorates the vessel shown in plate cxl, *a*, we find a new modification; the wings, instead of being attenuated into a diametric line or band, are in this case curved to form a loose spiral. Between them is the figure of a body and the three tail-feathers, while the triangular extensions which generally indicate the posterior of the body are simply two rounded knobs at the point of union of the wings and tail. There is no indication of a head.

The modifications in the figure of the bird shown in the last mentioned pictograph, and the highly conventionalized forms which the wings and other parts assume, give me confidence to venture an interpretation of a strange figure shown in plate cxli, *a*. This picture I regard as a representation of a bird, and I do so for the following resemblances to figures already studied. The head of the bird, as has been shown, is often replaced by a terraced rain-cloud symbol. Such a figure occurs in the pictograph under consideration, where it occupies the position of the head. On either side of what might be regarded as a body we find, at the anterior end, two curved appendages which so closely resemble similarly placed bodies in the pictograph last discussed that they are regarded as representations of wings. These extensions at the posterior end of the body are readily comparable with prolongations in that part on which we have already commented. The tail, although different from that in figures of birds thus far discussed, has many points of resemblance to them. The two circles, one on each side of the bird figure, are important additions which are treated in following pages.[145]

---

[145] At the present time the circle is the totemic signature of the Earth people, representing the horizon, but it has likewise various other meanings. With certain appendages it is the disk of the sun — and there are ceremonial paraphernalia, as annulets, placed on sand pictures or tied to helmets, which may be represented by a simple ring. The meaning of

From the study of the conventionalized forms of birds which I have outlined above it is possible to venture the suggestion that the star-shape figure shown in plate CLXVII, *b*, may be referred to the same group, but in this specimen we appear to have duplication, or a representation of the bird symbol repeated in both semi-circles of the interior of the bowl. Examining one of these we readily detect the two tail-feathers in the middle, with the triangular end of the body on each side. The lateral appendages duplicated on each side correspond with the band across the middle of the bowl in other specimens, and represent highly conventionalized wings. The middle of this compound figure is decorated with a cross, and in each quadrant there is a row of the same emblems, equidistant from one another.

It would be but a short step from this figure to the ancient sun symbol with which the eagle and other raptorial birds are intimately associated. The figure represented in plate CXXXIII, *c*, is a symbolic bird in which the different parts are directly comparable with the other bird pictographs already described. One may easily detect in it the two wings, the semicircular rain-cloud figures, and the three tail-feathers. As in the picture last considered, we see the two circles, each with a concentric smaller circle, one on each side of the mythic bird represented. Similar circular figures are likewise found in the zone surrounding the centrally placed bird picture.

In the food bowl illustrated in plate CXLI, *b*, we find the two circles shown, and between them a rectangular pictograph the meaning of which is not clear. The only suggestion which I have in regard to the significance of this object is that it is an example of substitution—the substitution of a prayer offering to the mythic bird represented in the other bowls for a figure of the bird itself. This interpretation, however, is highly speculative, and should be accepted only with limitations. I have sometimes thought that the prayer-stick or paho may originally have represented a bird, and the use of it is an instance of the substitution[146] of a symbolic effigy of a bird, a direct survival of the time when a bird was sacrificed to the deity addressed.

---

these circles in the bowl referred to above is not clear to me, nor is my series of pictographs sufficiently extensive to enable a discovery of its significance by comparative methods. A ring of meal sometimes drawn on the floor of a kiva is called a "house," and a little imagination would easily identify these with the mythic houses of the sky-bird, but this interpretation is at present only fanciful.

[146] The *paho* is probably a substitution of a sacrifice of corn or meal given as homage to the god addressed.

Food Bowls With Figures Of Birds And Feathers From Sikyatki

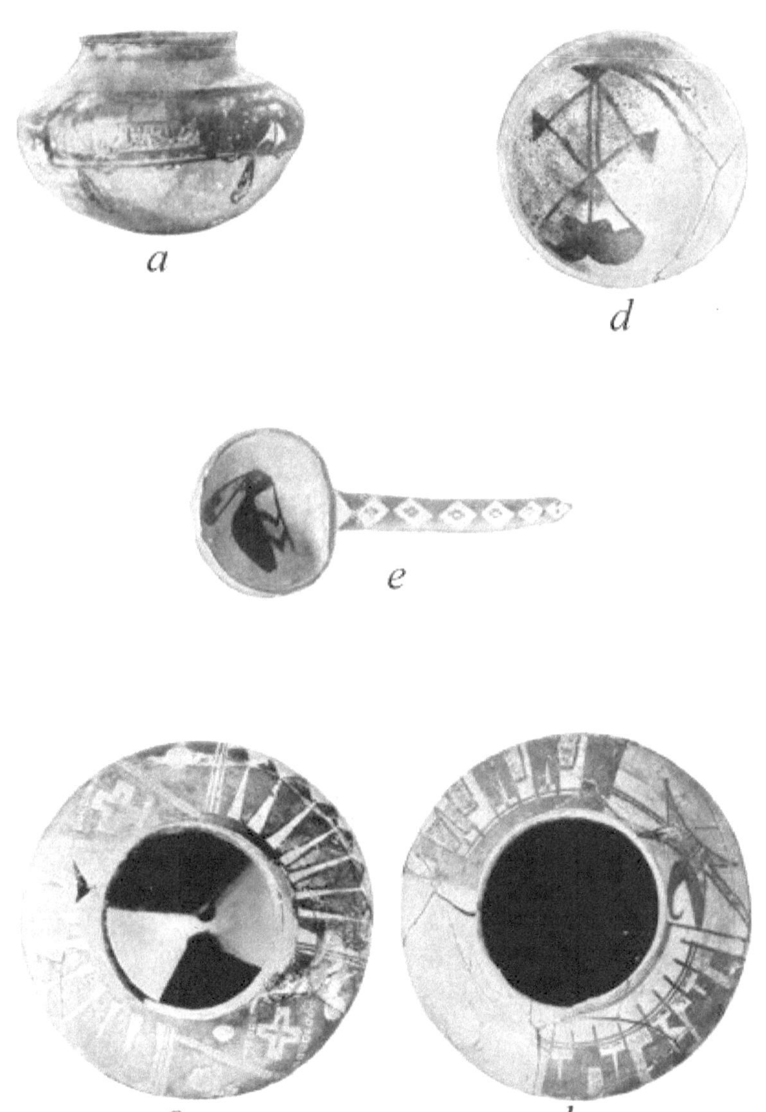

BUREAU OF AMERICAN ETHNOLOGY — — SEVENTEENTH ANNUAL RE-
PORT PL. CXLII

Vases, Bowl, And Ladle, With Figures Of Feathers, From Sikyatki

The studies of the conventional bird figures which are developed in the preceding pages make it possible to interpret one of the two pictures on the food bowl
represented in plate CLII, while the realistic character of the smaller figure leaves
no question that we can rightly identify this also as a bird. In the larger figure
the wings are of unequal size and are tipped with appendages of a more or less

decorative nature. The posterior part of the body is formed of two triangular extensions, to which feathers are suspended, and the tail is composed of three large pointed feathers. The head bears the terraced rain-cloud designs almost universal in pictographs of birds.

It is hardly necessary for me to indicate the head, body, wings, and legs of the smaller figure, for they are evidently avian, while the character of the beak would indicate that a parrot or raptorial genus was intended. The same beak is found in the decoration of a vase with a bird design, which will later be considered.

From an examination of the various figures of birds on the Sikyatki pottery, and an analysis of the appendages to the wings, body, and legs, it is possible to determine the symbolic markings characteristic of two different kinds of feathers, the large wing or tail feathers and the so-called breath or body feathers. There is therefore no hesitation, when we find an object of pottery ornamented with these symbols, in interpreting them as feathers. Such a bowl is that shown in plate CXLI, *c*, in which we find a curved line to which are appended three breast feathers. This curved band from which they hang may take the form of a circle with two pendent feathers as in plate CXLI, *d*.

In the design on the bowl figured in plate CXLI, *e*, tail-feathers hang from a curved band, at each extremity of which is a square design in which the cross is represented. It has been suggested that this represents the feathered rainbow, a peculiar conception of both the Pueblo and the Navaho Indians. The design appearing on the small food bowl represented in plate CXLI, *f*, is no doubt connected in some way with that last mentioned, although the likeness between the appendages to the ring and feathers is remote. It is one of those conventionalized pictures, the interpretation of which, with the scanty data at hand, must be largely theoretical.

Figures of feathers are most important features in the decoration of ancient Sikyatki pottery, and their many modifications may readily be seen by an examination of the plates. In modern Tusayan ceremonials the feather is appended to almost all the different objects used in worship; it is essential in the structure of the *tiponi* or badge of the chief, without which no elaborate ceremony can be performed or altar erected; it adorns the images on the altars, decorates the heads of participants, is prescribed for the prayer-sticks, and is always appended to aspergills, rattles, and whistles.

In the performance of certain ceremonials water from sacred springs is used, and this water, sometimes brought from great distances, is kept in small gourd or clay vases, around the necks of which a string with attached feathers is tied. Such a vase is the so-called *patne* which has been described in a memoir on the Snake ceremonies at Walpi.[147] The artistic tendency of the ancient people of Sikyatki apparently exhibited itself in painting these feathers on the outside of similar small vases. Plate CXLII, *a*, shows one of these vessels, decorated with an elaborate design with four breath-feathers suspended from the equator. (See also figure 273.) On

[147] *Journal of American Ethnology and Archæology*, vol. IV. These water gourds figure conspicuously in many ceremonies of the Tusayan ritual. The two girls personating the Corn-maids carry them in the Flute observance, and each of the Antelope priests at Oraibi bears one of these in the Antelope or Corn dance.

the vases shown in plate CXLII, *b*, *c*, are found figures of tail-feathers arranged in two groups on opposite sides of the rim or orifice. One of these groups has eight, the other seven, figures of these feathers, and on the two remaining quadrants are the star emblems so constantly seen in pottery decorated with bird figures. The upper surface of the vase (figure 274) shows a similar arrangement, although the feathers here are conventionalized into triangular dentations, seven on one side and three on the other, individual dentations alternating with rectangular designs which suggest rain-clouds. This vase (plate CXLIII, *a*, *b*) is also striking in having a well-drawn figure of a bird in profile, the head, wings, tail, and legs suggesting a parrot. The zone of decoration of this vessel, which surrounds the rows of feathers, is strikingly complicated, and comprises rain-cloud, feather, and other designs.

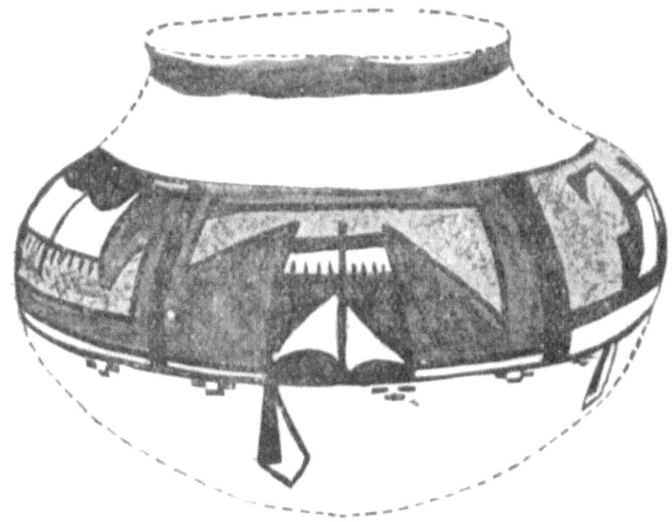

FIG. 273—PENDENT FEATHER ORNAMENTS ON A VASE.

In a discussion of the significance of the design on the food bowl represented in plate CXXXIX, *a*, *b*, I have shown ample reason for regarding it a figure of a highly conventionalized bird. On the upper surface of the vase (plate CXLIV, *a*, *b*) are four similar designs, representing birds of the four cardinal points, one on each quadrant. The wings are represented by triangular extensions, destitute of appendages but with a rounded body at their point of juncture with the trunk. Each bird has four tail-feathers and rain-cloud symbols on the anterior end of the body. As is the case with the figures on the food basins, there are crosses representing stars near the extended wings. A broad band connects all these birds, and terraced rain-cloud symbols, six in number and arranged in pairs, fill the peripheral sections between them. This vase, although broken, is one of the most beautiful and instructive in the rich collection of Sikyatki ceramics.

BUREAU OF AMERICAN ETHNOLOGY — — SEVENTEENTH ANNUAL RE-
PORT PL. CXLIII

Vase With Figures Of Birds From Sikyatki

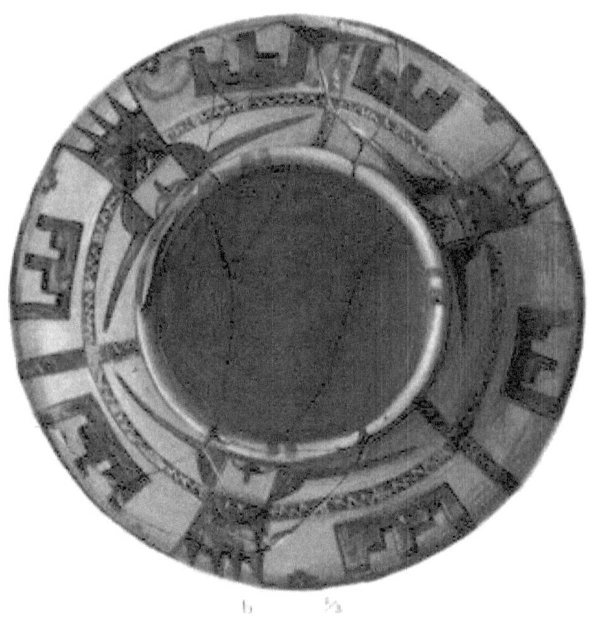

BUREAU OF AMERICAN ETHNOLOGY—— SEVENTEENTH ANNUAL RE-
PORT PL. CXLIV

Vase With Figures Of Birds From Sikyatki

BUREAU OF AMERICAN ETHNOLOGY — — SEVENTEENTH ANNUAL RE-
PORT PL. CXLV

Vases With Figures Of Birds From Sikyatki

FIG. 274—UPPER SURFACE OF VASE WITH BIRD DECORATION

I have not ventured, in the consideration of the manifold pictures of birds on ancient pottery, to offer an interpretation of their probable generic identification. There is no doubt, however, that they represent mythic conceptions, and are emblematic of birds which figured conspicuously in the ancient Hopi Olympus. The modern legends of Tusayan are replete with references to such bird-like beings which play important rôles and which bear evidence of archaic origins. There is, however, one fragment of a food bowl which is adorned with a pictograph so realistic and so true to modern legends of a harpy that I have not hesitated to affix to it the name current in modern Tusayan folklore. This fragment is shown in figure 275.

FIG. 275—KWATAKA EATING AN ANIMAL

According to modern folklore there once lived in the sky a winged being called Kwataka, or Man-eagle, who sorely troubled the ancients. He was ultimately slain by their War god, the legends of which have elsewhere been published. There is a pictograph of this monster near Walpi,[148] and pictures of him, as he exists in modern conceptions, have been drawn for me by the priests. These agree so closely with the pictograph and with the representation on the potsherd from Sikyatki, that I regard it well-nigh proven that they represent the same personage. The head is round and bears two feathers, while the star emblem appears in the eye. The wing and the stump of a tail are well represented, while the leg has three talons, which can only be those of this monster. He holds in his grasp some animal form which he is represented as eating. Across the body is a kilt, or ancient blanket, with four diagonal figures which are said to represent flint arrowheads. It is a remarkable fact that these latter symbols are practically the same as those used by Nahuatl people for obsidian arrow- or spearpoints. In Hopi lore Kwataka wore a garment of arrowpoints, or, according to some legends, a flint garment, and his

[148] "A few Tusayan Pictographs;" *American Anthropologist*, Washington, January, 1892.

wings are said to have been composed of feathers of the same material.

Bowls And Potsherd With Figures Of Birds From Sikyatki

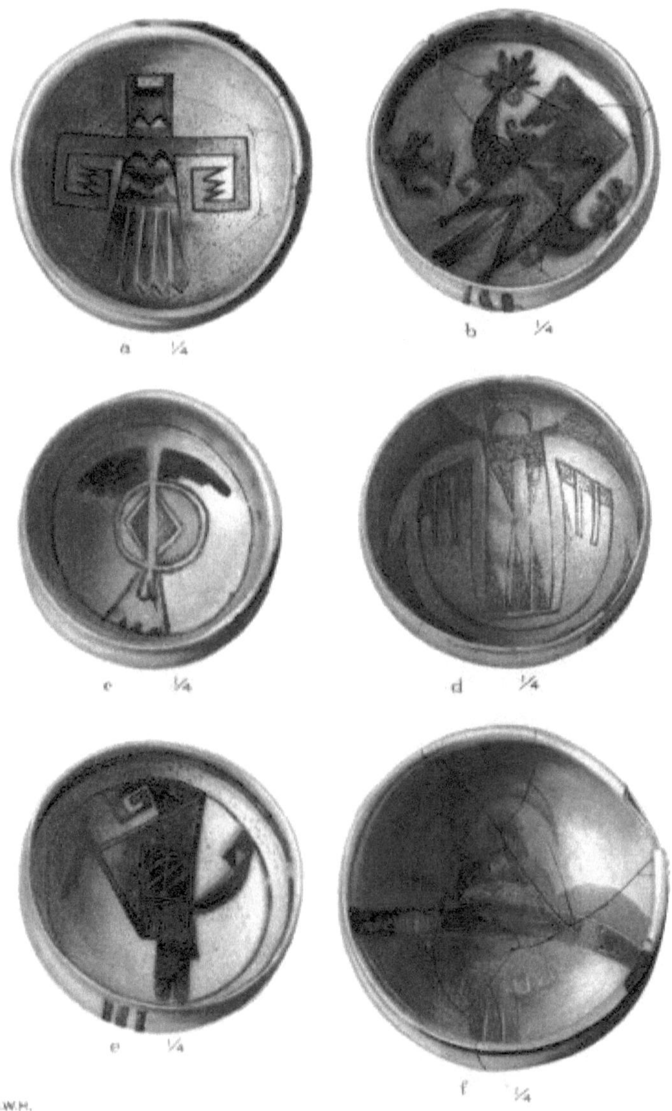

BUREAU OF AMERICAN ETHNOLOGY — — SEVENTEENTH ANNUAL RE-
PORT PL. CXLVII

Food Bowls With Figures Of Birds, From Sikyatki

From the pose of the figure and the various details of its symbolism there can
be little doubt that the ancient Sikyatki artists intended to represent this monster,
of which the modern Hopi rarely speak, and then only in awe. Probably several
other bird figures likewise represent Kwataka, but in none of these do the symbols
conform so closely to legends of this monster which are still repeated in the Tusay-

an villages. The home of Kwataka is reputed to be in the sky, and consequently figures of him are commonly associated with star and cloud emblems; he is a god of luck or chance, hence it is not exceptional to find figures of gaming implements[149] in certain elaborate figures of this monster.

By far the most beautiful of the many food bowls from Sikyatki, and, I believe, the finest piece of prehistoric aboriginal pottery from the United States, is that figured in plate CXLVI, *d*. This remarkable object, found with others in the sands of the necropolis of this pueblo, several feet below the surface, is decorated with a highly conventional figure of a bird in profile, but so modified that it is difficult to determine the different parts. The four appendages to the left represent the tail; the two knobs at the right the head, but the remaining parts are not comprehensible. The delicacy of the detailed crosshatching on the body is astonishing, considering that it was drawn freehand and without pattern. The coloring is bright and the surface glossy.

The curved band from which this strange figure hangs is divided into sections by perpendicular incised lines, which are connected by zigzag diagonals. The signification of the figure in the upper part of the bowl is unknown. While this vessel is unique in the character of its decoration, there are others of equal fineness but less perfect in design. Competent students of ceramics have greatly admired this specimen, and so fresh are the colors that some have found it difficult to believe it of ancient aboriginal manufacture. The specimen itself, now on exhibition in the National Museum, gives a better idea of its excellence than any figure which could be made. This specimen, like all the others, is in exactly the same condition as when exhumed, save that it has been wiped with a moist cloth to clean the traces of food from its inner surface. All the pottery found in the same grave is of the finest character, and although no two specimens are alike in decoration, their general resemblances point to the same maker. This fact has been noticed in several instances, although there were many exceptional cases where the coarsest and most rudely painted vessels were associated with the finest and most elaborately decorated ware.

The ladle illustrated in plate CXLII, *e*, is one of the most beautiful in the collection. It is decorated with a picture of an unknown animal with a single feather on the head. The eyes are double and the snout continued into a long stick or tube, on which the animal stands. While the appendage to the head is undoubtedly a feather and the animal recalls a bird, I am in doubt as to its true identification. The star emblems on the handle of the ladle are in harmony with known pictures of birds.

The feather decoration on the broken ladle shown in plate CXXXI, *f*, is of more than usual interest, although it is not wholly comprehensible. The representations include rain-cloud symbols, birds, feathers, and falling rain. The medially placed design, with four parallel lines arising from a round spot, is interpreted as a feather design, and the two triangular figures, one on each side, are believed to represent birds.

The design on the food bowl depicted in plate CXXXI, *e*, is obscure, but in it

[149] A beautiful example of this kind was found at Homolobi in the summer of 1896.

feather and star symbols predominate. On the inside of the ladle shown in plate cxxxi, *c*, there is a rectangular design with a conventionalized bird at each angle. The reduction of the figure of a bird to head, body, and two or more tail-feathers occurs very constantly in decorations, and in many instances nothing remains save a crook with appended parallel lines representing feathers. Examples of this kind occur on several vessels, of which that shown in plate cxlv, *a*, is an example.

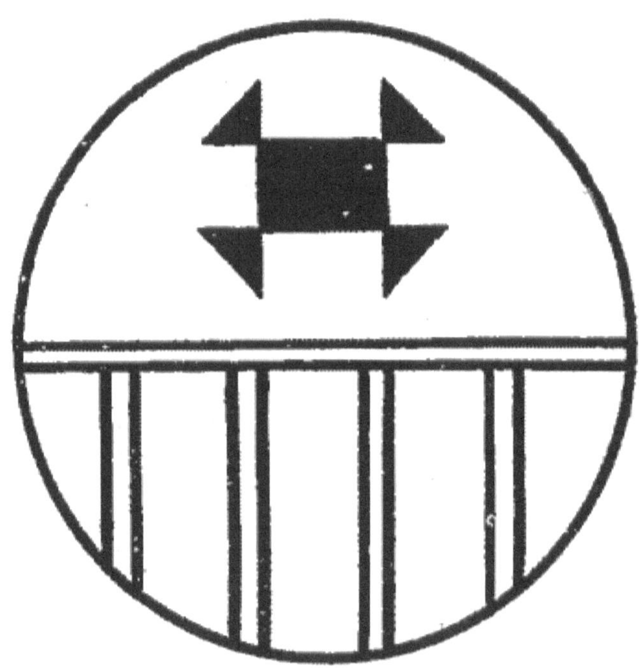

FIG. 276—DECORATION ON THE BOTTOM OF PLATE CXLVI, F

There are many pictures of birds and feathers where the design has become so conventionalized that it is very difficult to recognize the intention of the decorator. Plate cxlvii, *f*, shows one of these in which the feather motive is prominent and an approximation to a bird form evident. The wings are shown with a symmetric arrangement on the sides of the tail, while the latter member has the three feathers which form so constant a feature in many bird symbols. In *b* of the same plate there is shown a more elaborated bird figure, also highly modified, yet preserving many of the parts which have been identified in the design last described.

The beautiful design shown in plate cxlvi, *e*, represents a large breath feather with triangular appendages on the sides, recalling the posterior end of the body of the bird figures above discussed.

The interior of the saucer illustrated in plate clxvi, *f*, is decorated with feather symbols and four triangles. The remaining figures of this plate have already been considered.

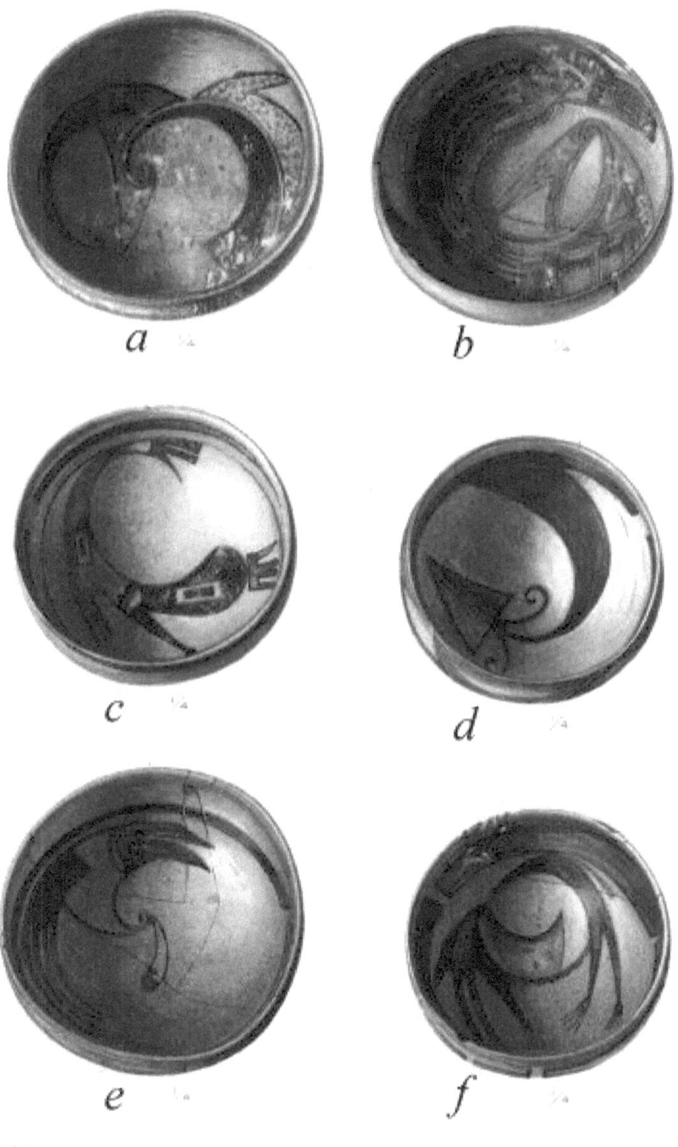

BUREAU OF AMERICAN ETHNOLOGY — — SEVENTEENTH ANNUAL RE-PORT PL. CXLVIII

Food Bowls With Symbols Of Feathers From Sikyatki

BUREAU OF AMERICAN ETHNOLOGY — — SEVENTEENTH ANNUAL RE-
PORT PL. CXLIX

Food Bowls With Symbols Of Feathers From Sikyatki

The figures on the vessel shown in plate CLXVII are so arranged that there can
be little question of their homologies, and from comparisons it is clear that they
should all be regarded as representations of birds. There appears no necessity of
discussing figures *a* and *b* of the plate in this interpretation. In figure *c* the center

of the design becomes circular, recalling certain sun symbols, and the tail-feathers are readily recognized on one side. I am by no means sure, however, that the lateral terraced appendages at the opposite pole are representations of wings, but such an interpretation can not be regarded as a forced one. Figure *d* shows the three tail-feathers, lateral appendages suggestive of wings, and a square body with the usual decorations of the body and head of a bird. The design shown in figure *f* suggests in many ways a sun-bird, and is comparable with those previously studied and illustrated. There is no question of the homologues of tail, head, and wings. The meridional band across the bowl is similar to those already discussed, and its relationship to the head and tail of the bird identical. This design is interpreted as that of one of the numerous birds associated with the sun. The crescentic extension above what is apparently the head occurs in many bird figures and may represent a beak.

Many food bowls from Sikyatki are ornamented on their interior with highly conventionalized figures, generally of curved form, in which the feather is predominant. Many of these are shown in plates CXLVIII to CLVII, inclusive, and in studying them I have found it very difficult to interpret the symbolism, although the figures of feathers are easy to find in many of them. While my attempt at decipherment is not regarded as final, it is hoped that it may at least reveal the important place which the feather plays in Tusayan ceramic decoration.

Plate CXLVIII, *a*, shows the spiral ornament worn down to its lowest terms, with no hint of the feather appendage, but its likeness in outline to those designs where the feather occurs leads me to introduce it in connection with those in which the feather is more prominent. Figure *b* of the same plate represents a spiral figure with a bird form at the inner end, and a bundle of tail-feathers at the outer extremity. On this design there is likewise a figure of the dragon-fly and several unknown emblems. Figure *c* has at one extremity a trifid appendage, recalling a feather ornament on the head of a bird shown in plate CXXXVIII, *a*. Figure *d* has no conventionalized feather decoration, but the curved line terminates with a triangle. Its signification is unknown to me. For several reasons the design in *e* reminds me of a bird; it is accompanied by three crosses, which are almost invariably found in connection with bird figures, and at the inner end there is attached a breath feather. This end of the figure is supposed to be the head, as will appear by later comparative studies. The bird form is masked in *f*, but the feather designs are prominent. This bowl is exceptional in having an encircling band broken at two points, one of the components of which is red, the other black.

Feather designs are conspicuous in plate CXLIX, *a*, *b*, in the former of which curved incised lines are successfully used. In *c*, however, is found the best example of the use of incised work as an aid in pottery decoration, for in this specimen there are semicircles, and rings with four triangles, straight lines, and circles. The symbolism of the whole figure has eluded analysis. Figure *d* has no feather symbols, but *e* may later be reduced to a circle with feathers. The only symbols in the design shown in *f* which are at all recognizable are the two zigzag figures which may have been intended to represent snakes, lightning, or tadpoles.

When the design in plate CL, *a*, is compared with the beautiful bowl shown in plate cxlvi, *d*, a treatment of somewhat similar nature is found. It is believed that both represent birds drawn in profile; the four bands (*a*) are tail-feathers, while the rectangle represents the body and the curved appendage a part of the head. From a similarity to modern figures of a turkey feather, it is possible that the triangle at the end of the curved appendage is the feather of this bird. An examination of *b* leads to the conclusion that the inner end of the spiral represents a bird's head. Two eyes are represented therein, and from it feathers are appended. The parallel marks on the body are suggestive of similar decorations on the figure of the Plumed Snake painted on the kilts of the Snake priests of Walpi. The star emblems are constant accompaniments of bird designs. Figure *c* has, in addition to the spiral, the star symbols and what appears to be a flower. The design shown in *d* is so exceptional that it is here represented with the circular forms. It will be seen that there are well-marked feathers in its composition. Figure *f* is made up of several bird forms, feathers, rectangles, and triangles, combined in a complicated design, the parts of which may readily be interpreted in the light of what has already been recorded.

The significance of the spiral in the design on plate cli, *a*, is unknown. It is found in several pictures, in some of which it appears to have avian relationship. Figure *b* of the same plate is a square terraced design appended to the median line, on which symbolic stars are depicted. As in many bird figures, a star is found on the opposite semicircle. There is a remote likeness between this figure and that of the head of the bird shown in plate cxlv, *d*. Plate cli, *c*, is a compound figure, with four feathers arranged in two pairs at right angles to a median band. The triangular figure associated with them is sometimes found in symbols of the sun. Figure *d* is undoubtedly a bird symbol, as may be seen by a comparison of it with the bird figures shown in plate cxxxviii, *a-f*. There are two tail-feathers, two outstretched wings, and a head which is rectangular, with terraced designs. The cross is triple, and occupies the opposite segment, which is finely spattered with pigment. This trifid cross represents a game played by the Hopi with reeds and is depicted on many objects of pottery. As representations of it sometimes accompany those of birds I am led to interpret the figure (plate clvii, *c*) as that of a bird, which it somewhat resembles. The two designs shown in plate cli, *e, f*, are believed to be decorative, or, if symbolic, they have been so worn by the constant use of the vessel that it is impossible to determine their meaning by comparative methods. Both of these figures show the "line of life" in a somewhat better way than any yet considered.

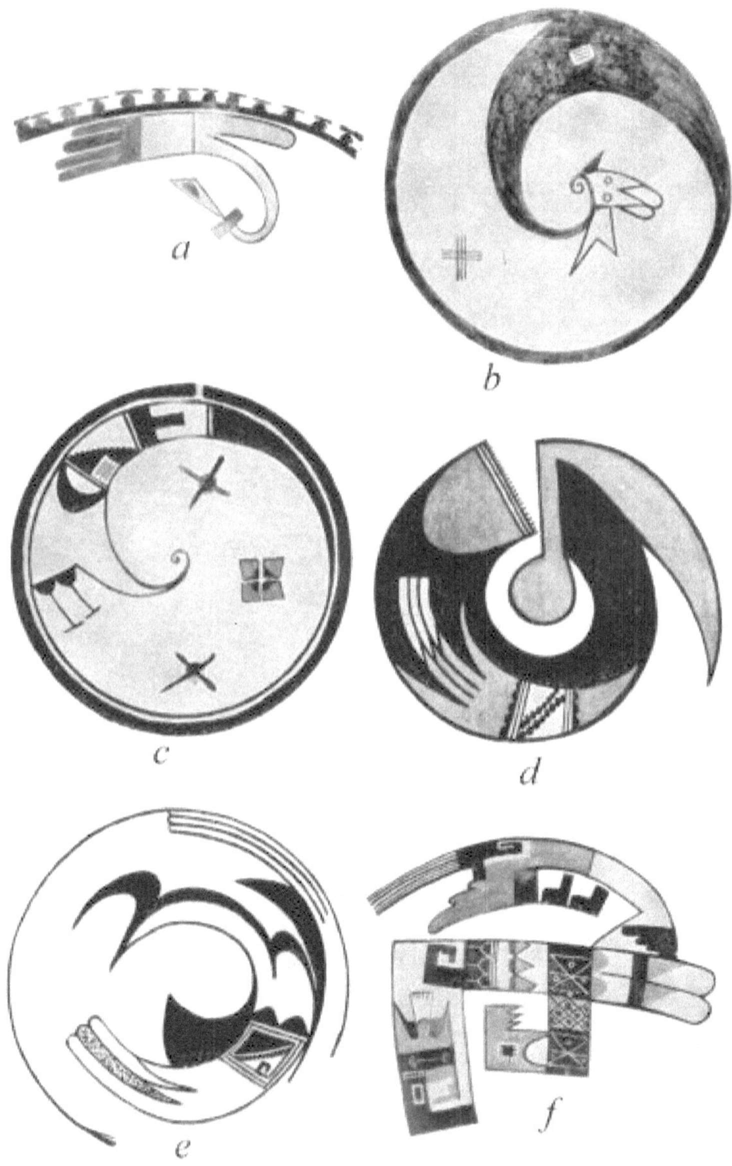

BUREAU OF AMERICAN ETHNOLOGY — — SEVENTEENTH ANNUAL RE-
PORT PL. CL

Figures Of Birds And Feathers From Sikyatki

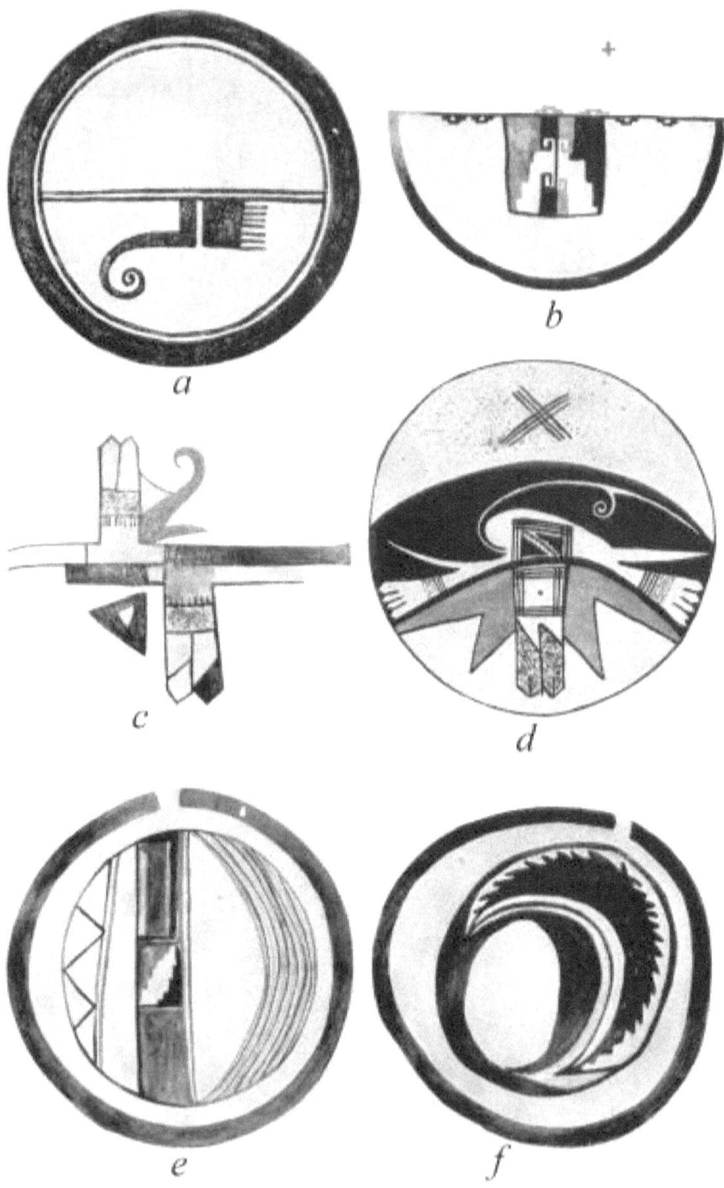

BUREAU OF AMERICAN ETHNOLOGY — — SEVENTEENTH ANNUAL RE-
PORT PL. CLI

Figures Of Birds And Feathers From Sikyatki

In plate CLII, *a*, is shown a compound figure of doubtful significance, made
up of a series of crescents, triangles, and spirals, which, in *c*, are more compactly
joined together, and accompanied by three parallel lines crossing three other lines.
The curved figure shown in *b* represents three feathers; a large one on each side,

inclosing a medially smaller member. In *d* is shown the spiral bird form with appended feathers, triangles, and terraced figures. Figure *f* of this plate is decorated with a design which bears many resemblances to a flower, the peripheral appendages resembling bracts of a sunflower. A somewhat similar design is painted on the side of the helmets of some *katcina* dancers, where the bracts or petals are colored in sequence, with the pigments corresponding to the six directions—north, west, south, east, above, and below. In the decoration on the ancient Sikyatki bowl we find seven peripheral bracts, one of which is speckled. The six groups of stamens(?) are represented between the triangular bracts.

The designs shown in plates CLIII to CLV, inclusive, still preserve the spiral form with attached feathers, some of them being greatly conventionalized or differentiated. In the first of these plates (figure *b*) is represented a bird form with triangular head with four feathers arranged in fan shape. These feathers are different from any which I have been able to find attached to the bodies of birds, and are thus identified from morphological rather than from other reasons.

The body of the conventionalized bird is decorated with terraced figures, spirals, flowers, and other designs arranged in a highly complicated manner. From a bar connecting the spiral with the encircling line there arises a tuft of feathers. Figure *a* of the same plate is characterized by a medially placed triangle and a graceful pendant from which hangs seven feathers. In this instance these structures take the form of triangles and pairs of lines. The relation of these structures to feathers would appear highly speculative, but they have been so interpreted for the following reason: If we compare them with the appendages represented in the design on the vase shown in CXLIII, *b*, we find them the same in number, form, and arrangement; the triangles in the design on this vase are directly comparable with the figures in plate CXLIII, *b*, in the same position, which are undoubtedly feathers, as has been shown in the discussion of this figure. Consequently, although the triangles on the pendant in plate CLIII, *a*, appear at first glance to have no relation to the prescribed feather symbol, morphology shows their true interpretation. The reduction of the wing feather to a simple triangular figure is likewise shown in several other pictures on food vessels, notably in the figure, undoubtedly of a bird, represented in plate CXLVI, *a*.

In the two figures forming plate CLIV are found simple bird symbols and feather designs very much conventionalized. The same is true of the two figures given in plate CLV.

The vessels illustrated in plate CLVI, *a*, *b*, are decorated with designs of unknown meaning, save that the latter recalls the modification of the feather into long triangular forms. On the outer surface this bowl has a row of tadpoles encircling it in a sinistral direction, or with the center of the bowl on the left. The design of figure *c* shows a bird's head in profile, with a crest of feathers and with the two eyes on one side of the head and a necklace. The triangular figure bears the symbolism of the turkey feather, as at present designated in Tusayan altar paraphernalia. As with other bird figures, there is a representation in red of the triple star.

Figure *d* is the only specimen of a vessel in the conventional form of a bird which was found at Sikyatki; it evidently formerly had a handle. The vessel itself is globular, and the form of the bird is intensified by the designs on its surface. The bird's head is turned to the observer, and the row of triangles represent wing feathers. The signification of the designs on *e* and *f* is unknown to me.

Figures *e* and *f* of plate CLVI are avian decorations, reduced in the case of the former to geometric forms. The triangular figure is a marked feature in the latter design.

The designs represented in plate CLVII are aberrant bird forms. Of these *a* and *b* are the simplest and *c* one of the most complicated. Figure *d* is interpreted as a double bird, or twins with a common head and tails pointing in opposite directions. Figure *e* shows a bird in profile with one wing, furnished with triangular feathers, extended. There is some doubt about the identification of *f* as a bird, but there is no question that the wing, tail, and breath feathers are represented in it. Of the last mentioned there are three, shown by the notch, colored black at their extremities.

VEGETAL DESIGNS

Inasmuch as they so readily lend themselves as a motive of decoration, it is remarkable that the ancient Hopi seem to have used plants and their various organs so sparingly in their pottery painting. Elsewhere, especially among modern Pueblos, this is not the case, and while plants, flowers, and leaves are not among the common designs on modern Tusayan ware, they are often employed. It would appear that the corn plant or fruit would be found among other designs, especially as corn plays a highly symbolic part in mythic conceptions, but we fail to find it used as a decoration on any ancient vessel.

Food Bowls With Bird, Feather, And Flower Symbols From Sikyatki

BUREAU OF AMERICAN ETHNOLOGY — — SEVENTEENTH ANNUAL RE-
PORT PL. CLIII

Food Bowls With Figures Of Birds And Feathers From Sikyatki

In a figure previously described, a flower, evidently an aster or sunflower, appears with a butterfly, and in the bowl shown in plate cxxxiv, *e*, we have a similar
design. This figure evidently represents the sunflower, the seeds of which were
ground and eaten in ancient times. The plant apparently is represented as growing
from the earth and is surrounded by a broad band of red in rudely circular form.
The totem of the earth today among the Hopi is a circle; possibly it was the same
among the ancients, in which case the horizon may have been represented by the
red encircling band, which is accompanied by the crook and the emblem of rain.
The petals are represented by a row of dots and no leaves are shown. From the kinship of the ancient accolents of Sikyatki with the Flute people, it is to be expected

that in their designs figures of asters or sunflowers would appear, for these plants play a not inconspicuous rôle in the ritual of this society which has survived to modern times.

THE SUN

Sun worship plays a most important part in modern Tusayan ritual, and the symbol of the sun in modern pictography can not be mistaken for any other. It is a circle with radiating feathers on the periphery and ordinarily with four lines arranged in quaternary groups. The face of the sun is indicated by triangles on the forehead, two slits for eyes, and a double triangle for the mouth. This symbol, however, is not always used as that of the sun, for in the Oraibi *Powalawû* there is an altar in which a sand picture of the sun has the form of a four-pointed star. The former of these sun symbols is not found on Sikyatki pottery, but there is one picture which closely resembles the latter. This occurs on the bowl illustrated in plate CLXI, *c*. The main design is a four-pointed star, alternating with crosses and surrounded by a zone in which are rectangular blocks. While the identification may be fanciful, its resemblances are highly suggestive. The existence of a double triangle adjacent to this figure on the same bowl, and its likeness to the modern mouth-design of sun pictures, appears to be more than a coincidence, and is so regarded in this identification.

In the design shown in plate CLVIII, *a*, one of the elaborate ancient sun figures is represented. As in modern symbols, the tail-feathers of the periphery of the disk are arranged in the four quadrants, and in addition there are appended to the same points curved figures which recall the objects, identified as stringed feathers, attached to the blanket of the maid (plate CXXIX, *a*). The design on the disk is different from that of any sun emblem known to me, and escapes my interpretation. I have used the distribution of the feathers on the four quadrants as an indication that this figure is a sun symbol, although it must be confessed this evidence is not so strong as might be wished. The triangles at the sides of two feathers indicate that a tail-feather is intended, and for the correlated facts supporting this conclusion the reader is referred to the description of the vessels shown in plate CXXXVIII.

It would appear that there is even more probability that the picture on the bowl illustrated in plate CLVIII, *b*, is a sun symbol. It represents a disk with tail and wing feathers arranged on the periphery in four groups. This recalls the sun emblems used in Tusayan at the present time, although the face of the sun is not represented on this specimen. There is a still closer approximation to the modern symbol of the sun on a bowl in a private collection from Sikyatki.

In plate CLVIII, *c*, the sun's disk is represented with the four clusters of feathers replaced by the extremities of the bodies of four birds, the tail-feathers, for some unknown reason, being omitted. The design on the disk is highly symbolic, and the only modern sun symbol found in it are the triangles, which form the mouth of the face of the sun in modern Hopi symbolism.

One of the most aberrant pictures of the sun, which I think can be identified with probability, is shown in the design on the specimen illustrated in plate CXXXiv, *b*. The reasons which have led me to this identification may briefly be stated as follows:

Among the many supernaturals with which modern Hopi mythology is replete is one called Calako-taka, or the male Calako. In legends he is the husband of the two Corn-maids of like name. The ceremonials connected with this being occur in Sichomovi in July, when four giant personifications enter the village as have been described in a former memoir. The heads of these giants are provided with two curved horns, between which is a crest of eagle tail-feathers.

Two of these giants, under another name, but with the same symbolism, are depicted on the altars of the *katcinas* at Walpi and Mishoñinovi, where they represent the sun. A chief personifying the same supernatural flogs children when they are initiated into the knowledge of the *katcinas*.

The figure on the bowl under discussion has many points of resemblance to the symbolism of this personage as depicted on the altars mentioned. The head has two horns, one on each side, with a crest, apparently of feathers, between them. The eyes and mouth are represented, and on the body there is a four-pointed cross. The meaning of the remaining appendages is unknown, but the likenesses to Calako-taka[150] symbolism are noteworthy and important. The figure on the food bowl illustrated in plate cxxxiv, *c*, is likewise regarded as a sun emblem. The disk is represented by a ring in the center, to which feathers are appended. The triangle, which is still a sun symbol, is shown below a band across the bowl. This band is decorated with highly conventionalized feathers.

---

[150] In this connection the reader is referred to the story, already told in former pages of this memoir, concerning the flogging of the youth by the husband of the two women who brought the Hopi the seeds of corn. It may be mentioned as corroboratory evidence that Calako-taka represents a supernatural sun-bird, that the Tataukyamû priests carry a shield with Tunwup (Calako-taka) upon it in the Soyaluña. These priests, as shown by the etymology of their name, are associated with the sun. In the Sun drama, or Calako ceremony, in July, Calako-takas are personated, and at Zuñi the Shalako is a great winter sun ceremony.

BUREAU OF AMERICAN ETHNOLOGY — — SEVENTEENTH ANNUAL RE-
PORT PL. CLIV

Food Bowls With Figures Of Birds And Feathers From Sikyatki

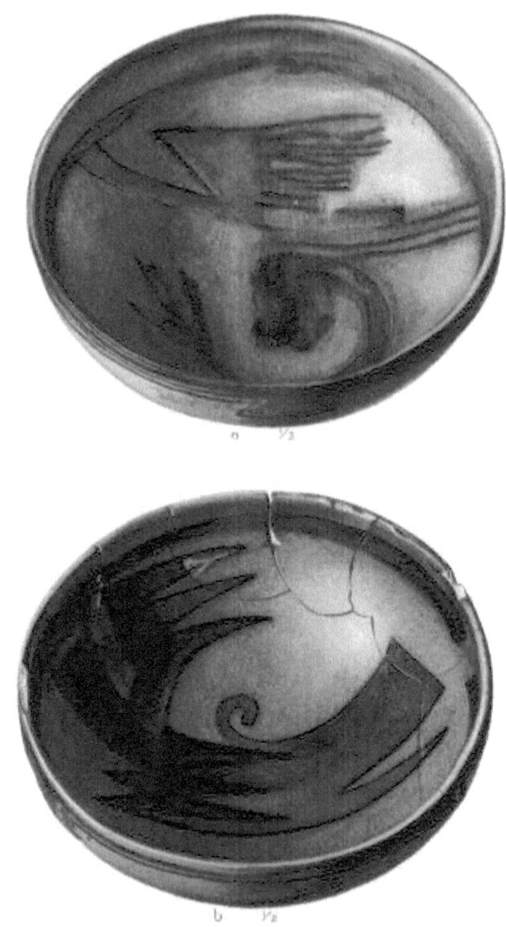

BUREAU OF AMERICAN ETHNOLOGY — — SEVENTEENTH ANNUAL RE-
PORT PL. CLV

Food Bowls With Figures Of Birds And Feathers From Sikyatki

BUREAU OF AMERICAN ETHNOLOGY— — SEVENTEENTH ANNUAL RE-
PORT PL. CLVI

Food Bowls With Figures Of Birds And Feathers From Sikyatki

It may be added that in this figure we have probably the most aberrant
sun-symbol yet recognized, and on that account there is a possibility that the validity of my identification is more or less doubtful.

The three designs shown in plate CLVIII, *c*, *d*, *e*, evidently belong in association
with sun or star symbols, but it is hardly legitimate to definitely declare that such

an interpretation can be demonstrated. The modern Tusayan Indians declare that the equal-arm cross is a symbol of the "Heart of the Sky" god, which, from my studies of the effigies of this personage on various altars, I have good reason to identify with the lightning.

GEOMETRIC FIGURES

Interpretation Of The Figures

Most of the pottery from Sikyatki is ornamented with geometric designs and linear figures, the import of many of which are unknown.

Two extreme views are current in regard to the significance of these designs. To one school everything is symbolic of something or some religious conception; to the other the majority are meaningless save as decorations. I find the middle path the more conservative, and while regarding many of the designs as highly conventionalized symbols, believe that there are also many where the decorator had no thought of symbolism. I have ventured an explanation of a few of the former.

Terraced figures are among the most common rectangular elements in Pueblo ceramic decorations. These designs bear so close a likeness to the modern rain-cloud symbol that they probably may all be referred to this category. Their arrangement on a bowl or jar is often of such a nature as to impart very different patterns. Thus terraced figures placed in opposition to each other may leave zigzag spaces suggesting lightning, but such forms can hardly be regarded as designed for symbols.

Rectangular patterns (plates CLXII-CLXV) are more ancient in the evolution of designs on Tusayan pottery than curved geometric figures, and far outnumber them in the most ancient specimens; but there has been no epoch in the development reaching to modern times when they have been superseded. While there are many specimens of Sikyatki pottery of the type decorated with geometric figures, which bear ornamentations of simple and complex terraced forms, the majority placed in this type are not reducible to stepped or terraced designs, but are modified straight lines, bars, crosshatching, and the like. In older Pueblo pottery the relative proportion of terraced figures is even less, which would appear to indicate that basket-ware patterns were secondary rather than primary decorative forms.

By far the largest element in ancient Tusayan pottery decoration must be regarded as simple geometric lines, triangles, spirals, curves, crosshatching, and the like, some of which are no doubt symbolic, others purely decorative (plate CLXVI). In the evolution of design I am inclined to believe that this was the simplest form, and I find it the most constant in the oldest ware. Rectangular figures are regarded as older than circular figures, and they possibly preceded the latter in evolution, but in many instances both are forms of reversion, highly conventionalized representations of more elaborate figures. Circles and crosses are sometimes combined, the former modified into a wavy line surrounding the latter, as in plate CLIX, *c, d,* where there is a suggestion (*d*) of a sun emblem.

Crosses

A large number of food bowls are decorated with simple or elaborate crosses, stars, and like patterns. Simple crosses with arms of equal length appear on the vessels shown in plate CLIX, *c, d*. There are many similar crosses, subordinate to the main design, in various bowls, especially those decorated with figures of birds and sky deities.

Plate CLX, *a*, exhibits a cruciform design, to the extremities of three arms of which bird figures are attached. In this design there are likewise two sunflower symbols. The modified cross figure in *b* of the same plate, like that just mentioned, suggests a swastica, but fails to be one, and unless the complicated design in figure *c* may be so interpreted, no swastica was found at Sikyatki or Awatobi. Plate CLX, *d*, shows another form of cross, two arms of which are modified into triangles.

On the opening of the great ceremony called *Powamû* or "Bean-planting," which occurs in February in the modern Tusayan villages, there occurs a ceremony about a sand picture of the sun which is called *Powalawû*. The object of this rite is the fructification of all seeds known to the Hopi. The sand picture of the sun which is made at that time is in its essentials identical with the design on the food bowl illustrated in plate CLXI, *c*; consequently it is possible that this star emblem represents the sun, and the occurrence of the eight triangles in the rim, replaced in the modern altar by four concentric bands of differently colored sands, adds weight to this conclusion. The twin triangles outside the main figure are identical with those in the mouth of modern sun emblems. These same twin triangles are arranged in lines which cross at right angles in plate CLXI, *d*, but from their resemblance to figure *b* they possibly have a different meaning.

The most complicated of all the star-shape figures, like the simplest, takes us to sun emblems, and it seems probable that there is a relationship between the two. Plate CLXI, *f*, represents four bundles of feathers arranged in quadrants about a rectangular center. These feathers vary in form and arrangement, and the angles between them are occupied by horn-shape bodies, two of which have highly complicated extremities recalling conventionalized birds.

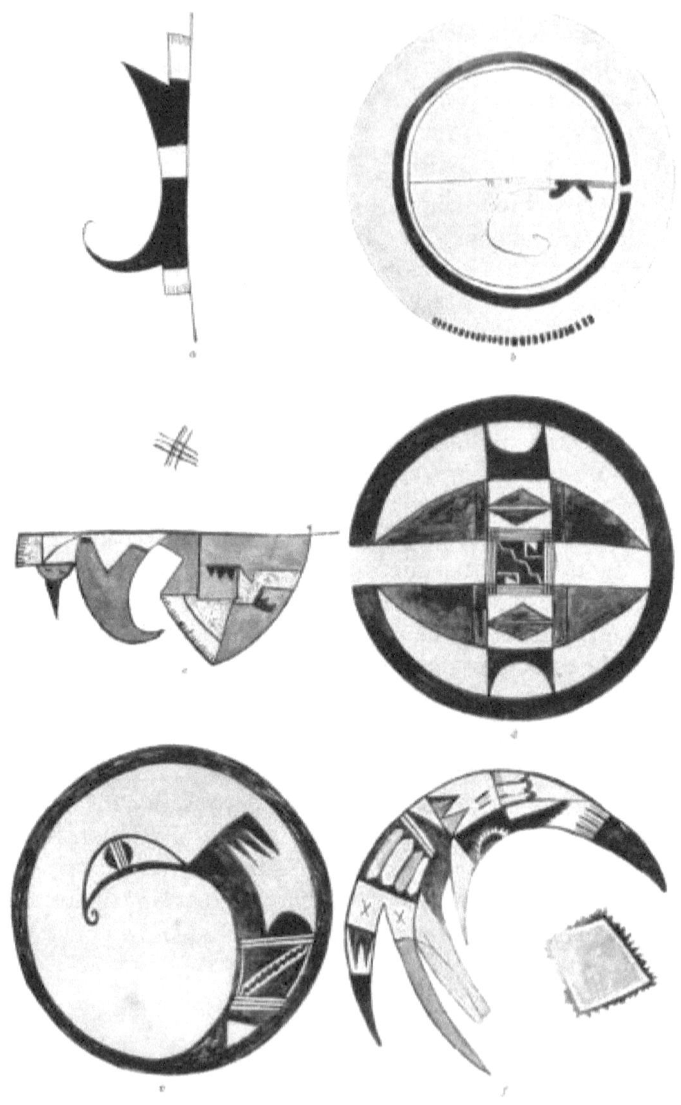

BUREAU Of AMERICAN ETHNOLOGY — — SEVENTEENTH ANNUAL RE-
PORT PL. CLVII

Figures Of Birds And Feathers From Sikyatki

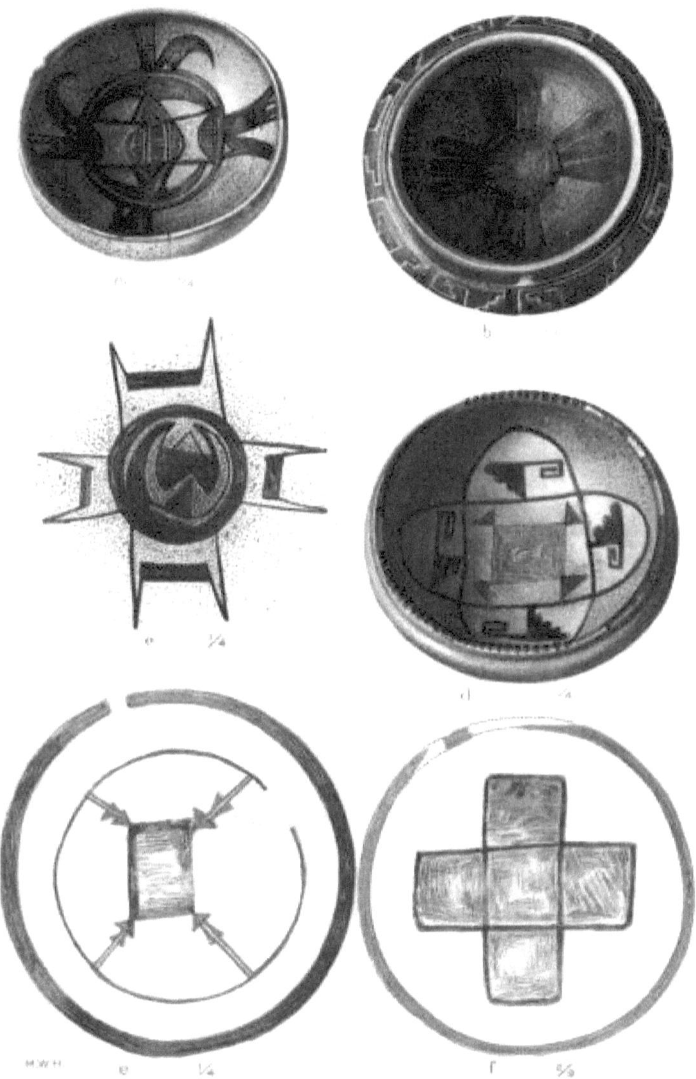

BUREAU OF AMERICAN ETHNOLOGY — — SEVENTEENTH ANNUAL RE-
PORT PL. CLVIII

Food Bowls With Figures Of Sun And Related Symbols From Sikyatki

A large number of crosses are represented in plate CLXII, *d*, in which the remaining semicircle is filled with a tessellated pattern. A spiral line with round
spots at intervals adorns the specimen shown in plate CLXI, *a*. Parallel lines with
similar spots appear on the vessel illustrated in plate CLXII, *e*, and a network of the
same is shown in *f* of the same plate. Plate CLXVII, *b*, represents a compound star.

While simple swasticas are not found on any of the Sikyatki pottery, modified and compound forms are well represented. There are several specimens of figures of the Maltese cross, and one closely approximating the Saint Andrew's cross. It is scarcely necessary to say that the presence of the various kinds of crosses do not necessarily indicate the influence of Semitic or Aryan races, for I have already shown[151] that even cross-shape prayer-sticks were in use among the Pueblos when Coronado first visited them.

Terraced Figures

Among the most common of all geometric designs on ancient Tusayan pottery none excel in variety or number those which I place in the above group. They form the major part of all decoration, and there is hardly a score of ornamented vessels in which they can not be detected. In a typical form they appear as stepped designs, rectangular figures with diagonals continuous, or as triangular designs with steps represented along their sides.

While it is probable that in some instances these figures are simply decorative, with no attempt at symbolism, in other cases without doubt they symbolize rain-clouds, and the same figures are still used with similar intent in modern ceremonial paraphernalia—altars, mask-tablets, and the like. Decorative modifications of this figure were no doubt adopted by artistic potters, thus giving varieties where the essential meaning has been much obscured or lost.

The Crook

Among the forms of geometric designs on ancient Tusayan pottery there are many jars, bowls, and other objects on which a crook, variously modified, is the essential type. This figure is so constant that it must have had a symbolic as well as a decorative meaning. The crook plays an important part in the modern ritual, and is prominent on many Tusayan altars. Around the sand picture of the rain-cloud, for example, we find a row of wooden rods with curved ends, and in the public Snake dance these are carried by participants called the Antelopes. A crook in the form of a staff to which an ear of corn and several feathers are attached is borne by *katcinas* or masked participants in certain rain dances. It is held in the hand by a personage who flogs the children when they are initiated into certain religious societies. Many other instances might be mentioned in which this crozier-like object is carried by important personages. While it is not entirely clear to me that in all instances this crook is a badge of authority, in some cases it undoubtedly represents the standing of the bearer. There are, likewise, prayer offerings in the form of crooks, and even common forms of prayer-sticks have miniature curved sticks attached to them.

Some of the warrior societies are said to make offerings in the form of a crook,

[151] *American Anthropologist*, April, 1895, p. 133. As these cross-shape pahos which are now made in Tusayan are attributed to the Kawaika or Keres group of Indians, and as they were seen at the Keresan pueblo of Acoma in 1540, it is probable that they are derivative among the Hopi; but simple cross decorations on ancient pottery were probably autochthonous.

and a stick of similar form is associated with the gods of war. There is little doubt that some of the crook-form decorations on ancient vessels may have been used as symbols with the same intent as the sticks referred to above. The majority of the figures of this shape elude interpretation. Many of them have probably no definite meaning, but are simply an effective motive of decoration.

In some instances the figure of the crook on old pottery is a symbol of a prayer offering of a warrior society, made in the form of an ancient weapon, allied to a bow.

The Germinative Symbol

The ordinary symbol of germination, a median projection with lateral extensions at the base (plate CXLIX, *e*), occurs among the figures on this ancient pottery. In its simplest form, a median line with a triangle on each side attached to one end, it is a phallic emblem. When this median line becomes oval, and the triangles elongated and curved at the ends, it represents the ordinary squash symbol,[152] also used as an emblem of fertility.

The triangle is also an emblem of germination and of fecundity—the female, as the previously mentioned principle represents the male. The geometric designs on the ancient Sikyatki ware abundantly illustrate both these forms.

Broken Lines

In examining the simple encircling bands of many of the food bowls, jars, and other ceramic objects, it will be noticed that they are not continuous, but that there is a break at one point, and this break is usually limited to one point in all the specimens. Various explanations of the meaning of this failure to complete the band have been suggested, and it is a remarkable fact that it is one of the most widely extended characteristics of ancient pottery decoration in the whole Pueblo area, including the Salado and Gila basins. While in the specimens from Sikyatki the break is simple and confined to one point, in those from other regions we find two or three similar failures in the continuity of encircling lines, and in some instances the lines at the point of separation are modified into spirals, terraces, and other forms of geometric figures. In the more complex figures we find the most intricate variations, which depart so widely from the simple forms that their resemblances are somewhat difficult to follow. A brief consideration of these modifications may aid toward an understanding of the character of certain geometric ornamental motives.

---

[152] In dolls of the Corn-maids this germinative symbol is often found made of wood and mounted on an elaborate tablet representing rain-clouds.

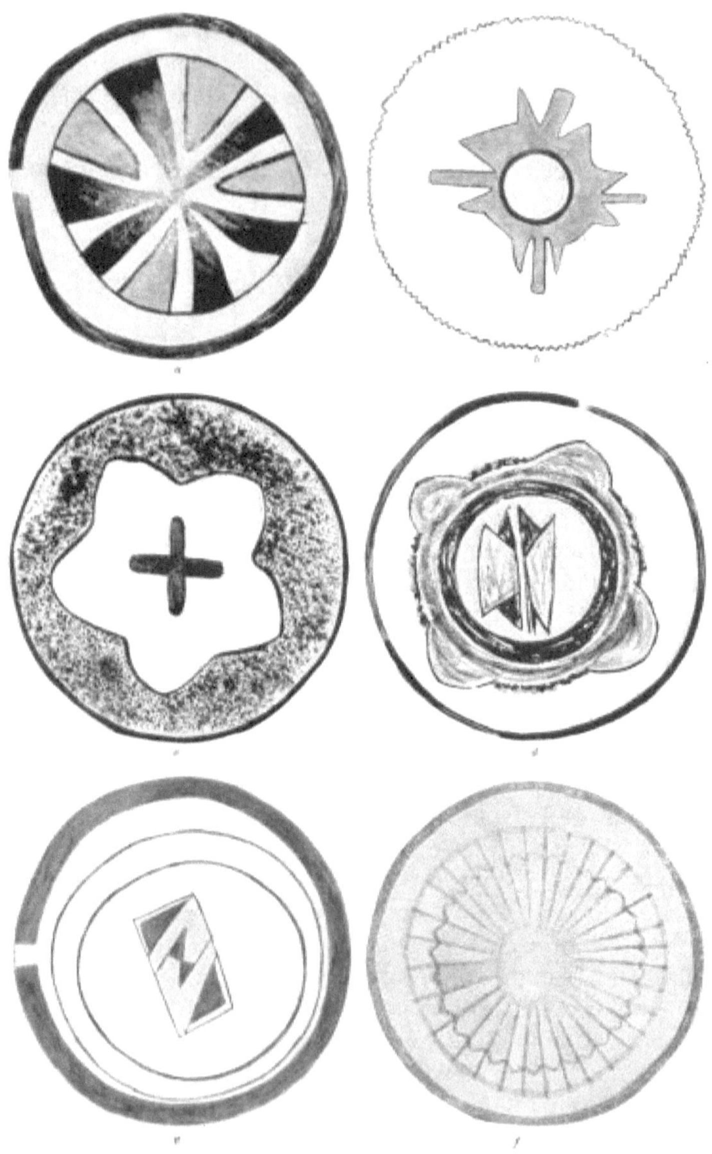

Cross And Related Designs From Sikyatki

BUREAU OF AMERICAN ETHNOLOGY—— SEVENTEENTH ANNUAL REPORT PL. CLX

Cross And Other Symbols From Sikyatki

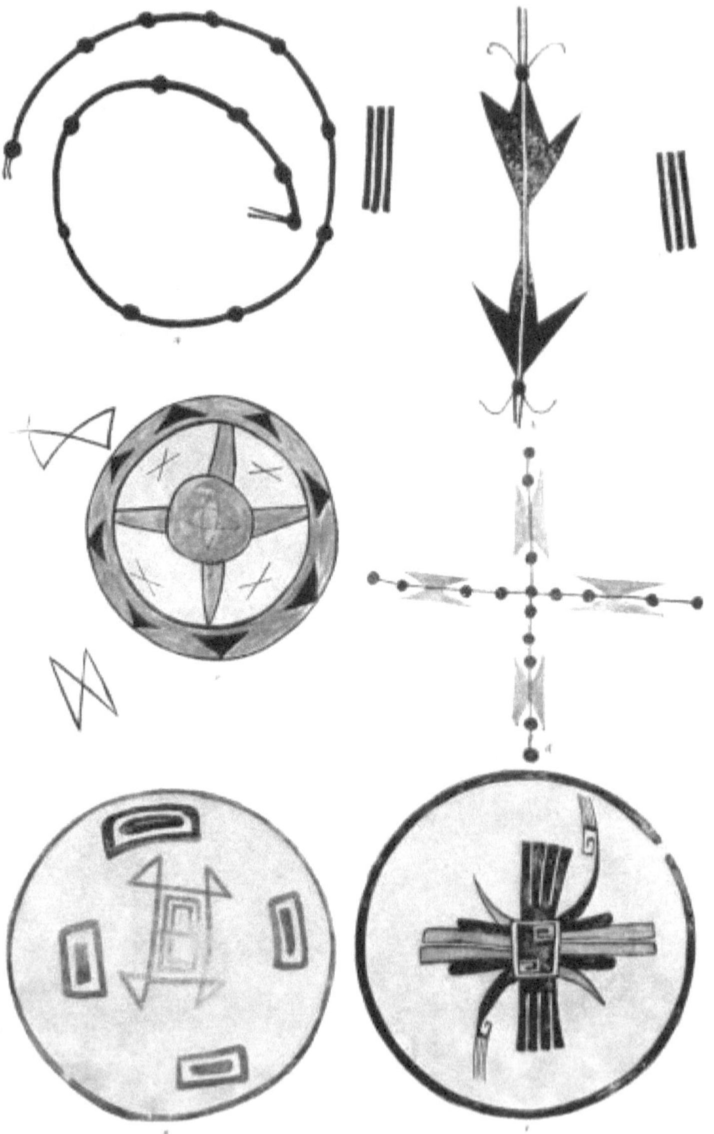

BUREAU OF AMERICAN ETHNOLOGY—— SEVENTEENTH ANNUAL RE-
PORT PL. CLXI

Star, Sun, And Related Symbols From Sikyatki

If any of the interlocking spirals on bowls or vases are traced, it is found that
they do not join at the center of the figure. The same is true when these spirals become frets. There is always a break in the network which they form. This break is
comparable with the hiatus on encircling bands and probably admits of the same

interpretation. In a simple form this motive appears as two crescents or two key patterns with the ends overlapping. This simple ornament, called the friendship sign, is commonly used in the decoration of the bodies of *katcinas*, and has been likened to the interlocking of fingers or hands of the participants in certain dances, the fingers half retracted with inner surfaces approximated, the palms of the hands facing in opposite directions and the wrists at opposite points. If the points be extended into an elaborate key pattern or curved into extended spirals, a complicated figure is produced in which the separation is less conspicuous although always present.

The same points may be modified into terraced figures, the separation then appearing as a zigzag line drawn across the figure, or they may have interlocking dentate or serrate prolongations imparting a variety of forms to the interval between them.[153] In order to trace out these modifications it would be necessary to specify each individual case, but I think that is unnecessary. In other words, the broken line appears to be a characteristic not only of simple encircling bands, but also of all geometric figures in which highly complicated designs extend about the periphery of a utensil.

DECORATIONS ON THE EXTERIOR OF FOOD BOWLS

The decorations on the exterior of the ancient food bowls are in most instances very characteristic and sometimes artistic. Generally they reproduce patterns which are found on the outside of vases and jars and sometimes have a distant relationship to the designs in the interior of the bowl upon which they occur. Usually these external decorations are found only on one side, and in that respect they differ from the modern food bowls, in which nothing similar to them appears.

The characteristics of the external decorations of food bowls are symbolic, mostly geometric, square or rectangular, triangular or stepped figures; curved lines and spirals rarely if ever occur, and human or animal figures are unknown in this position in Sikyatki pottery; the geometric figures can be reduced to a few patterns of marked simplicity.

It is apparent that I can best discuss the variety of geometric designs by considering these external decorations of food vessels at length. From the fact that they are limited to one side, the design is less complicated by repetition and seems practically the same as the more typical forms. It is rarely that two of these designs are found to be exactly the same, and as there appears to be no duplication a classification of them is difficult. Each potter seems to have decorated her ware without regard to the work of her contemporaries, using simple designs but com-

---

[153] Many similarities might be mentioned between the terraced figures used in decoration in Old Mexico and in ancient Tusayan pottery, but I will refer to but a single instance, that of the stuccoed walls of Mitla, Oaxaca, and Teotitlan del Valle. Many designs from these ruins are gathered together for comparative purposes by that eminent Mexicanist, Dr E. Seler, in his beautiful memoir on Mitla (*Wandmalereien von Mitla*, plate x). In this plate exact counterparts of many geometric patterns on Sikyatki pottery appear, and even the broken spiral is beautifully represented. There are key patterns and terraced figures in stucco on monuments of Central America identical with the figures on pottery from Sikyatki.

bining them in original ways. Hence the great variety found even in the grave of the same woman, whose handiwork was buried with her. As, however, the art of the potter degenerated, as it has in later times, the patterns became more alike, so that modern Tusayan decorated earthenware has little variety in ornamentation and no originality in design. Every potter uses the same figures.

FIG. 277—OBLIQUE PARALLEL LINE DECORATION

FIG. 278—PARALLEL LINES FUSED AT ONE POINT

FIG. 279—PARALLEL LINES WITH ZIGZAG ARRANGEMENT

The simplest form of decoration on the exterior of a food bowl is a band encircling it. This line may be complete or it may be broken at one point. The next more complicated geometric decoration is a double or multiple band, which, however, does not occur in any of the specimens from Sikyatki. The breaking up of this multiple band into parallel bars is shown in figure 277. These bars generally have a quadruple arrangement, and are horizontal, vertical, or, as in the illustration, inclined at an angle. They are often found on the lips of the bowls and in a similar position on jars, dippers, and vases. The parallel lines shown in figure 278 are seven in number, and do not encircle the bowl. They are joined by a broad connecting band near one extremity. The number of parallel bands in this decoration is highly suggestive.

BUREAU OF AMERICAN ETHNOLOGY — — SEVENTEENTH ANNUAL REPORT PL. CLXII

Geometric Ornamentation From Sikyatki

Four parallel bands encircle the bowl shown in figure 279, but they are so modified in their course as to form a number of trapezoidal figures placed with alternating sides parallel. This interesting pattern is found only on one vessel.

The use of simple parallel bars, arranged at equal intervals on the outside of food bowls, is not confined to these vessels, for they occur on the margin of vases, cups, and dippers. They likewise occur on ladle handles, where they are arranged in alternate transverse and longitudinal clusters.

FIG. 280—PARALLEL LINES CONNECTED BY MIDDLE BAR.

The combination of two vertical bands connected by a horizontal band, forming the letter H, is an ornamental design frequently occurring on the finest Hopi ware. Figure 280 shows such an H form, which is ordinarily repeated four times about the bowl.

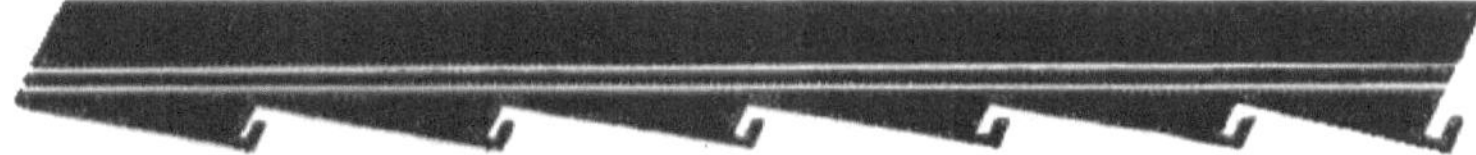

FIG. 281—PARALLEL LINES OF DIFFERENT WIDTH; SERRATE MARGIN

The interval between the parallel bands around the vessel may be very much reduced in size, and some of the bands may be of different width, or otherwise modified. Such a deviation is seen in figure 281, which has three bands, one of which is broad with straight edges, the other with serrate margin and hook-like appendages.

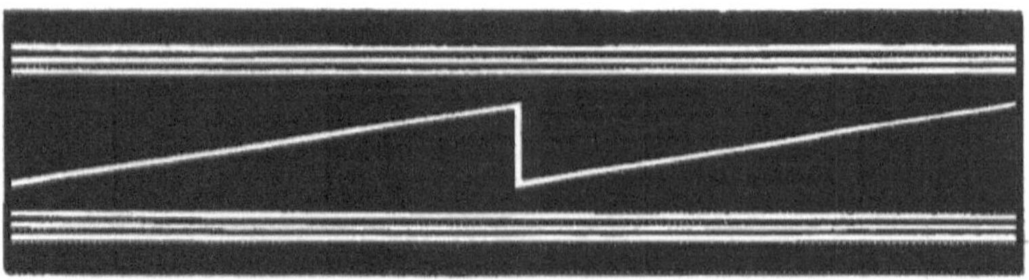

FIG. 282—PARALLEL LINES OF DIFFERENT WIDTH; MEDIAN SERRATE

FIG. 283—PARALLEL LINES OF DIFFERENT WIDTH; MARGINAL SERRATE

In figure 282 eight bands are shown, the marginal broad with edges entire, and the median pair serrated, the long teeth fitting each other in such a way as to impart a zigzag effect to the space which separates them. The remaining four lines, two on each side, appear as black bands on a white ground. It will be noticed that an attempt was made to relieve the monotony of the middle band of figure 282 by the introduction of a white line in zigzag form. A similar result was accomplished in the design shown in figure 283 by rectangles and dots.

FIG. 284—PARALLEL LINES AND TRIANGLES

The modification of the multiple bands in figure 283 has produced a very different decorative form. This design is composed of five bands, the marginal on each side serrate, and the middle band relatively very broad, with diagonals, each containing four round dots regularly arranged. In figure 284 there are many parallel, noncontinuous bands of different breadth, arranged in groups separated by triangles with sides parallel, and the whole united by bounding lines. This is the most complicated form of design where straight lines only are used.

FIG. 285—LINE WITH ALTERNATE TRIANGLES

We have thus far considered modifications brought about by fusion and other changes in simple parallel lines. They may be confined to one side of the food bowl, may repeat each other at intervals, or surround the whole vessel. Ordinarily, however, they are confined to one side of the bowls from Sikyatki.

FIG. 286—SINGLE LINE WITH ALTERNATE SPURS

FIG. 287—SINGLE LINE WITH HOURGLASS FIGURES

Returning to the single encircling band, it is found, in figure 285, broken up into alternating equilateral triangles, each pair united at their right angles. This modification is carried still further in figure 286, where the triangles on each side of the single line are prolonged into oblique spurs, the pairs separated a short distance from each other. In figure 287 there is shown still another arrangement of these triangular decorations, the pairs forming hourglass-shape figures connected by an encircling line passing through their points of junction.

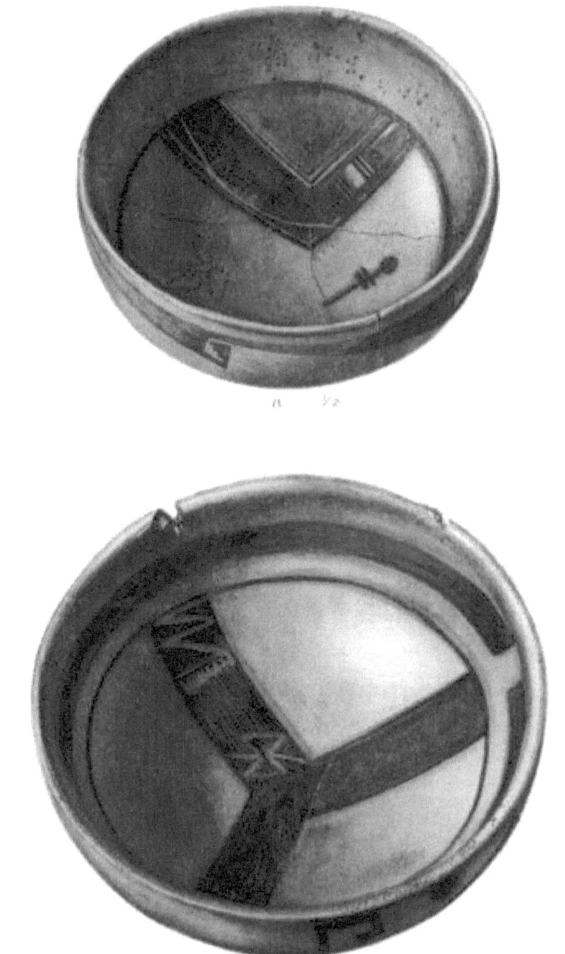

BUREAU OF AMERICAN ETHNOLOGY—— SEVENTEENTH ANNUAL RE-
PORT PL. CLXIII

Food Bowls With Geometric Ornamentation From Sikyatki

FIG. 288—SINGLE LINE WITH TRIANGLES

FIG. 289—SINGLE LINE WITH ALTERNATE TRIANGLES AND OVALS

FIG. 290—TRIANGLES AND QUADRILATERALS

FIG. 291—TRIANGLE WITH SPURS

In figure 288 the double triangles, one on each side of the encircling band, are so placed that their line of separation is lost, and a single triangle replaces the pair. These are connected by the line surrounding the bowl and there is a dot at the smallest angle. In figure 289 there is a similar design, except that alternating with each triangle, which bears more decoration than that shown in figure 288, there are hourglass figures composed of ovals and triangles. The dots at the apex of that design are replaced by short parallel lines of varying width. The triangles and ovals last considered are arranged symmetrically in relation to a simple band. By a reduction in the intervening spaces these triangles may be brought together and the line disappears. I have found no specimen of design illustrating the simplest form of the resultant motive, but that shown in figure 290 is a new combination comparable with it.

The simple triangular decorative design reaches a high degree of complication in figure 290, where a connecting line is absent, and two triangles having their smallest angles facing each other are separated by a lozenge shape figure made up of many parallel lines placed obliquely to the axis of the design. The central part is composed of seven parallel lines, the marginal of which, on two opposite sides, is minutely dentate. The median band is very broad and is relieved by two wavy white lines. The axis of the design on each side is continued into two triangular spurs, rising from a rectangle in the middle of each triangle. This complicated design is the highest development reached by the use of simple triangles. In figure 291, however, we have a simpler form of triangular decoration, in which no element other than the rectangle is employed. In the chaste decoration seen in figure 292 the use of the rectangle is shown combined with the triangle on a simple encircling band. This design is reducible to that shown in figure 290, but is simpler, yet not less effective. In figure 293 there is an aberrant form of design in which the triangle is used in combination with parallel and oblique bands. This form, while one of the simplest in its elements, is effective and characteristic. The triangle predominates in figure 294, but the details are worked out in rectangular patterns, producing the terraced designs so common in all Pueblo decorations. Rectangular figures are more commonly used than the triangular in the decoration of the exterior of the bowls, and their many combinations are often very perplexing to analyze.

FIG. 292—RECTANGLE WITH SINGLE LINE

FIG. 293—DOUBLE TRIANGLE; MULTIPLE LINES

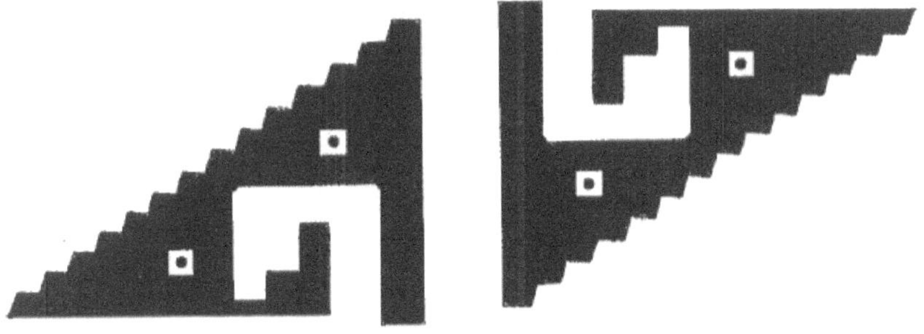

FIG. 294—DOUBLE TRIANGLE; TERRACED EDGES

FIG. 295—SINGLE LINE; CLOSED FRET

BUREAU OF AMERICAN ETHNOLOGY — — SEVENTEENTH ANNUAL RE-
PORT PL. CLXIV

Food Bowls With Geometric Ornamentation From Sikyatki

FIG. 296—SINGLE LINE; OPEN FRET

FIG. 297—SINGLE LINE; BROKEN FRET

FIG. 298—SINGLE LINE; PARTS DISPLACED

In figure 295, starting with the simple encircling band, it is found divided into alternating rectangles. The line is continuous, and hence one side of each rectangle is not complete. Both this design and its modification in figure 296 consist of an unbroken line of equal breadth throughout. In the latter figure, however, the openings in the sides are larger or the approach to a straight line closer. The forms are strictly rectangular, with no additional elements. Figure 297 introduces an important modification of the rectangular motive, consisting of a succession of lines broken at intervals, but when joined are always arranged at right angles.

FIG. 299—OPEN FRET; ATTACHMENT DISPLACED

FIG. 300—SIMPLE RECTANGULAR DESIGN

Possibly the least complex form of rectangular ornamentation, next to a simple bar or square, is the combination shown in figure 298, a type in which many changes are made in interior as well as in exterior decorations of Pueblo ware. One of these is shown in figure 299, where the figure about the vessel is continuous. An analysis of the elements in figure 300 shows squares united at their angles, like the last, but that in addition to parallel bands connecting adjacent figures there are two marginal lines uniting the series. Each of the inner parallel lines is bound to a marginal on the opposite side by a band at right angles to it. The marginal lines are unbroken through the length of the figure. Like the last, this motive also may be regarded as developed from a single line.

FIG. 301—RECTANGULAR REVERSED S-FORM

FIG. 302—RECTANGULAR S-FORM WITH CROOKS

Figures 301 and 302 are even simpler than the design shown in figure 300, with appended square key patterns, all preserving rectangular forms and destitute of all others. They are of S-form, and differ more especially in the character of their appendages.

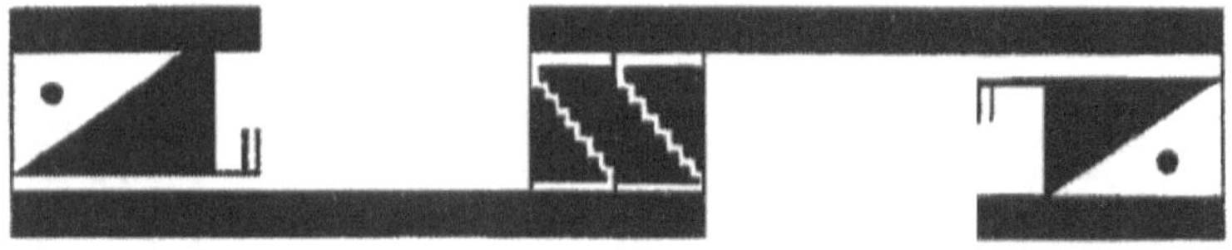

FIG. 303—RECTANGULAR S-FORM WITH TRIANGLES

FIG. 304—RECTANGULAR S-FORM WITH TERRACED TRIAN-GLES

While the same rectangular idea predominates in figure 303, it is worked out with the introduction of triangles and quadrilateral designs. This fairly compound pattern, however, is still classified among rectangular forms. A combination of rectangular and triangular geometric designs, in which, however, the former predominate, is shown in figure 304, which can readily be reduced to certain of those forms already mentioned. The triangles appear to be subordinated to the rectangles, and even they are fringed on their longer sides with terraced forms. It may be said that there are but two elements involved, the rectangle and the triangle.

FIG. 305—S-FORM WITH INTERDIGITATING SPURS

The decoration in figure 305 consists of rectangular and triangular figures, the latter so closely approximated as to leave zigzag lines in white. These lines are simply highly modified breaks in bands which join in other designs, and lead by comparison to the so-called "line of life" which many of these figures illustrate.

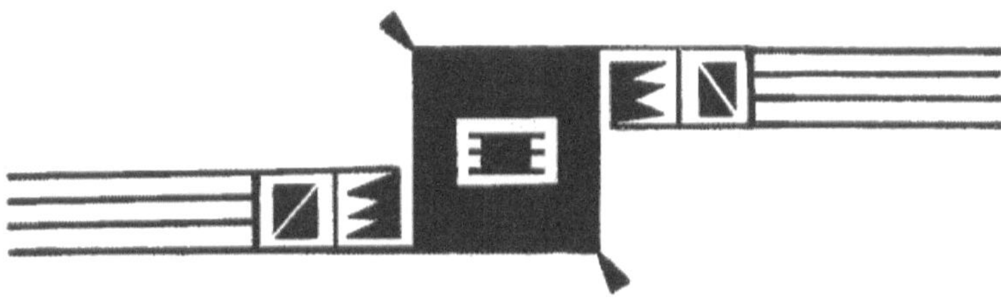

FIG. 306—SQUARE WITH RECTANGLES AND PARALLEL LINES

FIG. 307—RECTANGLES, TRIANGLES, STARS, AND FEATHERS

The distinctive feature of figure 306 is the square, with rectangular designs appended to diagonally opposite angles and small triangles at intermediate corners. These designs have a distant resemblance to figures later referred to as highly conventionalized birds, although they may be merely simple geometrical patterns which have lost their symbolic meaning.

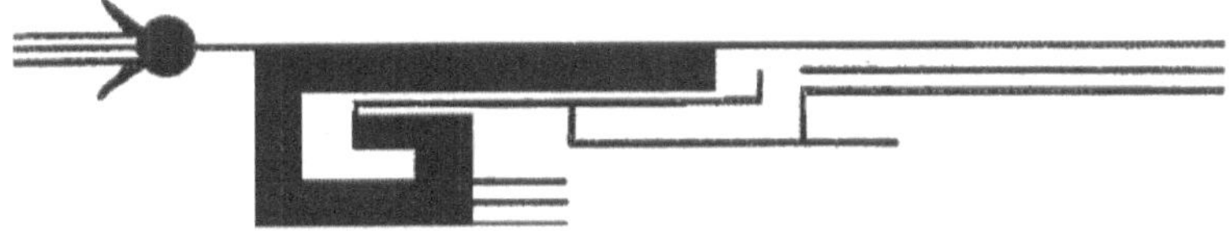

FIG. 308—CROOK, FEATHERS, AND PARALLEL LINES

Figure 307 shows a complicated design, introducing at least two elements in addition to rectangles and triangles. One of these is a curved crook etched on a black ground. In no other exterior decoration have curved lines been found except in the form of circles, and it is worthy of note how large a proportion of the figures are drawn in straight lines. The circular figures with three parallel lines extending from them are found so constantly in exterior decorations, and are so strikingly like some of the figures elsewhere discussed, that I have ventured a suggestion in regard to their meaning. I believe they represent feathers, because the tail-feathers of certain birds are symbolized in that manner, and their number corresponds with those generally depicted in the highly conventionalized tails of birds. With this thought in mind, it may be interesting to compare the two projections, one on each side of the three tail-feathers of this figure, with the extremity of the body of a bird shown in plate cxli, e. On the supposition that a bird figure was intended in this design, it is interesting also to note the rectangular decorations of the body and the association with stars made of three blocks in several bird figures, as already described. It is instructive also to note the fact that the figure of a maid represented in plate cxxix, a, has two of the round designs with appended parallel lines hanging to her garment, and four parallel marks drawn from her blanket. It is still customary in Hopi ceremonials to tie feathers to the garments of those who personate certain mythic beings, and it is possible that such was also the custom at Sikyatki. If so, it affords additional evidence that the parallel lines are representations of feathers.

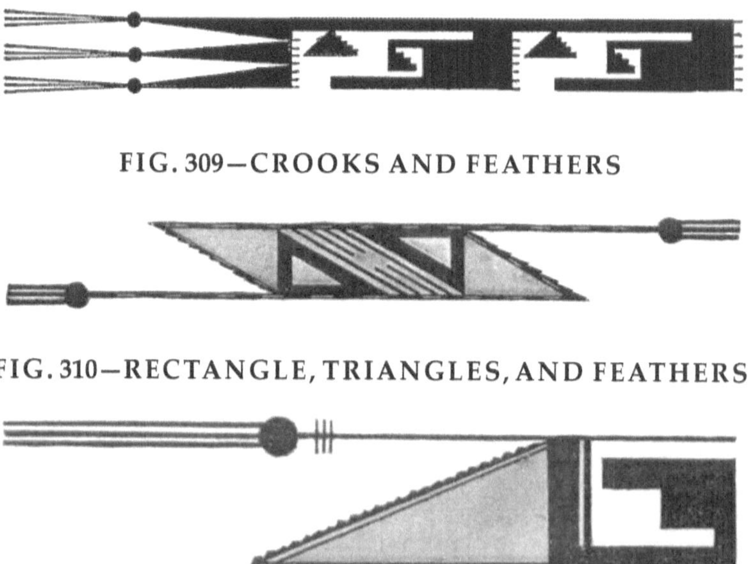

FIG. 309—CROOKS AND FEATHERS

FIG. 310—RECTANGLE, TRIANGLES, AND FEATHERS

FIG. 311—TERRACED CROOK, TRIANGLE, AND FEATHERS

Food Bowls With Geometric Ornamentation From Sikyatki

In figure 308 a number of these parallel lines are represented, and the general character of the design is rectangular. In figure 309 is shown a combination of rectangular and triangular figures with three tapering points and circles with lines at their tips radiating instead of parallel. Another modification is shown in figure 310 in which the triangle predominates, and figure 311 evidently represents one-half of a similar device with modifications.

FIG. 312—DOUBLE KEY

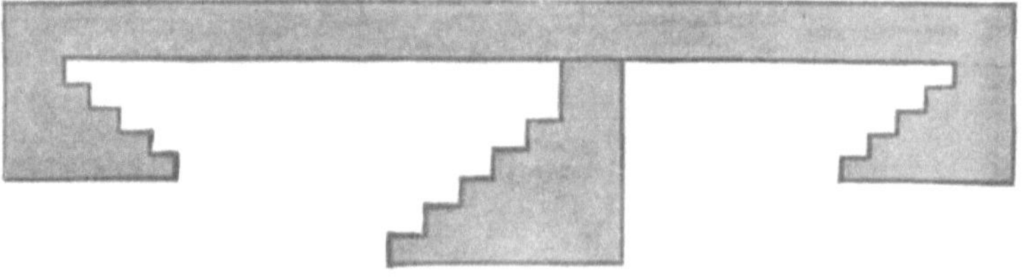

FIG. 313—TRIANGULAR TERRACE

One of the most common designs on ancient pottery is the stepped figure, a rectangular ornamentation, modifications of which are shown in figures 312-314. This is a very common design on the interior of food vessels, where it is commonly interpreted as a rain-cloud symbol.

FIG. 314—CROOK, SERRATE END

Of all patterns on ancient Tusayan ware, that of the terrace figures most closely resemble the geometrical ornamentation of cliff-house pottery, and there seems every reason to suppose that this form of design admits of a like interpretation. The evolution of this pattern from plaited basketry has been ably discussed by Holmes and Nordenskiöld, whose works have already been quoted in this memoir. The terraced forms from the exterior of food bowls here considered are highly aberrent; they may be forms of survivals, motives of decoration which have persisted from very early times. Whatever the origin of the stepped figure in Pueblo art was, it is well to remember, as shown by Holmes, that it is "impossible to show that any particular design of the highly constituted kind was desired through a certain identifiable series of progressive steps."

FIG. 315—KEY PATTERN; RECTANGLE AND TRIANGLES

FIG. 316—RECTANGLE AND CROOK

For some unknown reason the majority of the simple designs on the exterior of food bowls from Tusayan are rectangular, triangular, or linear in their character. Many can be reduced to simple or multiple lines. Others were suggested by plaited ware.

FIG. 317—CROOK AND TAIL FEATHERS

In figure 312 is found one of the simplest of rectangular designs, a simple band, key pattern in form, at one end, with a reentrant square depression at the opposite extremity. In figure 313 is an equally simple terrace pattern with stepped figures at the ends and in the middle. These forms are common decorative elements on the exterior of jars and vases, where they occur in many combinations, all of which are reducible to these types. The simplest form of the key pattern is shown in figure 314, and in figure 315 there is a second modification of the same design a little more complicated. This becomes somewhat changed in figure 316, not only by the modifications of the two extremities, but also by the addition of a median geometric figure.

FIG. 318—RECTANGLE, TRIANGLE, AND SERRATE SPURS

FIG. 319—W-PATTERN; TERMINAL CROOKS

FIG. 320—W-PATTERN; TERMINAL RECTANGLES

The design in figure 317 is rectangular, showing a key pattern at one end, with two long feathers at the opposite extremity. The five bodies on the same end of the figure are unique and comparable with conventionalized star emblems. The series of designs in the upper left-hand end of this figure are unlike any which have yet been found on the exterior of food bowls, but are similar to designs which have elsewhere been interpreted as feathers. On the hypothesis that these two parts of the figure are tail-feathers, we find in the crook the analogue of the head of a bird. Thus the designs on the equator of the vase (plate CXLV, *a*), which are birds, have the same crook for the head, and two simple tail-feathers, rudely drawn but comparable with the two in figure 317. The five dentate bodies on the lower left-hand end of the figure also tell in favor of the avian character of the design, for the following reason: These bodies are often found accompanying figures of conventionalized birds (plates CXLIV, CLIV, and others). They are regarded as modified crosses of equal arms, which are all but universally present in combinations with birds and feathers (plates CXLIV, *a*, *b*; CLIV, *a*), from the fact that in a line of crosses depicted on a bowl one of the crosses is replaced by a design of similar character. The arms of the cross are represented; their intersection is left in white. The interpretation of figure 317 as a highly conventionalized bird design is also in accord with the same interpretation of a number of similar, although less complicated, figures which appear with crosses. Thus the three arms of plate CLX, *a*, have highly conventionalized bird symbols attached to their extremities. In the cross figure shown in plate CLVIII, *d*, we find four bird figures with short, stumpy tail-feathers.

These highly conventionalized birds, with the head in the form of a crook and the tail-feathers as parallel lines, are illustrated on many pottery objects, nowhere better, however, than in those shown in plates cxxvi, *a*, and clx, *e*. Figure 318 may be compared with figure 317.

FIG. 321—W-PATTERN; TERMINAL TERRACES AND CROOKS.

FIG. 322—W-PATTERN; TERMINAL SPURS

Numerous modifications of a key pattern, often assuming a double triangular form, but with rectangular elements, are found on the exterior of many food bowls. These are variations of a pattern the simplest form of which is shown in figure 319. Resolving this figure into two parts by drawing a median line, we find the arrangement is bilaterally symmetrical, the two sides exactly corresponding. Each side consists of a simple key pattern with the shank inclined to the rim of the bowl and a bird emblem at its junction with the other member.

In figure 320 there is a greater development of this pattern by an elaboration of the key, which is continued in a line resembling a square spiral. There are also dentations on a section of the edge of the lines.

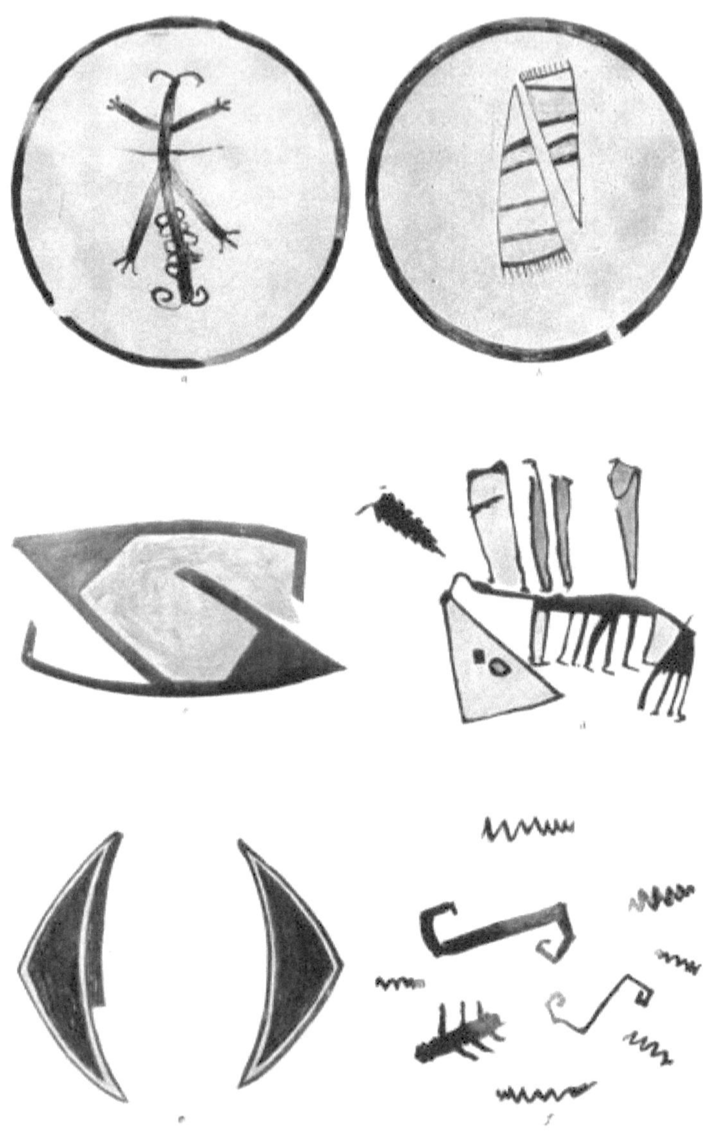

BUREAU OF AMERICAN ETHNOLOGY— — SEVENTEENTH ANNUAL RE-
PORT PL. CLXVI

Linear Figures On Food Bowls From Sikyatki

In figure 321 there is a still further development of the same design and a lack
of symmetry on the two sides. The square spirals are replaced on the left by three
stepped figures, and white spaces with parallel lines are introduced in the arms of
a W-shape figure.

FIG. 323—W-PATTERN; BIRD FORM

In figure 322 the same design is again somewhat changed by modification of the spirals into three triangles rimmed on one side with a row of dots, which are also found on the outer lines surrounding the lower part of the design.

FIG. 324—W-PATTERN; MEDIAN TRIANGLE

In figure 323 the same W shape design is preserved, but the space in the lower reentrant angle is occupied by a symmetrical figure resembling two tail-feathers and the extremity of the body of a bird. When this figure is compared with the design on plate CXLVI, *a*, resemblances are found in the two lateral appendages or wings. The star emblem is also present in the design. The median figure in that design which I have compared to the tail of a bird is replaced in figure 324 by a triangular ornament. The two wings are not symmetrical, but no new decorative element is introduced. It, however, will be noticed that there is a want of symmetry on the two sides of a vertical line in the figure last mentioned. The right-hand upper side is continued into five pointed projections, which fail on the left-hand side. There is likewise a difference in the arrangement of the terraced figures in the two parts. The sides of the median triangles are formed of alternating black and white blocks, and the quadrate figure which it incloses is etched with a diagonal and cross.

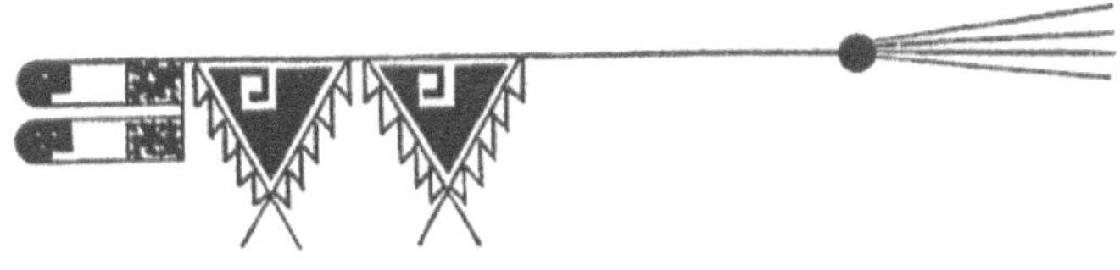

FIG. 325—DOUBLE TRIANGLE; TWO BREATH FEATHERS

FIG. 326—DOUBLE TRIANGLE; MEDIAN TRAPEZOID

The decoration in figure 325 consists of two triangles side by side, each having marginal serrations, and a median square key pattern. One side of these triangles is continued into a line from which hang two breath feathers, while the other end of the same line ends in a round dot with four radiating, straight lines. The triangles recall the butterfly symbol, the key pattern representing the head.

FIG. 327—DOUBLE TRIANGLE; MEDIAN RECTANGLE

**FIG. 328—DOUBLE COMPOUND TRIANGLE; MEDIAN RECTAN-
GLE**

In figure 326 there is a still more aberrant form of the W-shape design. The wings are folded, ending in triangles, and prolonged at their angles into projections to which are appended round dots with three parallel lines. The median portion, or that in the reentrant angle of the W, is a four-sided figure in which the triangle predominates with notched edges. Figure 327 shows the same design with the median portion replaced by a rectangle, and in which the key pattern has wholly disappeared from the wings. In figure 328 there are still greater modifications, but the symmetry about a median axis remains. The ends of the wings instead of being folded are expanded, and the three triangles formerly inclosed are now free and extended. The simple median rectangle is ornamented with a terrace pattern on its lower angles.

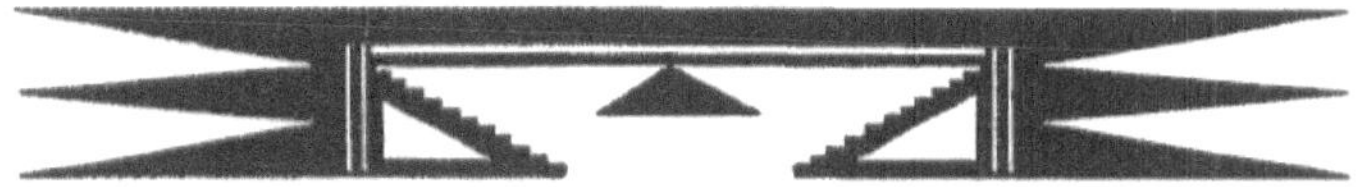

FIG. 329—DOUBLE TRIANGLE; MEDIAN TRIANGLE

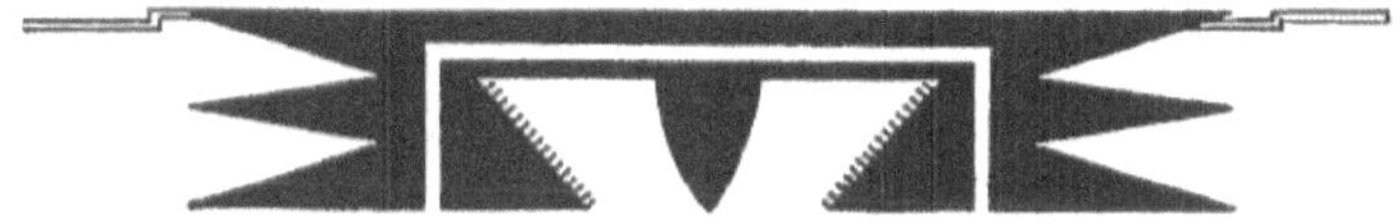

FIG. 330—DOUBLE COMPOUND TRIANGLE

Figure 329 shows a design in which the extended triangles are even more regular and simple, with triangular terraced figures on their inner edge. The median figure is a triangle instead of a rectangle.

FIG. 331—DOUBLE RECTANGLE; MEDIAN RECTANGLE

Figure 330 shows the same design with modification in the position of the median figure, and a slight curvature in two of its sides.

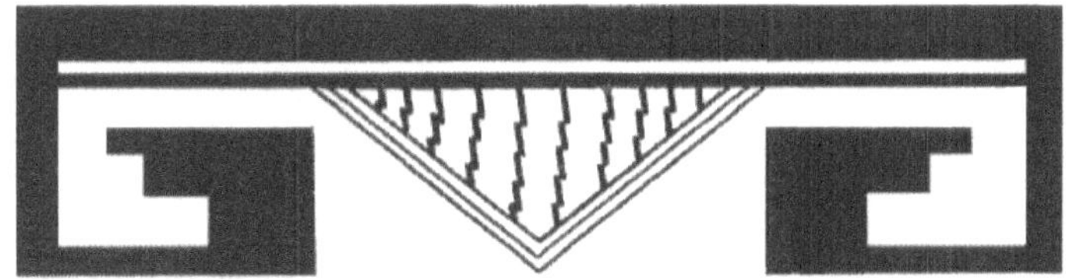

FIG. 332—DOUBLE RECTANGLE; MEDIAN TRIANGLE

FIG. 333—DOUBLE TRIANGLE WITH CROOKS

Somewhat similar designs, readily reduced to the same type as the last three or four which have been mentioned, are shown in figures 331 and 332. The resemblances are so close that I need not refer to them in detail. The W form is wholly lost, and there is no resemblance to a bird, even in its most highly conventionalized forms. The median design in figure 331 consists of a rectangle and two triangles so arranged as to leave a rectangular white space between them. In figure 332 the median triangle is crossed by parallel and vertical zigzag lines.

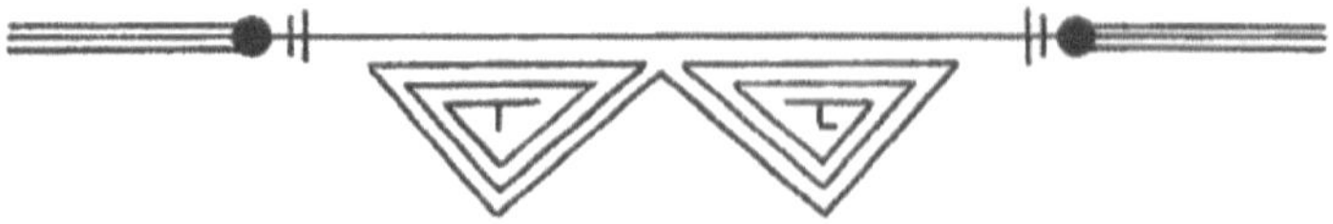

FIG. 334—W-SHAPE FIGURE; SINGLE LINE WITH FEATHERS

In the design represented in figure 333 there are two triangular figures, one on each side of a median line, in relation to which they are symmetrical. Each triangle has a simple key pattern in the middle, and the line from which they appear to hang is blocked off with alternating black and white rectangles. At either extremity of this line there is a circular dot from which extend four parallel lines.

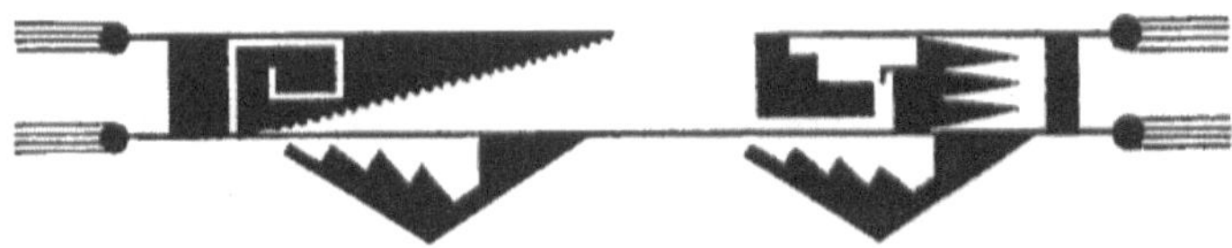

FIG. 335—COMPOUND RECTANGLE, TRIANGLES, AND FEATH-ERS

A somewhat simpler form of the same design is found in figure 334, showing a straight line above terminating with dots, from which extend parallel lines, and two triangular figures below, symmetrically placed in reference to an hypothetical upright line between them.

FIG. 336—DOUBLE TRIANGLE

Figure 335 bears a similarity to the last mentioned only so far as the lower half of the design is concerned. The upper part is not symmetrical, but no new decorative element is introduced. Triangles, frets, and terraced figures are inserted between two parallel lines which terminate in round dots with parallel lines.

BUREAU OF AMERICAN ETHNOLOGY— — SEVENTEENTH ANNUAL RE-
PORT PL. CLXVII

Geometric Ornamentation From Awatobi

FIG. 337—DOUBLE TRIANGLE AND FEATHERS

The design in figure 336 is likewise unsymmetrical, but it has two lateral triangles with incurved terrace and dentate patterns. The same general form is exhibited in figure 337, with the introduction of two pointed appendages facing the

hypothetical middle line. From the general form of these pointed designs, each of which is double, they have been interpreted as feathers. They closely resemble the tail-feathers of bird figures on several bowls in the collection, as will be seen in several of the illustrations.

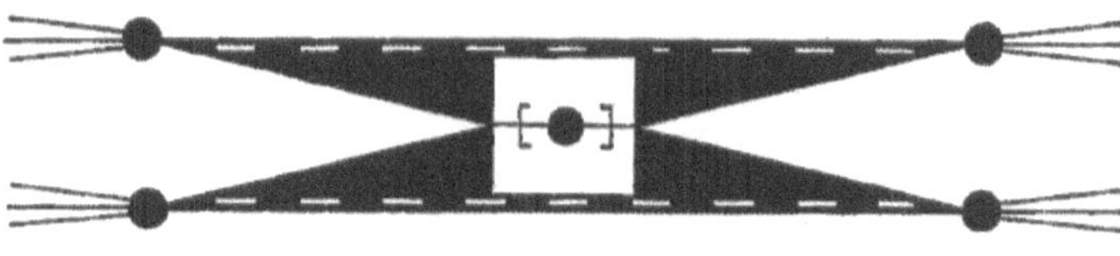

FIG. 338—TWIN TRIANGLES

FIG. 339—TRIANGLE WITH TERRACED APPENDAGES

FIG. 340—MOSAIC PATTERN

Figure 338 is composed of two triangular designs fused at the greatest angles. The regularity of these triangles is broken by a square space at the fusion. At each of the acute angles of the two triangles there are circular designs with radiating lines, a common motive on the exterior of food bowls. Although no new elements appear in figure 338, with the exception of bracket marks, one on each side of a circle, the arrangement of the two parts symmetrically about a line parallel with the rim of the bowl imparts to the design a unique form. The motive in figure 339 is reducible to triangular and rectangular forms, and while exceptional as to their arrangement, no new decorative feature is introduced.

The specimen represented in figure 340 has as its decorative elements, rectangles, triangles, parallel lines, and birds' tails, to which may be added star and crosshatch motives. It is therefore the most complicated of all the exterior decorations which have thus far been considered. There is no symmetry in the arrangement of figures about a central axis, but rather a repetition of similar designs.

FIG. 341—RECTANGLES, STARS, CROOKS, AND PARALLEL LINES

The use of crosshatching is very common on the most ancient Pueblo ware, and is very common in designs on cliff-house pottery. This style of decoration is only sparingly used on Sikyatki ware. The crosshatching is provisionally interpreted as a mosaic pattern, and reminds one of those beautiful forms of turquois mosaic on shell, bone, or wood found in ancient pueblos, and best known in modern times in the square ear pendants of Hopi women. Figure 340 is one of the few designs having terraced figures with short parallel lines depending from them. These figures vividly recall the rain-cloud symbol with falling rain represented by the parallel lines. Figure 341 is a perfectly symmetrical design with figures of stars, rectangles, and parallel lines. It may be compared with that shown in figure 340 in order to demonstrate how wide the difference in design may become by the absence of symmetrical relationship. It has been shown in some of the previous motives that the crook sometimes represents a bird's head, and parallel lines appended to it the tail-feathers. Possibly the same interpretation may be given to these designs in the following figures, and the presence of stars adjacent to them lends weight to this hypothesis.

FIG. 342—CONTINUOUS CROOKS

FIG. 343—RECTANGULAR TERRACE PATTERN

An indefinite repetition of the same pattern of rectangular design is shown in figure 342. This highly decorative motive may be varied indefinitely by extension or concentration, and while it is modified in that manner in many of the decorations of vases, it is not so changed on the exterior of food bowls.

There are a number of forms which I am unable to classify with the foregoing, none of which show any new decorative design. All possible changes have been made in them without abandoning the elemental ornamental motives already considered. The tendency to step or terrace patterns predominates, as exemplified in simple form in figure 343. In figure 344 there is a different arrangement of the same terrace pattern, and the design is helped out with parallel bands of different length at the ends of a rectangular figure. A variation in the depth of color of these lines adds to the effectiveness of the design. This style of ornamentation is successfully used in the designs represented in figures 345 and 346, in the body of which a crescentic figure in the black serves to add variety to a design otherwise monotonous. The two appendages to the right of figure 346 are interpreted as feathers, although their depart forms widely from that usually assumed by these designs. The terraced patterns are replaced by dentate margins in this figure, and there is a successful use of most of the rectangular and triangular designs.

FIG. 344—TERRACE PATTERN WITH PARALLEL LINES

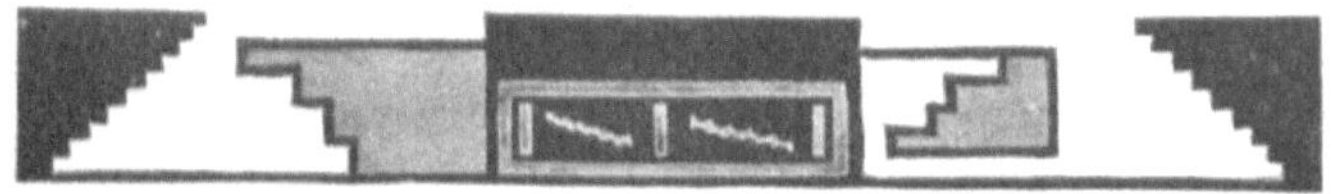

FIG. 345—TERRACE PATTERN

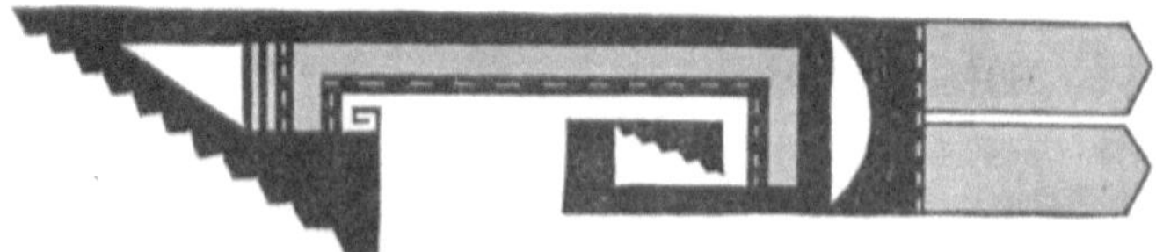

FIG. 346—TRIANGULAR PATTERN WITH FEATHERS

In the specimens represented in figures 347 and 348 marginal dentations are used. I have called the design referred to an S-form, which, however, owing to its elongation is somewhat masked. The oblique bar in the middle of the figure represents the body of the letter, the two extremities taking the forms of triangles.

FIG. 347—S-PATTERN

FIG. 348—TRIANGULAR AND TERRACE FIGURES

So far as decorative elements are concerned the design in figure 349 can be compared with some of those preceding, but it differs from them in combination. The motive in figure 350 is not unlike the ornamentation of certain oriental vases, except from the presence of the terraced figures. In figure 351 there are two designs separated by an inclined break the edge of which is dentate. This figure is introduced to show the method of treatment of alternating triangles of varying depth of color and the breaks in the marginal bands or "lines of life." One of the simplest combinations of triangular and rectangular figures is shown in figure 353, proving how effectually the original design may be obscured by concentration.

FIG. 349—CROOK, TERRACE, AND PARALLEL LINES

FIG. 350—TRIANGLES, SQUARES, AND TERRACES

In the foregoing descriptions I have endeavored to demonstrate that, notwithstanding the great variety of designs considered, the types used are very limited in number. The geometrical forms are rarely curved lines, and it may be said that spirals, which appear so constantly on pottery from other (and possibly equally ancient or older) pueblos than Sikyatki, are absent in the external decorations of specimens found in the ruins of the latter village.

Every student of ancient and modern Pueblo pottery has been impressed by the predominance of terraced figures in its ornamentation, and the meaning of these terraces has elsewhere been spoken of at some length. It would, I believe, be going too far to say that these step designs always represent clouds, as in some instances they are produced by such an arrangement of rectangular figures that no other forms could result.

BUREAU OF AMERICAN ETHNOLOGY— — SEVENTEENTH ANNUAL RE-
PORT PL. CLXVIII

Geometric Ornamentation From Awatobi

FIG. 351—BIFURCATED RECTANGULAR DESIGN

FIG. 352—LINES OF LIFE AND TRIANGLES

FIG. 353—INFOLDED TRIANGLES

The material at hand adds nothing new to the theory of the evolution of the terraced ornament from basketry or textile productions, so ably discussed by Holmes, Nordenskiöld, and others. When the Sikyatki potters decorated their ware the ornamentation of pottery had reached a high development, and figures both simple and complicated were used contemporaneously. While, therefore, we can so arrange them as to make a series, tracing modifications from simple to complex designs, thus forming a supposed line of evolution, it is evident that there is no proof that the simplest figures are the oldest. The great number of terraced figures and their use in the representation of animals seem to me to indicate that they antedate all others, and I see no reason why they should not have been derived from basketry patterns. We must, however, look to pottery with decorations less highly developed for evidence bearing on this point. The Sikyatki artists had advanced beyond simple geometric figures, and had so highly modified these that it is impossible to determine the primitive form.

As I have shown elsewhere, the human hand is used as a decorative element in the ornamentation of the interior of several food bowls. It is likewise in one instance chosen to adorn the exterior. It is the only part of the human limbs thus used. Figure 354 shows the hand with marks on the palm probably intended to represent the lines which are used in the measurement of the length of pahos or prayer-sticks. From between the index and the middle finger rises a line which recalls that spoken of in the account of the hand on the interior of the food bowl shown in plate cxxxvii.

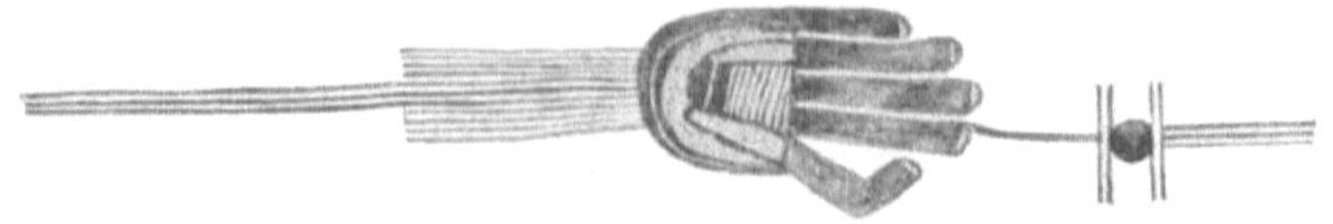

FIG. 354—HUMAN HAND

The limb of an animal with a paw, or possibly a human arm and hand, appears as a decoration on the outside of another food bowl, where it is combined with the ever-constant stepped figure, as shown in figure 355.

FIG. 355—ANIMAL PAW, LIMB, AND TRIANGLE

PIGMENTS

The ancient Sikyatki people were accustomed to deposit in their mortuary vessels fragments of minerals or ground oxides and carbonates, of different colors, used as paints. It thus appears evident that these substances were highly prized in ancient as in modern times, and it may be mentioned that the present native priests regard the pigments found in the graves as so particularly efficacious in coloring their ceremonial paraphernalia that they begged me to give them fragments for that purpose. The green color, which was the most common, is an impure carbonate of copper, the same as that with which pahos are painted for ceremonial use today. Several shallow, saucer-like vessels contained yellow ocher, and others sesquioxide of iron, which afforded both the ancients and the moderns the red pigment called *cuta*, an especial favorite of the warrior societies. The inner surface of some of the bowls is stained with the pigments which they had formerly contained, and it was not uncommon to find several small paint pots deposited in a single grave. The white used was an impure kaolin, which was found both in masses and in powdered form, and there were unearthed several disks of this material which had been cut into definite shape as if for a special purpose.

BUREAU OF AMERICAN ETHNOLOGY— — SEVENTEENTH ANNUAL RE-
PORT PL. CLXIX

Arrowshaft Smoothers, Selenite, And Symbolic Corn From Sikyatki

One of these disks or circular plates (figure 356) was found on the head of a
skeleton. The rim is rounded, and the opposite faces are concave, with a perforation in the middle. Other forms of this worked kaolin are spherical, oblong, or

lamellar, sometimes more or less decorated on the outer surface, as shown in plate CLXXII, *e*. Another, shown in *f*, of the same plate, is cylindrical, and other fragments of irregular shapes were found. A pigment made of micaceous hematite was found in one of the Sikyatki paint jars. This material is still used as coloring matter by the Tusayan Indians, by whom it is called *yayala*, and is highly prized by the members of the warrior societies.

FIG. 356—KAOLIN DISK (NATURAL SIZE)

STONE OBJECTS

Almost every grave at Sikyatki contained stone objects which were found either in the bowls or in the soil in the immediate neighborhood of the skeletons. Some of these implements are pecked or chipped, others are smooth—pebbles apparently chosen for their botryoidal shape, polished surface, or fancied resemblance to some animal or other form.

Many of the smooth stones were probably simply polishing stones, used by the women in rubbing pottery to a gloss before it was fired. Others were charm stones such as are still employed in making medicine, as elsewhere described. There were still other stones which, from their resemblance to animals, may have been personal fetishes. Among the unusual forms of stones found in this association is a quartz crystal. As I have shown in describing several ceremonies still observed, a quartz crystal is used to deflect a ray of sunlight into the medicine bowl, and is placed in the center of a sand picture of the sun in certain rites called *Powalawû*; the crystal is also used in divining, and for other purposes, and is highly prized by modern Tusayan priests.

A botryoidal fragment of hematite found in a grave reminds me that in the so-called Antelope rock[154] at Walpi, around which the Snake dancers biennially carry reptiles in their mouths, there is in one side a niche in which is placed a much larger mass of that material, to which prayers are addressed on certain ceremonial

[154] This pillar, so conspicuous in all photographs of Walpi, is commonly called the Snake rock.

occasions, and upon which sacred meal and prayer emblems are placed.

One or two mortuary bowls contained fragments of stalactites apparently from the Grand canyon of the Colorado or from some other locality where water is or has been abundant.

The loose shaly deposit which underlies the Tusayan mesas contains many cephalopod fossils, a collection of which was made in former years and deposited in the National Museum. Among these the most beautiful are small cephalopods called by the Hopi, *koaitcoko*. Among the many sacred objects in the *tiponi* baskets of the Lalakonti society, as described in my account[155] of the unwrapping of that fetish, there was a specimen of this ammonite; that the shell was preserved in this sacred bundle is sufficient proof that it is highly venerated. As a natural object with a definite form it is regarded as a fetish which is looked upon with reverence by the knowing ones and pronounced bad by the uninitiated. The occurrence of this fossil in one of the mortuary bowls is in harmony with the same idea and shows that it was regarded in a similar light by the ancient occupants of Sikyatki.

But the resemblance of these and other stones to animal fossils[156] is not always so remote as in the instances above mentioned. There was in one grave a single large fetish of a mountain lion, made of sandstone (plate CLXXII, *b*, *c*), in which legs, ears, tail, and eyes are represented, and the mouth still retains the red pigment with which it was colored, although there was no sign of paint on other parts of the body. This fetish is very similar to the one found at Awatobi, and is identical in form with those made by the Hopi at the present time.

It was customary to bury in Sikyatki graves plates or fragments of selenite or mica, some of which are perforated as if for suspension, while others are in plain sheets (plate CLXIX, *c*).

Among the stone implements used as mortuary offerings which were found in the cemeteries, was one made of the same fine lithographic limestone as the so-called *tcamahia* (plate CLXXI, *g*) which occur on the Antelope altar in the Snake ceremonies. The exceptional character of this fragment is instructive, and its resemblance to the finely polished stone hoes found in other ruins is very suggestive.

---

[155] *American Anthropologist*, April, 1892.
[156] I failed to find out how the Hopi regard fossils.

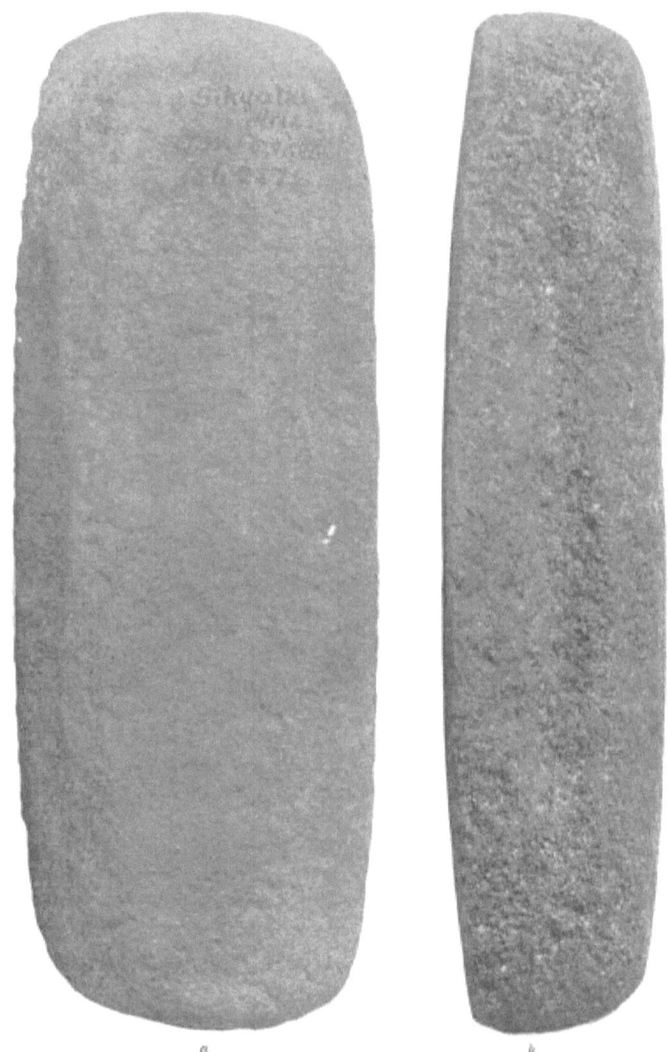

BUREAU OF AMERICAN ETHNOLOGY — — SEVENTEENTH ANNUAL RE-
PORT PL. CLXX

Corn Grinder From Sikyatki

There were found many disk-shape stones, pecked on the periphery as if used
in grinding pigment or in bruising seeds, and spheroidal stones with a facet worn
at one pole as if used for the same or a similar purpose (plate CLXXI, *b*, *c*). A few
stone axes and hatchets were also taken from the graves; most of these are rude
specimens of stone working, although one of them can hardly be excelled in any
other collection. Many arrowpoints were found, but these are in no respect peculiar. They are made of many different kinds of stone, but those of obsidian are the

most numerous. They were generally found in numbers, sometimes in bowls. Evidently they had not been attached to shafts when buried, for no sign of the reeds remained. Arrowheads sewed into a bandoleer are still worn as insignia of rank by warriors, and it is probable that such was also true in the past, so that on interment these arrowpoints might have been placed in the mortuary basin deposited by the side of the warrior, as indicative of his standing or rank, and the bandoleer or leather strap to which they were attached decayed during its long burial in the earth. Spearpoints of much coarser make and larger in size than the arrowheads were also found in the graves, and a rare knife, made of chalcedony, showed that the ancient, like the modern Hopi, prized a sharp cutting instrument.

Among the many large stones picked up on the mounds of Sikyatki there was one the use of which has long puzzled me. This is a rough stone, not worked save in an equatorial groove. The object is too heavy to have been carried about, except with the utmost difficulty, and the probability of the former existence of a handle is out of the question. It has been suggested that this and similar but larger grooved stones might have been used as tethers for some domesticated animal, as the eagle or the turkey, which is about the only explanation I can suggest. Both of these creatures, and (if we may trust early accounts) a quadruped about the size of a dog, were domesticated by the ancient Pueblo people, but I have found no survival of tethering in use today. Eagles, however, are tied by the legs and not confined in corrals as at Zuñi, while sheep are kept in stone inclosures. It is probable that this latter custom came with the introduction of sheep, and that these stones were weights to which the Sikyatki people tied by the legs the eagles and turkeys, the feathers of which play an important part in their sacred observances.

Certain small rectangular slabs of stone have been found, with a groove extending across one surface diagonally from one angle to another (plate CLXIX, *a, b.*) These are generally called arrowshaft polishers, and were used to rub down the surface of arrowshafts or prayer-sticks. Several of these polishers were taken from Sikyatki graves, and one or two were of such regular form that considerable care must have been used in their manufacture. A specimen from Awatobi is decorated with a bow and an arrow scratched on one side, and one of dark basaltic rock evidently came from a distance. A number of metates and mullers were found in the graves at Sikyatki. One of the best of the latter is shown in plate CLXX. These stones are of different degrees of fineness, and vary from simple triangular slabs of fine sandstone to very coarse lava. The specimen figured has depressions on the sides to facilitate handling.[157]

Perhaps the most significant of all the worked stones found in the Sikyatki cemeteries were the flat slabs the edges of which near the surface of the soil marked the presence of the graves. These slabs may be termed headstones, but they have a far different meaning from those that bear the name of the deceased with which we are most familiar, for when they have any marking on their faces, it is not a totem of the dead, but a symbol of the rain-cloud, which is connected with ancestor worship.

---

[157] These objects were eagerly sought by the Hopi women who visited the camps at Awatobi and Sikyatki.

One of the best of these mortuary slabs has its edge cut in such a way as to give it a terraced outline, and on one face a similar terrace is drawn in black pigment. These figures are symbols of rain-clouds, and the interpretation of the use of this design in graves is as follows:

The dead, according to current Tusayan thought, become rain-cloud gods, or powerful intercessors with those deities which cause or send the rains. Hence, the religious society to which the deceased belonged, and the members of the clan who survive, place in the mortuary bowls, or in the left hand of their friend, the paho or prayer emblem for rain; hence, also, in prayers at interment they address the breath body of the dead as a *katcina*, or rain god. These *katcinas*, as divinized ancestors, are supposed to return to the villages and receive prayers for rain. In strict accord with this conception the rain-cloud symbol is placed, in some instances, on the slab of rock in the graves of the dead at Sikyatki. It proves to me that the cult of ancestor worship, and the conception that the dead have power to bring needed rain, were recognized in Sikyatki when the pueblo was in its prime. One of these slabs is perforated by a small hole, an important fact, but one for which I have only a fanciful explanation, namely, to allow the escape of the breath body. Elsewhere I have found many instances of perforated mortuary stone slabs, which will be considered in a report of my excavations in 1896.

OBSIDIAN

Many fragments of obsidian, varying in size, are found strewn over the surface of the majority of ancient ruins in Tusayan, and the quantity of this material on some mounds indicates its abundance in those early habitations. This material must have been highly prized for knives, arrowpoints, and weapons of various kinds, as several of the graves contained large fragments of it, some more or less chipped, others in natural forms. The fact of its being deemed worthy of deposit in the graves of the Sikyatkians would indicate that it was greatly esteemed. I know of no natural deposit of obsidian near Sikyatki or in the province of Tusayan, so that the probability is that these fragments had been brought a considerable distance before they were buried in the earth that now covers the dead of the ancient pueblos.

BUREAU OF AMERICAN ETHNOLOGY — — SEVENTEENTH ANNUAL RE-
PORT PL. CLXXI

Stone Implements From Palatki, Awatobi, And Sikyatki

NECKLACES, GORGETS, AND OTHER ORNAMENTS

The Sikyatki people buried their dead adorned with necklaces and other ornaments as when living. The materials most highly prized for necklaces were
turquois and shell which were fashioned into beads, some of which were finely
made. These necklaces did not differ from those now worn, and the shells employed were mostly marine varieties of the genus *Pectunculus*. The turquois beads
are often as finely cut as any now worn, and their presence in the graves led to the
only serious trouble which I had with my native workmen, as they undoubtedly

appropriated many which were found. Some of these turquois beads are simply flat fragments, perforated at one end, others are well formed. Many skeletons had a single turquois near the mastoid process of the skull, showing that they had been worn as ear pendants. On the neck of one skeleton we found a necklace of many strands, composed of segments of the leg bones of the turkey, stained green. There were other specimens of necklaces made of turkey bones, which were smoothly finished and apparently had not been stained.

Necklaces of perforated cedar berries were likewise found, some of them still hanging about the necks of the dead, and in one instance, a small saucer like vessel (plate cxx, *d*) was filled with beads of this kind, as if the necklace had thus been deposited in the grave as a votive offering.

For gorgets the Sikyatki people apparently prized slabs of lignite (plate CLxxii, *d*) and plates of selenite. It was likewise customary to make small clay imitations of birds and shells for this and for other ornamental purposes; these, for the most part, however, were not found in the graves, but were picked up on the surface or in the débris within the rooms.

The three forms imitating birds shown in plate CLxxiii, *g*, *h*, *i*, are rude in character, and one of them is crossed by a black line from which depend parallel lines, representing falling rain; all of these specimens have a perforated knot on the under side for suspension, as shown in the figure between them.

The forms of imitations of shells, in clay, of which examples are shown in plate CLxxiii, *j*, *k*, *l*, are rude in character; they are often painted with longitudinal or vertical black lines, and have a single or double perforation for suspension. The shell imitated is probably the young *Pectunculus*, a Pacific-coast mollusk, with which the ancient Hopi were familiar.

TOBACCO PIPES

I have elsewhere mentioned that every modern Tusayan ceremony opens and closes with a ceremonial smoke, and it is apparent that pipes were highly prized by the ancient Sikyatkians.

The form of pipe used in most ceremonials today has a bowl with its axis at right angles to the stem, but so far as I have studied ancient Pueblo pipes this form appears to be a modern innovation.[158] To determine the probable ancient form of pipe, as indicated by the ritual, I will invite attention to one of the most archaic portions of the ceremonies about the altar of the Antelope priesthood, at the time of the Snake dance at Walpi:[159]

"The songs then ceased, and Wí-ki sent Ká-tci to bring him a light. Ká-tci went out, and soon returned with a burning corncob, while all sat silently awaiting Wí-ki's preparation for the great *Ó-mow-ûh* smoke, which was one of the most sacred

---

[158] The tubular form of pipe was almost universal in the pueblo area, and I have deposited in the National Museum pipes of this kind from several ruins in the Rio Grande valley.

[159] *Journal of American Ethnology and Archæology*, vol. IV, pp. 31, 32, 33.

acts performed by the Antelope priests in these ceremonials.

"The *wu-kó-tco-ño* is a huge, stemless pipe, which has a large opening in the blunt end, and a smaller one in the pointed. It is five inches long, one inch in diameter at the large aperture, and its greatest circumference is seven and a half inches. The pipe is made of some black material, possibly stone, and as far as could be seen was not ornamented. The bowl had previously been filled with leaves carefully gathered from such places as are designated by tradition. In the subsequent smokes the ashes, "dottle," were saved, being placed in a small depression in the floor, but were not again put in the pipe.

"Wí-ki took the live ember from Ká-tci and placed it in the large opening of the pipe, on the leaves which filled its cavity. He then knelt down and placed the pipe between the two *ti-po-nis*, so that the pointed end rested on the head of the large fetish, between the ears. Every one remained silent, and Wí-ki blew several dense clouds of smoke upon the sand altar, one after another, so that the picture was concealed. The smoke was made by blowing through the pipe, the fire being placed in the bowl next the mouth, and the whole larger end of the pipe was taken into the mouth at each exhalation.

"At the San Juan pueblo, near Santa Fé, where I stopped on my way to Tusayan, I purchased a ceremonial headdress upon which several spruce twigs were tied. Wí-ki received some fragments of these with gratitude, and they formed one of the ingredients which were smoked in the great *ó-mow-ûh* pipe. The scent of the mixture was very fragrant, and filled the room, like incense. The production of this great smoke-cloud, which is supposed to rise to the sky, and later bring the rain, ended the first series of eight songs.

BUREAU OF AMERICAN ETHNOLOGY — — SEVENTEENTH ANNUAL RE-
PORT PL. CLXXII

Paint Grinder, Fetish, Kaolin Disks, And Lignite From Sikyatki

"Immediately after this event, Há-ha-we filled one of the small-stemmed pipes lying near the fireplace with native tobacco, and after lighting it puffed smoke on the altar. He passed the pipe to Wí-ki, holding it near the floor, bowl foremost, as he did so, and exchanging the customary terms of relationship. Wí-ki then blew dense clouds of smoke over the two *tí-po-nis* and on the sand picture. Há-ha-we, meanwhile, lit a second pipe, and passed it to Kó-pe-li, the Snake chief, who enjoyed it in silence, indiscriminately puffing smoke on the altar, to the cardinal points, and in other directions. Kó-pe-li later gave his pipe to Ká-kap-ti, who sat at his right, and Wí-ki passed his to Na-syuñ-'we-ve, who, after smoking, handed the pipe to Kwá-a, who in turn passed it to Ká-tci, by whom it was given to Há-ha-we. Ká-tci, the last priest to receive it before it was returned to the pipe-lighter, smoked for a long time, and repeatedly puffed clouds of smoke upon the sand picture. Meanwhile Ká-kap-ti had handed his pipe to Há-ha-we, both exchanging terms of relationship and carefully observing the accompanying ceremonial etiquette. Há-ha-we, as was his unvarying custom, carefully cleaned the two pipes, and laid them on the floor by the side of the fireplace."

The form of pipe used in the above ceremony is typical of ancient Pueblo pipes, several of which were found at Sikyatki. One of these, much smaller than the *ó-mow-ûh* pipe, was made of lava, and bore evidence of use before burial. It is evident, however, that these straight pipes were not always smoked as above described. The most interesting pipes found at Sikyatki were more elongated than that above mentioned and were made of clay. Their forms are shown in plate CLXXIII, *b, c, d, f.* One of these (*b*) is very smooth, almost glazed, and enlarged into two lateral wings near the mouth end, which is perforated with a small hole. The cavity at the opposite end is large enough to hold sufficient for a good smoke, and shows evidence of former use. The whole median region of the exterior is formed by a collar incised with lines, as if formerly wrapped with fiber. In some of the modern ceremonials, as that of the Bear-Puma dramatization in the Snake dance, a reed cigarette is used, ancient forms of which have been found in sacrificial caves, and there seems no doubt that this pipe is simply a clay form of those reeds. The markings on the collar would by this interpretation indicate the former existence of a small fabric wrapped about it. The two pipes shown, in plate CLXXIII, *b, f,* are tubular in shape,[160] highly polished, and on one of them (*f*) we see scratches representing the same feature as the collar of *b*, and probably made with the same intent.

The fragment of a pipe shown in plate CLXXIII, *d*, is interesting in the same connection. The end of this pipe is broken, but the stem is intact, and on two sides of the bowl there are elevations covered with crosshatching. The pipe is of clay and has a rough external surface.

It is improbable that these pipes were always smoked as the *wu-kó-tco-ño* of the Snake ceremony, but the smaller end was placed to the mouth, and smoke taken into the mouth and exhaled. It is customary in ceremonials now practiced, to wind a wisp of yucca about the stem of a short pipe, that it may not become too hot to hold in the hand. This may be a possible explanation[161] of the scratches on the sides of the ancient tube pipes from Sikyatki.

PRAYER-STICKS

One of the most important objects made in the secret ceremonials of the mod-

---

[160] This form of pipe occurs over the whole pueblo area.

[161] Ancient cigarette reeds, found in sacrificial caves, have a small fragment of woven fabric tied about them.

ern Pueblos is sacrificial in nature, and is called a paho or "water wood," which is used as an offering to the gods (figure 357). These pahos are made of a prescribed wood, of length determined by tradition, and to them are tied appendages of symbolic meaning. They are consecrated by songs, about an altar, upon which they are laid, and afterward deposited in certain shrines by a special courier.

FIG. 357—MORTUARY PRAYER-STICK (NATURAL SIZE)

In modern times the forms of these pahos differ very greatly, the shape depending on the society which makes them, the god addressed, and the purpose for which they are used, as understood by the initiated. Among many other uses they are sometimes mortuary in character, and are deposited in the graves of chiefs, as offerings either to the God of Death, or to other deities, to whom they may be presented by the shade or breath body of the deceased. This use of pahos is of ancient origin in Tusayan, as shown by the excavations at Sikyatki, where they were found in mortuary bowls or vases deposited by the relatives or surviving members of the sacerdotal societies to which the deceased had belonged.

This pre-Spanish custom in Tusayan was discovered in my excavations at Awatobi, but the prayer-sticks from that place were fragmentary as compared with the almost perfect pahos from Sikyatki. These pahos are of many forms;[162] some of them are of considerable size, and the majority are of distinctive forms (plates CLXXIV-CLXXV). There are also many fragments, the former shapes of which could not be determined. When it is considered that these wooden objects with their neat carvings were fashioned with stone implements, the high character of the work is very remarkable. They show, in several instances, the imprint of attached strings and feathers, portions of which still remain; also, in one instance, fragments of a pine needle. They are painted with green and black mineral pigments, the former of which had undoubtedly done much to preserve the soft wood of which they were manufactured. As at the present day, cottonwood and willow were the favorite prescribed woods for pahos, and some of the best were made of pine. The forms of these ancient prayer offerings, as mentioned hereafter, differ somewhat from those of modern make, although in certain instances there is a significant resemblance between the two kinds.

---

[162] The so-called "implements of wood" figured by Nordenskiöld ("The Cliff Dwellers of the Mesa Verde," plate XLII) are identical with some of the pahos from Sikyatki, and are undoubtedly prayer-sticks.

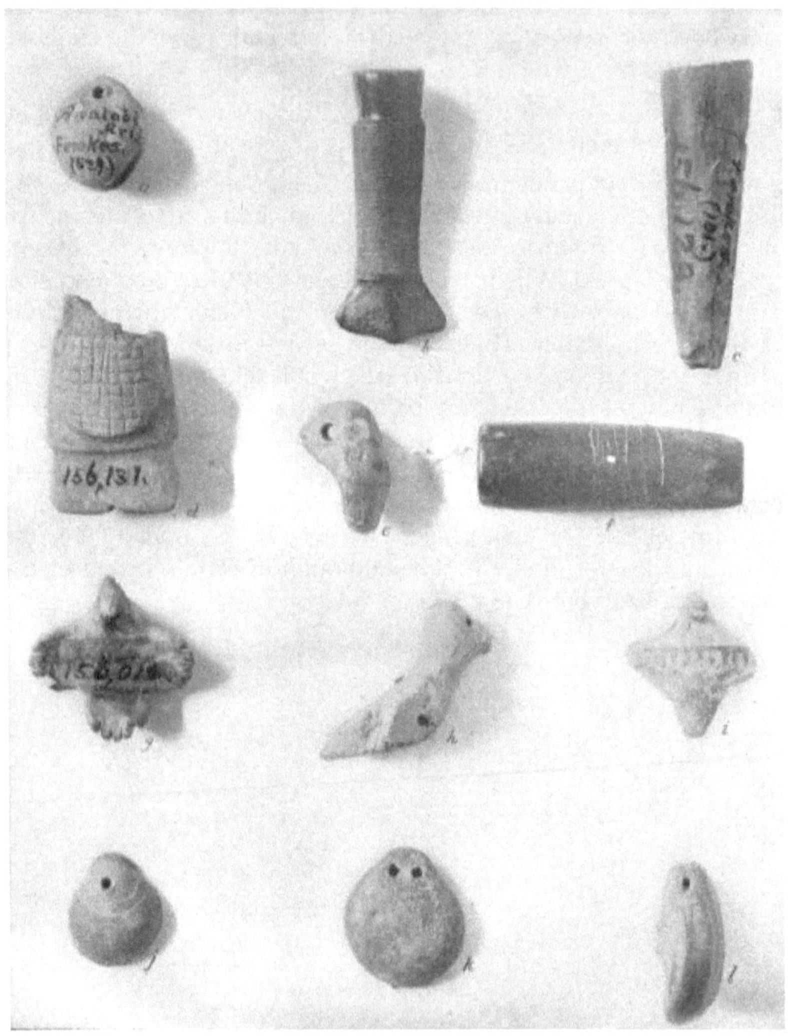

BUREAU OF AMERICAN ETHNOLOGY — — SEVENTEENTH ANNUAL RE-
PORT PL. CLXXIII

Pipes, Bell, And Clay Birds And Shells From Awatobi And Sikyatki

One of the most striking instances of resemblance between the old and the new is the likeness of some of these ancient pahos to those now made by the Flute society, and if this resemblance is more than a coincidence, the conclusion that the present flute paho is a survival of the ancient form may be accepted. As adding weight to this theory it may be mentioned that traditionally the Flute people claim to be the ancient people of Tusayan, and possibly contemporaries, in that province, with the ancient inhabitants of Sikyatki. There is likewise a most suggestive resemblance between these pahos and certain similar sticks from cliff dwellings, and it is a belief, which I can not yet demonstrate as true, that kindred people, or the same sacerdotal societies represented in cliff houses and in Sikyatki, manufactured ceremonial prayer offerings which are identical in design. Plate CLXXIV, *a*, represents a double stick paho, which closely resembles the prayer offering of the modern Flute society. The two rods were found together and originally had been attached, as indicated by the arrangement of the impression of the string midway of their length. The stick of the left has a facet cut on one side, upon which originally three dots were depicted to represent the eyes and the mouth. This member of the paho was the female; the remaining stick was the male. There are two deep grooves, or ferules, cut midway of their length, a distinctive characteristic of the modern flute paho. Both components are painted green, as is still customary in prayer-sticks of this fraternity. The pahos shown in *b*, *c*, and *d*, are likewise ascribed to the same society, and differ from the first only in length. They represent female sticks of double flute pahos. The length of these prayer-sticks varies on different ceremonial days, and is determined by the distance of the shrines for which they are intended. The unit of measurement is the length of certain joints of the finger, and the space between the tip of longest digit to certain creases in the palm of the hand. The length of the ancient Sikyatki pahos, ascribed to the Flute society, follows the same rule.

Plate CLXXIV, *e*, *f*, have the same ferules referred to in the description above, but are of greater diameter. They are unlike any modern paho except in this particular. In *g* is depicted a still larger prayer-stick, with two serrate incisions on each side of the continuation of the flattened facet.

Specimens *h* to *m* are forms of pahos which I can not identify. They are painted green, generally with black tips, round, flattened, and of small size. Figure *n* is a part of a paho which closely resembles prayer-sticks found in the cliff houses of Mesa Verde and San Juan valley of northern New Mexico.

Numerous specimens of a peculiar razor-shape paho were found, two of which are shown in plate CLXXV, *o*, *s*. The paho shown in figure *d* is flat on one side and rounded on the other, narrowing at one end, where it was probably continued in a shaft, and a hole is punctured at the opposite extremity, as if for suspension. It is barely possible that this may have been a whizzer or bull-roarer, such as are used at the present day to imitate the wind, and commonly carried by the performer in a public dance who personifies the warrior. Figure *t* differs from the ordinary flute paho in having five constrictions in the upper part, and in being continued into a very long shank.

The best preserved of all the pahos from the Sikyatki graves are represented in *u* and *v*, both of which were found in the same mortuary bowl. They are painted with a thick layer of green pigment, and have shafts, which are blackened and placed in opposite directions in the two figures. Their general form may be seen at a glance. The lower surface of the object shown in *u* is perfectly flat, and the part represented at the upper end is evidently broken off. This is likewise true of both extremities of the object shown in *v*; it is also probable that it had originally a serrated end, comparable with that shown in *c*. A similar terraced extremity survives in the corn paho carried by the so-called Flute girls in the biennial celebrations of the Flute ceremonies in the modern Tusayan pueblos.

I refer the paho to the second group of sacrifices mentioned by Tylor,[163] that of homage, "a doctrine that the gist of sacrifice is rather in the worshiper giving something precious to himself than in the deity receiving benefit. This may be called the abnegation theory, and its origin may be fairly explained by considering it as derived from the original gift theory."

While it is probably true that the Hopi barters his paho with the idea of receiving in return some desired gift, the main element is probably homage, but there is involved in it the third and highest element of sacrifice, abnegation. It is a sacrifice by symbolism, a part for the whole.

On this theory the query naturally is, what does a paho represent? While it is difficult to answer this question, I think a plausible suggestion can be made. It is a sacrifice by symbolic methods of that which the Hopi most prize, corn or its meal.

[163] Primitive Culture, vol. ii, p. 396.

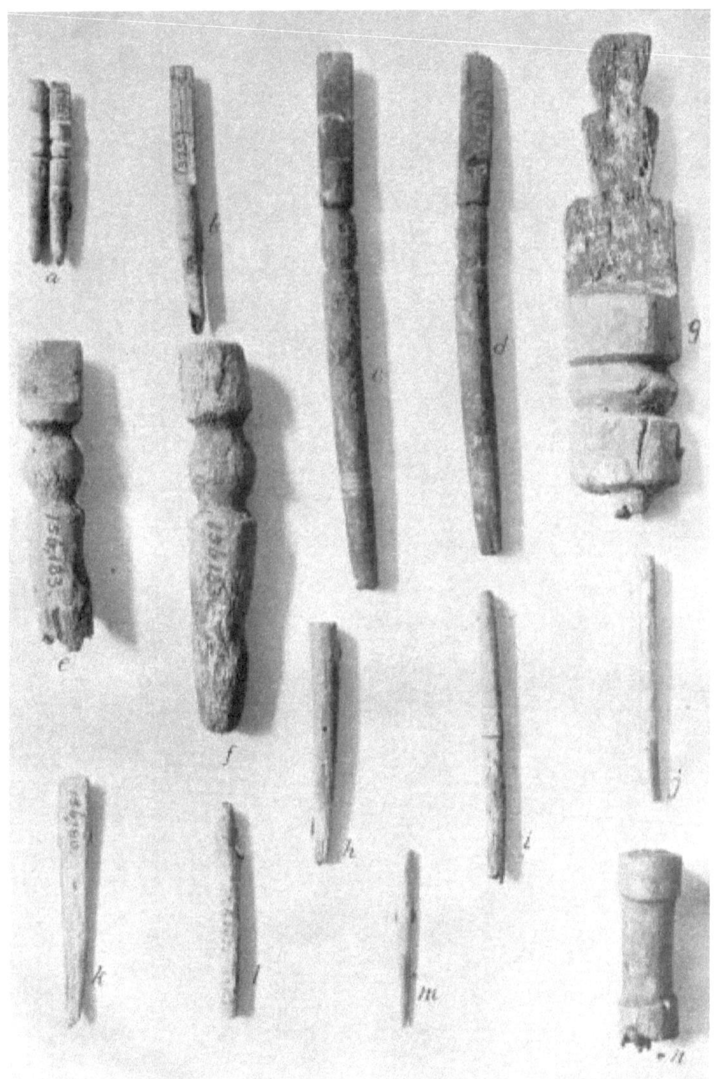

BUREAU OF AMERICAN ETHNOLOGY — — SEVENTEENTH ANNUAL REPORT PL. CLXXIV

Pahos Or Prayer-Sticks From Sikyatki

BUREAU OF AMERICAN ETHNOLOGY — — SEVENTEENTH ANNUAL RE-
PORT PL. CLXXV

Pahos Or Prayer-Sticks From Sikyatki

In a simple prayer the sacrifice is a pinch of meal thrown on the fetish or toward it. This is an individual method of prayer, and the pinch of meal, his prayer
bearer, the sacrifice.

When a society made its prayers this meal, symbolic of a gift of corn, is tied in
a packet and attached to two sticks, one male, the other female, with prescribed
herbs and feathers. Here we have the ordinary prayer-stick, varying in details but
essentially the same, a sacrifice to the gods appropriately designated by prescribed

accessories.

Frequently this packet of meal may be replaced by a picture of an ear of corn drawn on a flat slat, the so-called "corn paho" of the Flute maidens,[164] or we may have an ear of corn tied to the wooden slat. In the *Mamzrau* ceremony the women carry these painted slats in their hands, as I have elsewhere described.[165] It appears as if, in all these instances, there exists a sacrificial object, a symbolic offering of corn or meal.

The constant appearance of the feather on the paho has suggested an interpretation of the prayer-plumes as symbolic sacrifices of birds on the theory of a part for the whole; we know that among the Nahua sacrifices of birds were common in many ceremonials. The idea of animal sacrifice, and, if we judge from legends, of human sacrifice, was not an unknown conception among the Pueblos. While it is possible that the omnipresence of the feather on the prayer-sticks may admit of that interpretation, to which it must be confessed the male and the female components in double pahos lend some evidence,[166] I believe the main object was, as above stated, an offering of meal, which constituted the special wealth of an agricultural people.

MARINE SHELLS AND OTHER OBJECTS

The excavations at Sikyatki did not reveal a large number of marine shells, although some of the more common genera used in the ancient pueblos were found.

There were several fragments of *Pectunculus* cut into the form of wristlets, like those from the ruins on the Little Colorado which I have described. Two beautiful specimens of *Oliva angulata*, truncated at each pole, which occurred in one of the mortuary bowls, and a few conical rattles, made of the spires of *Conus*, were taken from the graves; there were also a few fragments of an unknown *Haliotis*. All of the above genera are common to the Pacific, and no doubt were obtained by barter or brought by migratory clans to Tusayan from the far south. One of the most interesting objects in Sikyatki food basins from the necropolis was a comparatively well preserved rattle of a rattlesnake. The Walpi Snake chief, who was employed by me when this was found and was present at the time it was removed from the earth, declared that, according to the legends, there were no Snake people living at Sikyatki when it was destroyed, but the discovery of the snake rattle shows that the rattler was not without reverence there, even if not in the house of his friends, and some other explanation may be suggested to account for this discovery. There are evidences that the ancient Hopi, like certain Yuman tribes, wore a snake's rattle as an ornament for the neck, in which case the rattle found in the Sikyatki food basin may have been simply a votive offering, and in no way connected with ceremonial symbolism.

Among many other mortuary offerings was one which was particularly sug-

[164] Journal of American Ethnology and Archæology, Vol. *ii*, p. 131.

[165] *American Anthropologist*, July, 1892.

[166] As stated in former pages, there is some paleographic evidence looking in that direction.

gestive. This specimen represented in plate CLXIX, *e*, is made of unbaked clay, and has a reticulated surface, as if once incrusted with foreign objects. The Hopi who were at work for me declared that this incrustation had been composed of seeds, and that the pits over the surface of the clay cone were evidence of their former existence. They identified this object as a "corn mound," and reminded me that a similar object is now used in the *Powamu, Lalakonti*, and certain other ceremonies. I have elsewhere mentioned the clay corn mound incrusted with seeds of various kinds in a description of the altar of the last-mentioned ceremony. These corn mountains (*ká-ü-tü'-kwi*) are made in the November ceremony called the *Nā-ác-nai-ya*, as described in my account of those rites from which I quote[167]—

> "The *Tá-tau-kya-mû* were very busy in their kib-va. Every member was shelling corn of the different colors as if on a wager. Each man made a figure of moist clay, about four or five inches across the base. Some of these were in the form of two mammæ, and there were also many wedge and cone forms, in all of which were embedded corn kernels, forming the cloud and other of the simpler conventional figures in different colors, but the whole surface was studded as full as possible with the kernels. Each man brought down his own *pó-o-tas* (tray), on which he sprinkled prayer-meal, and set his *ká-ü-tü'-kwi* (corn mountain) upon it. He also placed ears of corn on the tray."

These corn mountains were carried by the *Tá-tau-kya-mû* priesthood during an interesting ceremony which I have thus described:[168]

> "The whole line then passed slowly along the front of the village sideways, facing the north, and singing, and all the women came out and helped themselves to the clay molds and the ears of corn borne by the *Tá-tau-kya-mû*, bestowing many thanks upon the priests."

The fragment of polished stone shown in plate CLXIX, *d*, is perforated near the edge for suspension, and was found near the aural orifice of a skull, apparently indicating that it had been used as a pendant. With this object, many rude arrow-points, concretions of stone, and the kaolin disk mentioned above were also found. Small round disks of pottery, with a median perforation, were not common, although sometimes present. They are identified as parts of primitive drills.

No object made of metal was found at Sikyatki, nor is there any evidence that the ancient people of that pueblo ever saw the Spaniards or used any implement of their manufacture. While negative evidence can hardly be regarded as a safe guide to follow, so far as knowledge of copper is concerned, it is possible that the people of ancient Tusayan pueblos, in their trading expeditions to southern Arizona, may have met races who owned small copper bells and trinkets of metal. I can hardly believe, however, that the Tusayan Indians were familiar with the art of tempering copper, and even if objects showing this treatment shall be found hereafter in the

---

[167] *Journal of American Folk-Lore*, vol. v, no. xviii, p. 213.
[168] Op. cit., p. 214.

ruins of this province it will have to be proved that they were made in that region, and not brought from the far south.

No glazed pottery showing Spanish influence was found at Sikyatki, but there can hardly be a doubt that the art of glazing pottery was practiced by the ancestors of the Tusayan people. The modern potters of the East Mesa never glaze their pottery, and no fragment of glazed ware was obtained from the necropolis of Sikyatki.

PERISHABLE CONTENTS OF MORTUARY FOOD BOWLS

It is the habit of the modern Tusayan Indians to deposit food of various kinds on the graves of their dead. The basins used for that purpose are heaped up with paper-bread, stews, and various delicacies for the breath-body of the deceased. Naturally from its exposed position much of this food is devoured by animals or disappears in other ways. There appears excellent evidence, however, that the mortuary food offerings of the ancient Sikyatkians were deposited with the body and covered with soil and sometimes stones.

The lapse of time since these burials took place has of course caused the destruction of the perishable food substances, which are found to be simple where any sign of their former presence remains. Thin films of interlacing rootlets often formed a delicate network over the whole inner surface of the bowl. Certain of the contents of these basins in the shape of seeds still remain; but these seeds have not germinated, possibly on account of previous high temperatures to which they have been submitted. A considerable quantity of these contents of mortuary bowls were collected and submitted to an expert, the result of whose examination is set forth in the accompanying letter:

U. S. DEPARTMENT OF AGRICULTURE, DIVISION OF BOTONY,
Washington, D. C., March 25, 1896.

DEAR DR FEWKES: Having made a cursory examination of the samples of supposed vegetable material sent by you day before yesterday, collected at Sikyatki, Arizona, in supposed prehistoric burial places, I have the following preliminary report to make:

No. 156247. A green resinous substance. I am unable to say whether or not this is of vegetable origin.

No. 156248. A mass of fibrous material intermixed with sand, the fibers consisting in part of slender roots, in part of the hair of some animal.

No. 156249. This consists of a mixture of seed with a small amount of sand present. The seeds are, in about the relative order of their abundance, (*a*) a leguminous shiny seed of a dirty olive color, possibly of the genus *Parosela* (usually known as *Dalea*); (*b*) the black seed shells, flat on one side and almost invariably broken, of a plant apparently belonging to the family *Malvaceae*; (*c*) large, flat, nearly black achenia, possibly of a *Coreopsis*, bordered with a narrow-toothed wing; (*d*) the thin lenticular utricles of a

Carex; (*e*) the minute black, bluntly trihedral seeds of some plant of the family *Polygonaceae*, probably an *Eriogonum*. The majority of these seeds have a coating of fine sand, as if their surface had originally been viscous; (*f*) a dried chrysalis bearing a slight resemblance to a seed.

No. 156250. This bottle contains the same material as No. 156249, except that no larvæ are found, but a large, plump, brownish, lenticular seed 4 mm. in diameter, doubtless the seed of a *Croton*.

No. 156251. A thin fragment of matter consisting of minute roots of plants partially intermixed on one surface with sand.

No. 156252. This consists almost wholly of plant rootlets and contains a very slight amount of sand.

No. 156254. This consists of pieces of rotten wood through which had grown the rootlets of plants. The wood, upon a microscopical examination, is shown to be that of some dicotyledonous tree of a very loose and light texture. The plant rootlets in most cases followed the large ducts that run lengthwise through the pieces of wood and take up the greater part of the space.

No. 156255. The mass contained in this bottle is made up of (*a*) grains, contained in their glumes or husks, of some grass, probably *Oryzopsis membranacea*; (*b*) what appears to be the minute spherical spore cases of some microscopical fungus. The spore cases have a wall with a shiny brown covering, or apparently with this covering worn off and exhibiting an interior white shell. Within this is a very large number of spherical spore-like bodies of a uniform size; (*c*) a few plant rootlets.

No. 156256. The material in this bottle is similar to that in 156255 except that the amount of rootlets is greater, the grass seeds are of a darker color, seemingly somewhat more disorganized, and somewhat more slender in form, and that the spore cases seem to be entirely wanting.

No. 156257. The material in this bottle is similar to that in No. 156249, containing the seeds numbered *a*, *b*, *c*, and *d* mentioned under that number, besides a greater amount of plant rootlets and some fragments of corncob.

No. 156258. This consists almost entirely of plant rootlets and sand.

No. 156259. This consists chiefly of the leaves of some coniferous tree, either an *Abies* or a *Pseudotsuga*.

All the seeds with the exception of those of the leguminous plant are dead and their seed-coats rotten. The leguminous seeds are still hard and will be subjected to a germination test.[169]

For a specific and positive identification of these seeds it will be necessary either for a botanist to visit the region from which they came or to have at his disposal a complete collection of the plants of the vicinity. Under such conditions he could by process of exclusion identify the seeds with an amount of labor almost infinitely less than would be required in their identification by other means.

Very sincerely yours,
Frederick V. Coville, *Botanist.*

---

[169] They failed to germinate.

APPENDIX

The following list introduces the numbers by which the specimens illustrated in this memoir are designated in the catalog of the United States National Museum. Each specimen is also marked with a field catalog number, the locality in which it was found, and the name of the collector:

PLATE

CXI. *a*, 155895; *b*, 155897; *c*, 155898; *d*, 155896; *e*, 155900; *f*, 155916.

CXII. *a*, 155875; *b*, 155996; *c*, 155902; *d*, 155996; *e*, 155997.

CXIII. *a*, 155992; *b*, 155913; *c*, 155991; *d*, 155994; *e*, 155993.

CXIV. *a-g*, 156018; *h*, 156131; *i*, 156091; *j*, 156018.

CXIX. *a*, 155806; *b*, 155841; *c*, 155832; *d*, 155678; *e*, 155820; *f*, 155838.

CXX. *a*, 155867; *b*, 155866; *c*, 155871; *d*, 155856; *e*, 155861; *f*, 155460.

CXXI. *a*, 155694; *b*, 155698; *c*, 155719.

CXXII. *a*, 155702; *b*, 155684; *c*, 155688.

CXXIII. *a*, 155711; *b*, 155703; *c*, 155707; *d*, 155673.

CXXIV. *a*, 155674; *b*, 155683.

CXXV. *a*, 155750; *b*, 155753; *c*, 155751; *d*, 155752; *e*, 155749; *f*, 155747.

CXXVI. *a*, 155700; *b*, 155682.

CXXVII. *a*, 155718; *b*, 155714; *c*, 155723; *d*, 155691.

CXXVIII. *a*, 155745; *b*, 155744; *c*, 155746; *d*, 155735; *e*, 155734; *f*, 155733; *g*, 155736.

CXXIX. *a*, 155467; *b*, 155462; *c*, 155463; *d*, 155464; *e*, 155466; *f*, 155465.

CXXX.   *a,*   *b,*   *c,*   *d,*   *e,*   *f,*
155474; 155475; 155477; 155484; 155473; 155476.

CXXXI.   *a,*   *b,*   *c,*   *d,*   *e,*   *f*
155758; 155773; 155768; 155771; 155546; 155764.

CXXXII.   *a,*   *b,*   *c,*   *d,*   *e,*   *f,*
155482; 155483; 155481; 155480; 155479; 155485.

CXXXIII.   *a,*   *b,*   *c,*   *d,*   *e,*   *f,*
155614; 155757; 155502; 155772; 155758; 155781.

CXXXIV.   *a,*   *b,*   *c,*   *d,*   *e,*   *f,*
155570; 155597; 155567; 155507; 155575; 155505.

CXXXV.   *a,*   *b,*
155692; 155681.

CXXXVI.   *a,*   *b,*   *c,*
155687; 155737; 155695.

CXXXVII.   *a,*   *b,*   *c,*   *d,*   *e,*   *f,*
155488; 155450; 155468; 155732; 155776; 155740.

CXXXVIII.   *a,*   *b,*   *c,*   *d,*   *e,*   *f,*
155498; 155490; 155492; 155500; 155499; 155494.

CXXXIX.   *a,*   *b,*   *c,*   *d,*   *e,*   *f,*
155524; 155528; 155491; 155523; 155527; 155522.

CXL.   *a,*   *b,*   *c,*   *d,*   *e,*   *f,*
155529; 155489; 155540; 155541; 155606; 155410.

CXLI.   *a,*   *b,*   *c,*   *d,*   *e,*   *f,*
155501; 155503; 155509; 155511; 155510; 155512.

CXLII.   *a,*   *b,*   *c,*   *d,*   *e,*
155712; 155693; 155756; 155636; 155697.

CXLIII.   *a, b,*
155690.

CXLIV.   *a, b,*
155689.

CXLV.   *a,*   *b,*
155717; 155696.

CXLVI.   *a,*   *b,*   *c,*   *d,*   *e,*   *f,*
155538; 155508; 155802; 155537; 155487; 155653.

CXLVII.   *a,*   *b,*   *c,*   *d,*   *e,*   *f,*
155493; 155497; 155602; 155504; 155608; 155495.

CXLVIII.   *a,*   *b,*   *c,*   *d,*   *e,*   *f,*
155556; 155408; 155545; 155548; 155544; 155542.

CXLIX.   *a,*   *b,*   *c,*   *d,*   *e,*   *f,*
155554; 155549; 155573; 155607; 155572; 155581.

CL.   *a,*   *b,*   *c,*   *d,*   *e,*   *f,*
155565; 155519; 155518; 155569; 155551; 155574.

CLI.	*a,*	*b,*	*c,*	*d,*	*e,*	*f,*
	155535;	155532;	155539;	155526;	155613;	155615.

CLII.	*a,*	*b,*	*c,*	*d,*	*e,*	*f,*
	155555;	155547;	155571;	155553;	155536;	155521.

CLIII.	*a,*	*b,*
	155558;	155564.

CLIV.	*a,*	*b,*
	155560;	155568.

CLV.	*a,*	*b,*
	155543;	155557.

CLVI.	*a,*	*b,*	*c,*	*d,*	*e,*	*f,*
	155562;	155561;	155562;	155796;	155601;	155588.

CLVII.	*a,*	*b,*	*c,*	*d,*	*e,*	*f,*
	155531;	155530;	155525;	155585;	155563;	155552.

CLVIII.	*a,*	*b,*	*c,*	*d,*	*e,*	*f,*
	155628;	155742;	155632;	155633;	155587;	155634.

CLIX.	*a,*	*b,*	*c,*	*d,*	*e,*	*f,*
	155583;	155598;	155516;	155629;	155590;	155520.

CLX.	*a,*	*b,*	*c,*	*d,*	*e,*	*f,*
	155577;	155576;	155622;	155594;	155647;	155654.

CLXI.	*a,*	*b,*	*c,*	*d,*	*e,*	*f,*
	155642;	155506;	155517;	155472;	155589;	155600.

CLXII.	*a,*	*b,*	*c,*	*d,*	*e,*	*f,*
	155637;	155618;	155643;	155621;	155534;	155533.

CLXIII.	*a,*	*b,*
	155611;	155612.

CLXIV.	*a,*	*b,*
	155610;	155609.

CLXV.	*a,*	*b,*
	155593;	155592.

CLXVI.	*a,*	*b,*	*c,*	*d,*	*e,*	*f,*
	155641;	155616;	155617;	155619;	155584;	155640.

CLXVII.	*a,*	*b,*	*c,*	*d,*	*e,*	*f,*
	155877;	155878;	155892;	155882;	155890;	155881.

CLXVIII.	*a,*	*b,*	*c,*	*d,*	*e,*	*f,*
	155876;	155891;	155884;	155914;	155940;	155880.

CLXIX.	*a,*	*b,*	*c,*	*d,*	*e,*	*f,*
	156095;	156098;	156175;	156174;	156154;	156065.

CLXX.	*a, b,*
	156227.

CLXXI.	*a,*	*b, c,*	*e,*	*f,*
	156270;	156303;	156199;	156043.

CLXXII.   *a,*   *b,*   *c,*   *d,*   *e,*   *f,*
156042; 156169; 156169; 156170; 156184; 156164.

CLXXIII.   *a,*   *b,*   *c,*   *d,*   *e, f,*   *g,*   *h-l,*
155999; 155154; 156128; 156131; 1561?0; 156010; 156130.

CLXXIV.   *a,*   *b, c,*   *d,*   *e-g,*   *h-j,*   *k,*   *l, m,*   *n,*
156191; 156183; 156185; 156183; 156194; 156180; 156191; 156182.

CLXXV.   *o,*   *p,*   *q,*   *r,*   *s,*   *t,*   *u,*   *v,*   *w,*
156188; 156185; 156191; 156186; 156180; 156188; 156181; 156179; 156187.

INDEX

A

B

Lector House believes that a society develops through a two-fold approach of continuous learning and adaptation, which is derived from the study of classic literary works spread across the historic timeline of literature records. Therefore, we aim at reviving, repairing and redeveloping all those inaccessible or damaged but historically as well as culturally important literature across subjects so that the future generations may have an opportunity to study and learn from past works to embark upon a journey of creating a better future.

This book is a result of an effort made by Lector House towards making a contribution to the preservation and repair of original ancient works which might hold historical significance to the approach of continuous learning across subjects.

HAPPY READING & LEARNING!

LECTOR HOUSE LLP
E-MAIL: lectorpublishing@gmail.com

www.ingramcontent.com/pod-product-compliance
Lightning Source LLC
Chambersburg PA
CBHW020901160726
47993CB00005B/1767